SEAN MICHAEL WHITE

FINANCIAL AND COST ANALYSIS FOR ENGINEERING AND TECHNOLOGY MANAGEMENT

ETM WILEY SERIES IN ENGINEERING & TECHNOLOGY MANAGEMENT

Series Editor: Dundar F. Kocaoglu, Portland State University

Badiru/PROJECT MANAGEMENT IN MANUFACTURING AND HIGH TECHNOLOGY OPERATIONS

Baird/MANAGERIAL DECISIONS UNDER UNCERTAINTY: AN INTRODUCTION TO THE ANALYSIS OF DECISION MAKING

Edosomwan/INTEGRATING INNOVATION AND TECHNOLOGY MANAGEMENT

Eschenbach/CASES IN ENGINEERING ECONOMY

Gerwin and Kolodny/MANAGEMENT OF ADVANCED MANUFACTURING TECHNOLOGY: STRATEGY, ORGANIZATION, AND INNOVATION

Gönen/ENGINEERING ECONOMY FOR ENGINEERING MANAGERS

Jain and Triandis/MANAGEMENT OF RESEARCH AND DEVELOPMENT ORGANIZATIONS: MANAGING THE UNMANAGEABLE

Lang and Merino/THE SELECTION PROCESS FOR CAPITAL PROJECTS

Martin/MANAGING INNOVATION AND ENTREPRENEURSHIP IN TECHNOLOGY-BASED FIRMS

Messina/STATISTICAL QUALITY CONTROL FOR MANUFACTURING MANAGERS

Morton and Pentico/HEURISTIC SCHEDULING SYSTEMS: WITH APPLICATIONS TO PRODUCTION SYSTEMS AND PROJECT MANAGEMENT

Niwa/KNOWLEDGE BASED RISK MANAGEMENT IN ENGINEERING: A CASE STUDY IN HUMAN-COMPUTER COOPERATIVE SYSTEMS

Porter et al./FORECASTING AND MANAGEMENT OF TECHNOLOGY

Riggs/FINANCIAL AND COST ANALYSIS FOR ENGINEERING AND TECHNOLOGY MANAGEMENT

Rubenstein/MANAGING TECHNOLOGY IN THE DECENTRALIZED FIRM

Sankar/MANAGEMENT OF INNOVATION AND CHANGE

Streeter/PROFESSIONAL LIABILITY OF ARCHITECTS AND ENGINEERS

Thamhain/ENGINEERING MANAGEMENT: MANAGING EFFECTIVELY IN TECHNOLOGY-BASED ORGANIZATIONS

FINANCIAL AND COST ANALYSIS

FOR ENGINEERING AND TECHNOLOGY MANAGEMENT

HENRY E. RIGGS
Harvey Mudd College
Claremont, California

A WILEY-INTERSCIENCE PUBLICATION

JOHN WILEY & SONS, INC.
NEW YORK   CHICHESTER   BRISBANE   TORONTO   SINGAPORE

Library of Congress Cataloging in Publication Data

Riggs, Henry E.
    Financial and cost analysis for engineering and technology management / by
Henry E. Riggs.
        p.   cm. — (Wiley series in engineering and technology
    management)
    ISBN 0-471-57415-5
    1. Accounting.   I. Title.   II. Series.
HF5635.R564   1994
657—dc20   93-42806
                                                                                        CIP

Printed in the United States of America

10 9 8 7 6 5 4 3 2

To **GAYLE**

*For her love, patience, encouragement,
and occasional gentle upbraiding*

PREFACE

Financial and Cost Analysis is written for managers and aspiring managers who must make decisions based upon information drawn from the financial statements and accounting reports of organizations with and for whom they work. It assumes no prior knowledge of either accounting procedures or management, and is intended to be the first, and very possibly the only, book on accounting that the reader will study.

This book combines in a single volume both financial and managerial/cost accounting, topics that are more typically the subjects of two books for two separate courses. It minimizes, but does not eliminate, discussion of accounting techniques and mechanics, instead focusing on, first, the concepts that underpin the accounting systems, statements, and reports most commonly encountered in industry today, and, second, the extraction of meaning from (that is, the analysis of) those statements and reports.

Rather than commencing the study of accounting with a set of dogmatic rules, this book asks the reader to consider the objectives of the financial reports—that is, why keep financial score? Then, because most accounting controversies turn on the question of valuation of what is owned and owed by the organization, the concept of—and alternative definitions of—*value* are discussed. Rules and mechanics are put off until Chapters 5 and 6. The struggles of valuation are again the focus of Chapters 7, 8, and 9. Financial statement analysis is the subject of Chapters 10 and 11; analysis of budgets is covered in Chapters 12 and 13. After cost accounting is introduced in Chapters 14 and 15, the analysis and interpretation of product (and service) cost data and cost accounting reports are the focus again of the final three chapters of the book. While avoiding much accounting jargon, each chapter summary is followed by a list of defined key terms, since the reader needs to be thoroughly acquainted with the language of accounting.

This book seeks to instill in the reader both a respect for the usefulness of financial information and accounting reports and a healthy skepticism regarding the precision and relevance of certain financial data. As procedures and analytical techniques are introduced, the role of compromises, estimates, assumptions, and omissions is stressed. Since the book does not purport to be comprehensive, it omits a number of subjects of great interest to professional accountants but of only marginal use to managers (for example, consolidated and consolidating statements, accounting for minority interests, and transfer pricing). On the other hand, sophisticated topics relevant to managers—such as price-level adjustments and activity-based costing—are discussed concisely, with an emphasis on conceptual understanding rather than theory.

This book, organized to serve both as a textbook and as a professional book for practicing managers, grew out of a one-quarter course in industrial accounting at Stanford University. Parts or all of this manuscript have been used productively in semester-long courses in engineering and business, beginning graduate-level courses, continuing education courses (particularly for engineers ascending to management positions), and introductory courses at liberal arts colleges.

All readers—whether in a formal class or engaged in self-study—will find that the discussion questions at the end of each chapter will engage them in thinking actively about the chapter's key topics. A large number and range of end-of-chapter problems permit homework assignments of varying length and complexity. The four cases included at the end of the book are excellent vehicles for in-class discussion of analytical techniques presented in the book, as well as the many accounting dilemmas that are inescapable for both accountants and their audiences. A comprehensive instructor's manual is available from the publisher for use by those who adopt the book for their classes.

I am indebted beyond explanation to the bright, energetic, challenging students and teaching assistants whom I have been privileged to know and work with over the 25 years that I have been teaching engineering management. Their responses to this material as it has evolved over the years have run the gamut from delight to surprise to puzzlement to annoyance. Those responses are the wellspring of the format and content of this book, and, coupled with the enthusiasm, questioning, and encouragement of both students and colleagues, they have brought me much enjoyment from this project. My sincere thanks to them all.

I extend hearty thanks also to the many associates and assistants who have read, critiqued, typed, proofread, and otherwise helped shape this book, particularly to Mary Neu, who has devoted herself to the successful completion of this project, and to the staff at Wiley. Despite their best efforts, mistakes inevitably remain and they are my responsibility. Finally, special thanks to my wife, Gayle, who is patient with, and encouraging of, the joy I derive from writing.

HENRY E. RIGGS

Claremont, California

CONTENTS

FINANCIAL AND COST ANALYSIS FOR ENGINEERING AND TECHNOLOGY MANAGEMENT

___1
INTRODUCTION: WHY KEEP SCORE?

Accounting. You probably already have a set of conceptions about the subject of accounting. You may think it is the lifeblood of a modern industrial enterprise. Alternatively, you may view accounting information as merely history, with little relevance for forward-looking management. You may think that accounting data are precise and represent indisputable facts about an operation; or you may feel that, since accountants themselves often disagree, the results of their labors must represent little more than their individual opinions. You may equate accounting with your checkbook and monthly bank statement; or your savings account passbook; or your paycheck with its stub indicating amounts withheld from pay; or the record of receipts and expenses for your club, charity, or association. You may be accustomed to reading published financial statements of corporations, perhaps in connection with common stock investments you have made or contemplate making. Or, you may feel totally lost when confronted by these published financial statements, replete with large numbers and financial jargon that seem to speak only to the initiated.

Accountant. Again, the word may bring a variety of thoughts or images to your mind. Your mental image may be of the Victorian clerk working for Ebenezer Scrooge, leaning over his desk, perched atop his tall stool. Alternatively, you may view the modern accountant as commanding a massive computer database with high-speed laser printers spitting forth financial facts at lightning speed.

Each of us is in contact with accounting information nearly every day of our lives. These frequent encounters—many of them baffling, and some simply unpleasant—form our opinions on what accounting is and is not, what it can and cannot do for us or to us, and what accountants must be like.

For now, keep an open mind about both accounting and accountants. Those of you who are skeptics now may be persuaded that accounting information, properly analyzed and interpreted, can be of substantial benefit. Those who are now enthusiastic believers in accounting's value may, after further study, want to temper that enthusiasm. You may conclude that accounting information, like most other information, has its significant limitations.

INTRODUCTION TO THE BOOK

This book is addressed to those seeking to understand the framework of accounting. It is designed for the present and the future *user* of accounting information rather than for the accountant. This user—you—may now be a business, engineering, or liberal arts major in college or graduate school; or a manager (or aspiring manager) in business, industry, government, or in one of the many other types of organizations, both public and private, that dominate our society. For every professional accountant, there are a host of others of us who need to understand basic accounting concepts because we must interpret accounting reports and make use of financial data both in our personal lives and in our jobs.

Some of you will proceed no further than this book in your study of accounting or financial control; for you, this text provides both a satisfactory introduction and a conclusion. You will gain an understanding of the fundamental concepts and the managerial uses of accounting information. Importantly, you will also come to appreciate the inherent limitations of accounting techniques and therefore, of the resulting information.

For others who want to study further, this book provides an understanding upon which to build both greater technical skills and greater sophistication in financial analysis. Of course, for a few readers this book will awaken an interest in accounting as a career. This discovery may surprise them, for they may have approached the study of accounting with reluctance, thinking it a dry and lifeless subject with limited practicality.

This book is in a number of ways quite unlike traditional accounting books. First, as just stated, it assumes that you are or will be a manager, not a person preparing for a professional accounting career. Second, the book seeks to develop within you a healthy skepticism regarding the precision and reliability of accounting data—as well as an appreciation of the benefits. Third, it omits any serious discussion of a number of subjects of great interest to the professional accountant but of only marginal usefulness to the manager.

Fourth, and most importantly, this book is nontraditional in its organization. It asks you first to consider the need for and purposes of financial information before studying a set of dogmatic accounting rules. Accounting can be taught, and often is, by a pedantic presentation of rules and procedures that you are asked to apply to a set of simplified and generally unrealistic exercises. The rules and procedures are slow to sink in if you have little appreciation of the condition or dilemma that gave rise to them. Moreover, if you do not wrestle with the dilemmas, you are likely to fight the rules as unnecessarily arbitrary.

So this book creates a need to know by exploring financial data requirements, first in the area of general, or financial, accounting and then later in cost and managerial accounting. This problem-first technique is analogous to providing food only after you are hungry and is the opposite of the more common practice of introducing detailed technical material and then illustrations and exercises. This flow is intended to create an awareness on your part that there is a need for data, that a body of knowledge has developed for compiling these data, and that some quite arbitrary rules and procedures are necessary to permit the accountant to communicate with his or her audience.

This book will not try to convince you to become an accountant nor teach you basic bookkeeping skills. Rather, its purpose is to make you a better user of accounting and financial information—gaining all that you can, while being mindful of the shortcomings and limitations of the information.

SCOREKEEPING

Accounting is analogous to scorekeeping. Managers in business are interested in the financial score; managers of athletic teams are interested in the game score. Non-management members of the business enterprise, like their athletic counterparts, the players, are also interested in the score. Besides the active participants, a host of other individuals are also interested in the score—in athletics, the fans, the sports-writers, and the concessionaires selling beer and hot dogs; in business, the share-holders, the bankers, the customers, and the government.

We are interested in the score for a variety of reasons, but most importantly because it helps us make better decisions. Managers—whether in business or athletics—change strategies and tactics depending on the score. The score can cause customers, employees, and sports fans to renew their allegiances to a company or team, or to change allegiances. The score also influences the operating plans of concessionaires at the playing field, just as it influences plans of employees of, and suppliers to, the business.

DEFINITION OF ACCOUNTING

A useful definition of accounting, or financial scorekeeping, should both describe and circumscribe the task and responsibility of accountants. It should tell us what we can expect from our scorekeeping system, and what kinds of information or insights are simply beyond its reasonable scope.

Accounting is Historical

The score of an athletic contest gives the results of the game thus far, not an estimate of what may take place in the next period, inning, or minute; similarly, accounting information shows only what has gone on in the enterprise up to the date of the reports. Thus, an accountant is an historian.

Of course, history is relevant to the future. Plans for virtually all human endeavors—business, athletics, and international diplomacy, for example—are better formulated after a careful analysis of history. You should recognize, however, that accounting cannot provide a crystal-ball view of the future. Sales forecasts, production plans, and expense budgets—all prospective, and all describing what we expect, hope, or plan to occur in the future—are not in the accounting records. On the other hand, the best financial forecasts, plans, and budgets build on solid knowledge of the past as revealed by the historical financial score.

Accounting Measures and Reports in Money Terms

Much of importance about an enterprise cannot easily or usefully be expressed in **monetary terms.** These events are not less important than others that can be expressed monetarily, and they are no less relevant to the enterprise's future. Hiring a respected design engineer may be much more significant for the company than purchasing a new piece of laboratory equipment; however, we have a good deal less trouble valuing laboratory equipment in monetary terms than a newly hired engineer. Similarly, obtaining an appointment with the president of a major potential customer company may be more significant than shipping just another order to a present customer, but clearly the first event is more difficult to value in monetary terms (an appointment is not a sale) than is the second (we can value both the goods shipped—the sale—and the resulting reduction in inventory).

Accounting is for a Defined Entity

The entity may be a retail shop, an industrial concern, a church, the city government, the local fire department (a segment of the city government), the senior high school, a parish affiliated with an archdiocese, your family or just you, an individual. But in each case the entity must be precisely defined. Then, both the accountant and the user of the accounting information must not confuse that entity with other entities of close association or particular affinity.

For example, when you account for a partnership (say, a law firm), you account for the partnership's activities and not the personal activities of the partners. The partners probably have other incomes and they surely have other expenses, but these are not incomes or expenses of the partnership. If the accounting entity is your family, you include the earnings and expenses of all family members, and the result is different than if the accounting entity is you alone. If you are accounting for your parish, you are concerned only with that organization—not the archdiocese and certainly not the worldwide Catholic Church. And you should make sure that you include all activities of this parish, including, for example, the membership committee and the social committee.

For accounting purposes, a large enterprise is frequently broken up into elements, with each treated as an accounting entity. For example, normally a single division of a large, multidivision industrial enterprise is an accounting entity; the division manager and his or her associates need to know the division's score separate from the score of the larger enterprise. Of course, the score must also be kept for the overall enterprise, but that can be readily accomplished by combining divisional accounting information.

Another example: we might define the social committee of the parish as a separate entity. If so, we would isolate the financial transactions of this committee and design an accounting system to produce quite different financial reports than those for the parish as a whole—reports tailored, incidentally, to the information needs of the social committee chairperson, not to those of the parish priest.

Accounting is an Action Process

What verbs define accounting actions? The first verb that comes to mind is *record.* We speak of accounting records, and therefore the accounting process must record what goes on in the entity. But, before the goings-on can be recorded, they must be *observed:* What of monetary significance is happening? Once observed, the goings-on must be translated into monetary terms so they can be recorded; that is, they must be measured in monetary units.

Once the goings-on are recorded, however, the accountant's job is not completed. A sequential log of all that transpired in a business might satisfy certain legal requirements for records, but it would be so long and unorganized as to be unreadable. Thus, the accountant *classifies* and then *summarizes* the data, so that data become information.

To recap, the action verbs in the definition, listed in the order in which the actions are taken, are **observe, measure, record, classify,** and **summarize.**

Now, to what are these actions directed? We need to be more specific than goings-on. What kinds of goings-on need to be observed, measured, recorded, classified, and summarized? Surely, transactions to which the entity is a party: for example, making a sale, paying a bill, receiving a check from a customer, lending or borrowing money, paying the payroll, acquiring inventory, buying a machine tool. Can we draw a boundary line around the accounting entity and concentrate solely on transactions with other entities outside the boundary? Not quite. While such transactions trigger the great majority of accounting entries, we also need to take accounting action to recognize changed conditions internally, changes that have not—at least not yet—involved transactions with outside persons or organizations. Consider these several examples of occurrences or changed conditions:

- A piece of production equipment grows older and thus becomes less useful to the company.
- Certain inventory items fail to sell for many months, signaling that their worth to the company has diminished or disappeared.
- The company's obligation to pay salaries or taxes arises before the date when they must actually be paid.

Stringing these elements together, then, we arrive at the following definition of accounting:

Accounting is the process of observing, measuring, recording, classifying, and summarizing the changes occurring in an entity, expressed in monetary terms, and interpreting the resulting information.

The final clause of this definition, ("interpreting the resulting information,") is, of course, not solely the accountant's task; managers and all others interested in the financial score of the entity also interpret the resulting information. Nevertheless, this final clause is included in the definition to emphasize that part of the accountant's job is to extract meaning from the recorded history. Indeed, this book places major emphasis on interpretation.

LIMITATIONS OF ACCOUNTING INFORMATION

Read again the definition of accounting. Does it suggest that the accounting score tells the entity's full story? Does it imply that accountants themselves never disagree on the financial score? To many people it does; such is most assuredly not the case. Accounting information is limited both in scope (or completeness) and in precision.

Too frequently, readers of accounting reports assume they have in hand the truth about the organization's financial state. Even worse, they believe the reports present the *whole* truth. Unfortunately, some accountants, perhaps understandably, do little to dispel these erroneous impressions.

The first limitation arises because observing and recording is limited to those activities—transactions or changed conditions—that can be expressed in monetary terms. As mentioned earlier, much of importance cannot be so expressed. Second, we limit our attention to history. Third, we focus on a particular entity; but that entity will be much affected by what goes on outside—for example, in the economy as a whole or within a competing organization.

Finally, the process of observing and measuring inevitably demands estimates, assumptions, compromises, and even intentional omissions. This situation is aggravated by the fact that the accountant is always under time constraints, since the usefulness of accounting information is, in part, a function of its timeliness. For example, consider the following dilemmas. How precisely can you value obsolescing inventory? Can you be certain that no one has entered into an agreement that obligates the company without informing the accounting department? Can you be certain that all your customers will pay their bills? Is it not likely that reasonable people will disagree on the precise value to your company of a five-year-old piece of machinery?

In truth, accounting can only *estimate* the financial state of the enterprise. Don't expect the accounting documents to reflect all that is important about the enterprise —even its history—or to reflect that history in absolutely indisputable terms. Because accounting reports are often presented in very precise terms—down to the hundredth part of a dollar—they imply a higher level of precision than they deliver. It is possible to be precisely wrong; it is also true that vague accuracy can be highly useful!

AUDIENCES FOR ACCOUNTING INFORMATION

Because so many people and institutions are interested in an entity's financial score, the accountant serves many constituencies. That is, accounting reports address multiple audiences. Consider an industrial manufacturing corporation. Who are the audiences of the financial reports of such a company, and for what kinds of questions do they seek input? That is, who cares, and what do they want to know?

Management

Managers make the most extensive demands for financial scorekeeping. Charged with the responsibility for both day-to-day operations and long-range direction, managers are concerned with a broad array of issues and questions. They need rapid feedback to determine whether the company is operating according to plan. Are sales and expenses on target? If not, where are they out of line? Managers face a host of marketing decisions. Should a product be added? Should another be deleted? Should a particular order be accepted or declined? What price should the company bid on job X? Should it adjust prices on product line Y? Should it increase or decrease sales promotion expenditures?

In addition to using information to improve operating decisions, managers also must monitor the current financial health of the company. How much cash does the corporation have? How much do customers owe it? Are they paying on time? How much does the company owe its suppliers? Is the company paying them on time? How much inventory does it hold? Does it have the ability to borrow additional money from the bank?

Furthermore, managers had best be alert to the messages that the company's financial statements are conveying to the following others audiences seeking information on the company's financial score.

Investors

The corporation's present shareholders are of course already investors, but any persons or institutions who might buy shares of the company's stock are potential investors, and both groups seek financial information. Is the company profitable? Is it sufficiently profitable to sustain or increase the dividend? What are the risks that the company will cut or eliminate the dividend, or, much worse, become bankrupt?

Security analysts and brokers who advise present and potential investors are an important segment of this audience. Indeed, the market prices for a company's securities are determined by a relatively few professional investors and analysts who become thoroughly knowledgeable of the company's financial score. Thus, this audience segment is both highly demanding and of critical importance.

Creditors

As you think of a company's creditors, you probably think first of the bank. In addition, trade suppliers—companies selling on credit to the manufacturing company—

are also creditors. All creditors are interested in being repaid on time and, in the case of formal loans, being paid interest; but they do not share, as investors (owners) do, in the future growth and profits of the company.

The sooner the creditor expects to be repaid—that is, the shorter the maturity of the credit—the greater the focus on immediate financial position (liquidity) and the less the concern with longer-term prospects. Conversely, if repayment is scheduled in the distant future—that is, if the loan has a long maturity—the lender is increasingly concerned with the company's long-term prospects, since the long-term lender may not be repaid if the borrower incurs a string of loss years and fails as a viable business unit.

Tax Collector

Various taxes are incurred by the corporation as a function of sales, profits, property owned, payroll, and occasionally other factors as well. In the United States, taxes on profit—income taxes—are exacted by the federal government, certain state governments, and a few municipal governments. Typically, property taxes are collected by the county or municipal government, while sales and payroll taxes may be imposed by several levels of government—federal, state, county, and municipal.

The basis for calculating and subsequently verifying tax liabilities is accounting records. Thus, the preparer of a company's various tax returns is a user of accounting data; also, government tax auditors routinely demand access to accounting records to verify the correctness of the company's tax payments.

Two preliminary comments regarding taxes are in order, although taxes are discussed at several points in this book. First, in virtually all cases, managers strive to minimize the company's current liability for taxes of all kinds. This effort leads both to postponing the payment as long as possible and taking advantage of every tax law provision to reduce taxes. Note the world of difference between avoiding unnecessary taxes and evading required taxes! Be aware, too, that the exact applicability of the tax law (particularly the income tax law) is often unclear. Thus, a company's tax liability may not be determinable with certainty. For an adversary relationship to arise between company management and tax collectors is inevitable.

Second, tax laws must not dictate accounting practice, particularly accounting for profits. Governments enact income tax laws to raise revenue and, in certain instances, to further national economic goals by providing incentives to taxpayers. Thus, the definition of profit in the income tax laws is typically at variance to some degree with the definition of profit that is useful to managers and investors. As a result, a company normally has to maintain in its accounting records certain information solely for the purpose of calculating its tax liability.

Others

Aside from these primary audiences, many others are interested in the financial score. Customers are interested in the company's financial viability, particularly if they are dependent upon the company for long-term source of supply. Employees have similar interests; a growing, profitable, and financially strong company is an attractive employer. Labor unions, as representatives of the employees, have an avid interest in financial results, particularly just prior to contract negotiations, when the union is formulating demands based at least in part on what it feels the company can afford. Managements of competing companies are also eager readers of published financial statements.

Government regulatory bodies look to the company's accounting records for information. Companies are, of course, subject to varying amounts of regulation, depending primarily on their lines of business. Public utilities (electric, natural gas distribution, telephone, and so forth), some transportation companies (airlines and railroads) and most broadcasting companies (radio and TV) are regulated by both federal and state agencies. All companies whose securities are actively traded in organized markets (for example, the New York Stock Exchange) are subject to financial reporting requirements stipulated by the Securities and Exchange Commission, and both federal and state securities agencies exercise some control over the financial information that must be supplied in connection with the sale of all newly issued securities. Antitrust legislation, whole affecting primarily large companies, constrains the actions (particularly pricing actions) of even relatively small concerns. In their interactions with each of these regulatory bodies, managers rely to a great extent on financial information obtained from the accounting records to advance the company's cause or to defend its position.

DIFFERENT MESSAGES FOR DIFFERENT AUDIENCES

This discussion should both convince you that different audiences are interested in quite different types of financial information and also alert you that a company may legitimately wish to convey quite different messages to different audiences.

For example, while wanting to report a strong profit picture to shareholders, management seeks to minimize taxes calculated as a percentage of profits. The desired message to creditors may be that the company is in a strong financial position, entitled to more liberal credit terms, at just the time that the desired message to the labor union is that the company would be hard pressed to meet demands for substantial wage or fringe benefit increases.

This book will emphasize frequently that, in fact, the accountant has considerable latitude in reporting both profits and financial position. Consider again the example of obsolescing inventory. If the accountant is relatively pessimistic about the value of this inventory, both profits and financial position will be reported less glowingly to both shareholders and the income tax collector than if the accountant takes a more optimistic view of its value. Of course, this and similar situations present opportunities for deception or, far worse, fraud. But no matter how honest and objective the accountant attempts to be, judgments are colored by the conscious or unconscious consideration of the message that the resulting financial reports convey to key audiences. After all, the accountant is subject to the same human frailties and is buffeted by the same human motivations that affect us all!

ACCOUNTING IN THE WORLD OF BUSINESS

The accounting function in business is a service function, not an end in itself. The accounting department does not create sales, fabricate products, or engineer new products. It keeps score and provides information and analyses.

Within the business environment, accounting is useful to the extent it assists managers in achieving the company's objectives. An important (although not necessarily the prime) objective of business is to earn a profit.* The accountant is the scorekeeper with respect to that objective.

Most businesses, of course, articulate other objectives to accompany the profit objective. At the risk of opening up arguments over the appropriateness of various objectives, we can say that managers pay attention to:

- Meeting budgets,
- Maximizing sales or market share,
- Increasing economic power through sheer size,
- Creating or maintaining technical leadership,
- Developing enhanced reputations or prestige,
- Perpetuating the enterprise for the benefit of employees, the community, the management, or the founding family, and
- Assuring that present management members retain their jobs.

Accounting may not help much in keeping score on certain of these objectives. Try quantifying in monetary terms economic power or reputation or prestige. Remember, accounting reports tell only part of the company's total story.

The fundamental economic decisions that must be made by all economic enterprises involve the efficient allocation of available resources, since resources are inevitably scarce. These scarce productive resources are money, existing productive capacity, and labor, including technical expertise, management expertise, and human muscle. Many analytical techniques, some quite sophisticated and requiring extensive computing power, inform these resource allocation decisions. Much, though not all, of the data utilized in these mathematical models can and should be available from the accounting records, for example, costs and revenues for certain products, for certain departments, or for certain geographic regions. Indeed, designers of accounting systems should have in mind the various input data required by the company's present and future analytical and planning tools, such as:

- Discounted cash flow analyses of alternative investment opportunities,
- Simulation of segments of the company's operations,

---

*Actual behavior suggests that maximizing profits is not a widespread objective. Rather, managers seem to act as though they want their companies to be adequately (perhaps comfortably) profitable, but not necessarily maximally profitable.

- Economic order quantity and other scheduling analyses, and
- Linear programming of the company's distribution activities.

ACCOUNTING IN NONPROFIT AND GOVERNMENTAL ORGANIZATIONS

The primary focus of this book is on businesses—manufacturers, service organizations, and sales organizations—that seek to make a profit. Of course, our society is replete with organizations that are not profit-seeking: government units, educational institutions, charities, certain hospitals, churches and synagogues, clubs, foundations, fraternal and service organizations, political parties, and consumer or farmer cooperatives. The accounting requirements, and therefore accounting systems, of these organizations are somewhat, but not fundamentally, different from those of profit-seeking companies. With different objectives, they require different sorts of data and reports to track progress. Yet all of them take in revenue and incur expenses. The well-managed among them operate on a plan, and the plan involves a budget in monetary terms. Their managers have the same needs as their profit-seeking counterparts to monitor actual financial performance as compared to the budget. Nevertheless, some accounting conventions are different for governmental, educational, or other types of nonprofit organizations.*

USEFUL NONACCOUNTING INFORMATION

Our definition limits accounting information to that which can be stated in monetary terms. Yet nonmonetary measures and records are vitally important to managers of both for-profit and nonprofit organizations. Thus, a caveat: You should seek out insightful *non*accounting measures of both performance and condition to supplement and amplify accounting information.

Consider again the analogy with athletic teams. Sports fans are concerned with other information about the team besides simply the score of the games played and the related statistics on individual team members. They are interested in the age and health of the athletes, and the depth of backup personnel for each critical position. They are interested in which athletes perform best under varying climatic, competitive, or time conditions.

Similarly, business managers are interested in such nonmonetary measures as the number of potential new customers contacted, frequency of late deliveries, frequency of stock outs, employee turnover, employee absenteeism, market share vis-à-vis competitors, educational background of technical and managerial personnel, number of sales calls per salesperson per day, percentage of contract proposals accepted,

---

*In general, these organizations place a good deal more emphasis on the flow of cash, where profit-seeking businesses place more emphasis on the measurement of profit.

percentage of production capacity utilized, and quality yield. Indeed, most businesses can define a handful of nonmonetary key indicators of performance that should be monitored every bit as closely as accounting data. The most significant of these key indicators are those that provide early warning signals—that is, those that foretell operating problems.

IMPORTANCE OF PERSONAL MOTIVATIONS

Managing is often defined as the process of planning, supervising, and controlling an organization in pursuit of its objectives. To repeat, this book focuses on accounting's role in providing data and analyses to assist managers, particularly in their efforts to plan and control.

Bear in mind however, that an organization is not an impersonal machine, but rather a collection of human beings. These people—middle- and lower-level managers, salespersons, scientists and engineers, clerks, machine operators, and everyone else in the organization—have their individual and collective objectives. Every student of human behavior knows that each of us is motivated to satisfy our own needs, whatever those needs may be. Accounting information may help us to satisfy certain of our needs (e.g., you need to demonstrate that your department can operate on budget, and the accounting report verifies that it has) or it can threaten our need satisfaction (e.g., you committed to lowering overtime costs in your department, and the last accounting report shows no improvement). Inevitably, readers of accounting reports react based on their motivations; those reactions may be constructive to the organization's overall goals and objectives (e.g., you are going to take corrective steps to increase sales of certain products because sales have been below target) or they may be destructive (e.g., you will subcontract certain production activities at a sacrifice in total costs rather than incur additional overtime costs, since the high subcontract costs will not be charged to your department and management is on your back about overtime costs). The net benefit of accounting reports is very much a function of how managers use them. They can be used to threaten or coerce middle- and lower-level managers, or they can be used to provide feedback to those managers to permit them to do a better job. More about these motivational issues in Chapter 12.

Accountants themselves are of course in turn influenced by how managers react to their reports. Too frequently, an adversarial relationship builds up between accounting managers and operating managers. If operating managers dispute the veracity of the accounting numbers, the accounting department may become defensive. Operating managers may withhold unfavorable information from the accounting department. Accounting personnel may delight in highlighting areas of poor operating performance. By contrast, a healthy relationship exists when operating managers look to the accounting department for feedback and assistance, and the accounting department readily admits that accounting is not an exact science, that there may be valid explanations why actual results deviated from plan.

SUMMARY

Accounting is the process of financial scorekeeping. More comprehensively, accounting is defined as the process of observing, measuring, recording, classifying, and summarizing the changes occurring in an entity, expressed in monetary terms, and interpreting the resulting information.

This book is primarily for managers, those seeking to understand the accounting framework in order to make more effective use of accounting and financial information. It is not for those who seek to learn basic bookkeeping skills.

Accounting is not a complete story—or history—of the enterprise. It ignores those activities that cannot be measured and expressed in monetary terms. Furthermore, to a significant extent, it ignores events or conditions outside of the entity, even though they may affect importantly the future of the enterprise. Remember that nonmonetary, and therefore nonaccounting, measures of a company's activities and condition can also prove both revealing and useful.

While accounting reports serve a myriad of audiences, the primary audience consists of the managers of the enterprise. Secondary, but very key, audiences include investors (present and potential) in the company's securities, creditors to the company, and the various governmental taxing authorities. Other interested parties include customers, employees, trade unions, government regulatory bodies, and competitors. The informational requirements of these audiences vary widely.

The value of accounting reports to the primary audience, managers, is as an aid in tracking the company's progress toward one or more of the corporate objectives. Furthermore, accounting data are the key inputs for most analytical and planning techniques that assist decisions regarding the optimum allocation of the enterprise's scarce productive resources.

Accounting techniques for government, education, charity, and other nonprofit organizations are not fundamentally different than those for profit-seeking enterprises. However, informational requirements and certain accounting conventions do vary, since these nonprofit organizations pursue quite different objectives from those of private-sector businesses.

NEW TERMS

Accounting. The process of observing, measuring, recording, classifying, and summarizing the changes occurring in an entity, expressed in monetary terms, and interpreting the resulting information.

Classify. To categorize within the accounting system similar transactions, occurrences, or conditions.

Entity. The definition of the organizational unit for which the accounting is being performed.

Measure. To value in monetary terms the transaction, occurrence, or condition to be recorded in the entity's accounting system.

Monetary terms. The measure used in valuing all that is to be included in the accounting records.

Observe. To determine what transactions, occurrences, or conditions represent changes to be recorded in the entity's accounting system.

Record. To evidence in the accounting system those transactions, occurrences, and changed conditions that have been observed and measured (valued).

Summarize. To combine and condense data in the accounting system in order to supply meaningful information to the various audiences.

DISCUSSION QUESTIONS

1.1   Who are the internal users of an organization's accounting data and reports?

1.2   Who are the external users of an organization's accounting data and reports?

1.3   As a product design engineer, what questions are important to you that the accounting system may be able to answer? Do you think the information you require would be different from that required by a person in marketing? How?

1.4   How do the following individuals interact with—provide information to, and get information from—the accounting system?
  (a)   The inventory clerk in the stockroom.
  (b)   The project manager in design engineering.
  (c)   The shop floor foreman.
  (d)   The sales engineer who calls on customers.
  (e)   The secretary to the president of the company.
  (f)   The manager of a regional sales office.
  (g)   The purchasing agent.
  (h)   The product line manager in the marketing department.
  (i)   The manager of warehousing and shipping.
  (j)   The quality manager.
  (k)   The new products design engineer.
  (l)   The marketing manager.
  (m)   A securities analyst.
  (n)   A tax auditor.

1.5   Identify two examples of data expressed in monetary terms that are important for:
  (a)   An automobile manufacturing company.
  (b)   A fast-food restaurant.
  (c)   A university.

(d) An apartment complex.

(e) An appliance distributor.

(f) A hotel.

(g) A photocopier service business.

(h) A janitorial services company.

(i) A bank.

(j) A telephone company.

(k) A nonprofit health clinic.

(l) A street vendor selling tie-dyed shirts.

(m) A small TV repair shop.

(n) A recycling operation.

1.6 What nonmonetary measures (that is, data not expressed in monetary terms) would you consider important for each of the types of enterprises listed in question 1.5?

1.7 You are a securities analyst for a major stock brokerage firm and have the responsibility for writing a report on the Kaplan Company. You have just received the Kaplan Company's published annual financial statements. What specific questions do you think will be answered by a careful review of these statements? You now have an opportunity to interview the president of the Kaplan Company for one hour. What are some of the questions you would ask the president? What are the differences between the two types of questions? Do you think these questions complement one another? How?

1.8 You are a shareholder of the Kaplan Company. You have just received the latest published annual financial statements for the company but you have no access to anyone in the management of the company. Where would you look for additional information on the company to decide whether to increase or reduce your stock holdings in the company? How would you judge the reliability of this information?

1.9 You are an investigator for the antitrust division of the Justice Department. You are investigating a large manufacturer of computers. What published financial information from that manufacturer, and from its competitors, would be useful in your investigation?

1.10 You are a sales tax auditor for the state. You are to begin auditing a company that sells both taxed and nontaxed goods to the public. What documents would you ask the accountant to provide for your investigation?

1.11 You are a government auditor charged with auditing a publicly held bank and reporting to the federal government any irregularities in its operations. What type of documents would you review during your audit? Would you seek information beyond that provided by the bank? Why?

1.12 How difficult would it be to measure, in monetary terms, the following transactions:

(a) The purchase of a used truck.

(b) The exchange of a parcel of land owned by the company for a 15-year lease in a newly constructed facility.

(c) The sale of newly issued common stock to an outside investor.

(d) The acceptance of an interest-bearing five-year note from a customer in settlement for his past due account.

(e) The signing of a five-year employment contract with the company's chief scientist.

(f) The negotiation of a ten-year license on a product developed by the company to another company who agrees to pay 4 percent royalty on all sales of the product.

(g) The acceptance of an order for 120 units of product X to be delivered at the rate of 10 units per month over the next year.

(h) The shipment of the first 10 units in connection with the order described in (g).

(i) The receipt of 400 kg of raw material Z.

(j) The purchase of a one-year insurance policy providing comprehensive coverage on the company's facilities.

(k) The filing of a lawsuit seeking $200,000 in damages from a supplier for breach of contract.

(l) The on-the-job injury of one of the company's workers.

(m) The return of defective goods to the company by the company's best customer.

(n) The expiration of a copyrighted brand name for a product.

(o) The purchase of an extended warranty for the company's computers.

(p) The purchase of advertising space in the local newspaper.

(q) The delivery of 500 kg of product to a customer.

(r) The enactment of an environmental law that will require all company-owned cars to have a higher fuel efficiency in five years.

(s) The bankruptcy of the company's best customer.

(t) The lowering of tariffs in a foreign market.

(u) The lowering of tariffs (applicable to competing imports) in the home market.

(v) The recall of a product the company manufactures.

1.13 Evaluate and comment on the following quotation:

Accountants are simply historians focusing on past events. Management is concerned with charting the future course of the company, not with worrying about past successes or failures. Therefore, the accountant's function is not vital to management, except to the extent that it causes the company to comply with various government regulations.

1.14 You have just received the monthly bill for your gasoline credit card. You recall signing each of the slips that are included with your bill. Describe the probable progress of the slips from the time you signed them to the time they appeared in your monthly bill. What transactions have occurred? What accounting actions were taken at the gas station? And at the gasoline company? What transactions remain to be completed?

1.15 Most modern supermarkets use automatic scanners to check out groceries. What monetary and nonmonetary information would you expect to be updated every time at item is scanned?

1.16 If you were applying for a loan at a bank, what personal financial information would you provide the bank to try to obtain a favorable outcome? What nonmonetary information about yourself would you like the bank to take into account before making its decision?

1.17 A well-established fast-food restaurant has offered you a franchise in a nearby town. What kind of information, both monetary and nonmonetary, would you like them to provide you to help you make a decision about acquiring the franchise?

1.18 What are the five tasks that must be performed in accounting? Explain each.

____2
THE ACCOUNTING FRAMEWORK: THE CONCEPT OF VALUE

In Chapter 1, we defined the accountant's task as observing, measuring in monetary terms, recording, classifying, and summarizing the changes occurring in an entity. This chapter focuses on the first two action words in that definition: observe and measure, but in particular, the second—measuring, or valuing, in monetary terms. We'll put off the discussion of recording, classifying, and summarizing to subsequent chapters.

How does an accountant value what the enterprise owns, as well as its obligations? How is a monetary value assigned to the many and varied transactions to which the enterprise is a party? Some valuations are straightforward and relatively indisputable. Others present very real dilemmas. You need to understand three valuation methods.

But before considering the three primary valuation methods, you need to understand the framework for incorporating these values into our accounting system.

THE ACCOUNTING EQUATION

Every entity for which we account owns property and rights; it also has obligations that it must discharge. That which the entity owns are called *assets;* that which it owes—its obligations—are called *liabilities*.

Assets are defined as physical property, rights, and financial resources that hold the promise of providing ongoing future benefits. Examples are securities, promises of customers to pay, production facilities like machine tools and plant space, rights to use patents, and protection under a one-year insurance policy. Cash (whether in the drawer or in the bank) and inventory are obviously critically important assets to all merchandising and manufacturing companies, and, by the way, are not difficult to value. On the other hand, other important assets such as customer orders and employment contracts with key personnel are a good deal more difficult to value, as we shall see.

The point is that a company owns a great number of physical things and intangible rights that we call *assets*. The company also has certain obligations—to its bank for money it has borrowed, to its vendors for inventory or services rendered, to its employees for wages and benefits earned but not yet paid, to customers in connection with product warranty provisions, and to others as well. These obligations to outside persons* or organizations are referred to as liabilities. Most company liabilities are discharged by the payment of cash, but some are discharged by the performance of a service, such as warranty repair. Liabilities comprise all that the accounting entity owes.

Thus, to repeat, assets are what the entity *owns,* and *liabilities* are what the entity *owes.* You feel one way about assets—you are better off to own them—and the opposite way about liabilities—you like to avoid them. Put another way, liabilities represent a call on the assets; to discharge liabilities, you utilize the assets owned. A healthy company owns more than it owes: the value of its assets exceeds the value of its liabilities. Moreover, the difference between what it owns and owes, the net amount of assets not required to offset liabilities, is a measure of the company's *worth.* This worth accrues to the benefit of the company's owners—in the case of a corporation, its shareholders. So, the greater this difference between assets and liabilities, the better off are the shareholders collectively. This difference between assets and liabilities is **owners' equity,** and the fundamental **accounting equation** is

$$\text{Assets} - \text{liabilities} = \text{owners' equity}$$

This statement must be true at all times. If assets of the company increase with no change in liabilities, owners' equity increases; that is, the owners collectively are in a better position. If, on the other hand, the liabilities of the corporation increase with no change in assets, then the owners' equity declines.

Using simple algebra, rearrange the terms in the equation shown above to restate the accounting equation

$$\text{Assets} = \text{liabilities} + \text{owners' equity}$$

This form is, in fact, the typical one. You may already be aware that most published financial statements in this country follow this format: assets listed first (or on the left), liabilities and owner's equity shown below (or on the right), with equal totals. Another way to describe the fundamental accounting equation is that the assets represent the entity's investments in physical property, intangible rights, and financial resources, while the liabilities and owner's equity represent the sources of funds used to make the investments. The left-hand side of the equation shows what the

*Are employees part of, or outside, the entity? While essential to the operation of the enterprise, they personally earn income and incur expenditures independent of the business entity and so are separate and distinct accounting entities.

company owns, and the right-hand side shows how the ownership of the assets was financed.

MORE ON OWNERS' EQUITY

But how, in fact, is owners' equity created? How can assets increase without an increase in liabilities, or how can liabilities decrease without a corresponding decrease in assets? Both events increase owners' equity. Two ways:

(1) The owners can invest additional capital in the enterprise. In a sole proprietorship or partnership, the owners are the sole proprietor or the partners, and they simply agree to put more funds into the business. In a corporation, additional shares of stock are created and sold to investors.

(2) The enterprise can earn a profit. Take the simple example of a company selling for three dollars merchandise it bought for two dollars. The inventory asset decreases by two dollars, and the cash asset increases by three dollars. If this one dollar of profit is not removed by the owners, it adds to owners' equity.

These are the two important ways that owners' equity is increased. You quickly see the two primary ways owners' equity is decreased.

(1) The owners withdraw funds from the business, for example by paying dividends to the owners of the corporation's capital stock.

(2) The company incurs a loss. If in the example above the merchandise purchased for two dollars is sold for $1.50, the company has a loss of fifty cents.

Therefore, owners' equity is defined both as the difference between assets and liabilities, and as

The sum of capital invested by the owners plus profits earned, less the sum of any losses incurred and any funds paid by the enterprise back to its owners.

Unfortunately, the meaning of owners' equity often gets confused. What is it *not?* First, owners' equity is not a pool of cash, not liquid funds available to be spent or repaid to shareholders. You must look to the company's assets, not its owners' equity, to determine whether cash exists for spending or for return to shareholders. If today the owners put additional capital into the company, the company's financial resources—assets in the form of cash—increase by exactly the same amount as owners' equity increases. If tomorrow the company uses this cash to purchase inventory, it trades one asset for another: owners' equity remains unchanged but the company no longer has the liquid funds.

What else is owner's equity *not?* It is not the value that the financial markets assign to the ownership of the company. For a publicly traded corporation, the market value of the entire corporate entity is equal to the current trading price of a single share of stock times the total number of shares owned by all investors. This *trading value* may be considerably at odds with—higher or lower than—the value arrived at by subtracting liabilities from assets. Thus, the value of owners' equity provides you no indication of the price at which you could buy or sell a few shares—or a very large number of shares. Recall that trading (market) prices for common stocks are a function of the investors' collective expectations about the future flow of benefits (primarily dividends) from ownership. Moreover, the stock trading price applies only to fairly small trades, 100 or 200 shares. If you sought to purchase all the shares of a corporation, your demand would greatly exceed the available supply of shares and would cause the trading price to increase; conversely, if you sought to sell a very large number of shares, your supply might swamp demand and depress the trading price.

Thus, for reasons having to do both with the mechanics of establishing the share trading prices and with the difficulties in valuing the assets and liabilities of the corporation, you can't reasonably expect that the two evaluations of owners' equity will agree—that is:

$$(\text{Assets} - \text{liabilities}) \text{ typically won't} = (\text{trading price per share} \times \text{number of common shares})$$

VALUATION METHODS

The accounting framework—the fundamental accounting equation—requires that we value both assets (what the entity owns) and liabilities (what it owes). Valuing assets and liabilities is the fundamental accounting task and the one that draws most of the arguments among accountants and most of the controversies between accountants and their audiences.

These arguments and controversies typically center on which one of the following three valuation methods is most appropriate in a particular circumstance:

(1) The *time-adjusted value* method. It views values as a function of future benefits and costs arising from the item owned or from the obligation.
(2) The *market value method.* It equates value to the price at which the item owned could now be bought or sold.
(3) The *cost value method.* It equates value to the price paid for the item when it was originally acquired.

You need to keep in mind a few blunt facts about these alternative methods. They do not typically result in the same values. No single method is inherently more correct than the other two. The cost value method is the predominant method used, but is in some sense the least appealing intellectually. To better understand the advantages and shortcomings of each method, you need to understand all three.

Let's begin with an explanation of the time-adjusted value method. It is most easily visualized by valuing a promise to pay. Note that a promise to pay is an asset to the lender and a liability to the borrower.

VALUING A LOAN (OR NOTE)

Consider valuing a debt from the point of view of the lender or creditor.

How does the lender go about valuing the borrower's promise to repay the principal at maturity and, in the meantime, interest on the outstanding balance? These two cash flow streams—interest and principal—are fixed by agreement between lender and borrower, both as to amount and timing. Thus, the flows are very predictable, assuming the borrower is a good credit risk. Because money has a time value (i.e., you would prefer to receive one dollar now rather than a year from now, since you can make use of that dollar in the intervening year), those flows of cash that the lender is scheduled to receive in the distant future are of less value today than those flows that are due to be received sooner. Interest tables permit the lender to calculate the equivalent value today of flows occurring at various dates in the future, at any interest rate that the lender selects as appropriate. Such values are referred to as *present values of futures cash flows* or **time-adjusted values.** Thus, the term *time-adjusted* value refers to today's equivalent value, at a specific interest rate, of a flow of cash (inflow or outflow) that will occur in the future.

For example, assume that $1000 has been lent in return for the borrower's promise to make interest payments of $50 at the end of each of the next three years and a principal repayment of $1000 at the end of the third year. What is the value to the lender of this borrower's promise to pay? That depends on the lender's **equivalency rate.** That rate, in turn, is a function of the lender's other opportunities to deploy money. If the lender can earn only 5 percent (at equivalent risk*), then 5 percent is the lender's equivalency rate, and the time-adjusted value of this series of flows is $1000, since the lender will be receiving interest at the rate of 5 percent from now until the principal balance of the loan is repaid. Put another way, the lender is indifferent between having $1000 now or the promise from a creditworthy borrower to pay the following amounts:

$50 at the end of 12 months
$50 at the end of 24 months
$1050 at the end of 36 months

Now suppose the lender has opportunities to invest at 8 percent with risk no greater than the risk inherent in the loan. The lender's equivalent rate goes from 5 to

*We will consider differences in risk in a moment.

8 percent and the time-adjusted value of that stream of promised payments is now less than $1000. The lender would be willing to "sell" this note for less than $1000. How much less? Standard inte.est rate tables tell us that at 8 percent the time-adjusted value of the payment stream is about $923. Conversely, if a lower rate is used—because the lender's equivalency rate is lower—the time-adjusted value will be greater: at 3 percent it is about $1057. Here the lender is indifferent between owning $1057 in cash or the borrower's note. This simple table helps explain this concept:

Equivalency Value Now of the Cash Flows at Alternative Equivalency Rates

Cash Flow	Timing	3%	5%	8%
$ 50	End of 12 months	48.54	47.62	46.30
$ 50	End of 24 months	47.13	45.35	42.87
$1050	End of 36 months	960.90	907.03	833.52
		$1056.57	$1000.00	$922.69

Therefore, a lender values this note differently depending upon the equivalency interest rate applicable to the situation. If 8 percent is the appropriate rate, the lender is willing to sell the borrower's promise to pay for any amount above $923 or, what amounts to the same thing, is willing to cancel the borrower's note if the borrower pays $923 or more now (that is, the lender is willing to discount the note from its face value of $1000 in order to get early payment.)*

This illustration assumes a creditworthy borrower. Suppose that the lender learns that the borrower's financial position and employment prospects are such that on-time repayment is by no means assured. Now the lender regards this loan as more risky than the average. Lenders routinely charge higher interest rates on riskier loans. Put another way, a higher interest return is necessary to compensate for the higher risk. Therefore, the lender concludes that the equivalency interest rate should be higher—say 10 percent—to allow for this greater risk. Using a 10 percent equivalency rate, the lender values the note at about $876, and is willing to discount the note all the way to $876 if by doing so the lender can secure immediate payment of that amount. The lender would also be willing to sell this loan to another lender (or lending institution) for $876, a considerable discount from the $923 equivalency value at 8 percent.

Lenders typically have portfolios of notes, each having different risks and different payment schedules. This technique of valuing the notes provides information useful to the lender in negotiating with borrowers or in selling (discounting) the notes to other lenders.

Of course, borrowers use the same technique to value their own promises to pay interest and principal, that is, to value their loan liabilities. A borrower whose equivalency interest rate is 8 percent is willing to pay not more than $923 right now to be relieved of the obligation to make the scheduled payment of principal and

*For further discussion of these concepts, see the appendix to this chapter.

interest. On the other hand, a borrower whose equivalency rate is 3 percent is better off paying any amount up to $1057 now (a premium of up to $57 over the face value of the note), since a 3 percent equivalency rate indicates that the borrower doesn't have other opportunities to invest cash at a return higher than 3 percent. Note that the repayment of a debt is essentially a risk-free investment.

VALUING COMMON STOCK SECURITIES

Move now to the more complex case of valuing a share of common stock.* If the stock is publicly traded in organized markets (e.g., the New York Stock Exchange), the value is determined by auction: it is equal to what the buyer is willing to pay and the seller is willing to take for the share.

But how do buyers and sellers judge value and thus decide whether they should buy or sell? Like the lender, the shareholder (or investor contemplating purchase) estimates what benefits will flow from ownership of the share of stock: dividends while the stock is owned and the market price (less selling commissions) at the time the owner elects to sell the stock (ignoring income taxes). Thus, the stock value is the time-adjusted value of the future cash flow calculated at the shareholder's equivalency interest rate. That rate is influenced by the riskiness of the investment—that is, by the shareholder's assessment of the risk that the anticipated dividend payments and selling price will be realized—and by the returns available from competing investment opportunities.

As shareholders lower their interest rate equivalencies, they bid up the price of shares. Moreover, those investors who are averse to high risks are attracted to companies with secure dividend payments and they calculate the time-adjusted values at relatively low equivalency rates, thus placing a high value on the security.

CALCULATING TIME-ADJUSTED VALUES

If this all sounds too hypothetical, it is not. Time-adjusted values are calculated routinely. In a rational market, the price that future buyers will pay for the stock will also be a function of the expected cash returns. If all future buyers are treated as one, the future cash returns from ownership of the share of common stock are limited to dividends paid plus the liquidation payment to shareholders when the company is liquidated. Thus, even for a company currently paying no dividends, the value of its common stock security is a function of shareholders' expectations as to the amount and timing of all future cash dividends.

The truism on which this valuation method is based is that money has a time value. You would rather receive a certain amount of money today than the same amount at a later date, say a year from today, since you can earn a return† on

*Evidence of partial ownership.
†The return may be in the form of interest earned or in the form of wants satisfied by spending the money.

money during the intervening year. Similarly, you would prefer to delay the payment of a specified amount as long as possible so that you can earn a return on the money during the period of the delay.

If you know the rate of the available return, you can calculate the advantage or disadvantage associated with accelerating or delaying receipts and payments. Thus, values of cash flows (receipts or payments) are a function of their timing; timing differences have monetary value consequences. The time-adjusted valuation method values, as of today, future cash flows that will arise because of assets owned or obligations undertaken, utilizing an appropriate equivalency (interest) rate.

Suppose, for example, that you are the manager of a retail store. When the store has a small amount of excess cash, you invest it in a short-term deposit or security that earns interest at a specified rate, r percent per year; when the store runs short of cash, you withdraw (disinvest) from this deposit or security the amount necessary to cover the cash deficiency. Now suppose that the owner of your building offers to reduce (or discount) the store's rent if you agree to pay the rent a year in advance. You need to determine the rent discount that would be attractive; that is, you need to know how much to pay in rent today in lieu of a $20,000 rental payment otherwise due a year from today.

If you do not make the advance rental payment, the money will remain in the deposit or security that earns at the rate r. Your equivalency rate is r. Therefore, the maximum amount that you would be willing to pay today is that amount that would otherwise grow at the rate of r per year to $20,000 at the end of the year; that is, you will leave the money in the interest-bearing deposit or security if the advance rental payment is not made. Therefore, an equation for the advance payment P is

$$P(1 + r) = \$20,000$$

$$P = \frac{20,000}{(1 + r)}$$

If r is 8 percent

$$P = \frac{20,000}{(1.08)} = \$18,520$$

Your decision? If the building owner will accept today $18,520 or less in lieu of $20,000 a year from today, you should pay the rent in advance. P is referred to as the present worth or time-adjusted value of the future rental payment at rate r. The time-adjusted value today of $20,000 a year from now is $18,520, assuming an interest rate of 8 percent.

Now suppose the building owner asks you to consider paying in advance the rentals due at the end of each of the next three years. Certainly you will demand a greater discount on the second year's rent than on the first, and a still greater discount on the rent otherwise due at the end of year three. Therefore, you need to know the time-adjusted value (or present value) P of a stream of three payments, each of $20,000, occurring at one-year intervals, assuming an interest rate of r. P is the sum of the individual time-adjusted values for each of the three years:

$$P = \frac{20,000}{(1 + r)} + \frac{20,000}{(1 + r)^2} + \frac{20,000}{(1 + r)^3}$$

If r is once again 8 percent, this equation produces a value for P of $51,540. You are willing to pay an amount up to $51,540—but not more—to be relieved of the obligation to make the three annual rental payments of $20,000 each.

Assume now that the building owner, badly needing cash, will have to borrow money at very high interest rates if you don't prepay the rent. Under these conditions the owner might be willing to accept substantially less than $51,540. That is, the owner undoubtedly has an equivalency rate well above 8 percent and thus a time-adjusted value of these future cash flow that is less than yours. Assuming an r of 12 percent, P for the building owner—the time-adjusted value of the next three annual rental payments—is $48,040.

Note that the higher the interest, or equivalency rate, r used in the calculation, the lower the time-adjusted value of future cash flows. Standard present value tables for calculating time-adjusted values are included in an appendix to this chapter. Illustrations of how to use these tables, based on the examples just discussed and others as well, are also in the appendix.

VALUING PERSONAL AND COMPANY ASSETS

With this background on the time-adjusted valuation of securities, loans, and pre-payments, consider valuing other assets owned by individuals by this method. We'll illustrate with assets typically owned by individuals, but ownership by individuals is no different than ownership by profit-seeking companies: time-adjusted values are as applicable to individuals as to businesses.

As mentioned earlier, the term *asset* encompasses all physical property, rights (e.g., patent and trademark rights), and any other resources that hold the promise of providing ongoing future benefits to the owner. Certainly, shares of common stock and debt instruments are assets to the investor. An automobile or household furniture or an account at the savings bank or even a pantry full of canned foods is an asset to the person who owns it: each holds the promise of delivering future benefits. The car may become wrecked or the canned food in the pantry may spoil, but at the moment the owner has a reasonable expectation of future benefits flowing from ownership of each. Each asset has a value, and our task is to consider alternative methods for determining that value.

Can the time-adjusted value of an automobile be calculated? Yes; at least in concept. The ownership of the automobile gives rise to certain future cash outflows and inflows and provides transportation benefits. These transportation benefits can be valued by reference to the cost of alternative transport methods such as taxicab, train, or bicycle. Other benefits, more difficult to value in monetary terms, include convenience, or status, or time saved. If the owner's time-adjusted valuation of the car is less than the amount it would sell for on the secondhand market, the owner will probably sell it; conversely, if the time-adjusted value is higher than its value to potential buyers, as reflected by its secondhand price, the owner will retain the car.

The automobile example highlights the importance of the viewpoint of the evaluator. You may feel that the convenience of automobile ownership is very important, while your neighbor who seldom requires travel to out-of-the-way places or at odd hours places little value on convenience. If so, you will place a higher time-adjusted value on an automobile than will your neighbor.

About now you are probably thinking that a far easier and more practical way to value your automobile is simply to value it at its secondhand price; in this country, values of recent-vintage cars are published monthly. Or, if your car is almost brand new, you might argue that the value of the car is what you paid for it. Clearly, these are alternative valuation methods—to be defined in just a moment. But, these methods of valuation are not inherently any more or less correct than the method based upon the time-adjusted value of the future flow of benefits.

Consider now the difficulty of valuing another asset that you own, your household furniture. Again, the time-adjusted value of the future benefits derived from owning this furniture is one evidence of value, although one not easily calculated. Secondhand prices are another, but used household furniture does not have the same organized secondhand market or readily ascertainable resale prices that used automobiles do. As in the case of your automobile, the price you originally paid for the asset represents still another indication of value.

What about the pantry full of canned goods? You probably filled the pantry either because you were able to get a very attractive price on the food or because you like the security of having a stock of food in the event of a tornado, hurricane, earthquake, enemy attack, or food shortage. In any case, the benefits of owning this large stock of food are stretched out into the future, and you have some idea of the timing and magnitude of the financial benefits to be derived from owning it. Thus, calculating a time-adjusted value for this stock of food is feasible; indeed you probably went through an intuitive time-adjusted valuation when you purchased it. Of course, you could also value this hoard of food at its replacement price or you could value it at the actual acquisition cost. Again, as in the case of the automobile and the household furniture, all three valuation methods are applicable.

Let's look more closely at each of these valuation methods: the time-adjusted value method, the **market value** method and the **cost value** method.

Time-Adjusted Value

To apply the time-adjusted method the asset's owner (or the accountant for the owner) must forecast the future benefits derived from ownership. For certain assets, such as loans, investments in common stock, paid-up insurance policies, or customers' promises to pay, estimating future benefits is easy. These benefits are either future cash inflows or the elimination of future cash outflows that would be required in the absence of the asset. Payment in advance of one year's rent on a building creates an asset—the right to use the building for one year or, equivalently, the elimination of the requirement to make rental payments during the year.

This valuation method is particularly useful for assets that have a long life and a predictable benefit flow. What is the value of a loan requiring the borrower to make level payments, incorporating both principal and interest, at the rate of $1000 per year for 10 years? The value of the loan depends upon the equivalency rate that the lender assigns to loans (investments) of this type. Its value is $10,000 only under the very unlikely assumption that the lender has a zero interest equivalency rate, implying that the lender has nothing else productive to do with the money. The higher the equivalency interest rate assumed, the lower the value of the loan:

Equivalency Interest Rate	Time-Adjusted Value
6%	$7360
8%	6710
10%	6144
12%	5650
15%	5019

Consider this valuation method for other assets, for example, a machine tool owned by a manufacturing company and a cellar of fine wines owned by an individual. In both cases asset ownership promises benefits stretched out into the future, but measuring these benefits is a real challenge.

The benefits of the machine tool depend upon a host of factors, including:

(1) The rate of obsolescence of the tool, which in turn depends upon the rate of technological development by machine tool builders.

(2) The future demand for the product or products produced on the machine tool (this demand in turn depends on the rate of change in the company's product lines, changes in the competitive climate, the strength of the economy, and changing consumer preferences).

The cellar of fine wines may be even more troublesome to value. The benefits are the personal pleasure of consuming the wine and serving it to friends, but here value is also dependent upon factors such as how well the wine ages, the volume and quality of wines to be produced in upcoming years, and future supply–demand imbalances that may affect the cost of wines.

So, this method of valuation, while appealing in concept, may be less useful in practice, at least for valuing such assets as machine tools and wine cellars.

We have been focusing on valuing assets. Does the time-adjusted valuation method apply also to liabilities? Yes; recall the borrower's valuation of a promise to pay under a loan agreement. The borrower's equivalency rate (determined by reference both to uses for the borrowed money and also to alternative sources of funds) is applied to the future cash flows to which the borrower is obligated.

What other obligations (liabilities) might be similarly valued? Consider a company's obligation to perform warranty service on the products it sells. If the company has some experience with the warranted product, it can estimate the timing and extent of the warranty service that will have to be provided. Once the pattern of warranty expenditures—future cash flows—has been estimated, the time-adjusted valuation method can be applied to arrive at a present-day equivalent value.

Similarly, a company's obligation to make payments to employees who have retired (i.e., pensions) or to others on vacation or sick leave can be valued on a time-adjusted basis. Typically, the timing and amounts of these flows are predictable.

You may feel that these future obligations—warranty and employee leave—need not be valued as liabilities. Why not postpone any accounting for warranty or leave until the product is returned for repair or the employee commences the leave? The reason is quite simple: it is today's shipments of products that give rise to the warranty service obligations and today's employment of personnel that requires the company to make certain payments at the time of promised leave. There is little doubt that the company will incur these expenditures, since inevitably a certain percentage of products will fail during the warranty period and employees do indeed take vacations or get sick or otherwise become entitled to paid leave. Activities today are creating these future company obligations and the timing and amount of these future expenditures are quite predictable. Thus, the obligations should be valued and recorded as a liability.

Other obligations that are more contingent or unpredictable might not be valued and recorded. Examples are the possibility of infringing another company's patent, the possibility that an income tax audit will result in the imposition of additional taxes, or the possibility that a current dispute with a supplier will result in additional payments to that supplier. Obviously, certain types of obligations will fall in a gray area—that is, reasonable people might disagree whether the obligation should be recorded. We'll come back to this issue in later chapters.

Market Value

Another indicator of value of both assets and obligations is market value, or the price at which similar assets and obligations currently trade in the market place. That is, if you can determine the price at which the asset can be purchased or sold, that price is a basis for valuing the asset.

Recall the example of the used automobile for which there exists a ready second market. Because used automobiles are regularly traded in the secondhand market in this country, information is collected, compiled, and published as to typical, or market, prices for a variety of makes and models.

Of course, actively traded common stocks (referred to as being publicly held) have market prices. Loans are also bought and sold among financial institutions and thus have a market price. On the other hand, common shares in a company predominantly owned by a single family, or loans of a specialized nature, or loans between individuals, are not actively traded in any organized market, and thus do not have an easily determinable market price. Nevertheless, even these securities do have some market price, that is, a price at which they could be bought or sold.

Looking back over the other examples used in this chapter, we see that:

(1) Household furniture surely has a market value. The newspaper classified advertisements evidence a relatively active, though largely unorganized, market for secondhand furniture. Persons knowledgeable about the used furniture market—including appraisers of antiques—can reliably estimate market values.

(2) The pantry full of canned foods can easily be valued at market prices by a simple reference to today's prices at the food market.

(3) Secondhand machine tools of a standard configuration have a very ready market at predictable prices, much like used automobiles. However, market prices of machine tools fluctuate widely, depending upon the state of the economy and the delivery schedules for equivalent new machine tools. These fluctuations are troublesome; if we use this valuation method in accounting records, we will be forever changing recorded values in our attempt to reflect these fluctuations. Also, specialized machine tools—tools that were custom-made for a particular user—may have a very limited market and accordingly a low market value even though they are certainly delivering benefits to the user. Can we arrive at reliable market prices for such assets?

(4) The cellar of fine wines can be valued by reference to today's prices for a bottle of the same wine from the same vineyard in the same year. In fact, vintage fine wines are sold and traded quite regularly.

What about valuing obligations? We saw earlier how the time-adjusted valuation method applies to warranty and employee leave obligations. Can the market value method also value these obligations?

Is there a market for warranty obligations? A manufacturer of devices subject to warranty could contract with another organization, perhaps one with an extensive network of service centers, to undertake the warranty work. Such a contract fixes a market price for this obligation: the price the manufacturer will pay to be relieved of the obligation to repair during the warranty period. In fact, contracts of this nature are entered into regularly in certain industries, such as the telecommunications industry.

How about employee pension obligations? Contracting with outside firms, generally insurance companies, to fulfill employee pension obligations is widespread—another example of paying a market price to be relieved of a future obligation. Many organizations also contract with insurance companies to pay wages to employees in the event of extended sickness.

Therefore, valuing in terms of current market price for both assets and liabilities is feasible; in many instances undue effort or research is not required and the resulting values are quite defensible. This evaluation method has some strong appeal: it does not require predictions about the future, as the time-adjusted value method does; it is rooted in the reality of today's marketplace; and it is understandable, explainable, and not complex.

However, the method does have its shortcomings. Recall the example of the specialized machine tool for which the market is very limited. The company might receive quite a low price for the asset in a sale. Does this imply that the specialized tool has little value to the owning company, which, in fact, has no intention of selling it? Indeed, just how relevant are current market prices to the task of valuing an asset, if its owner does not intend to sell it? The value of the specialized machine tool resides in its use, not in its resale. The fact that there may exist no other potential users of the specialized tool does not denigrate or destroy its usefulness to the company that now owns it.

At the other end of the scale, suppose that an asset has a high resale, or market value, but for any of a number of reasons its owner cannot consider selling the asset. Again, the value in use is more relevant to the accountant's task of asset valuation than is the higher market value that may exist but not be realizable.

Similarly, the household furniture, the pantry full of canned foods, and the wine cellar may have values to their particular owners that are higher than the market prices of strictly comparable items today. The furniture may have a sentimental value, the emergency supply of food a security value, and the wine cellar a prestige value—important values to their owners, but not reflected in the market prices that others are willing to pay.

Thus, the market value method of valuation, while appealing, has limitations, as did the time-adjusted value method. How about the cost value method?

Cost Value

A more complete name for this method is the historical cost method, since it calls for assets to be valued at the prices paid at the time they were acquired.

A decided advantage of the cost value method is that typically you can determine with both ease and accuracy what was actually paid for the asset. The acquisition prices of the securities, the automobile, the household furniture, the pantry full of canned goods, the machine tools (whether standard or custom), and the cellar of fine wines are known.

Note, however, that these historical cost values bear no necessary relationship to the values arrived at by the time-adjusted value or market value methods. If the automobile or household furniture was purchased long ago, its cost value may be considerably higher than its current market value. On the other hand, if the automobile is now considered a classic or if the owner of the fine wine made a particularly astute purchase, current market prices may be considerably above the acquisition or historical cost value. Consider valuing a parcel of land, a building site. If the land was acquired some time ago, its original cost is probably much below today's current market values, unless of course the development of the community or roadway system has left the parcel in less desirable surroundings, in which case the reverse may be true.

If the decline in an asset's value is caused simply by the passage of time—for example, wear, tear, and obsolescence on buildings or machine tools or vehicles—we could value the asset at a declining percentage of its original cost, as the asset ages. You probably already know that this procedure is in fact widely followed: Cost values in the accounting records are reduced each year by an amount called *depreciation*. Don't worry about that for now; we'll come back to depreciation in Chapter 8.

Even if we undertake a systematic write-down of an asset's value over its life, this procedure takes care of only one set of causes of value decline. A number of other factors create wide differences between market value and historical cost value. The most important is inflation.* Inflation can cause an old asset recorded at historical cost to appear in accounting records to have substantially less value to the company than its replacement cost. This condition frequently affects public utilities (electric, gas distribution, telephone). The facilities built by these companies many years ago may continue to be very productive, but inflation in land and construction costs causes them to be valued very much below the cost value of newly con-structed, equivalent facilities. This dilemma has been widely discussed by the accounting profession, but with essentially no resolution.

Can the cost method be used to value liabilities? By their nature obligations are settled in the future and have no historical cost; history has not yet caught up with the obligations. A strict interpretation of the cost value method might then suggest omitting from accounting records any such obligations that require the future expen-diture of cash or the future performance of services. Such an interpretation, how-ever, is simply unsatisfactory, as liabilities such as bank loans, promises to pay vendors, obligations under warranty provisions, and wage payments to employees on sick leave have major effects on the company's financial condition. Moreover, it is not unduly difficult to measure the future cost of meeting these obligations.

CHOOSING AMONG THE VALUATION METHODS

What are the advantages and disadvantages of the three valuation methods just discussed? Which one does the best job of valuing the assets and liabilities of the company? By now you realize that different valuation methods fit different situa-tions. The time-adjusted value method well suits the valuation of common stocks, notes, and other investment securities. The market value method seems workable in valuing automobiles, standard machine tools, a pantry full of canned goods, and perhaps even a cellar of fine wines. The cost value method seems widely applicable, but the longer the time between acquisition date and evaluation date and the higher the rate of inflation, the less comfort we can have in this method of valuation.

We need some criteria to compare these three valuation methods. Here are seven useful ones.

*Or, more generally, changes in purchasing power, both inflation and deflation. The history of virtually all organized economies is one of persistent inflation at various rates, punctuated by relatively few periods of deflation.

Currently Relevant

The accounting information resulting from the valuation of assets and liabilities is used to make decisions, such as operating decisions by management, investment decisions by shareholders, and credit decisions by lenders. These decisions require currently relevant data, data that reflect today's situation and expectations. Almost by definition, the historical cost method suffers in fulfilling this criterion and the more ancient the history, the more it is likely to suffer.

Feasible

You have to be able to develop the data required by the valuation method. If the future flow of an asset's benefits simply cannot be quantified, the time-adjusted value method is infeasible for that asset. An example is a patent on one feature of a potential new product. If the remaining design work is never completed, or the resulting product proves to have no market or to be too expensive to produce, the patent in question may provide very modest future benefits, or none. Alternatively, if the product gets designed, is producible, and meets a market need, the flow of benefits may be long and large. The accountant simply can't know at the time of the invention what the future holds for the patent.

Market values are readily ascertainable for some assets, but not others. Some liabilities (obligations) can be transferred for a (market) price; others can't.

The cost value method is typically the most feasible—historical cost data are readily available.

Effective

While it may be feasible to develop certain data for time-adjusted valuation or market valuation, it is not always practical to do so. The expense incurred to engage expertise, computing power, or the service of outside appraisers may be prohibitive. For example, it is certainly possible for you to develop the current market value of a chemical processing plant or of a trademark; you can advertise the asset for sale, and solicit offers. But the process is costly; much discussion and negotiation would transpire before a bona fide offer would be received. Moreover, a bona fide offer might never be forthcoming, if it became known that you had no intention of selling the asset.

You cannot afford to spend more to develop accounting information than the information is worth to you. As a result, the time-adjusted and market value methods are ineffective for valuing very many assets and liabilities that do not have a predictable flow of future benefits and readily available market prices.

Timely

The usefulness of accounting information declines rapidly with time. Management needs information to make today's operating decisions, to correct problems, and to seize opportunities. Investors need information to decide to buy, sell, or hold securities, and they want it as soon as possible. A month-end accounting report that takes six months to prepare is much less useful than one that is available in one week following month-end. To get rapid valuation, therefore, accountants are willing to sacrifice some accuracy.

Free from Bias

By now you undoubtedly see that an accountant has a good deal of latitude in deciding what should be recorded and at what value. The ideal valuation method is objective and little affected by an accountant's conscious or unconscious bias.

Repeatable

This criterion is closely related to the previous one. If the valuation method is objective, it should be repeatable. If an asset valuation done today and the one performed next month or next year are consistent (but of course not necessarily identical), you can have more confidence in the resulting information. If valuation by another accountant leads to the same result, both the method and the information are more reliable.

Verifiable

Financial records and statements of major enterprises are audited by independent, professional accountants. For these auditors to fulfill their role of confirming that the financial reports fairly represent the company's position, the valuations of assets and liabilities by the company's own accountants must be verifiable by the outside accountants. That is, tangible evidence that is subject to independent verification must be used. Again, if the method used is objective, it will probably satisfy the final three criteria—it will be free from bias, repeatable, and verifiable.

THE CHALLENGE OF ALTERNATIVE VALUATION METHODS

Clearly, none of the three valuation methods—time-adjusted value, market value, cost value—satisfies all seven criteria. The first criterion, that data be currently relevant, seems best satisfied by the time-adjusted value and market value methods, and least satisfied by the cost value method. However, the remaining criteria are well satisfied by the cost value method:

Uncovering historical cost data is clearly feasible.

The data can be arrived at in a timely manner.

Historical costs are relatively free from bias; arguments sometimes arise as to what constitutes cost, but these are minor compared to disagreements on the future flow of benefits.

Cost value determinations are repeatable; once determined, they don't change with time, and thus they are consistent and reliable.

Cost data are tangible evidence subject to independent verification.

Yet, the market value method also satisfies most, if not all, criteria in valuing certain assets such as automobiles or standard machine tools. Market values of these assets are certainly currently relevant; arriving at the data is feasible and cost-effective; the data are quickly available, objective, free from bias, repeatable, and verifiable.

The time-adjusted value method also satisfies substantially all of the criteria in certain instances, such as the valuation of a loan or an employee pension, where the data required are available, objective, verifiable, and so forth. Moreover, the time-adjusted value method provides information that is most relevant to today's decision. The problem is that the method is extraordinarily difficult to apply to very many assets and liabilities. The data required are not readily or inexpensively available, biases are inevitable, and as a result different individuals, each doing the most conscientious job possible, arrive at different values.

The challenge that faces the accountant is to develop accounting information and reports that combine the relevancy and usefulness inherent in time-adjusted values with the efficiency and reliability inherent in cost values.

DOMINANCE OF THE COST VALUE METHOD

We must deal with reality, and reality is that current accounting practices and rules are built to a very large degree on the cost value method. In the vast majority of cases today, accountants use historical cost data as the best evidence of what the company owns—the value of its assets—and what the company owes—the value of its liabilities. While expedient and pragmatic, most agree that the method is not wholly adequate. It is precise but, in the view of many, not sufficiently accurate.

As a result, accountants are embracing, to an increasing degree, the other two valuation methods. Market values, or replacement values of assets, are seen as relevant to the business and financial communities, particularly in times of rapid inflation when values escalate or in times of recession when market values plummet, often to values well below cost. The future flow of benefits and costs is now considered the most appropriate way to value certain liabilities.

Thus, we are likely to see a continuing, although gradual, move away from strict adherence to historical cost valuations. The accountants' rule-making bodies, both public and private, have been conspicuously active in the last several years in promulgating new rules that attempt to overcome some of the deficiencies in the cost value methodology and to provide more objectivity to alternative methodologies. As you proceed through this book, then, you should question the rules and conventions now in use; because these rules and conventions are built largely on cost value methodology, they are subject to change.

SUMMARY

In this chapter we have focused on the valuing part of the accounting task: valuing the various assets and obligations (liabilities) of the accounting entity, preparatory to recording the events and conditions of the enterprise.

The resulting valuations determine what the company owns (assets) and what it owes (liabilities); the difference between the two is the worth attributable to the owners. Thus, the fundamental accounting equation can be written

$$\text{Assets} - \text{liabilities} = \text{owners' equity}$$

The two fundamental sources of financing for the assets owned by the enterprise are (1) the funds obtained from the company's creditors, as represented by the company's liabilities and (2) funds obtained from the company's owners, either as cash invested over the years by the owners or profits earned but not paid out. Thus, the accounting equation can also be stated as

$$\text{Assets} = \text{liabilities} + \text{owners' equity}$$

The simplest view of owners' equity is that it is just the difference between assets owned and liabilities owed. But it is also equal to capital invested in the business by its owners, plus the net of profits earned less losses incurred in operating the business, and less any amounts returned to the owners.

The three valuation methods are:

(1) The time-adjusted value method, which determines the equivalency value today of the future flow of benefits or costs that will arise as a result of owning the asset or being subject to the liability.

(2) The market value method, which equates value with the price at which the asset or liability, in its present state, could be bought or sold in the market today.

(3) The cost value method, which relies on historical cost—that is, the cost of the asset or liability at the time it was originally acquired—to represent its value.

The relative advantages and disadvantages of each of the three valuation methods are judged by seven criteria. The ideal valuation method provides information that is (1) relevant to current decisions; (2) feasible in its derivation; (3) cost-effective (worth more than the cost to generate it); (4) timely; (5) free from bias; (6) repeatable; and (7) verifiable by independent persons. None of the three valuation methods is clearly the best in all circumstances. The time-adjusted value method provides the most currently useful data, but is often difficult to implement. The cost value method best satisfies those criteria dealing with objectivity and verifiability of the data, but historical costs are frequently not relevant to today's decisions.

Today accepted valuation rules and techniques adhere closely to the cost value methodology; but increasingly both accountants and financial audiences are pressuring for a correction of some shortcomings of the cost value method. The time-adjusted value and market value methods are now accepted in more and more circumstances.

NEW TERMS

Accounting equation. Assets = liabilities + owners' equity.

Asset. The name given to all property and rights owned by the accounting equity.

Cost value. The value of an asset or liability based on the price at which it was originally purchased (asset) or will be discharged (liability).

Equivalency rate. The interest rate used in time-adjusted valuations to adjust future benefits and costs to their value today (present value).

Liability. The name given to obligations of (amounts owed by) the accounting equity.

Market value. The value of an asset or liability based on the price at which it could be bought or sold today.

Owners' equity. The net value or worth of the owners' interest in the entity as expressed in the accounting records. Owners' equity is the sum of capital invested by the owners plus profits earned (less losses incurred) less any funds repaid by the entity to its owners. Owners' equity also equals the difference between the total value of assets and total value of liabilities.

Time-adjusted value. The value of an asset or liability based on the future stream of benefits and costs associated with it, with appropriate adjustments for their timing.

DISCUSSION QUESTIONS

2.1 How are liabilities and owners' equity similar? How are they different?

2.2 Why must the basic accounting equation always balance?

2.3 Are long-term interest rates generally higher or lower than short-term interest rates? Why?

2.4 Describe how you would value your car and your family home using three methods:

   (a) Time-adjusted value.

   (b) Market value.

   (c) Cost value.

   Which of these methods results in the highest value?

2.5 Is it possible for a company to have a large owners' equity and be short of cash? Why? How?

2.6 Make a list of five assets your own; then indicate the valuation method most appropriate to determine the monetary value of each for the purpose of insuring each asset.

2.7 Which of the valuation methods (time-adjusted, market, and cost) would you use to value the following:

(a) Your personal wardrobe.

(b) Your half interest ownership in a pleasure sailboat.

(c) A stereo system, assuming you assembled it yourself.

(d) A three-year time savings account that earns interest at 7 percent per year (an interest penalty will be charged against the account if you withdraw the funds before the end of three years).

(e) The installment loan on your car, which requires that you pay $200 per month for the next 24 months.

(f) Your health.

(g) Your used computer.

(h) Your textbooks for courses you have completed.

(i) A student loan, payable over 10 years after graduation.

(j) Ten shares of common stock in a company whose shares are listed on the New York Stock Exchange.

(k) 10 shares of common stock in a small company of which 80 percent of the shares are owned by your brother-in-law.

2.8 Consider yourself as an accounting entity. Can you calculate your own owners' equity? If so, what assets and liabilities would you need to consider in arriving at your owners' equity?

2.9 The following *things* or *rights* are owned by a particular company. Do you think they should be valued in the company's accounting records? And if so, what valuation method would you propose to use?

(a) A trade name that is widely known and trusted by consumers.

(b) A two-year employment contract with a well-known scientist employee.

(c) A contract with a major supplier that requires the supplier to deliver 14,000 metric tons of material to the company at a fixed price over the next year; that fixed price is 20 percent below the price the company would now have to pay to other suppliers for equivalent materials.

(d) A small parcel of land that is not large enough to serve as a building site.

(e) 200 dozen pencils, representing about a 15-month supply, for use by office personnel.

(f) A simple conveyor system that was built by the plant maintenance person during her spare time from scrap material she found around the plant.

(g) Obsolete material in inventory that was originally purchased for $3000 and could now be sold to a salvage dealer for $400.

(h) The five-year lease on the company's building, which has 4.5 years remaining and calls for monthly rent of $20,000.

(i) Electrical power distribution equipment that was installed at a cost of $50,000 in the company's leased building, but could not be removed if the company vacates the building.

(j) An option to purchase the company's building at the end of the current lease at a predetermined price.

(k) A list of names of the 200 customers with whom the company has traded for 10 years or more.

(l) A five-year site license for several software products.

(m) A 10-year contract with a waste treatment company to dispose of all of your company's hazardous waste.

2.10 The following liabilities or obligations are owned by a particular company. Do you think they should be valued in the company's accounting records? And if so, what valuation method would you use?

(a) The company's promise to deliver 10 units of product A by the fifteenth of next month.

(b) As part of the contract described in (a), the company agrees to pay a $1000 penalty for every day that it is late in its delivery.

(c) A two-year employment contract with a well-known scientist.

(d) The expectation by the company's employees that they will receive a handsome end-of-year bonus.

(e) The $5000 bill from the electrical contractor who installed power distribution facilities in the company's leased building.

(f) The five-year lease on the company's building, which has 4.5 years remaining and calls for monthly payments of $20,000.

(g) A contract with a major supplier that requires the company to accept delivery of and pay for 14,000 metric tons of material over the next year. The fixed price on the contract is 20 percent below the price the company would now have to pay to other suppliers for equivalent material.

(h) A three-year contract with a consulting firm to assist in improving quality in all plant operations.

(i) Warranty provisions on a product that has recently been shown to require warranty repair on about 30 percent of all units supplied to customers over the past two years.

(j) Your company's promise to customer N to rebate $2000 if the customer is not fully satisfied with products shipped to the customer this month.

2.11 Is it possible for a company to have negative owners' equity? If so, how might this condition come about? What does this condition imply about the total value of assets owned and liabilities owed by the company?

2.12 Banks are business entities, just as are manufacturing and retailing companies. What are the main assets a bank owns? What are its principal liabilities? Who are the owners' of a bank; that is, who benefits from the bank owners' equity? If a bank's borrower fails to pay back the money borrowed, how would this situation affect the bank's assets, liabilities, and owners' equity?

2.13 What are the principal assets of a law firm? What are its principal liabilities? Who are its owners?

2.14 Suppose you belong to a private social or tennis club. What are the principal assets owned by the club? What are its principal liabilities? Does the club have owners? If so, who are they? If not, is there no amount equivalent to owners' equity for your club?

2.15 You own a bond that pays you interest at the rate of 6 percent per year. Since you purchased the bond, prevailing interest rates have increased to about 8 percent. Would you now be inclined to value your bond at more or less than you paid for it? (You can verify your answer by noting the relationship between bond prices and interest rates quoted on the financial pages of a newspaper such as the *Wall Street Journal*.)

2.16 Are current market prices of assets generally equivalent to the cost to replace them? Why?

2.17 Suppose that the market value method leads to a valuation of $4000 for an asset that has an original cost of $5000. If we use the cost value rather than the market value method of valuation, what effect will this decision have on the company's assets, liabilities, and owners' equity? Is this effect desirable or undesirable? To whom?

2.18 Since the time-adjusted value requires the accountant to forecast the future flows of benefits and costs, is this method of valuation inconsistent with the view that the accountant is a historian? Discuss your answer.

2.19 Suppose you are the independent auditor for a company, charged with the responsibility of verifying the valuations placed on the items below. For each of the three valuation methods, how would you go about the process of verification?

(a) The promise of a customer to pay $100 per month for the next 25 months to repay the $2500 now owed by her to the company.

(b) A five-year-old office building owned by the company and utilized as its sales office in Des Moines.

(c) An inventory of merchandise that the company expects to sell to customers over the next three months and that will be replaced as it is sold by equivalent merchandise purchased from suppliers.

2.20   Consider the promise of a customer to pay $100 per month for 25 months to repay the $2500 now owed by her to the company. Which of the three valuation methods is likely to lead to the highest value for this promise to pay? Under what set of conditions would you expect the time-adjusted value to be lower than the market value?

2.21   Consider a five-year-old office building owned by the company and utilized as its sales office in Des Moines. What factors might cause the building's time-adjusted value to its present occupants to be above its market value?

2.22   Consider an inventory of merchandise that the company expects to sell to customers over the next three months and that will be replaced as it is sold by equivalent merchandise purchased from suppliers. Would you expect the market value to exceed the cost value, to be less than the cost value, or to be typically the same as the cost value? Why?

2.23   Assume you are a banker considering making a five-year loan to a medium-sized manufacturing company. Would you prefer to have financial statements for the company prepared on the basis of time-adjusted values, market values, or cost values?

2.24   Assume you are a banker considering a loan of $5000 to a middle-income family. The money is to be used to remodel the family's home. Would you prefer to have the family's financial statement prepared on the basis of time-adjusted values, market values, or cost values?

2.25   Identify each of the following as an asset, a liability, or owners' equity (from the point of view of the company):

(a)   Income taxes for last year which have not been paid.

(b)   Vacation leave for employees, earned by them but not yet taken.

(c)   Amounts owed to the company by its suppliers for faulty merchandise that has been returned to the suppliers.

(d)   A license granted by a governmental regulatory agency that permits the company to engage in a certain business.

(e)   A loan by the bank to the company.

(f)   A loan by the company to one of its employees.

(g)   Common stock owned by this company in another, unrelated company.

(h)   Products that have been manufactured and are now in inventory awaiting sale.

(i)   Interest on a loan due to the corporation by an employee.

(j)   Deposit paid to an equipment supplier for specialized equipment to be delivered next year.

(k)   Amounts owed to the company's outside lawyers for legal services received.

(l) Trucks used to provide delivery service to customers.

(m) Life insurance policy on the company president's life that will pay $1,000,000 to the company in the event of the president's death.

(n) A house owned by the company and rented by the company to the sales manager's son.

(o) A loan from a shareholder to the corporation.

(p) An order from a customer for equipment to be manufactured and delivered next year and billed to the customer at that time.

(q) Earnings of the company during the first six months of this year when no dividends have been paid.

(r) The obligation to provide warranty repair for one year after delivery on certain products shipped to the company.

(s) An amount paid last month to the insurance company for one year of comprehensive coverage.

2.26 Provide three examples of transactions that would:

(a) Decrease an asset and decrease a liability.

(b) Increase owners' equity and increase an asset.

(c) Increase one asset and decrease another.

(d) Decrease owners' equity and decrease an asset.

(e) Increase an asset and increase a liability.

PROBLEMS

2.1 The Hume Company is a small retailing firm. During one month the following events occurred. Analyze the effect of each event on the assets, liabilities, and owners' equity of the Hume Company. For each, consider the appropriateness of the cost value as the measure of the value of the event.

Example

Hume paid $2600 to Security Bank: $2400 as partial payment of the remaining principal balance of a loan, and $200 in interest for the month.

Answer

Assets: Decrease by $2600
Liabilities: Decrease by $2400
Owners' Equity: Decrease by $200

(a) A customer to whom goods were sold last month made a partial payment of $3100.

(b) Excess equipment carrying a value on the accounting records of $2000 was sold for $2000.

    (c) Sales of goods totaled $16,500, of which $3000 was received in cash and $13,500 represented credit sales. The inventory sold in these transactions had been purchased by Hume for $12,300.

    (d) Wages earned by the employees and paid during the month totaled $2500. In addition, as required by law, Hume paid $450 in employment taxes.

    (e) Hume paid $2700 to suppliers for goods received in previous months.

    (f) New inventory having an original cost of $11,000 was ordered and received. Of this amount, $4500 was paid in cash and $6500 remained owing to the suppliers. In addition, Hume placed orders during the month for inventory costing $8000, but none of this inventory has been received.

    (g) A supplier to whom Hume owed $5000 agreed to defer payment for one year, provided Hume agreed to pay interest on the balance at 8 percent per year.

    (h) At the end of the month, 25 shares of common stock were sold to an employee for a cash payment of $5000.

2.2 The Calistoga Corporation is a television repair firm located in a medium-sized town. During one month, the following events occurred. Analyze the effect of each described event on the assets, liabilities, and owners' equity of the corporation. For each, consider the appropriateness of the cost value as the measure of the value of the event.

    (a) One repairperson was paid a $100 bonus for making an evening visit to fix a customer's TV, which had not been properly repaired in the shop.

    (b) A shipment of invoice forms bearing the company's name and other specialized information was received. This supply of invoices cost $850 and should be sufficient to last for 18 months.

    (c) A bill for $70 was received from Turlock Trucking for delivery of the invoices mentioned above.

    (d) The company paid dividends totaling $1000 to its shareholders.

    (e) The company invested $1000 in excess cash in a short-term U.S. government note.

    (f) The company purchased for cash materials used in the repair of TV sets. These materials cost $1150.

    (g) The company purchased for $10,000 in cash a new truck that had a list price of $11,400.

    (h) The president of Calistoga purchased for $3000 in cash 10 shares of common stock in Calistoga that were owned by the president's cousin.

    (i) An employee to whom Calistoga had lent $200 disappeared and was rumored to have moved to another city.

    (j) A young customer who owed $150 to Calistoga painted the woodwork on the exterior of the store in full "payment" of his account.

(**k**) The accountant for Calistoga estimated that the value of the repair equipment owned by the company had declined by $550 during the month.

2.3 A flower stand operated by an enterprising student in a shopping mall near the college was in the following financial position at the end of September:

Assets:	Cash	$500
	Flower stand structure	2500
Liabilities:	Owed to suppliers	600

During the month of October the events listed below occurred:

(**a**) Sales totaled $3400. All sales were for cash.

(**b**) Flowers were purchased fresh every day, and the total of all flowers purchased for the month was $1800. Purchases were on credit.

(**c**) Rental of $200 was paid to the shopping mall in cash.

(**d**) Wages paid in cash to the stand attendants totalled $1200.

(**e**) Payments on account to the flower suppliers totaled $1750.

(**f**) The student estimated that the value of the flower stand had declined by $100 during the course of the month.

Trace through the effects on the assets, liabilities, and owners' equity of all of these events, and determine the financial position of the flower stand at the end of the month.

2.4 A foreign language school, La Casa de Juan, has been operating for several years. In the month of March 1994, the following transactions took place:

(**a**) Tuition for the month for all students was $22,700. Payment for tuition is due at the end of each month and $13,700 of this amount was received in March.

(**b**) Late payment of the previous month's tuition totaled $6700.

(**c**) The monthly rent for the school building was paid in cash, $3500.

(**d**) Expenses for miscellaneous materials purchased on credit totaled $1600 for the month.

(**e**) Salaries for the teachers and staff totaled $13,000 and were paid in cash.

(**f**) Taxes on salaries for teachers and staff were paid to the state, totaling $1300.

Trace through the effects on the assets, liabilities, and owners' equity of all of these events, and determine the extent to which the financial position of the school changed during the month of March.

2.5 With the new emphasis on environmental awareness, The Green Thumb, a company that sells natural foods, wants to start managing a recycling program in the city in which it operates. In order to start this business, the owners have created a new business entity, The Green Hand. The following transactions all took place in January 1995. Employees hired by the company will begin work on February 1, when the first recyclable materials will arrive for processing.

(a) Purchased 0.5 acre of land to be used for sorting recyclable materials for $20,000, financed entirely through a bank loan.

(b) Paid for "help wanted" ads in the newspaper at a cost of $275.

(c) Purchased a prefabricated shed to be installed on the new property. The shed was purchased for $1500 cash; the installation was done on credit and cost $600.

(d) Transportation, separating, and packing equipment was purchased. Part of the purchase, $27,000, was on credit, while another portion, $5000, was paid in cash.

(e) Three large billboards urging the general population to recycle were rented for two years. The rent per year is $860, and was paid in advance for the first year.

(f) A contract for trash removal from the site was signed with the local garbage company. The contrast is for five years and calls for weekly trash pickup. The Green Hand must pay a monthly fee of $250 for the service. No payments have yet been made.

(g) The Green Hand paid filing fees with the county for the creation of a new business, $300 in cash.

(h) The county returned $250 of the filing fees under a program to provide incentives to environmentally conscious businesses.

Trace through the effects of these transactions on the assets, liabilities, and owners' equity of The Green Hand. What is the financial position of the company on January 31? How much do you think The Green Thumb has had to invest in this new business?

INTEREST TABLES TO CALCULATE TIME-ADJUSTED (PRESENT WORTH) VALUES

Table 2A.1 contains factors for calculating the time-adjusted value of one dollar to be received or paid at various dates in the future and at various interest rates. Table 2A.2 contains factors for calculating the time-adjusted value of a stream of payments or receipts, each of one dollar, occurring at annual intervals for the periods (n) indicated; these factors are also shown for various interest rates.

The use of these tables is illustrated with the examples discussed in Chapter 2:

(a) The time-adjusted value today of a cash flow of $20,000 occurring a year from today can be calculated from Table 2A.1; the factor in the 8% column and the one-year row is 0.926. Therefore $P = 20,000\ (0.926) = \$18,520$.

(b) The time-adjusted value today of a stream of three $20,000 cash flows occurring at the end of each of the next three years can be calculated from Table 2A.2; the factor in the 8% column and the three-year row is 2.577. Therefore: P at 8 percent $= 20,000\ (2.5770) = \$51,540$. The factor in the 12% column and the three-year row is 2.402. Therefore P at 12 percent $= 20,000\ (2.402) = \$48,040$.

For purposes of accounting valuations, we are typically concerned with making time adjustments of future cash flows (inflows or outflows) to value them as of today. However, these same tables can also provide answers to the following types of questions.

(1) If you place $100 today in an investment earning 10 percent per year, what will be the value of that investment in five years? Since the factors in Table 2A.1 indicate the value today of $100 to be received at some date in the future, the inverse of the factors indicates the value in the future of an

TABLE 2A.1 Time-Adjusted (Present) Value of One Dollar at the End of n Years

Year (n)	1%	2%	3%	4%	5%	6%	7%	8%	9%	10%	12%	14%	15%	Year (n)
1	0.990	0.980	0.970	0.962	0.952	0.943	0.935	0.926	0.917	0.909	0.893	0.877	0.870	1
2	0.980	0.961	0.943	0.925	0.907	0.890	0.873	0.857	0.842	0.826	0.797	0.769	0.756	2
3	0.971	0.942	0.915	0.889	0.864	0.840	0.816	0.794	0.772	0.751	0.712	0.675	0.658	3
4	0.961	0.924	0.888	0.855	0.823	0.792	0.763	0.735	0.708	0.683	0.636	0.592	0.572	4
5	0.951	0.906	0.863	0.822	0.784	0.747	0.713	0.681	0.650	0.621	0.567	0.519	0.497	5
6	0.942	0.888	0.837	0.790	0.746	0.705	0.666	0.630	0.596	0.564	0.507	0.456	0.432	6
7	0.933	0.871	0.813	0.760	0.711	0.665	0.623	0.583	0.547	0.513	0.452	0.400	0.376	7
8	0.923	0.853	0.789	0.731	0.677	0.627	0.582	0.540	0.502	0.467	0.404	0.351	0.327	8
9	0.914	0.837	0.766	0.703	0.645	0.592	0.544	0.500	0.460	0.424	0.361	0.308	0.284	9
10	0.905	0.820	0.744	0.676	0.614	0.558	0.508	0.463	0.422	0.386	0.322	0.270	0.247	10
11	0.896	0.804	0.722	0.650	0.585	0.527	0.475	0.429	0.388	0.350	0.287	0.237	0.215	11
12	0.887	0.788	0.701	0.625	0.557	0.497	0.444	0.397	0.356	0.319	0.257	0.208	0.187	12
13	0.879	0.773	0.681	0.601	0.530	0.469	0.415	0.368	0.326	0.290	0.229	0.182	0.163	13
14	0.870	0.758	0.661	0.577	0.505	0.442	0.388	0.340	0.299	0.263	0.205	0.160	0.141	14
15	0.861	0.743	0.642	0.555	0.481	0.417	0.362	0.315	0.275	0.239	0.183	0.140	0.123	15
16	0.853	0.726	0.623	0.534	0.458	0.394	0.339	0.299	0.252	0.218	0.163	0.123	0.107	16
17	0.844	0.714	0.605	0.513	0.436	0.371	0.317	0.270	0.231	0.198	0.146	0.108	0.093	17
18	0.836	0.700	0.587	0.494	0.416	0.350	0.296	0.250	0.212	0.180	0.130	0.095	0.081	18
19	0.828	0.686	0.570	0.475	0.396	0.331	0.277	0.232	0.194	0.164	0.116	0.083	0.070	19
20	0.820	0.673	0.554	0.456	0.377	0.312	0.258	0.215	0.178	0.149	0.104	0.073	0.061	20
21	0.811	0.660	0.538	0.439	0.359	0.294	0.242	0.199	0.164	0.135	0.093	0.064	0.053	21
22	0.803	0.647	0.522	0.422	0.342	0.278	0.226	0.184	0.150	0.123	0.083	0.056	0.046	22
23	0.795	0.634	0.507	0.406	0.326	0.262	0.211	0.170	0.138	0.112	0.074	0.049	0.040	23
24	0.788	0.622	0.492	0.390	0.310	0.247	0.197	0.158	0.126	0.102	0.066	0.043	0.035	24
25	0.780	0.610	0.478	0.375	0.295	0.233	0.184	0.146	0.116	0.092	0.059	0.038	0.030	25

Year (n)	16%	18%	20%	22%	24%	25%	26%	28%	30%	35%	40%	50%	Year (n)
1	0.862	0.847	0.833	0.820	0.806	0.800	0.794	0.781	0.769	0.741	0.714	0.667	1
2	0.743	0.718	0.694	0.672	0.650	0.640	0.630	0.610	0.592	0.549	0.510	0.444	2
3	0.641	0.609	0.579	0.551	0.524	0.512	0.500	0.477	0.455	0.406	0.364	0.296	3
4	0.552	0.516	0.482	0.451	0.423	0.410	0.397	0.373	0.350	0.301	0.260	0.198	4
5	0.476	0.437	0.402	0.370	0.341	0.328	0.315	0.291	0.269	0.223	0.186	0.132	5
6	0.410	0.370	0.333	0.303	0.275	0.262	0.250	0.227	0.207	0.165	0.133	0.088	6
7	0.354	0.314	0.279	0.249	0.222	0.210	0.198	0.178	0.159	0.122	0.095	0.059	7
8	0.305	0.266	0.233	0.204	0.179	0.168	0.157	0.139	0.123	0.091	0.068	0.039	8
9	0.263	0.225	0.194	0.167	0.144	0.134	0.125	0.108	0.094	0.067	0.048	0.026	9
10	0.227	0.191	0.162	0.137	0.116	0.107	0.099	0.085	0.073	0.050	0.035	0.017	10
11	0.195	0.162	0.135	0.112	0.094	0.086	0.079	0.066	0.056	0.037	0.025	0.012	11
12	0.168	0.137	0.112	0.092	0.076	0.069	0.062	0.052	0.043	0.027	0.018	0.008	12
13	0.145	0.116	0.093	0.075	0.061	0.055	0.050	0.040	0.033	0.020	0.013	0.005	13
14	0.125	0.099	0.078	0.062	0.049	0.044	0.039	0.032	0.025	0.015	0.009	0.003	14
15	0.108	0.084	0.065	0.051	0.040	0.035	0.031	0.025	0.020	0.011	0.006	0.002	15
16	0.093	0.071	0.054	0.042	0.032	0.028	0.025	0.019	0.015	0.008	0.005	0.002	16
17	0.080	0.060	0.045	0.034	0.026	0.023	0.020	0.015	0.012	0.006	0.003	0.001	17
18	0.069	0.051	0.038	0.028	0.021	0.018	0.016	0.012	0.009	0.005	0.002	0.001	18
19	0.060	0.043	0.031	0.023	0.017	0.014	0.012	0.009	0.007	0.003	0.002		19
20	0.051	0.037	0.026	0.019	0.014	0.012	0.010	0.007	0.005	0.002	0.001		20
21	0.044	0.031	0.022	0.015	0.011	0.009	0.008	0.006	0.004	0.002	0.001		21
22	0.038	0.026	0.018	0.013	0.009	0.007	0.006	0.004	0.003	0.001	0.001		22
23	0.033	0.022	0.015	0.010	0.007	0.006	0.005	0.003	0.002	0.001			23
24	0.028	0.019	0.013	0.008	0.006	0.005	0.004	0.003	0.002	0.001			24
25	0.024	0.016	0.010	0.007	0.005	0.004	0.003	0.002	0.001	0.001			25

TABLE 2A.2 Time-Adjusted (Present) Value of One Dollar per Year for _n_ Years

Year (n)	1%	2%	3%	4%	5%	6%	7%	8%	9%	10%	12%	14%	15%	Year (n)
1	0.990	0.980	0.971	0.962	0.952	0.943	0.935	0.926	0.917	0.909	0.893	0.377	0.870	1
2	1.970	1.942	1.914	1.886	1.859	1.833	1.808	1.783	1.759	1.736	1.690	1.647	1.626	2
3	2.941	2.884	2.829	2.775	2.723	2.673	2.624	2.577	2.531	2.487	2.402	2.322	2.283	2
4	3.902	3.808	3.717	3.630	3.546	3.485	3.387	3.312	3.240	3.170	3.037	2.914	2.855	4
5	4.854	4.713	4.580	4.452	4.330	4.212	4.100	3.993	3.890	3.791	3.605	3.433	3.352	5
6	5.796	5.601	5.417	5.242	5.076	4.917	4.767	4.623	4.486	4.355	4.111	3.889	3.785	6
7	6.728	6.472	6.230	6.002	5.786	5.582	5.389	5.206	5.033	4.868	4.564	4.288	4.160	7
8	7.652	7.325	7.020	6.733	6.463	6.210	5.971	5.747	5.535	5.335	4.968	4.639	4.487	8
9	8.566	8.162	7.786	7.435	7.108	6.802	6.515	6.247	5.985	5.759	5.328	4.946	4.772	9
10	9.471	8.963	8.530	8.111	7.722	7.360	7.024	6.710	6.418	6.145	5.650	5.216	5.019	10
11	10.368	9.787	9.253	8.760	8.306	7.887	7.498	7.139	6.805	6.495	5.938	5.453	5.234	11
12	11.255	10.575	9.954	9.385	8.863	8.384	7.943	7.536	7.161	6.814	6.194	5.660	5.421	12
13	12.134	11.348	10.635	9.966	9.394	8.853	8.358	7.904	7.487	7.103	6.424	5.842	5.583	13
14	13.004	12.106	11.296	10.563	9.899	9.296	8.745	8.244	7.786	7.367	6.628	6.002	5.725	14
15	13.865	12.849	11.938	11.118	10.380	9.712	9.108	8.560	8.061	7.606	6.811	6.142	5.847	15
16	14.718	13.578	12.561	11.652	10.838	10.106	9.447	8.851	8.313	7.824	6.974	6.265	5.954	16
17	15.562	14.292	13.166	12.166	11.274	10.477	9.763	9.122	8.544	8.022	7.120	6.373	6.047	17
18	16.398	14.992	13.753	12.659	11.690	10.828	10.059	9.372	8.756	8.201	7.250	6.467	6.128	18
19	17.226	15.678	14.324	13.134	12.085	11.158	10.336	9.604	8.950	8.365	7.366	6.550	6.198	19
20	18.046	16.351	14.877	13.590	12.462	11.470	10.594	9.818	9.129	8.514	7.469	6.623	6.259	20
21	18.857	17.011	15.415	14.029	12.821	11.764	10.836	10.017	9.292	8.649	7.562	6.687	6.313	21
22	19.661	17.658	15.937	14.451	13.163	12.042	11.061	10.201	9.442	8.772	7.645	6.743	6.359	22
23	20.456	18.292	16.444	14.857	13.489	12.303	11.272	10.371	9.580	8.883	7.718	6.792	6.399	23
24	21.244	18.914	16.936	15.247	13.799	12.550	11.469	10.529	9.707	8.985	7.784	6.835	6.434	24
25	22.023	19.523	17.413	15.622	14.094	12.783	11.654	10.675	9.823	9.077	7.843	6.873	6.464	25

Year (n)	16%	18%	20%	22%	24%	25%	26%	28%	30%	35%	40%	50%	Year (n)
1	0.862	0.848	0.833	0.820	0.807	0.800	0.794	0.781	0.769	0.741	0.714	0.667	1
2	1.605	1.566	1.528	1.492	1.457	1.440	1.424	1.392	1.361	1.289	1.225	1.111	2
3	2.246	2.174	2.107	2.042	1.961	1.952	1.923	1.868	1.816	1.696	1.589	1.407	3
4	2.796	2.690	2.589	2.494	2.404	2.362	2.320	2.241	2.166	1.997	1.849	1.605	4
5	3.274	3.127	2.991	2.864	2.745	2.689	2.635	2.532	2.436	2.220	2.935	1.737	5
6	3.685	3.496	3.326	3.167	3.021	2.951	2.885	2.759	2.643	2.385	2.168	1.824	6
7	4.039	3.812	3.605	3.416	3.242	3.161	3.083	2.937	2.802	2.508	2.263	1.883	7
8	4.344	4.078	3.837	3.619	3.421	3.329	3.241	3.076	2.925	2.596	2.331	1.922	8
9	4.607	4.303	4.031	3.786	3.566	3.463	3.366	3.184	3.019	2.665	2.379	1.948	9
10	4.833	4.494	4.103	3.923	3.682	3.571	3.465	3.269	3.092	2.715	2.414	1.965	10
11	5.029	4.656	4.327	4.035	3.776	3.656	3.544	3.335	3.147	2.752	2.438	1.977	11
12	5.197	4.793	4.439	4.127	3.851	3.725	3.606	3.387	3.190	2.779	2.456	1.985	12
13	5.342	4.910	4.533	4.203	3.912	3.780	3.656	3.427	3.223	2.799	2.469	1.990	13
14	5.468	5.008	4.611	4.265	3.962	3.824	3.695	3.459	3.249	2.814	2.478	1.993	14
15	5.576	5.092	4.676	4.315	4.001	3.859	3.726	3.483	3.268	2.826	2.484	1.995	15
16	5.669	5.162	4.730	4.357	4.033	3.887	3.751	3.503	3.283	2.834	2.489	1.997	16
17	5.749	5.222	4.775	4.391	4.059	3.910	3.771	3.518	3.295	2.840	2.492	1.998	17
18	5.818	5.273	4.812	4.419	4.080	3.928	3.786	3.529	3.304	2.844	2.494	1.999	18
19	5.878	5.316	4.844	4.442	4.097	3.942	3.799	3.539	3.311	2.848	2.496	1.999	19
20	5.929	5.353	4.870	4.460	4.110	3.954	3.806	3.546	3.316	2.850	2.497	1.999	20
21	5.973	5.384	4.891	4.476	4.121	3.963	3.816	3.551	3.320	2.852	2.498	2.000	21
22	6.011	5.410	4.909	4.488	4.130	3.971	3.822	3.556	3.323	2.853	2.499	2.000	22
23	6.044	5.432	4.925	4.499	4.137	3.976	3.827	3.559	3.325	2.854	2.499	2.000	23
24	6.073	5.451	4.937	4.507	4.143	3.961	3.831	3.562	3.327	2.855	2.499	2.000	24
25	6.097	5.467	4.948	4.514	4.147	3.965	3.834	3.564	3.329	2.856	2.499	2.000	25

amount placed at interest today. The factor in the 10% column and five-year row is 0.621; the future value after five years of $100 placed at 10 percent interest today is

$$100 \times \frac{1}{0.621} = \$161$$

(2) If you borrow $10,000 today at an interest rate of 12 percent, what equal annual payments (at year end) will you be required to make (principal plus interest) so as to just repay the loan in eight years? The typical home-mortgage borrowing agreement or installment purchase of an automobile or appliance follows this form. Since the factors in Table 2A.2 indicate the value today of a stream of future payments or receipts, the inverse of the factors indicates the amounts to be paid or received in the future that are equivalent to a certain value today. In this example, the factor in the 12% column and eight-year row is 4.968; the stream of eight future annual payments required to discharge a $10,000 loan taken out today at 12 percent interest is

$$10,000 \times \frac{1}{4.968} = \$2013$$

(3) If you place $10,000 today in an investment earning 12 percent, how much can you withdraw at the end of each of the next eight years and just deplete the investment at the end of the eighth year? This is the same question as in (2) above, now phrased from the point of view of an investor rather than a borrower. You can remove $2013 per year for each of the eight years; the investment account will be zero at the end of eight years.

(4) If the seller of a residential building site agrees to accept either a lump-sum payment of $25,000 now or a payment schedule of $5000 now and $3300 per year at the end of each of the next 10 years, the seller is, in effect offering to lend $20,000 (the difference between $25,000 and $5000) to the buyer in return for the 10 annual payments of $3300. What is the interest rate inherent in this borrowing? Table 2A.2 provides factors to adjust to today's value the 10 annual payments. The factors in the 10-year row are

@ 10%:6.145
@ 12%:5.650

Thus:

P (@ 10%) = 6.145 × $3300 = $20,279
P (@ 12%) = 5.560 × $3300 = $18,645

Since the amount of the loan ($20,000) lies between these two values of P, the inherent interest rate on the loan must also lie between 10 and 12 percent.

By interpolation the rate is 10.3 percent. Thus, the tables can be used to estimate returns (interest rates) when both the time-adjusted (present) values and future values are known.

PROBLEMS TO THE APPENDIX

2A.1 You have made a loan to a small business that is due one year from now. At the end of the year you are to receive $1100, $1000 for principal and $100 interest. A new investment opportunity has appeared that will pay 12 percent instead of the 10 percent on your loan. What is the minimum amount you should be willing to accept now in full payment of the original loan so that you can invest in this new project?

2A.2 You currently hold a note receivable due at the end of two years providing for a lump-sum payment of $3250. The person who owes you the money has offered to pay $2750 to you now instead of waiting until the end of the two years. Is this an attractive offer? Be specific as to the implied interest rate in this offer.

2A.3 You hold an 8 percent note of $12,000 with interest payable annually (at year end) and principal payable at the end of five years. The company that owes you the money operates in a high-risk industry. With new information now available you feel the interest rate should have been 12 percent. For what amount should you be willing to sell this note in order to reduce your exposure to losses?

2A.4 You have asked the bank for a $1200 loan. The bank offers you a five-year note requiring payments of $80 at the end of each of the next four years, with a final payment of $1580 at the end of the fifth year. What is the effective interest rate on this loan?

2A.5 Your business has accumulated $10,000 in a savings account that pays 6 percent interest. Your landlord has offered to let you discount next year's rent if you pay in advance. Normal rent is $2000 due at the end of the year. What is the minimum discount you should require of your landlord?

2A.6 As a landlord you find yourself short of cash to meet $2500 of obligations. You have two alternatives. You can either borrow money from the bank at 12 percent to meet these obligations, or you can try to get early rent payment from your properties. You have various rental income payments due to you one year from now. How much less should you be willing to accept as rent payment now to help you meet your current obligations?

2A.7 As a supplement for your retirement income, you plan to save $1500 at the end of each year until you retire. If the rate that you can earn on this investment is 9 percent, how much will the account be worth in five years? In 10 years?

2A.8 Consider again the situation in (2A.7) above. If you want to have accumulated $30,000 in this manner when you retire, for how many more years will you have to work?

2A.9 How much will an investment of $2500 be worth at the end of one year if it earns at an annual rate of 8 percent? At the end of two years? At the end of five years?

____3
AN ACCOUNTING SYSTEM PRODUCT: THE BALANCE SHEET

Following our discussion of valuation, we turn now to the accountant's tasks of recording, classifying, and summarizing. To gain useful information from the accounting records and to avoid a jumble of financial data, values must be recorded in a systematic and organized way and with some thought to the accounting reports required. While a wide variety of accounting reports prove useful to managers, owners, creditors, and others, two are fundamental to all systems: the **balance sheet,** discussed in this chapter, and the **income statement,** discussed in the next.

KEY ACCOUNTING REPORTS

The balance sheet details the firm's financial position at a particular date. Its form is the accounting equation:

$$\text{Assets} = \text{liabilities} + \text{owners' equity}$$

A balance sheet tells how much the business owns and owes as of a particular date and therefore, by deduction, the value of owners' equity. A comparison of a company's balance sheet at two different dates reveals the change in financial position, including the change in total owners' equity. Recall that changes in owners' equity are occasioned by either (1) investment or withdrawal of funds by the owners or (2) the earning of a **profit** or **loss** by the company. Thus, if owners' equity has increased and the owners neither invested nor withdrew funds, the company was profitable for the period between the two balance sheet dates.

Note that one can derive profit/loss information from the balance sheet. But, the other accounting report, the income statement, is the more convenient and comprehensive source of information about a business's **earnings** (profits) or losses. It helps you analyze why the company was or was not profitable, critical information for the various audiences who read the statements. Thus, the income statement amplifies one section—the owners' equity section—of the balance sheet.

THE BALANCE SHEET

The balance sheet is sometimes more formally called a **statement of financial position.** It shows what you own and owe as of a single, particular date. Every balance sheet is dated and provides a snapshot of the entity's financial condition at that date. By the next day the stream of events and transactions will have changed that financial position, however modestly. Of course, most businesses don't draw up a balance sheet each day; monthly or even quarterly (three-month interval) balance sheet provide management, owners, and creditors with sufficiently timely information.

Each major section of the balance sheet—assets, liabilities, and owners' equity —can display as much or as little detail as you think useful. Surely you want more than simply the aggregate value of all assets owned by the company; values by asset category are useful. How much cash does the company hold? How much **inventory?** What is the total value of productive plant and equipment? Similarly, you want detail about liabilities. How much is owed to trade creditors (vendors)? To the bank? To taxing authorities? Finally, with respect to owners' equity you typically want to separate the amount of owners' equity attributable to funds invested by the owners from the amount attributable to operating profits or losses.

But you could provide a lot more detail. Perhaps in your manufacturing company you want separate inventory categories for raw material, work in process, and finished goods. And perhaps the balance sheet should distinguish between cash in the bank and cash in the cash registers, or between amounts due soon from customers and amounts that won't be received for some time. Of course, more detail requires more accounting work and thus you need to balance the usefulness of the detail with the cost of operating a more elaborate accounting system. Many companies err on the side of collecting and disseminating more detail than is truly useful.

Figure 3-1 provides a sample balance sheet of the Robinson Company. Some of the nomenclature of this typical balance sheet needs defining.

Definition of Current and Noncurrent

Virtually all accounting systems, including the Robinson Company's, draw an important distinction between so-called current and noncurrent (or long-term) assets and liabilities. **Current assets** are those assets that will, in the normal course of business, be converted into cash or used up within the next 12 months. Thus, amounts that customers owe and are likely to pay within the next year (typically labeled **accounts receivable**) are considered current. If Robinson permits a customer to discharge its receivables by monthly payments over the next three years, only

FIGURE 3-1   The Robinson Company, Inc., Balance Sheet, June 30, 1994.

Assets		
Current assets		
Cash	$6,233	
Accounts receivable	46,525	
Inventory	23,270	
Prepaids	1,950	
Total current assets		$77,978
Investments		18,250
Property and equipment		56,825
Intangibles		6,675
Total assets		$159,728
Liabilities and Owners' Equity		
Current liabilities		
Accounts payable	$13,375	
Salaries and employee benefits payable	6,201	
Taxes payable	4,637	
Notes payable within one year	12,500	
Total current liabilities		$36,713
Long-term debt		37,500
Owners' equity		
Invested capital	37,500	
Retained earnings	48,015	
Total owners' equity		85,515
Total liabilities and owners' equity		$159,728

payments to be received during the next year are considered current; the remainder are noncurrent or long-term. Inventory typically qualifies as a current asset, as it will be sold in the next several months. The primary current assets for both manufacturing and merchandising firms are cash, accounts receivable, and inventory. Companies that sell only for cash (no credit sales) have no accounts receivable; service companies often have little or no inventory.

The definition of **current liabilities** parallels that of current assets: those liabilities that must be discharged within the next 12 months. Amounts owed to vendors (typically labeled **accounts payable**) are current since they are usually due within 90 days or less. If Robinson has a bank loan requiring monthly principal repayments over five years (generally referred to as a **term loan**), that portion of the principal due to be repaid within the next year is a current liability and the remainder is a long-term (noncurrent) liability.

What is the magic of the one-year time frame? There is none, in particular. This definition of current and noncurrent is simply one of the many widely accepted accounting conventions that we will encounter. Obviously, the job of reading and interpreting financial reports issued by a variety of companies is facilitated by the uniform adoption of such conventions.

Do you really care if your company's assets are predominantly current rather than noncurrent? Or if your liabilities are due within the next 12 months or thereafter? The distinction between current and noncurrent does not affect your owners' equity—owners' equity is still the difference between assets and liabilities. Surely your creditors care about these distinctions. If your company has a high value of current assets and few liabilities due within the next 12 months, the probability that your company will be able to meet its liabilities on schedule is a good deal higher than for another company that has high current liabilities and low current assets. Your company is *liquid* and the second company *illiquid*. A liquid company has less risk of running out of cash and being unable to meet the string of obligations inherent in every business operation: meeting the payroll, acquiring supplies, paying (on schedule) the utilities.

Therefore, the relationship between current assets and current liabilities is really more important than the absolute level of either. A measure of **liquidity** is the ratio of current assets to current liabilities, defined as the *current ratio,* and discussed further in Chapter 10. The difference between current assets and current liabilities is **working capital.**

Companies with low, or negative, working capital may encounter difficulty meeting their day-to-day commitments and frequently must scramble for cash to pay their bills. A company with a strong working capital position knows that, even if a temporary business slowdown occurs, or the collection of accounts receivable lags for a month or two, the company will probably still be able to pay its bills. But we must not overdo this generalization; suppliers' bills and the payroll must be paid with cash, not with inventory! Thus, the composition of current assets—particularly the amounts of cash and of accounts receivable to be collected soon—in relationship to current liabilities is critical.

Figure 3-1 indicates that the Robinson Company's current assets total $77,978, more than twice the total current liabilities of $36,713. Its working capital is $41,265—the difference between current assets and current liabilities.

In summary, a careful review of current assets and liabilities is revealing: for an employee anxious about getting paid on time, for a banker considering making a short-term loan, for a supplier contemplating providing credit terms. For these decisions, information regarding current assets and liabilities is more useful than information about company profitability or the value of owners' equity. A company may be profitable and growing, and yet be unable to meet its short-term liabilities because it simply has inadequate cash.

Statement Format

The typical balance sheet format lists assets first, followed by liabilities and owners' equity. Again, this convention represents simply a convenience, not a law of either nature or the government. Some companies present their balance sheets in the format: assets − liabilities = owners' equity. Still others use the format: working capital plus noncurrent assets equal to noncurrent liabilities plus owners' equity. Each of these formats is simply a variation on the equation: assets = liabilities +

owners' equity. While good arguments favor each of these variations in format, this book adheres to the traditional U.S. format illustrated in Figure 3-1.

The subcategories of assets and liabilities are listed in order of liquidity, with the most liquid assets and the most immediate liabilities listed first. Cash, the ultimate in liquidity, is listed first among the Robinson Company's assets. Accounts receivable are more liquid than inventory, which when sold creates an account receivable. **Prepaids,** typically not large in amount, represent advance payments for services or rights not yet received; for example, rent or insurance protection paid in advance are prepaid expenses. More about prepaids later.

Long-term, or noncurrent, assets of manufacturing or merchandising companies consist largely of land and building facilities—offices, manufacturing plants, warehouses, and salesrooms—and of equipment—machine tools, display cases, automobiles and trucks, and office machines. Investments in shares of other companies or in loans (with maturities longer than one year) to employees or customers are examples of other noncurrent assets. Finally, a company may own patents, trademarks, or other intangible rights having an ongoing life. For the Robinson Company these are lumped together as **intangibles.**

You might reasonably argue that certain noncurrent assets are in one sense more liquid than some current assets. For example, a used pickup truck (a noncurrent asset) may have a ready secondhand market; the company could realize cash from its sale without delay. The reason we classify the truck as noncurrent is that, assuming normal continuation of the business, the truck will in fact not be sold. That is, the truck is owned because it's useful and used; unlike inventory it is not owned to be sold.

Of course, not all inventory is immediately salable. Nevertheless, in-process and raw material inventory are classified as current because the manufacturing company expects to complete and sell the inventory within the next 12 months.

The liability side of the balance sheet is arranged in a parallel manner. The labels used are, for the most part, self-explanatory. Recall that accounts payable are amounts owing to suppliers as the result of purchasing supplies, inventory, and services for day-to-day business operations. Within the owners' equity section of the balance sheet a distinction is made between (1) capital contributed by the company's owners and (2) the company's accumulated earnings net of dividends.

Once Again: What is Owners' Equity?

Figure 3-1 lists two items in the owners' equity section of Robinson Company's balance sheet:

Invested capital
Retained earnings

For a corporation, **invested capital** is the sum of all monies received from shareholders as new shares of common stock were from time to time sold by the corporation (by the way, perhaps at quite different prices per share). In a partnership, invested capital is the sum of all investments by the partners. **Retained earnings** is the cumulative total of all earnings reinvested in the business (that is, not paid out to shareholders) since the corporation's formation. Thus, retained earnings equals:

Cumulative profits earned

Less: any cumulative losses incurred

Less: cumulative dividends paid to the company's shareholders.

Recall that owners' equity is also simply the difference between total assets and total liabilities. That's not a coincidence; accounting procedures result in the two definitions of owners' equity being compatible.

Recall, too, that owners' equity is not a pool of cash available to management or the owners. Furthermore, bear in mind that owners' equity rarely equals the aggregate market value of the corporation's shares of common stock. If shareholder A decides, two years after purchasing new shares from the Robinson Company, to sell the shares to investor B, the price per share is not determined by the owners' equity section of the balance sheet. The market price per share may be higher or lower than the balance sheet value per share, depending upon how eager A is to sell and B is to buy.

Note that the transaction between shareholder A and investor B has no effect on Robinson's owners' equity. A and B are different accounting entities than Robinson, and Robinson was not a party to the transaction. The sale from A to B may have been at a higher or lower price than shareholder A paid for the shares originally, but this is not recorded in Robinson's accounting records. The capital invested in the Robinson Company is whatever A originally paid in cash for the shares.

Incidentally, owners' equity is often referred to as **net worth,** or, for corporations, **shareholders' equity.** These three terms are used interchangeably in this book.

MORE ON ACCOUNTING DEFINITIONS AND CONVENTIONS

Before turning from the balance sheet to the income statement, we need to focus on some additional accounting definitions and on the conventions that have built up around them.

Double Entry

You may have heard the phrase **double-entry** bookkeeping. It describes the accepted method for recording accounting data. It is not mysterious and, like the format of the balance sheet, derives from the accounting equation.

Recall that if assets increase with no increase in liabilities, owners' equity must increase—that is, the owners now own more without owing more, and are therefore better off. To record this event—an increase in assets and an increase in owners' equity—requires two entries, hence the name double entry. Another event may trigger both an increase in an asset and an increase in a liability: for example, the company borrows money. Here both the increase in cash and the increase in loans payable must be recorded. Notice that owners' equity is unaffected—the company owns the additional cash (an asset) but it owes the same amount to the lender (a liability) and therefore the entity is neither better nor worse off. Thus, no entry is made to owners' equity, but only the double entry to Cash and to Loans Payable.

Another example may help: assume that a customer pays an amount owed to the company. One asset has been swapped for another; cash increases and accounts receivable decrease. We need the following double entry:

Increase in Cash, by the amount received

Decrease in Accounts Receivable, by the amount received.

Here, neither the liabilities nor owners' equity section of the balance sheet is affected, but two entries are nevertheless required to record completely the transaction.

How does double-entry accounting differ from single-entry accounting? Your bank check stubs represent a common single-entry system. You record a deposit as a single entry and a withdrawal as a single entry. Your checkbook can still be balanced making only these single entries. Implicitly, however, when you make a deposit you are increasing your worth and when you make a withdrawal you are decreasing it. This simple accounting system, probably quite adequate for your purposes, involves a single asset, cash; when you increase cash, you increase your worth or equity. In a more complex accounting system than your checkbook, one designed to provide extensive financial information, a double-entry system is imperative.

Accounts, Ledgers, and T-Accounts

Accounts classify entries by putting like entries in the same **account.** Each subcategory of asset, liability, or owners' equity is represented by a separate account in the accounting records. Some typical account names are:

Cash on Hand
Cash on Deposit, First Bank
Cash on Deposit, Fidelity Savings and Loan
Accounts Receivable—Trade
Accounts Receivable—Employees
Raw Material Inventory
Finished Goods Inventory
Supplies Inventory
Inventory on Consignment at Customers.

All of these accounts are current assets. On published balance sheets, the first three accounts listed above are typically combined simply as Cash, the next two as Accounts Receivable. Although combined on published financial statements, separate accounts provide useful additional detail. The treasurer of the company, responsible for managing the company's cash, needs to know how much cash is located where. Similarly, the manager of inventories needs detail on the value of inventory of various kinds; yet on published financial statements, combining the last four accounts on the list into a single account, Inventory, is typically satisfactory.

A listing of all accounts that are available within a particular accounting system to receive entries is the system's **chart of accounts,** a kind of road map of the accounting system. It shows the nature and extend of classification, or categorization, in the accounting records. Simple accounting systems may have only 20 or 30 accounts, but as the size and complexity of both the organization and the accounting system increase, it is not unusual for the chart of accounts to grow to hundreds of separate accounts.

The **general ledger** is that set of accounting documents that details the increases, decreases, and current status of each of the accounts. Thus, all entries ultimately find their way to the general ledger. Accounting reports—the balance sheet and income statement among them—are constructed from the balances in the general ledger. Chapter 6 will illustrate the detailed format of the general ledgers used in actual accounting systems. For now, keep in mind that the general ledger shows the amount and cause of all increases and decreases in each account so you can trace what is happening in the account and calculate its balance at any time.

Accountants use a shorthand for general ledger accounts, the **T-account.** Its name describes its appearance:

Account Name

Each account in the general ledger has its own T-account, but the T-account omits some of the detail of an actual general ledger. We'll be using T-accounts to illustrate accounting entries.

Debits and Credits

The accounting equation implies that assets are recorded on the left and liabilities on the right:

$$\text{Assets} = \text{liabilities} + \text{owners' equity}$$

Accordingly, asset accounts have balances on the left-hand side of their T-accounts, and liabilities and owners' equity accounts have right-hand side balances in their respective T-accounts. As a result, the sum of all the left-hand balances will equal the sum of all the right-hand balances. The double-entry convention assures that this equality is always true.

The terms *left-hand balance* and *right-hand balance* are neither convenient nor

FIGURE 3-2   Partial General Ledger of The Robinson Company, Inc. (In T-Account Format)

Cash	Accounts Receivable	Inventory	Prepaids
6233	46,525	23,270	1950

Accounts Payable	Wages and Employee Benefits Payable	Taxes Payable	Notes Payable within One Year
13,375	6201	4637	12,500

Note: The sum of these debit balances is not equal to the sum of the credit balances because this is only a partial balance sheet.

elegant. We use instead the names **debit** balance for left-hand balances and **credit** balance for right-hand balances. To repeat, asset accounts typically have debit balances, and liability and owners' equity accounts credit balances; the sum of all debit balances always equals the sum of all credit balances.

All professions promulgate their own particular conventions and definitions, and the accounting profession is no exception. You may ask, "Why can't I put assets on the right, and call the balances in asset accounts Charlie?" You can, so long as you remember what rules you establish for your system and so long as no one else has to work with or seek information from it. As a practical matter, conventions greatly facilitate communication; please accept these conventions and definitions and express your creativity in other ways!

In T-account format, the current assets and current liabilities of the Robinson Company at June 30, 1994, appear in Figure 3-2.

How are transactions or events recorded in the T-accounts? If a company borrows $2000 on a short-term note, the transaction is recorded in the company's T-accounts as follows:

Cash	Notes Payable
Balance*	Balance
2000	2000

Here an asset, cash, is increased and a liability, notes payable, is increased. An addition is made both to the debit balance of the asset and to the credit balance of the liability. A debit entry is made to Cash, an a credit entry to Notes Payable. The equality demanded by the accounting equation is maintained. Obviously the double-entry concept requires equal debit and credit entries for a complete recording of a transaction in the general ledger.

*The term *balance* is shown to indicate that the account had a debit (or credit) balance before the particular transaction was noted.

Note that this transaction would be recorded by the bank making the loan in essentially the opposite way. The note is a receivable to the bank—an asset—and the company's cash deposit is a bank liability. The debit entry is to the Note Receivable account and the credit entry is to the Customer Deposit (liability) account. More on this in a moment.

Take another example: a customer pays $150 on her account. This transaction is recorded by the company receiving the payment as follows:

Cash		Accounts Receivable	
Balance		Balance	150
150			

An increase in an asset, cash, is matched by a decrease in another asset, accounts receivable. The increase in cash is a debit and the decrease in accounts receivable is a credit entry. A debit entry matches a credit entry; the accounting equality holds.

Still another example: the company pays $850 to a vendor; since the company previously recorded this obligation, $850 is currently in the accounts payable balance. The company records this transaction:

Cash		Accounts Payable	
Balance	850	850	Balance

Both assets and liabilities are decreased, and no change in owners' equity occurs. The decrease in the asset, cash, is a credit entry, and the decrease in the liability, accounts payable, is a debit entry. Again, the debit and credit entries are equal.

We can generalize that:

- Asset accounts typically have debit balances.
- Liability and owners' equity accounts typically have credit balances.
- An increase in an asset is created by a debit entry.
- A decrease in an asset is created by a credit entry.
- An increase in a liability or owners' equity account is created by a credit entry.
- A decrease in a liability or owners' equity account is created by a debit entry.

Accordingly, we define debit and credit entries as follows:

- A debit entry increases an asset account or decreases a liability or owners' equity account.
- A credit entry increases a liability or owners' equity account or decreases an asset account.

Notice that, again by convention, we do not use negative entries. That is, a decrease in assets is not represented by a negative debit entry, but rather by a credit entry. Of course, a credit entry is the opposite of a debit entry, just as would be a negative debit entry—if such were used.

While asset accounts typically have debit balances, could they have credit balances, and, if so, what would a credit balance mean? Yes, certain asset accounts can temporarily have credit balances—that is, their typical debit balances can be forced by excessive credit entries to a negative (credit) position. A credit balance will occur in the account, Cash on Deposit, First Bank, when the bank account is overdrawn. Conceivably, an account receivable could incur a temporary credit balance if customers overpaid their accounts; this condition signals that the company owes refunds. Similarly, liability accounts can have temporary debit balances. Finally, if a company earns a cumulative loss or pays dividends in excess of cumulative profits, the retained earnings account in owners' equity will carry a debit balance.

Are you puzzled by the names, *debit* and *credit,* chosen for both balances and entries? Your past associations with these terms may cause you to think of debits as bad and credits as good: you have always been eager to earn credits and you may have experienced the bank debiting your checking account for service charges. Yet now assets—which you probably think of as good—have debit balances and liabilities—which you try to avoid—have credit balances.

Can we reconcile the popular connotations of these terms with their accounting definitions? Think of the terms in the context of the owners' equity accounts. Owners' equity accounts typically carry credit balances; an increase in owners' equity (a good event) is recorded by a credit entry, and a decrease in owners' equity is recorded as a debit entry. If that perspective on the terms debit and credit doesn't help, simply block from your mind their emotional connotations.

Incidentally, when the bank tells you that it is crediting (increasing) your account or debiting (decreasing) it, the bank, from its viewpoint, is consistent with our definitions. Your checking account is the bank's liability (since it is obligated to give you your money on request). An increase in your account is an increase in the bank's liability, a credit entry. Similarly, a decrease in your account, represented by a credit entry to your asset account, Cash, is a debit entry (decrease) to the bank's liability account, Customer Deposits.

SUMMARY

While a wide assortment of accounting reports are useful to various audiences, the two key reports are the balance sheet and the income statement. The balance sheet, a statement of financial condition, provides a snapshot as of a particular date of the assets owned, liabilities owed, and balance of owners' equity. The comparison of two balance sheets, one at the beginning of an accounting period and the other at the end, reveals the total change in the company's retained earnings during the period. This change represents profit for the accounting period (assuming no dividends were paid to the owners). However, this single profit figure tells little about the company's operations and thus a separate report, the income statement, which is discussed in the next chapter, is developed.

The typical format for the balance sheet follows the accounting equation: assets = liabilities + owners' equity. The company's assets and liabilities are each listed on the balance sheet in order of decreasing liquidity, and a careful distinction is made between their current and noncurrent components. The difference between these two amounts, the working capital of the company, indicates the company's overall liquidity, that is, its ability to meet near-term obligations.

The double-entry system of accounting is widely used. Again, the fundamental accounting equation leads directly to the double-entry method: A full accounting entry must involve equal debit and credit entries in order to preserve the equation. Typically, asset accounts carry debit balances, and both liabilities and owners' equity accounts carry credit balances. A debit entry increases an asset or decreases a liability or owners' equity account; a credit entry increases a liability or owners' equity account or decreases an asset account.

NEW TERMS

Account. The fundamental element of the accounting system that permits categorization and combination of like transactions and of like assets and liabilities. All accounts appear in the company's general ledger.

Accounts payable. The liability account showing the amounts due to suppliers.

Accounts receivable. The asset account showing the amounts due from customers.

Balance sheet. Statement of condition of an enterprise as of a particular date, expressed in the form of the accounting equation: assets = liabilities + owners' equity. An alternative name is *statement of financial position.*

Chart of accounts. The listing of all accounts available in the general ledger.

Credit (credit entry; credit balance). Liability, owners' equity, and revenue (sales) accounts typically carry credit balances. A credit entry increases a credit balance or decreases a debit balance.

Current assets. Those assets that will be converted to cash within the next 12 months.

Current liabilities. Those obligations of the enterprise that will be discharged within the next 12 months.

Debit (debit entry; debit balance). Asset and expense accounts typically carry debit balances. A debit entry increases a debit balance or decreases a credit balance.

Double entry. The type of accounting system that requires that each debit entry be balanced with a credit entry in order to preserve the accounting equation.

Earnings. Alternative name for profit.

General ledger. The set of accounting records that details the current status of all of the accounts.

Income statement. Statement of performance of an enterprise for an accounting period, indicating the profit or loss earned by the entity during the period. Alternative names are *operating statement, profit and loss (P&L) statement,* and *earnings statement.*

Intangibles. The asset accounts showing the values of certain rights or other intangible property such as patents, trademarks, and licenses.

Inventory. The asset account for materials or merchandise owned by the enterprise and available for resale or for use in manufacturing operations.

Invested capital. The owners' equity account showing the cumulative value of all investment in the enterprise by its owners. In a partnership, this account is often called partners' capital, and in a corporation common stock or capital stock.

Liquidity. An enterprise's condition with respect to its ability to meet near-term obligations. Liquid assets include cash, marketable securities, certain accounts receivable, and any other assets that will be or can be converted to cash in the near-term.

Loss. The amount by which entries that decrease owners' equity exceed those that increase owners' equity. The opposite of a profit.

Net worth. An alternative name for owners' equity.

Prepaid (or prepaid expenses). Current asset accounts showing amounts paid in advance of the accounting period when the corresponding expenses will be recognized. (Examples: prepaid rent and prepaid insurance.)

Profit. The amount by which entries that increase owners' equity exceed those that decrease owners' equity. An alternative name is *earnings*.

Retained earnings. The owners' equity account showing cumulative earnings retained by the corporation. Net income increases retained earnings and dividends reduce retained earnings.

Shareholders' equity. An alternative name for a corporation's owners' equity.

Statement of financial position. Alternative name for the balance sheet.

T-account. A shorthand notation for a general ledger account.

Term loan. A loan (liability) having a maturity greater than one year.

Working capital. An amount equal to the difference between current assets and current liabilities. Working capital is negative if current liabilities exceed current assets.

DISCUSSION QUESTIONS

3.1 What does the word *current* imply in the definition of current assets and current liabilities?

3.2 What are the two ways to calculate total owners' equity?

3.3 Is it possible for a company to have negative working capital? Explain.

3.4 Why does the balance in your bank checking account appear as a debit balance in your personal general ledger and a credit balance in the bank's general ledger?

3.5 What fixed assets do you own? How about current assets? What current liabilities do you owe? How about long-term liabilities?

3.6 What is the difference between accounts payable and accounts receivable? What are the similarities between them?

3.7 What type of information would you expect to obtain from a typical balance sheet?

3.8 If you had to compare the performance of two companies based solely on their balance sheets, how would you do it? What types of financial performance measures could you use that would not be influenced by the size of the firm?

3.9 Classify the following assets and liabilities of a corporation as either current or noncurrent (in certain instances, a portion may be current and the balance noncurrent), and explain why.

(a) Prepayment of $800 for a six-month insurance policy.

(b) A loan payable to the bank, requiring monthly payments on the principal over two years.

(c) An automobile owned by a manufacturing company and used by one of the salespersons.

(d) An automobile owned by a used car dealer and available for resale.

(e) Dividends declared by the company's board of directors and payable next month.

(f) Investment in common stock of an unrelated corporation whose shares are widely traded on the New York Stock Exchange.

(g) Investments in U.S. Treasury securities that trade actively and mature in 15 months.

(h) Production equipment that has now been retired after many years of use and is available for sale.

(i) A loan to the company from its president; the loan has a stated maturity of six months but both the president and others in the company feel that several years will pass before the company will be in a position to repay the loan.

(j) A lease between the company and one of its customers, requiring the customer to pay $7400 per month for 36 months.

(k) The $8000 payment for a license to use a particular patent.

(l) Vacation wages payable; employees accrue vacation at the rate of one day per month worked.

3.10 Classify the following into assets (fixed or current), liabilities (current or noncurrent), and owners' equity.

(a) A loan for $10,000 payable as a lump sum in three years.

(b) A computer leased from the manufacturer for two years.

(c) Prepaid rent for the next two years.

(d) A loan from the bank payable in bimonthly installments over the next three years.

(e) Money owed to a supplier for raw materials payable in 30 days.

(f) Cash on hand of $13,000.

(g) Retained earnings of $17,000.

(h) Buildings and land valued at $90,000.

(i) Overpayment of income taxes, to be used as a tax credit in the next fiscal year.

(j) Utility bills payable in two weeks.

3.11 The following three events are somewhat unusual, and present problems both as to valuation and as to the particular accounts in the general ledger that will be affected. Indicate which accounts you think will be affected, if any, and whether the entry will be a debit or a credit. Then describe how you would arrive at the value or values required for the entries.

(a) The Brown Co. acquires from a local inventor a patent on a new device that Brown will produce in the coming years, in exchange for issuing to the investor 500 shares of Brown Co. common stock.

(b) The Redding Corporation leases a specialized machine tool from a lease financing company for five years, the estimated life of the machine tool. Redding estimates that the machine tool will have no value at the end of five years. The lease requires 60 monthly payments of $275.

(c) Mans Electronics, Inc. files a lawsuit against one of its suppliers for $50,000 for breach of contract. The supplier has offered to settle for $10,000 but Mans has decided to take the matter to court.

3.12 Which of the following produces a change in owners' equity? Explain.

(a) A loan was obtained to buy equipment for $25,000.

(b) Payments totaling $5000 were made to suppliers on account.

(c) Salaries for the month totaling $4000 were paid.

PROBLEMS

3.1 Prepare the T-account entries (in double entry format) for the following transactions:

(a) Received $545 worth of raw materials on credit from suppliers.

(b) Paid a $600 principal payment on a loan.

(c) Collected $745 from customers on account.

(d) Delivered $1250 of finished goods to customers.

(e) Bought an automobile on credit for $10,000.

(f) Purchased office furniture for $578 and paid cash.

(g) Paid a dividend of $12,000.

3.2 The following balances have been taken from the balance sheet of the Godfrey Company as of the end of its most recent fiscal year:

Current assets	$900,000
Invested capital	400,000
Long-term liabilities	300,000
Other noncurrent assets	100,000
Property, plant, and equipment	650,000
Retained earnings	550,000
Total assets	1,650,000

Construct a balance sheet and determine the amount of Godfrey's current liabilities at year's end. What was the company's working capital at year's end?

3.3 The Earle Company, a manufacturing company, has total current assets of $500,000. Below are listed the balances in all accounts classified as either current assets or current liabilities except for the Cash account. Determine the balance in the Cash account.

Accounts payable	$ 70,000
Accounts receivable	150,000
Inventories	260,000
Loans payable	100,000
Prepaid expenses	60,000
Salaries and wages payable	40,000

3.4 The ending account balances for ARS, Inc. for all asset accounts, except cash, and some liability accounts are given below. If the total value of assets is $110,000, how much cash does the company hold?

Accounts payable	$14,000
Accounts receivable	22,000
Finished goods inventories	13,500
Income tax payable	7,500
Municipal bonds	6,000
Plant and equipment	52,000
Prepaid rent	1,800

3.5 Prepare a balance sheet for the Ralph Wendell Company using the information provided below:

Accounts payable	$17,800
Accounts receivable	24,000
Capital stock	29,700
Cash	4,500

Notes payable	12,000
Plant and equipment	43,000
Retained earnings	12,000

3.6 Using the information presented below, construct a balance sheet in conventional format for the Cheney Corporation at the end of the fiscal year 1996.

Accounts payable	$34,000
Accounts receivable	34,000
Building and equipment	18,000
Cash	12,000
Income taxes payable	5,000
Inventory—finished goods	11,000
Investments	14,000
Invested capital	23,300
Land	45,000
Loans payable	25,000
Notes payable	13,000
Rent payable	1,200
Retained earnings	20,000
Salaries payable	12,500

3.7 Prepare a balance sheet in conventional format for the Leopold Corp. as of August 31, 1994 using the following data:

Accounts payable	$ 80,000
Accounts receivable	110,000
Accrued vacation and holiday pay	16,000
Cash	20,000
Dividends payable	10,000
Estimated tax liability	20,000
Interest payable	6,000
Inventories	172,000
Invested capital	200,000
Investment in marketable securities	10,000
Investment in Ramsey Corp. (represents	
20% ownership)	20,000
Land	24,000
Loan to Ramsey Co.	10,000
Notes payable	60,000
Patents and trademarks	30,000
Plant and equipment	72,000
Prepaid insurance premiums	4,000
Retained earnings	80,000

3.8 Prepare a balance sheet in conventional format for the Laval Company (a partnership providing data-processing services) as of March 31, 1996 using the following data:

Accounts payable	$ 4,000
Accounts receivable	36,000
Accrued insurance premiums payable	2,000
Cash	14,000
Computer programs (developed by Laval Co.)	20,000
Data processing equipment (leased)	60,000
Improvements in rented office space	6,000
Lease payable (data processing equipment)	56,000
License to use computer programs (developed by others)	6,000
Office furniture	10,000
Office supplies inventory	4,000
Partnership equity (at 1/1/96)	90,000
Prepaid rent	2,000
Profit (before partner withdrawals) 1/1/1996 through 3/31/1996	10,000
Taxes payable (property)	2,000
Withdrawals by partners 1/1/1996 through 3/31/1996	6,000

3.9 Fill in the blanks before the account names with either "debit" or "credit" according to the required entry for the transaction described.

(a) Purchase a cement mixer on credit. _____ accounts payable, and _____ plant and equipment.

(b) Pay off a bank loan by borrowing on a note from the credit union. _____ notes payable, and _____ loans payable.

(c) Receive raw materials on credit. _____ raw materials inventory, and _____ accounts payable.

(d) Purchase a computer for cash. _____ cash, and _____ plant and equipment.

(e) Receive payment from customers. _____ cash, and _____ accounts receivable.

(f) Declare a dividend. _____ retained earnings, and _____ dividends payable.

(g) Purchase fire insurance for the year. _____ cash, and _____ prepaid insurance.

3.10 The founders of Nettleship and Sons, Inc. invested a total of $500,000 upon formation of the company two years ago. No dividends have been paid. Now the company has total assets of $170,000, current assets of $70,000, current liabilities of $100,000, and long-term liabilities of $60,000. Would you say that the company has been successful during its first two years of operations? Explain.

3.11 The working capital of the Hurley Co. at May 31, 1993 is $70,000. Current assets are $120,000, total assets are $250,000, and the company owes no long-term liabilities. What is the balance of owners' equity at May 31, 1993?

3.12 The management of the Jonsson Corporation wishes to maintain a ratio of current assets to current liabilities equal to two, reducing its short-term borrowing so as to achieve this result. The corporation's cash balance is currently $30,000. Accounts payable are equal to $60,000 and the company is now borrowing $30,000 from the bank on a short-term loan. Inventory totals $100,000 and accounts receivable total $40,000. The only current asset accounts are Cash, Accounts Receivable, and Inventory; and the only current liability accounts are Accounts Payable and Short-term Bank Loan Payable. How much of its short-term bank loan should the company repay?

3.13 The Ralston Company expanded rapidly during 1992 by investing in new plant and equipment and in manufacturing inventory. As a result, total assets increased from $400,000 at the beginning of the year to $700,000 at the end of the year. Total owners' equity at the beginning of the year was $200,000 and the company's net profit for the year was $50,000. Assuming the company paid no dividends during 1992:

  (a) What were the company's total liabilities at the end of the year, if no additional capital stock of the company was sold during the year?

  (b) What were the company's total liabilities at the end of the year, if the company received $300,000 during the course of 1992 from the sale of additional capital stock?

3.14 The Marchik Company earned a profit of $25,000 for the year 1993, while the total assets of the company declined by $20,000 from the beginning to the end of the year. If the company sold no additional capital stock and paid no dividends during the year, by how much did the company's liabilities change? How is it possible that the company's assets could decline during the same year that a profit was earned?

3.15 In certain countries the typical balance sheet is presented in such a manner that the left-hand side of the accounting equation reads (instead of simply "assets"):

$$\text{Working capital} + \text{noncurrent assets.}$$

How would the right hand side of the equation read?

____4
THE OTHER ACCOUNTING PRODUCT: THE INCOME STATEMENT

The income statement is an elaboration, or an expanded clarification, of the changes in the Retained Earnings account within the owners' equity section of the balance sheet. Recall that certain events or transactions increase owners' equity, while others decrease owners' equity. If, between one balance sheet date and the next, the cumulative effect of the increasing transactions exceeded that of the decreasing transactions, then the company earned a profit for the period. The balance sheet account, Retained Earnings, increased by the amount of this profit, less any dividends paid to shareholders.

Then why do we need an income statement? The balance sheet shows only the net effect on owners' equity of the very many transactions that serve to both increase and decrease owners' equity. It alone simply does not provide all necessary information. It tells us nothing about the magnitude and classification of either the increasing or decreasing transactions. It is this additional information that various audiences need and that the income statement provides.

Whereas the balance sheet is a statement of *condition* as of a particular date, the income statement is a statement of *performance,* detailing how the company performed during the period covered by the statement. Thus, while a balance sheet is a snapshot as of a particular date, the income statement is a "moving picture" of what happened during the period. Just as a balance sheet must carry a specific date to be meaningful, an income statement must specify the exact period for which it details the changes in owners' equity.

The income statement is also commonly referred to as a **profit and loss statement** or **P&L;** or an **operating statement;** or an **earnings statement.** This book uses these terms interchangeably, but with a preference for the term *income statement.*

DEFINITION OF REVENUE, SALES, AND EXPENSES

The term for increases in owners' equity is **revenue.** Typically, the most important revenue source is sales of goods or services to customers. Decreases in owners' equity are **expenses.** If revenues exceed expenses for a particular period, the company earns a profit; conversely, if expenses exceed revenues, the company incurs a loss for the period.

While sales transactions with customers are the key source of revenue, the company may also earn interest on its savings, or on its investments, or on its loans to employees or customers; interest thus earned is another source of revenue. The company may rent to others excess plant or office space, or may sell an old physical asset for more than its value currently reflected in the company's general ledger; these events also create revenue.

Expenses are categorized to help management judge the performance of the various segments or departments of the business. A primary expense category is **cost of golds sold (COGS), or cost of sales (COS):** the expenses that can be traced directly to the goods or services provided to customers. For a merchandising company using the cost value method, cost of goods sold equals the amount the company spent to acquire the particular inventory items now sold to the customer.

Determining cost of goods sold for manufacturing or service companies is more difficult than for merchandising companies. Manufacturers or service firms need to include in cost of goods sold (or cost of services rendered) wages and related expenses of those personnel directly involved in creating the particular product or service being sold. Valuing services and manufactured products is a complex process, referred to as *cost accounting,* to which we will return later. For now our illustrations are drawn primarily from merchandising companies.

Of course, both merchandising and manufacturing firms incur many other expenses not traceable directly to the product or service involved in the sales transactions. Typically these include selling expenses and administrative expenses. Depending upon how the business is financed, it may incur significant interest expenses. Tax obligations are still another form of expense.

Note, however, that dividend payments to shareholders, although an appropriate and necessary form of return on invested capital, are traditionally not shown as an expense of the company. Although dividend payments do result in a decrease in the company's Retained Earnings account, they do not represent a diminution in the collective financial position of the shareholders; cash formerly held by the corporation for the benefit of the shareholders is now paid to them as dividends.

STATEMENT FORMAT

Figure 4-1 presents the Robinson Company's income statement in typical format. Note that the net income, or net profit, of the firm was $10,306 for the six-month period January 1 through June 30, 1994. Figure 3-1 shows that the retained earnings for Robinson Company at June 30, 1994 was $48,015. Although we do not have the

FIGURE 4-1 The Robinson Company, Inc., Income Statement (first half 1994) Period January 1, 1994 through June 30, 1994.

Sales, Gross	$291,025	
less: Returns and Allowances	7,688	
Net Sales		$283,337
Cost of Goods Sold		196,708
Gross Profit		86,629
Operating Expenses		
Selling and Promotion	45,013	
General and Administration	22,275	
Total Operating Expenses		67,288
Operating Profit		19,341
Other Income and Expense		
Interest and Dividend Income	908	
less: Interest Expense	2,293	
		1,385
Income before Taxes		17,956
Taxes on Income		7,650
Net Income		$10,306

balance sheet for Robinson Company at December 31, 1993,* we know that, if no dividends were paid during the six-month period, the retained earnings at December 31, 1993 must have been $37,709—$48,015 at June 30 less than $10,306 earned during these past six months.

The income statement tells much more, however, than simply the single profit figure. It begins with information on the sales transactions. Since Robinson is a merchandising company, it encounters sales returns and is required to make certain adjustments for quality, delivery problems, incorrect merchandise, and so forth. Because the total of such returns and allowances is significant for this company— about 2.6 percent of gross sales for the first half of 1994—Robinson's accountants have provided this information in the accounting records and on the income statement. For other companies where returns are minimal, this income statement refinement may not be warranted.

Next, the income statement provides information on the cost of goods sold and **gross profit.** Gross profit, sometimes referred to as **gross margin,** is simply the difference between sales revenue and the corresponding cost of goods sold. Remember that the Cost of Goods Sold account carries the cost of merchandise sold during the period, not the cost of merchandise acquired during the period. In that sense the Sales account matches the Cost of Goods Sold account. Thus, the gross profit represents the cumulative total difference between purchase cost and sales price of all merchandise sold during the period, obviously useful information to management.

*The balance sheet at the close of business on December 31, 1993, must be the same as the balance sheet at the start of business on January 1, 1994.

A great deal more detail could be provided in the revenue and expense sections of the accounting records, if the cost of generating this detail is warranted. For example, information on sales by major product category, or by department, or by region, or even by individual salesperson, might be useful; indeed, most data-processing systems permit multiple categorization of sales. A parallel set of details could be developed for cost of goods sold, so that gross profit could be calculated by product line, by department, or by region. This level of detail could be very helpful in making decisions about adding or deleting products, or allocating the promotional budget among the products or outlets, or determining whether salespersons should be dropped or added.

RECORDING SALES TRANSACTIONS

What entries are required to record a sales transaction? Again, we must be true to the double-entry convention and to the accounting equation. A $25 merchandise sale for cash is recorded as follows:

The debt entry is to the asset account, Cash, and the credit entry is to the Sales account. The assets of the company have increased with no increase in liabilities, so owners' equity has increased. If the sales had been on account (on credit)—that is, if the customer did not pay cash, but promised to pay in the near future—the debit would have been to Accounts Receivable, but the credit would still have been to Sales.

The entries required to record cost of goods sold are not quite so obvious. Typically a company like Robinson will sell merchandise from its inventory; if so, the sale creates a decrease in the asset account, Inventory. In order to match the cost of merchandise sold with the sales revenue, the following entries are made:

The debit entry is to the Cost of Goods Sold account, an expense account; the credit entry reduces the asset account, Inventory. This double entry decreases owners' equity, just as the double entry to record the sale increases owners' equity. (The debit balance in the Inventory account was created when the merchandise was purchased from the company's suppliers.)

Here, the sales price of the merchandise exceeded its purchase cost—a desirable condition! That is, the credit to the Sales account was greater than the debit to the Cost of Goods Sold account. The owners of the business are better off to the extent of the difference, the gross profit, since that equals the net increase in owners' equity as a result of this transaction.

You may detect a possible shortcut through these entries: record simply a credit to a Gross Profit account for the difference between the sales value and the cost value of the merchandise. The accounting entries would then be as follows:

Here, two credit entries balance a single debit entry, but, since the sum of the two credit entries equals the single debit entry, the accounting equation is preserved: the net difference in assets (differences between accounts receivable increase and inventory decrease) is balanced by the increase in gross profit (equivalent to an increase in owners' equity). However, this is an undesirable shortcut: information is lost. The shortcut permits determination of neither total sales nor total cost of goods sold for the company. Figure 4-1 shows that net sales for the six months were $283,337 and the gross profit was $86,629, or 30.6 percent of sales. That information is both more complete and more useful than the information on gross profit alone.

To summarize, then, the $25 cash sale of merchandise that was valued in inventory at $15 is properly recorded as follows:

Two double entries are required: one to record the sale and one to record the matched cost of goods sold. Note that no account entitled Gross Profit is used here. The gross profit shown on the income statement (Figure 4-1) was derived in preparing the statement.

The last several paragraphs have mentioned increases and decreases in owners' equity arising from this combined sales and cost of goods sold transaction. Note, however, that no debit or credit entries were made directly to an owners' equity account. You can think of the revenue and expense accounts as being, in effect, owners' equity accounts. Thus, an increase in owners' equity is signaled both by the fact that a credit was made to a sales account and by the fact that assets (cash or accounts receivable) were increased with no change in liabilities. Similarly, a decrease in owners' equity is signaled both by the debit entry to an expense account and by the fact that an asset account (merchandise inventory) was decreased with no change in liabilities.

OPERATING EXPENSES

Refer again to Figure 4-1. Operating expenses for the Robinson Company are shown here as Selling and Promotion expenses and General and Administrative expenses. Within each of these expense categories, the Robinson Company undoubtedly has a number of individual expense accounts, each appearing in Robinson's chart of accounts. Within the Selling Expense section of the chart of accounts the following individual expense accounts might appear:

Salaries of Sales Personnel
Sales Bonuses and Commissions—Sales Personnel
Office Salaries Expense
Rent Expense
Depreciation Expense
Telecommunications Expense
Automotive Expense
Other Travel Expense
Postage Expense
Supplies Exchange
Advertising Expense
Brochure Expense
Miscellaneous Expense

Again, more or less detail can be included. For example, separate accounting of hotel expenses and air travel expenses, rather than combining them as Other Travel Expense, might be useful, or advertising and brochure expenses might be combined as a single account, Promotional Expenses.

The entries to record these expenses are straightforward. Assume the company pays in cash a $100 bonus to salesperson X:

Cash			Commissions Expense	
Balance	100		100	

The decrease in the asset (credit entry) is balanced by a decrease in owners' equity (debit entry to an expense account). If the company purchases promotional brochures on open account for $175:

Accounts Payable			Brochure Expenses	
	Balance		175	
	175			

No change in assets has occurred, but the increase in liabilities (credit entry) is balanced by a decrease in owners' equity (debit entry to an expense account).

Figure 4-1 shows that Robinson earned an **operating profit** of $19,341 for the six months. Operating profit is calculated before considering other revenue and expenses that did not arise directly from Robinson's merchandising operations. Thus, the interest and dividend revenue from Robinson's investments (see the assets on Figure 3-1) are not part of operating profit, since holding investments is not

FIGURE 4-2   The Robinson Company, Chart of Accounts

Number	Names	Number	Names
	Assets		Revenues
1001	Cash on Hand	5010	Sales—Department X
1051	Cash on Deposit, First Bank	5015	Sales Returns and Allowances
1110	Accounts Receivable—Trade		—Department X
1115	Accounts Receivable—Other	5020	Sales—Department Y
1210	Inventory—Department X		—Department Y
1220	Inventory—Department Y		
1301	Prepaids	5025	Sales Returns and Allowances
1510	Land	5100	Interest Income
		5200	Dividend Income
1520	Warehouse and Store Facilities	5400	Gain (Loss) on Sale of Physical Assets
1525	Depreciation—Warehouse and Store Facilities		Expenses
1530	Fixtures and Equipment	6000	Cost of Goods Sold Expenses
1535	Depreciation—Fixtures and Equipment	6010	Cost of Goods Sold— Department X
1540	Transportation Equipment	6020	Cost of Goods Sold— Department Y
1545	Depreciation—Transportation Equipment	7000	Selling Expenses
1701	Investments—Shares in Unrelated Companies	7110	Salaries of Sales Personnel
		7130	Sales Bonuses & Commissions- Sales Personnel
1711	Investments—Municipal Bonds		
1901	Intangibles—Trademark	7150	Office Salaries Expense
		7200	Rent Expense
	Liabilities	7300	Depreciation Expense
2010	Accounts Payable—Trade	7410	Telecommunications Expense
2020	Accounts Payable—Other	7420	Automotive Expense
2110	Salaries Payable	7430	Other Travel Expense
2120	Commissions and Bonuses Payable	7510	Postage Expense
		7520	Supplies Expense
2210	Payroll Taxes Payable	7600	Promotional Expense
2220	Sales Tax Payable	7900	Miscellaneous Expense
2230	Property Taxes Payable	8000	General and Administrative Expense
2410	Short-term Notes Payable—Bank		
2420	Short-term Notes Payable—Other	8110	Salaries—Executive
		8150	Salaries—Clerical
2701	Long-term Debt	8200	Rent Expense
	Owners' Equity	8250	Insurance Expense
3001	Invested Capital	8300	Depreciation Expense
3100	Retained Earnings		

(*continued*)

FIGURE 4-2 (*Continued*)

Number	Names	Number	Names
8410	Telephone and Telegraph Expense	8700	Professional Fees Expense
		8900	Miscellaneous Expense
8430	Travel and Entertainment Expense	9000	Other Expenses
		9110	Interest Expense
8510	Postage Expense	9210	Other Nonoperating Expenses

Robinson's primary line of business. Similarly, interest obligations on the company's long-term and short-term debts (again, see Figure 3-1) are nonoperating expenses, although clearly very real expenses to the company. While these other incomes and expenses are not included in the calculation of operating profit, the tax laws require that they be included in determining taxable income. Thus, the next item on the income statement is Income (or Profit) before Taxes. Taxes on Income, a function of the profit earned, is the last expense item shown on the income statement. The net income—the bottom line on the income statement—represents the net improvement in the shareholders' position for the period, before any dividend return to those shareholders.

Good arguments can be made for presentation of the income statement in other formats. However, Figure 4-1 is currently the most widely accepted format for merchandising companies. Income statements for manufacturing companies follow a very similar format; income statements for other types of businesses sometimes look quite different. For example, the primary revenue and expense categories for an insurance company or commercial bank are vastly different from those of a manufacturing or merchandising firm, and a bank's or insurance company's income statement is designed to highlight information relevant to that particular business.

We have now touched on each of the major account categories that appear in the Robinson's Company's chart of accounts: asset, liability, owners' equity, revenue (sales), and expense. To repeat, the revenue and expense accounts are really subsets of the owners' equity category; the net difference between the two subsets becomes a part of retained earnings. Figure 4-2 presents a simplified chart of accounts for Robinson. (We'll consider later the use of certain of these accounts, such as Depreciation.) The account numbers appearing along side the account names facilitate data processing in Robinson's accounting department.

It should be apparent now why a company's chart of accounts can involve hundreds of individual general ledger accounts: the company wants much detail on revenues and expenses.

Finally, notice that the statements appearing in both Figures 3-1 and 4-1 show amounts only to the nearest whole dollar; that is, the cents have been omitted for presentation purposes. This practice is typical, although the accounting records themselves carry figures to the hundredth part of a dollar. Indeed, large companies may, for statement purposes, round off to the nearest thousand dollars, or even to the nearest million dollars.

THE ACCOUNTING PERIOD

Figure 4-1 is Robinson's income statement for the six-month period from January 1, 1994 to June 30, 1994. That is, the **accounting period** to which this statement applies is six months long. An accounting period, the time period for the company's income statements, can be of any length. The most typical is the calendar month. While most publicly-owned companies publish financial statements for shareholders every three months (that is, each quarter), for internal use they generally produce financial statements monthly. The Robinson Company produces monthly statements; by simple combination it can then develop income statements for longer periods, such as the six-month statement in Figure 4-1.

Most companies focus particular attention on their annual income statements and year-end balance sheets. Also, for convenience or because of business seasonality, many companies define their financial, or fiscal, year differently than a calendar year. Retailers often end their years on January 31, so that the busy holiday season is fully reflected, whole other companies select September 30, June 30, or another date.

In recent years, accounting periods not tied to calendar months have come into wide acceptance. The year may be divided into 13 four-week periods, with each four-week segment treated as an accounting period, or into four 13-week periods. This definition of the accounting period assures that each period has the same number of business days, ignoring holidays, and thus operating results are comparable year-to-year since they are unaffected by the number of Saturdays and Sundays that happen to fall in the period. Periods defined in this way are particularly useful for retailing firms and some service firms.

Income statements for accounting periods shorter than one year are generally referred to as **interim statements.**

A one-year period permits a full seasonable cycle to be included in each accounting year, but some years may be adversely affected by the economic cycles (recessions) while others are favorably affected (prosperity). Thus, one might argue for accounting periods longer than one year so as to encompass a full economic cycle. Because the frequency, duration, and severity of economic cycles remain quite unpredictable, and because tax laws require companies to file tax returns annually, 15-month, 18-month, or longer accounting periods are generally impractical.

A more convincing argument can be made for accounting periods shorter than a month. Much can happen in a month, and managers often need feedback on operations more frequently than monthly. However, you must balance the cost of developing frequent, detailed financial reports with the benefits that these reports might have. You will probably conclude that partial financial statements on a more frequent basis—perhaps even daily—are necessary supplements to the more detailed monthly or four-week statements. Daily reports might pertain to cash position, sales, sales returns, and a host of other nonaccounting data such as equipment downtime, number of overtime hours, rejection rates on production lines, and new orders received.

WHEN IS INCOME EARNED?

The Robinson Company is a retailer, a merchandising operation. When customers come to one of Robinson's stores, they select merchandise, purchase it for cash or on credit, and take the merchandise away. Robinson does not typically receive orders from its customers in advance of delivery time, and direct selling activity is limited to the time when the customer is in the store. When should the Robinson Company account for the gross profit on the merchandise sold (the difference between sales price and purchase cost)? Is it all earned at the moment that the customer buys and carries away the merchandise?

The cost valuation method does indeed require that the full amount of the gross profit be recognized as earned when the sale to the customer is consummated—no part before, and none later. The Robinson managers may have done a clever job of selecting merchandise or negotiating price, and may have spent thousands of dollars over several weeks on newspaper and radio advertising to promote the merchandise. Nevertheless, 100 percent of the gross profit is assumed to be earned at the moment of the sale.

The time-adjusted value method views the situation quite differently. Effective promotion and advertising for certain merchandise inventory increases the chance that it will be sold at attractive prices and decreases the risk that it will have to be disposed of at distress prices; as a result, the merchandise increases in value even before the sale. Similarly, if the managers obtained particularly attractive prices, perhaps by placing large orders or by making early commitments, the time-adjusted value method records a portion of the total realizable gain long before the final sale. The market value method also causes earlier recognition of a portion of the gain. Moreover, both methods imply that Robinson should record something less than the full gain as the customer leaves the store, since Robinson still carries the risk that the customer may return the merchandise or keep it but not pay for it.

For a manufacturer of large equipment, rather than a merchandising company, the differences among the time-adjusted value, the market value, and the cost value methods are still more pronounced. The manufacturer of large equipment receives orders from customers well in advance of delivery date, and the equipment ordered is typically manufactured over a period of weeks or months. The cost value method insists that the critical moment in the entire transaction between buyer and seller is the moment of delivery; at that moment the sale is recorded and the gross margin earned. The time-adjusted and market value methods recognize that receipt of the order itself is a valuable event—the company (and its owners) are almost surely better off with the order than without it. In addition, both methods recognize that gross profit is earned progressively during those weeks or months that the equipment is being manufactured.

One can reasonably argue that income is earned in small steps, in the course of developing, selling, manufacturing, order processing, shipping, and after-sale servicing. However, reaching agreement on just how much of the income is earned at each step might be very difficult. The engineering design, embodied in drawings, has value; the inventory increases in value as manufacturing occurs; the selling process adds value; and after-sales services may be critical to keeping the product sold. But to measure each increment of value objectively, consistently, and without bias is exceedingly difficult. As a result, accountants revert back to the cost value method as being objective, verifiable, efficient, and timely.

In summary, the cost value method concentrates the recognition of earnings in any sales transaction at that moment when the goods are delivered or services provided in response to a firm order from the customer. Such a convention, although unquestionably arbitrary, simplifies the accounting task.

ACCRUAL CONCEPT OF ACCOUNTING

Consider again the simple accounting method you use for your bank checking account. You equate your worth with your cash balance. As your cash balance increases, you are better off. You earn wages as you work, but acknowledge those earnings only when your paycheck increases your bank balance. Similarly, when you purchase $30 worth of food, you consider that you have incurred $30 of expense, even though you take home an inventory of food to consume over the coming days. You operate a simple **cash basis** accounting system.

Such a system works equally well for certain businesses, particularly professional services, such as doctors' or lawyers' offices. These businesses have essentially no inventory, only minimal physical assets, and one dominating expense category: salaries and wages.

The great majority of business enterprises must utilize a more complex accounting concept: the **accrual concept.** This concept:

(1) Recognizes revenue at the time that goods are delivered or services rendered, regardless of when the customer orders or pays for them. The customer may pay in advance, simultaneously with delivery, or 30 or more days after being billed.

(2) Recognizes expenses as soon as they are incurred, regardless of when the cash outflow occurs. An expense is incurred when the service is received. For example, rent expense for a company's rented facilities is incurred in the period the facilities are used, regardless of whether the rent was actually paid during the previous period or will be paid in a future period; similarly, management salaries expense is incurred when the work is performed by the managers, regardless of when the salaries are actually paid in cash.

Thus, in accrual accounting, in contrast to your checkbook accounting, the flow of revenues and expenses is not the same as the flow of cash into and out of the business. To properly determine the profit earned during an accounting period and to value assets and liabilities at the period end, revenues and expenses must be matched to the accounting period.

Therefore, revenue for the accounting period includes only those sales for which merchandise or services were delivered during the period. Similarly, all expenses must be properly assigned to the period. The expenses that were incurred in the previous period and paid for in this period are omitted, as are the expenses properly assigned to a future period even if the associated cash outflow occurred in this period.

Examples of the Accrual Concept

A few examples will clarify the accrual concept. The simplest example is a credit sale. The critical transaction—delivery of merchandise—occurs during this period, although cash from the customer will be received in a subsequent period. As illustrated earlier, the appropriate entries are:

> Debit to Accounts Receivable
> Credit to Sales

The entries associated with giving up the merchandise to the customer also must be recorded in this period. Assume the merchandise was acquired in a previous period. When the merchandise was received, the translation was recorded as follows:

> Debit to Inventory
> Credit to Accounts Payable (or Cash)

The cost of goods sold transaction in this period is recorded as follows:

> Debit to Cost of Goods Sold
> Credit to Inventory

Another example: a customer makes a $100 down payment on an order that will be delivered in the next accounting period. The $100 received is not revenue to the company in this accounting period; the critical sales transaction has not yet occurred (according to the cost value method). Rather, the receipt of the $100 has created a liability for the company: it must either make the delivery in the upcoming accounting period or return the customer's deposit. The appropriate entries are:

> Debit $100 to Cash
> Credit $100 to Customer Advance (a liability account)

Note here that the increase in the asset is exactly matched by the increase in the liability; no gross margin has been earned and thus owners' equity is unaffected.

What entries will be required when the merchandise is finally delivered, that is, when the sale is completed and the revenue appropriately recorded? Assume that the total sale is $1000 and the customer pays the remaining $900 in cash at the time of delivery. The appropriate entries at that time will be:

Cash		Customer Advances		Sales	
Balance		100	Balance		1000
900					

Here, two debit entries balance the single credit entry to the Sales account. (Here we ignore the cost of goods sold.)

Now an example involving expenses, not revenue: today the company purchases and pays for a one-year comprehensive insurance policy providing protection commencing with the next accounting period. To record the $1200 annual premium payment:

> Debit $1200 to Prepaid Expenses (an asset)
> Credit $1200 to Cash

One asset was swapped for another; no change occurs in either liabilities or owners' equity. Some cash was given up in return for another asset, the right to future insurance protection.

What will be the appropriate entry next month when $1/12$ of the insurance benefit will have expired? At that time the asset, Prepaid Expenses, will have declined in value to $1100; an insurance expense of $100 will need to be included in next month's expenses:

Insurance Expense		Prepaid Expenses (an asset)	
100		Balance	100

Obviously, at the end of 12 months, the prepaid expense account will have been written down to zero; each of the months will have been charged with $100 of insurance expense.

A final example: by agreement with the owner of the building, a company may delay monthly rental payments until 15 days following month end. If the company uses a monthly accounting period, it needs to recognize that this month it received the benefit of the property, even though it does not have to pay rent until the next accounting period. The use this month creates a liability, an obligation to the property owners. The appropriate accounting entries this month are

> Debit the monthly rent to Rental Expense
> Credit the monthly rent to Rent Payable (or Accounts Payable)

Next month, when the rent for this month is finally paid, the entries will be

> Debit to Rent Payable (or Accounts Payable)
> Credit to Cash

FIGURE 4-3   Accrual Entries Under Alternative Cash Flow Conditions

	Transaction Neutralizes Prepayment	Cash Simultaneous With Transaction	Transaction now with Future Cash Payment
Revenue: Merchandise or service delivered this period	Debit to Customer Advances (liability)	Debit to Cash	Debit to Accounts Receivable (asset)
	Credit to Sales	Credit to Sales	Credit to Sales
Expense: Incurred this period (service or benefits received this period)	Debit to Expense	Debit to Expense	Debit to Expense
	Credits to Prepaid expense (asset)	Credit to Cash	Credit to Accounts Payable (liability)

Notice that these entries next month—a decrease in an asset and a decrease in a liability—do not affect owners' equity. The effect on owners' equity—the expense—is recorded this month.

Review again these four examples:

(1) A sale this period, with the inflow of cash occurring in a subsequent period.

(2) Cash inflow this period, with the corresponding sale recognized in a subsequent period.

(3) Cash outflow prior to the accounting period in which the expense will be recognized.

(4) Expense recognized this period, although cash outflow occurs in a subsequent period.

Figure 4-3 summarizes the accounting entries to recognize revenues and expenses under alternative assumptions as to the flow of cash. Adherence to the accrual concept of accounting is essential for accurate profit reporting, and consequently for accurate valuation of assets and liabilities. However, it is the day-to-day application of this concept that creates most of the disagreement among accountants and between accountants and their audiences; in practice it is often far from clear just when a sale is consummated or an expense incurred. The next chapter looks at some rules to assist in resolving these disagreements.

EXAMPLE: ACCOUNTING FOR A FULL PERIOD

A simple example will illuminate the relationship between the balance sheet and the income statement: accounting for a small business for a full accounting period, one month. The example also illustrates the use of T-accounts (representing general ledger accounts) and debit and credit entries.

FIGURE 4-4   T-Accounts for Flower Stand

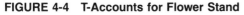

Assets

	Cash		Stand (Fixed Asset)
250	100 (c)	1250	50(f)
(a) 1700	600 (d)		
	850 (e)		

Liabilities and Owners' Equity

	Accounts Payable		Owners' Equity
(e) 850	300		1200
	900 (b)		

Revenue

Sales	
	1700 (a)

Expenses

Cost of Goods Sold Expense		Rent Expense	Wages Expense
(b) 900		(c) 100	(d) 600

Decline in Value of Fixed Asset (expense)
(f) 50

(a) Sales for cash totaled $1700. (While the operator of the stand makes daily bank deposits, the entry is shown as if only a single deposit were made at month end.) The credit to Sales is balanced with the debit to Cash.

(b) Flowers were purchased fresh each day, and the total of all purchases (on credit) was $900. Since the stand had no beginning or ending inventory, these purchases represent cost of goods sold. The debit to Cost of Goods Sold (expense) is balanced with the credit to Accounts Payable.

(c) A $100 payment was made to the shopping center for rent. The debit to the expense account, Rent Expense, is balanced with a credit to Cash.

(d) Wages paid in cash to the stand's attendants totaled $600. The debit to the expense account, Wages Expense, is balanced with a credit to Cash.

(e) Payments in cash to the flower suppliers aggregated $850. Recall that flowers are purchased on credit; payments to suppliers during the month were less than credit purchases, and thus the Accounts Payable balance is higher at month-end. This transaction does not affect the income statement. The credit to Cash is balanced with a debit to Accounts Payable.

(f) The flower stand operator estimates that the value of the fixed asset (the physical stand) declined by $50 during the month. No tranaction is involved here; rather, a review of the assets owned reveals that one of those assets should be valued lower at the end of the month than at the beginning. The credit entry to the fixed asset account is balanced with a debit to an expense account.

FIGURE 4-5   Financial Statements for Flower Stand

Income Statement for April

Sales, gross		$1700
Cost of goods sold		900
Gross margin		800
Operating Expenses		
Rent	100	
Wages	600	
Decline in value of fixed asset	50	750
Profit		$ 50

Balance Sheet at April 30

Assets

Cash		$ 400
Flower stand structure		$1200
Total Assets		$1600

Liabilities and Owners' Equity

Accounts payable		$ 350
Owners' equity as of March 31	1200	
Profit for April	50	
Total owners' equity (at April 30)		1250
Total Liabilities and Owners' Equity		$1600

You are accounting for a flower stand for the month of April. The flower stand sells all flowers for cash, and thus has no accounts receivable. It buys new flowers each day, and thus carries no inventory over from one day to the next. The balance sheet for the flower stand at March 31 is

Assets

Cash	$ 250
Stand (fixed asset)	1250
Total assets	$1500

Liabilities

Accounts payable	$ 300
Owners' equity	1200
Total liabilities and owners' equity	$1500

Figure 4-4 shows the T-accounts for the flower stand. The balances at March 31 are shown in the four accounts listed on the balance sheet above. Each entry in the T-accounts is labeled with the letter describing the entry as shown in the footnotes to the figure.

The accounting process for April is complete and we can construct an April income statement and a balance sheet as of April 30, utilizing the balances that appear in the T-accounts (general ledger accounts). These statements are shown in Figure 4-5.

Note that the flower stand made a $50 profit for the month of April. This profit amount does not appear in any T-account but is derived on the income statement as the difference between sales and expenses. The profit amount also appears in the owners' equity section of the balance sheet as the balancing item—here is the linkage between the income statement and the balance sheet.

Note also that total assets increased during the month of $100. This $100 increase in assets is balanced by a $50 increase in liabilities (accounts payable) and a $50 increase in owners' equity (profit for the month). Is this good or bad? Neither. The balance sheet shows the flower stand's condition at month end—it is quite solvent—but says little about its performance. Performance—a $50 profit—is revealed by the income statement.

SUMMARY

While summary information on profit can be derived by comparing balance sheets at the beginning and end of the accounting period, this single profit figure tells little about the company's operations. The income statement is designed to do just that. While the balance sheet is a snapshot of financial condition as of a date, the income statement is a statement of performance for a particular accounting period.

On the income statement, expenses directly attributable to sales made during the period (i.e., cost of goods sold) are matched against those sales to permit the calculation of gross profit. The operating expenses (e.g., selling and administrative) for the period are then subtracted from gross profit to derive operating profit. The bottom line of the income statement—net income after nonoperating income and expenses and after income tax expense—increases the Retained Earnings account of owners' equity.

Recall that the cost value method of valuation dominates actual accounting practice in this country, in preference to the time-adjusted value or market value methods. So also does the accrual concept in preference to cash-basis accounting. The accrual concept requires that revenues and expenses be matched to the accounting period when the revenues are earned and the expenses incurred, regardless of when cash is received or paid out. The cost value method assumes that income is earned only when a sale is realized: at the single point in time when the goods or services are delivered to the customer. Thus, the delivery transaction with an external party, the customer, gives rise to revenue and earnings.

The categories of general ledger accounts are assets, liabilities, owners' equity, revenue, and expense. Each category has from several to hundreds of individual accounts, depending upon the size and nature of the business and upon management's preferences. A full listing of all accounts utilized in the company's accounting system is the chart of accounts and the set of records containing this account-by-account information is the general ledger.

NEW TERMS

Cash basis. The accounting concept that, in contrast to the accrual basis, requires that revenues and expenses be recognized in the accounting period when the corresponding cash flow occurs.

Cost of goods sold (COGS). The expense account containing costs directly identifiable with the sales for the accounting period. An alternative name for *cost of sales.*

Cost of sales (COS). An alternative name for *cost of goods sold.*

Earnings statement. Alternative name for *income statement.*

Expense. A decrease in owners' equity as a result of operations.

Gross margin. An alternative name for *gross profit.* Gross margin may be expressed as a percentage: the percentage that gross profit is of net sales.

Gross profit. An amount equal to the difference between sales and cost of goods sold.

Interim statements. Income statements for accounting periods shorter than one year and balance sheets at dates other than fiscal year-end.

Operating profit. The amount of profit (or earnings) derived from normal operations of the enterprise, before the recognition of other (nonoperating) income and expense and before taxes on income.

Operating statement. Alternative name for the income statement.

Profit and loss (P&L) statement. Alternative name for the income statement.

Revenue. An increase in owners' equity as a result of operations.

DISCUSSION QUESTIONS

4.1 Describe the type of information you would expect to find in an income statement. How does it relate to and complement the balance sheet?

4.2 What would your personal income statement look like? What categories of income and expenses would you include? What time period would you use (one month, six months, and so on)? Why?

4.3 If you were preparing to invest in a computer manufacturing company, what information would you try to gain from a review of the company's income statement?

4.4 If you had to compare the financial performance of two firms based solely on their income statements, how would you do it? What types of financial measures might you use that would eliminate the effects of firm size in your analysis?

4.5 Identify a sales transaction for which cash-basis accounting would recognize revenue earlier than would accrual-basis accounting.

4.6 Identify an expenditure transaction for which accrual-basis accounting would recognize the expense later than would cash-basis accounting.

4.7 When the total value of goods manufactured by a company during a particular accounting period exceeds the total value of goods sold for the period, what values appear on the income statement and how, if at all, is the balance sheet affected?

4.8 Why might a company choose to define its accounting fiscal year as 13 four-week interim periods rather than 12 monthly interim periods?

PROBLEMS

4.1 Classify the following into income and expenses, and separate expenses into cost of goods sold, selling expenses, general and administrative expenses, and miscellaneous income and expenses.

(a) Sales of $22,000.

(b) Purchase of postal supplies for $240.

(c) Salaries for sales personnel totaling $2200.

(d) Return of defective materials to a supplier for $400 credit.

(e) Travel expenses for sales representatives totaling $230.

(f) Returns of defective products from clients totaling $143.

(g) Interest received on savings account of $25.

(h) Payment of $97 to leasor for rent of a computer used by the accounting department.

(i) Dividends of $100 received on stock owned in a publicly traded company.

4.2 The Stepp Company's general ledger contained the following account balances (partial listing) at the end of June, 1994. Construct an income statement in conventional format using the following data:

Administrative expenses	$ 2,800
Cost of goods sold	16,500
Development expenses	1,100
Interest expense	500
Sales	25,000
Selling expenses	3,300

What was Stepp's gross margin for the period? Profit before tax?

4.3 Use the following information to construct an income statement in conventional format. The company's income tax rate is 22 percent.

Administration expenses	$ 200
Cost of goods sold	1,250
Gross sales	2,200
Interest expense	100
Rent income	200
Sales returns	50
Selling and promotion expenses	100

4.4 The key problem in determining profit for an accounting period is that of timing: deciding when revenues and expenses should be recognized. Insert, as appropriate, "increase" or "decrease" in the first blank of each of the following statements, and asset, liability, revenue, expense, or owners' equity in the second blank of each statement.

(a) If an expenditure of cash occurs in the accounting period prior to the period when the corresponding expense is incurred, the expenditure serves to _____ a (an) _____ account and decrease the account Cash.

(b) If cash is received in the accounting period following the period when the corresponding revenue was recognized, the receipt of cash serves to _____ a (an) _____ account and increase the account Cash.

(c) If cash is received in the accounting period prior to the period when the corresponding revenue will be recognized, the receipt of cash reserves to _____ a (an) _____ account and increase the account Cash.

(d) If an expenditure of cash occurs in the accounting period following the period when the corresponding expense was incurred, the expenditure serves to _____ a (an) _____ account and decrease the account Cash.

4.5 The Marks Consultants account for both revenues and expenses on the cash basis, rather than the accrual basis. Expenses consist solely of salaries and office rent, and totaled $74,000 in 1993. Total cash revenue from clients for the same year was $90,000. In addition, the company purchased $1000 of new office equipment and determined that the value of the existing equipment declined by $500 during the year. The balance sheet for the Marks Consultants at the beginning of the year 1993 was as follows:

Cash	$5,000
Office equipment	4,000
Total Assets	$9,000
Liabilities	0
Owners' equity	9,000
Total liabilities and owners' equity	$9,000

Construct the company's balance sheet at the end of the year 1993 and the income statement for the year.

4.6 Record in T-account format the following events or transactions, each of which is independent of all others. You should make only those entries required to record a particular event or transaction; do not include balances that may exist in the accounts as a result of earlier entries. Be certain that the sum of your debit entries is equal to the sum of your credit entries. Label each T-account with the account name that you think is appropriate and indicate whether the account is an asset, liability, owners' equity, income, or expense account.

(a) The Davis Co. sells (on credit) for $11,000 merchandise that was valued in the company's inventory at $6400.

(b) The Davis Co. purchases inventory valued at $9800, paying cash to the supplier.

(c) The Davis Co. pays $1600 rent on office space—$800 for this month and $800 for next month.

(d) The Davis Co. pays wages and salaries totaling $5400; one-half of this amount was earned by employees for work performed this month and one-half for last month.

(e) The Davis Co. pays the Bank of Centerville $5200: $5000 principal repayment on a loan and $200 interest for the current month.

(f) The Davis Co. pays dividends to its shareholders totaling $1100.

(g) The Davis Co. purchases on open account inventory valued at $4700.

(h) The Davis Co. pays to its suppliers $3000 for merchandise purchased on open account in previous months.

(i) The Davis Co. receives $6000 in cash from the sale of 100 shares of newly issued capital stock of the company.

(j) The Davis Co. determines that the value of its equipment has declined by $450 during the month.

4.7 Following the instructions for problem 4.6 above, record the following events or transactions.

(a) The Sky Co. receives a bill for $550 for janitorial services for the month.

(b) The Sky Co. pays $450 in payroll taxes for the previous month.

(c) The Sky Co. receives $1700 from customer X in partial payment of that customer's account.

(d) The Sky Co. sells on open account merchandise having an aggregate sales price of $2320.

(e) The Sky Co. borrows $8000 from First Bank on a five-year term loan.

(f) The Sky Co. declares dividends totaling $3500, with the intention of paying the dividend next month.

(g) The Sky Co. returns to its suppliers merchandise that is defective. Sky was originally billed $700 for the merchandise by the supplier, but the bill has not yet been paid.

(h) The Sky Co. purchases an insurance policy for $1500 in cash for one year of comprehensive coverage, commencing next month.

(i) The Sky Co. receives supplies having a purchase cost of $900. These supplies were ordered last month, and the vendor's invoice is expected to arrive just after the end of this month.

(j) The Sky Co. receives $150 as down payment from a customer who has requested delivery of certain merchandise next month.

4.8 Following the instructions for problem 4.6 above, record the following events or transactions.

(a) The House of Threads Co. accepts a used vehicle valued at $4000 in full settlement of a customer's account receivable that has been valued at $4500.

(b) The House of Threads Co., after a careful review of all merchandise in inventory, determines that certain items that have been valued at $450 are now worthless.

(c) The House of Threads Co. accepts from one of its customers the return of merchandise having an original sales value of $350. The customer had previously paid for the merchandise, but has agreed to accept a credit against future purchases rather than a cash refund.

(d) A one-year insurance policy purchased last month by House of Threads Co. for $4800 in cash now has only 11 months of protection left.

(e) The House of Threads Co. makes a $750 travel advance (loan) to one of its managers for a business trip that will be taken next month.

4.9 The Centurion Company specialized in the repair of foreign-made auto- mobiles. The company's general ledger at the end of 1993 carried the follow- ing balances:

Accounts payable	$ 9,600
Accounts receivable	30,200
Cash	7,400
Decline in value of tools and equipment, 1994	400
Insurance expense	400
Inventory of parts	17,400
Owners' equity (at January 1, 1993)	39,000
Parts expense	8,400
Prepaid rent expense	1,200
Property tax expense	600
Property taxes payable	3,000

Rent expense	600
Repair income	58,000
Telephone and utilities expense	1,000
Tools and equipment	6,600
Salaries expense	8,000
Wages and salaries payable	6,200
Wages expense	33,600

Construct in conventional format both an income statement for the year 1993 and a balance sheet at year end, using the data above. What was Centurion's profit for the year?

4.10 The Gold Delivery Company specialized in the delivery of products from local manufacturers to retail shops. The company's general ledger at the end February 1994 carried the following balances:

Accounts payable	$10,200
Accounts receivable	23,000
Cash	8,000
Capital stock	25,000
Delivery equipment	22,000
Delivery expenses (gas, oil)	1,300
Delivery revenues	12,000
Insurance expense	500
Loans payable	10,500
Notes payable	3,500
Office equipment	3,700
Prepaid insurance	2,000
Rent expense	1,500
Retained earnings (at January 31)	8,000
Wages expense	7,200

Construct in conventional format both an income statement for the month of February 1994 and a balance sheet at month end, using the data above. What was Gold's profit for the month?

____5
DEVELOPING THE RULES
OF FINANCIAL ACCOUNTING

By now you should begin to see that wide differences of opinion exist on how best to record in monetary terms a particular event or transaction. These differences arise because different individuals observe and measure the same event in different ways. Also, both the audiences for and the uses of financial information influence the specific debit and credit entries. For example, if the primary focus is on data for the company's creditors, you might choose to record a transaction one way, and quite a different way if your objective is data useful for product pricing decisions.

We need now to evolve and understand those basic concepts—rules, if you will—that are widely followed in accounting practice today. This chapter also discusses the various rule-making bodies in the United States that interpret these concepts and promulgate specific constraints and rules to guide professional accountants in their day-to-day practice.

A BRIEF REVIEW

As you consider accounting concepts and rules, bear in mind:

- The valuation of assets and liabilities determines the valuation of owners' equity, as owners' equity is simply the difference between assets and liabilities.
- The income statement is an amplification of the sources and magnitude of changes in owners' equity.
- Therefore, the valuation of assets and liabilities ultimately determines the magnitude and timing of revenues and expenses on the income statement.
- The two basic accounting products—the balance sheet and the income statement—form one integral whole: the balance sheet is a snapshot of assets

owned and liabilities owed on a certain date; the income statement details changes in assets and liabilities (and thus owners' equity) for an accounting period.

Recall that the three bases for valuing assets and liabilities are:

(1) The time-adjusted value method: the present value of the future stream of positive benefits (for assets) and negative benefits (for liabilities), discounted at an interest rate appropriate to the particular entity.
(2) The market value method: the current market value of each asset and liability; for assets this often approximates replacement cost.
(3) The cost value method: the original cost of the asset or liability. This method recognizes certain adjustments to original cost as fixed assets age, inventory obsolesces, and so forth.

Recall also our conclusion regarding the advantages and disadvantages of these three methods. The time-adjusted value method is the most intellectually satisfying basis for valuation. It best recognizes the future in today's valuation, and thus best supports the notion that the major benefit of financial data and reports is input for decisions regarding the future. Nevertheless, after struggling with the problems inherent in estimating the magnitude and timing of the future benefit streams, most accountants lose confidence in their ability to apply this method. The cost value method, on the other hand, minimizes the need to assess the future; this very real advantage greatly mitigates its disadvantages.

Professional accountants have for years struggled with these and other dilemmas; the struggles continue today. These struggles and debates have led to both basic concepts and specific rules that now provide a framework for resolving many, but certainly not all, accounting valuation questions. This framework, based largely, but not entirely, on the cost value method, undergoes continuous evolution in a series of small steps as the accounting profession attempts to resolve recurring dilemmas.

Remember that this framework of concepts and rules incorporates compromises between conflicting accounting objectives. You need to understand this framework, and the reasons behind its various rules, in order to interpret intelligently the financial data you encounter as manager, stockholder, and member of the voting public. You may not always agree with the rules, but you should at least understand them. As you interpret financial information, be alert to the limitations imposed by these concepts and rules.

BASIC CONCEPTS

The basic concepts evolve directly from the accounting definition in Chapter 1 and the distinction drawn in Chapter 4 between accrual and cash accounting systems.

Expression in Monetary Terms

Only those events and transactions that can be expressed in monetary terms can be recorded. The resulting accounting story about the business is necessary incomplete, since many of the most important business events cannot be reduced to monetary terms: hiring and leaving of personnel; discovery of a new process, product, or technique; resolution of a key management disagreement.

Entity

The entity being accounted for, be it a business, a nonprofit organization, a person, a family, or a government unit, must be carefully delineated, and only events affecting that specific entity should be measured and recorded in the accounting system. For a business, accounting is restricted to those events affecting that business; the effects of the same events on outside individuals and organizations— including employees, stockholders, customers, labor unions, and suppliers—are ignored. For a governmental unit, accounting is confined to those events affecting that governmental unit, and ignores the effects that the same events have on citizens served or individuals employed by the organization.

Going-Concern Assumption

Unless you know for a fact to the contrary, your accounting procedures should assume that the entity will continue to operate for an indefinite future period, providing essentially the same services that it does today. This **going-concern assumption** means that the valuations of assets and liabilities need not reflect the amount that could be realized if the entity sold its plants, equipment, or other producing assets, since the assumption is that the entity has no intention of selling them. Instead, the focus is on the value of those assets in the context of their present use.

Of course, should the entity decide to liquidate or sell its assets, the going-concern assumption is no longer valid; the assets and liabilities must then be re-valued under this new assumption, and the resulting values are likely to be considerably different than under the going-concern assumption. The assets will be valued substantially higher if they are currently very productive, but much lower if they are generally unproductive and are to be abandoned or sold at a distress price. In recent years many large corporations have decided to discontinue certain lines of business. Such a decision negates the going-concern assumption and triggers a reevaluation of the assets and liabilities in the particular line of business, typically resulting in a substantial decrease in owners' equity.

Conservatism

When faced with reasonable doubt as to whether an asset or revenue should be stated at one value or another *lower* value, the accountant should choose the conservative lower value; correspondingly, when faced with reasonable doubt as to whether a liability or expense should be stated at one value or another *higher value,* the accountant should choose the conservative higher value. That is, opt for the choice that results in lower owner's equity. The key phrase in the first sentence is "reasonable doubt."

This concept does not direct the accountant to understate purposely owners' equity, although some understatement may result from the application of this concept. Rather, it demands reasonable precaution: Provide for probable losses and do not record revenues before they are earned.

The application of this concept leads to many heated arguments between accountants and business executives. The executive is typically optimistic; this concept demands that the accountant lean in the direction of pessimism. Quite apart from accounting theory or logic, the concept has another desirable feature: it provides a useful balance to the optimistic nature of most of us. The surprises that occur in business—unexpected or unanticipated events—most frequently, although by no means always, have the effect of reducing ownership equity, rather than increasing it. Thus, in practice this concept of conservatism results in greater realism in financial statements.

Realization

The **realization** concept dictates that revenue is all earned at the single moment when the particular goods or services are delivered or furnished.

In the absence of this concept, you might record a portion of the revenue as earned when the customer's order is received, additional portions as earned at each step in the manufacturing or servicing process, still more as earned when the product is shipped, and the final increment as earned when the customer's payment is received. The daunting task is to determine the timing and amount of revenue to be recognized at each step in the complete sales and collection cycle.

Intuitively you may feel that not all of the revenue, and thus not all of the profit, from a sales transaction is earned at one single moment in time. You know, and economists confirm, that each segment of the business has a hand in producing value. Nevertheless, we rely on the simplifying convention that all the revenue is recognized at the date of exchange of the goods or services between seller and buyer.

There are, however, exceptions to this generalization. When in-process manufacturing time is very long and the value added at various process stages can be accurately and objectively measured, portions of the revenue may be recognized in advance of final delivery or exchange. Examples include large building or other construction projects or the fabrication of complex equipment such as space vehicles or nuclear power generators. Also, if there is considerable doubt that the supplier of the goods or services will ever be paid—for example, because of financial failure of the customer or because the customer retains the right to return the goods following evaluation—revenue recognition may be delayed beyond the date of delivery, perhaps until the cash is finally received.

Accrual

Recall that an accounting system can operate on either the accrual concept or the cash concept. The cash concept requires that expenses be recorded only when the corresponding cash outflows occur, and that revenues be recorded only when the corresponding cash inflows occur.

By contrast, the accrual concept requires that expenses be recorded when, and as soon as, they are incurred, regardless of when cash flows. Sometimes the expense and the cash outflow occur simultaneously; in these cases, the cash and accrual concepts lead to the same result. At other times, the expense occurs before the expenditure is made—for example, when goods or services are purchased on credit and consumed prior to payment; here the accrual concept acknowledges the expense at the time of consumption, while the cash concept recognizes it when the vendor's invoice is ultimately paid. In other situations, the cash outflow occurs before the goods or services are consumed; for example, rent on a building may be prepaid and wages may be paid to production workers in connection with goods now in finished-goods inventory and thus not yet shipped. Under these circumstances, the accrual concept records the expense at the time the rented building is ultimately used and the finished goods inventory ultimately sold; in the meantime, the cash outflows create assets, here a prepaid expense and inventory, respectively.

The accrual concept recognizes revenue when the goods or services are provided to the customer, regardless of whether the customer obtains them on credit, or for cash at the time of delivery, or by advance payment.

Note that while the distinction between these two concepts is only a matter of timing, timing is most important. As we shall see, most valuation disagreements among accountants simply revolve around the question of timing. Even under the accrual concept, reasonable persons frequently disagree as to just when goods or services are actually consumed or delivered.

The accounting systems illustrated in this book all utilize the accrual concept. Nevertheless, there are many entities that do use the cash concept, and quite reasonably so. As mentioned in Chapters 3 and 4, you probably run your personal set of books (your checkbook) on a cash basis. Certain professional and service companies maintain their records on a cash-concept basis; these entities have few or no fixed assets and little or no inventory and their primary expenses are wages and salaries which are paid regularly and frequently. In such cases, there are minimal timing differences between incurring an expense and making the corresponding cash payment, and between delivering goods or services and receiving payment for them. Since the accrual and cash concepts yield similar results, the entity uses the simpler and less costly cash-basis accounting system.

The concepts of accrual accounting and realization point up the need to match revenues and expenses within an accounting period. That is, when revenue is realized from a certain transaction, all related expenses should also be recognized. Here again, reasonable persons frequently differ as to just which expenses are properly matched to what revenues; practices differ somewhat among companies and accountants.

While in theory expenses are recognized neither before nor after the precise date when the associated revenue is recognized, in practice the key is to match the revenues and expenses to the same accounting period, not necessarily to the same day.

Consistency

Since these concepts or guidelines are at best vague and general, accountants are left with a great deal of discretion in recording particular transactions and events. Specific accounting rules only narrow, they do not eliminate, this discretionary area. The **consistency** concept requires that, once having decided how to account for a particular transaction within a particular company, you must consistently employ that method for all similar transactions. The concept requires consistency over time as well as consistency among similar transactions. Consistency over time facilitates comparisons of financial data from one accounting period to another. You will soon see that comparisons and trend analyses are two primary means of interpreting financial data. If the concept of consistency is relaxed, comparability is lost and analysts find themselves comparing the apples of one accounting period to the oranges of another.

Of course, conditions change over time; to prohibit entirely any change in accounting policies and procedures would thwart efforts to present more useful and meaningful data to various audiences, particularly managers and stockholders. The concept of consistency requires, instead, that when a change in accounting practice or procedure would enhance the usefulness of the financial data, accountants must thoroughly disclose the nature of the change and estimate its effect on the financial reports.

Materiality

The concept of **materiality** instructs accountants to focus time and attention on the significant, or material, events in the business. Measuring, valuing, and recording financial data costs money; if the benefit of the resulting information is less than the cost of collecting and processing the data, then collection and processing should cease. Rather than incurring the expenses inherent in detailed measurement, the accountant may simply decide to estimate the value of the event or transaction.

For example, it is typically inefficient and uneconomic to track the use of low-value parts in an assembly process—parts such as nuts, bolts, and washers. Estimating the value of these inventory items for a particular job is typically quite satisfactory, if the value of the parts is immaterial in the context of the total enterprise; even a substantial estimating error has only an immaterial effect on the final financial statements.

Another example: if you are billed monthly for certain services such as utilities and telephone, it is typically unnecessary to separate charges among the current accounting period, the past accounting period, and the next accounting period. If the bill is for about the same amount each month and you are careful to record one bill in each monthly accounting period, you don't need to allocate the bill between this month and last month or this month and next month. Such allocations are expensive because you have to collect additional information upon which to base the allocations. Their effect is generally immaterial in your reported financial statements.

SPECIFIC RULES

In addition to these general concepts, certain specific rules have been promulgated by the accounting profession and agencies of the U.S. federal government to provide additional guidelines in particularly troublesome and controversial accounting areas.

The primary purpose of these rules is to promote consistency among companies in reporting to shareholders operating results and financial positions. For internal management purposes, you are free to develop data in any manner you deem useful. Public reporting of financial information, however, must follow rather comprehensive guidelines.

The **American Institute of Certified Public Accountants (AICPA),** an association of professional, or certified, accountants, has been a strong force in this country in formulating accounting policies and procedures. For many years, this association issued informal and nonbinding recommendations. In the late 1950s, the need for more standardized procedures led the institute to organize the **Accounting Principles Board (APB).** From 1959 to 1973 this board issued 31 formal opinions that **certified public accountants (CPAs)** were required to follow. Controversy surrounding the APB's work grew steadily during its 14-year existence, as the opinions issued dealt with very sensitive and difficult issues.

The need for a more independent rule-setting body, one with industry and academic representation as well as CPA representation, led in 1973 to the formation of the **Financial Accounting Standards Board (FASB),** a board of seven full-time members appointed by a Board of Trustees. As with APB opinions, FASB pronouncements must be followed by professional accountants in this country. The FASB continues to tackle many thorny and unresolved accounting issues. Thus far, the FASB's rules have been met with a good deal of both opposition and support, a condition likely to continue. Since different audiences for financial statements have different needs and objectives, it is unrealistic to expect that any rule aimed at settling conclusively a highly controversial issue will be warmly embraced by all. The hope of most accountants and businesspersons is that the FASB will prove sufficiently effective and efficient so that rule making will remain in the private sector rather than be taken over by the government. We cannot be certain, of course, that this hope will be realized.

Indeed, a governmental regulatory agency, the **Securities and Exchange Commission (SEC),** in its role as watchdog for the investing public, has become increasingly active in requiring that certain standardized accounting procedures be followed in financial statements issued to public shareholders. While these procedures and guidelines need be followed by only those companies whose securities are traded in interstate commerce, virtually all major U.S. corporations fall into this category; thus the requirements of the SEC become de facto guidelines for the entire accounting profession. The SEC's growing impact suggests that it will become more dominant if the FASB proves ineffective or slow to resolve the many remaining accounting dilemmas.

Typically, the formal rules and procedures set forth by the FASB and the SEC are so specialized that we won't worry about them here. Among the areas these rules now cover are the calculation of earnings per share, accounting for the value of fluctuating international currencies, accounting for research and development expenses, accounting for leases, accounting for taxes, and accounting for stock options and other management incentive payments. The FASB and the SEC will continue to promulgate new rules in an attempt to reduce the diversity of accounting treatments, to improve comparability among financial statements, and to reduce what some perceive to be accounting abuses (valuations that are not conservative).

Other agencies of the U.S. government also insist on certain standardized accounting procedures for those companies that they regulate or with whom they contract. For example, companies, universities, and research institutes that perform contract research for the government and defense and aerospace contractors must submit to certain specified accounting procedures.

THE ROLE OF THE CPA AUDITOR

The independent and certified accountant plays a key role in ensuring that both the generalized concepts and the specific rules of accounting are followed by companies issuing financial statements. All companies whose securities are widely traded—virtually all companies of significant size—engage CPAs to audit their accounting records and systems and certify their financial statements.

Certified public accountants must demonstrate, through formal education, on-the-job experience, and rigorous testing, a level of accounting competency that warrants certification, or licensing, by the state. As members of a profession, CPAs are required to observe a code of professional ethics. Similar procedures are followed in other countries; chartered accountants in England or Canada are generally equivalent in background and function to CPAs in the United States.

CPAs practice public accounting by offering their services for a fee, while remaining independent of the clients whose financial statements they certify. Although CPAs are hired and paid by their clients, their independent status requires that they not simply be advocates of the client, as would a lawyer. Rather, the CPA code of ethics requires the CPA to discharge an obligation to the general public, while performing a service to the client. Thus, in certifying the correctness and fairness of publicly reported financial statements, the CPA is asserting that he or she has performed sufficient review of the accounting procedures and individual records to be able to assert that the financial statements fairly represent the position and condition of the firm. Should this assertion prove incorrect, and a member of the general public (typically an investor) who relies on the accountant's certification suffer financial loss, the individual suffering the loss may bring legal action against the CPA for malpractice or incompetence. Therefore, the potential liability to which the independent CPA is exposed by virtue of this public responsibility is very large indeed.

The process of certifying the accuracy and fairness of financial statements is called **auditing,** and the audit function is central to the independent CPA's public practice. CPAs do not prepare the companies' financial statements (indeed, a CPA who prepared the statements would no longer be independent), but rather they review and test the accuracy of the statements prepared by the companies' own managements. Further, auditing does not involve a review of each specific accounting entry, an effort that would be prohibitively time consuming and expensive. Rather, CPAs employ well-developed and standardized procedures that involve such activities as (1) reviewing a random sample of routine transactions, assets and liabilities (e.g., inventory, accounts receivable, and accounts payable), (2) testing the accounting systems, including computer programs, to assure their reliability and completeness, (3) reviewing other routine daily procedures of the accounting department, (4) checking out in detail any unusual transactions or accounting entries, and (5) making other such tests as may seem necessary or prudent given the nature of the particular company being audited. Further, to protect shareholders, creditors, and honest and competent company employees, the independent CPA tests for conditions that might facilitate fraud.

As a part of the audit, the independent CPA must be certain that the company is following both basic concepts (e.g., the company is properly and conservatively matching revenues and expenses) and the specific rules of the FASB and, if applicable, the SEC. Thus, the CPA is expected to guard against the intentional or unintentional over- or understatement of profit or misstatement of financial position. He or she has a responsibility to the shareholder not to permit overstatement of profit, to the taxing authorities not to permit understatement of profit, and to the company's creditors not to permit an unrealistic presentation of the company's financial position. Surely by now you have gathered that many opportunities exist for disagreements between the CPA performing the audit and the company's managers who prepared the financial statements being audited. The relationship between the independent CPA and the client is unusual, often delicate, and sometimes stormy.

A CPA may practice professionally as an individual or as a member of a partnership. Partnerships vary in size from local two-person partnerships to very large, worldwide partnerships. The profession is dominated by six large firms that practice throughout the world—the so-called *Big Six*—but many strong regional and local firms also provide competent client service. In addition to performing audits, the larger accounting firms all provide consulting or advisory services, generally in the areas of tax return preparation, tax planning, management-information systems, data-processing systems, routine or special accounting procedures, and general consulting.

HOW GOOD ARE THESE CONCEPTS AND RULES?

Readers of financial statements, even sophisticated and experienced financial analysts, have a strong tendency to accept formal statements as representing truth within only a small margin of error. Yet this book stresses that accountants must utilize estimates and approximations if they are to provide useful financial data in a timely manner. The concepts and rules discussed here help accountants exercise reasonable judgment, but they surely do not resolve all accounting dilemmas.

Since input data contain estimates and approximations, the output of the accounting system, the financial statements, are at best estimates—the balance sheet is an estimate of the value of assets and liabilities at a moment in time, and the income statement is an estimate of profit performance (change in owners' equity) during the particular accounting period. To repeat, they are only estimates. To be completely certain of the amount of profit and thus the value of owners' equity, a company would have to cease operations, liquidate the assets, and pay off all liabilities. Only then could you know for certain how much value remained for the owners of the company.

Nevertheless, by following these rules and concepts, particularly the concept of consistency, accountants provide extremely useful data to their audiences: to managers for making operating decisions; to stockholders for making investment decisions; and to lenders for making credit decisions.

As an interpreter of financial statements you must strike a balance: Use the financial data to make decisions but retain a healthy skepticism. Financial statements simply cannot convey absolute truth about the business's financial position or profitability.

SUMMARY

As accountants wrestle with the problem of valuing assets and liabilities, and thereby owners' equity (changes in owners' equity are defined as revenues and expenses), they follow certain generalized concepts and specific rules.

Among the alternative valuation methods, the cost value method is the most practical and widely used. Accounting concepts are built on the cost value method. Nevertheless, the time-adjusted value and market value methods are appropriate in certain situations and are in some circumstances required by rules promulgated by professional authorities.

The key concepts that assist in resolving day-to-day accounting dilemmas are:

> Expression in monetary terms
> Entity
> Going-concern assumption
> Conservatism
> Realization

Accrual

Consistency

Materiality

These key concepts improve comparability among financial statements emanating from *different* companies and ensure even greater comparability among financial statements emanating over time from the same firm. Valuation procedures assume that a firm will continue in its present business. Accountants must exercise care not to overstate either profit or the overall financial health of the firm. Several of the concepts aim at the pivotal question of when revenues and expenses—and therefore profits—should be recognized.

In a further step to meet these laudable objectives, the Financial Accounting Standards Board was organized within the private (nongovernment) sector in the United States to establish specific rules to resolve (or at least help to resolve) crucial accounting dilemmas. The Securities and Exchange Commission, the federal agency watchdog for the investing public, also formulates guidelines for financial statements presented to shareholders and potential investors.

Independent certified public accountants (CPAs) are employed by major companies to audit the companies' accounting systems and attest that their financial statements can be relied upon by the public. In fulfilling their responsibilities to both client companies and the public, CPAs make certain that companies' accounting practices are in accord both with the general concepts discussed here and with the specific rules that are issued by the professional and governmental regulatory authorities.

NEW TERMS

AICPA (American Institute of Certified Public Accountants). An association of professional certified accountants in the United States.

Auditing. The process carried out by certified public accountants of testing and verifying the resulting financial statements.

Certified public accountant (CPA). An accountant who has, through formal education, on-the-job experience, and rigorous testing, demonstrated competency in accounting and been awarded state certification.

Conservatism. The accounting concept that requires the accountant, when in doubt as to the value of assets and liabilities, to lean in the direction of understating revenues and assets and overstating expenses and liabilities.

Consistency. The accounting concept that requires that similar transactions and conditions be accounted for in the same manner over time.

FASB (Financial Accounting Standards Board). An independent rule-setting body within the private (nongovernment) sector in the United States responsible for promulgating accounting regulations to which accountants and CPAs must adhere.

Going-concern assumption. The accounting concept that requires accountants to value assets and liabilities assuming the enterprise will continue its present set of activities, unless or until a decision to the contrary is made by the enterprise.

Materiality. The accounting concept that advises the accountant to focus time and attention on valuing the material, or important, events or changes in condition that affect assets and liabilities, and to rely on estimates and approximations as expedients in the valuation of immaterial events and changes in condition. Materiality is judged in relationship to total values appearing on the particular company's financial statements.

Realization. The accounting concept that requires revenue to be recognized as earned only at the particular time when the goods or services are delivered or furnished.

SEC (Securities and Exchange Commission). A U.S. government regulatory agency responsible for regulating securities markets and certain relationships between publicly owned companies and their shareholders.

DISCUSSION QUESTIONS

5.1 How would each of the eight principles presented in this chapter affect you if you applied them in accounting for your personal affairs? Give two examples for each principle.

5.2 Under what set of conditions is a cash-basis accounting system preferable to an accrual-basis system?

5.3 Even when a company is following the cost value method, accepted accounting procedures require that the company value inventory (and other selected assets) at the lower of cost or market value. What is the justification for imposing this lower of cost or market rule? What effects would this policy have in times of high inflation?

5.4 Assume that you must pay a 6 percent export duty on a certain export sale. When you record the export duty expense at the same time that you record the sale, what accounting concept are you following?

5.5 Assume that the decision has been made to liquidate a company (i.e., go out of business). What effect does this decision have on the accounting concepts followed by the company? What effects, if any, do you think this decision would have on the valuation of the company's assets and liabilities?

5.6 Some manufacturing companies treat property taxes as a part of cost-of-goods-sold expense, while others treat them as operating expenses. Does this difference in practice violate the principle of consistency? If so, under what conditions?

5.7 What accounting concept states that revenue is recognized not when a sales order is received, nor when a contract is signed, nor when the goods are manufactured, but only when the product is shipped or delivered to the customer?

5.8 Explain the problems that you might encounter in applying the following concepts:

(a) Realization

(b) Matching

(c) Conservatism

to the following business:
Your company produces and markets compact discs and tapes of popular music groups. You contract with a music group, paying the group a fixed amount plus a percentage of the sales revenue. You sell to record and tape distributors who have the right to return any unsold CDs or tapes within 12 months following purchase.

5.9 How might the principal of materiality affect accounting for expenses in:

(a) A fast-food restaurant

(b) An auto repair shop

5.10 In certain instances, companies may treat research and development expenditures for new products as an asset (typically referred to as capitalizing research and development) rather than as an expense. In terms of the accounting concepts discussed, what are the arguments in favor of such treatment? What are the opposing arguments?

5.11 How might an independent certified public accountant (CPA) go about obtaining verification of

(a) Amounts owed to the company by its customers (accounts receivable)

(b) Value of inventory

(c) Amounts owed by the company to its suppliers (accounts payable)

(d) Value of cash

(e) Value of loans payable

5.12 Imagine that you are the president of the student association. The association runs the campus grocery store, and rents space to a marketer of T-shirts and a ticket outlet. The association is also currently considering starting up a recycling program on campus. Would you account for these as separate entities or a single entity? Why?

5.13 Following a period of high inflation in the late 1970s and early 1980s, many companies did not adjust the value of their assets, and as a result, the value of their assets reflected in the general ledger was substantially below the assets' market value. Many acquisitors then proceeded to buy out companies and sell them as individual pieces at their higher market value. Do you think the principles of consistency and conservatism, and the use of the cost value method, helped make this process possible? Do you think the application of these principles should be modified? Why? How?

5.14 Many government contracts include *milestones* in the project under contract. As each milestone is met, a certain amount of money is paid to the contractor, even though the project may not be complete in its entirety. For example, if the armed forces order a nuclear submarine, they do not hold back payment until the submarine is delivered. Why is this? Do you think the process is a reasonable one?

5.15 If you were running a business and you prepaid six months of insurance, how often would you expect the accounting system to reflect using up the insurance? Every day? At the end of six months? Why?

5.16 What types of problems do you think a fluctuating exchange rate for international currencies presents to an accounting system?

5.17 Following the savings and loan industry crisis in the late 1980s, many investors who lost money filed lawsuits against the accounting firms that audited the savings and loan companies before they went bankrupt. What do you suppose were the bases for those lawsuits?

5.18 What are some primary differences in objectives between the Financial Accounting Standards Board (FASB) and the Securities and Exchange Commission (SEC)?

5.19 Should you have a great deal more confidence in financial statements that are certified by independent auditors than in those that are not? Explain.

5.20 Give three examples of expenditures that, at the time the expenditures are made, are not expenses for the business firm. Give three examples of expenses that, at the time the expenses are recognized, do not involve cash expenditures by the firm.

5.21 *Multiple choice:* Circle the letter that best answers the question. Circle only one letter for each question.
 (A) How do auditors verify the accuracy of a client company's accounts receivable?
  (a) By checking all credit invoices sent to the customer
  (b) By checking all cash receipts from customers
  (c) By checking both invoices sent to and cash receipts from customers
  (d) By verifying balances directly with a random sample of customers
  (e) By verifying balances directly with all customers
 (B) In relying on the published financial statements of a company in which you own common stock, you are relying on the:
  (a) Integrity of the company's managers

(b) Scrutiny by the Securities and Exchange Commission (SEC)

(c) Bookkeeping done by the company's auditors

(d) The principle of conservatism

(e) All of the above

(C) The time-adjusted value method will yield a higher value for an asset than the market-value method when the asset is owned by X and:

(a) X's equivalency interest rate is lower than the rate for other typical owners.

(b) The typical owner of such assets is willing to pay more for the asset than X is willing to pay.

(c) The economy is experiencing rapid inflation.

(d) Prevailing interest rates in the economy are low.

(e) None of the above

5.22 Indicate the accounting concept that requires the accountant to:

(a) Lean toward understating revenues and overstating expenses.

(b) Use prepaid expense accounts.

(c) Ignore historical cost when valuing an asset that will no longer be used by a manufacturing company because of a change in the manufacturing company's business.

(d) Refrain from changing accounting practice from period to period.

(e) Record the expected electric expense for this month, even though the corresponding electric bill itself will not be received from the electric company until next month.

(f) Treat as an expense of this month the utility bill for the period from the 20th of last month to the 20th of this month.

PROBLEMS

5.1 Suppose you are the accounting manager for a magazine company that offers three-year subscriptions to the magazine for $65. Show how you would account for the receipt of such a $65 payment. What entries would be required in future accounting periods?

5.2 The Howell Mixer Sales Company sells three basic models of a very popular mixer for restaurant use. It also sells miscellaneous parts, supplies, and accessories for the mixer. Opening balances in the company's general ledger at May 1, 1995, were as follows:

Account	Debit	Credit
Cash	$3,520	
Accounts receivable	4,440	
Inventory—Light use model (11 units)	6,600	

Inventory—Heavy use model (1 unit)	1,000	
Inventory—Medium use model (7 units)	3,500	
Inventory—Miscellaneous	2,500	
Accounts payable		$2,900
Invested capital		12,000
Retained earnings		6,660
	$21,560	$21,560

The balances in accounts receivable and accounts payable were composed of the following:

Accounts receivable
S. Statts	$1360
Y. Williams	800
P. Baricci	400
L. Elanndes	600
A. Correos	900
M. Bausenn	380
	$4440

Accounts payable
Howard Machine Co.	$2640
Daily Gazette	260
	2900

Other accounts used by Howell (that is, included in the company's chart of accounts) are as follows:

Advertising expense
Cost of goods sold—Other
Cost of goods sold—Mixers
Salaries expense
Rent expense
Sales—Other
Sales—Mixers

Set up T-accounts for the accounts listed above and enter the following May transactions directly in these accounts.

(a) Enter the opening balances in their respective accounts.

(b) Paid rent for store and store equipment to T. Takata, $500.

(c) Received $600 from S. Statts, $600 from L. Elanndes, and $300 from A. Correos, a total of $1500.

(d) Sold four light use mixers, each for $900, for cash.

(e) Paid Howard Machine Co. $1600 on account.

(f) Sold parts, supplies, and other miscellaneous inventory for a total sales value of $1420, all received in cash.

(g) Sold one heavy use mixer for $2600 on credit to P. Baricci. Sold one medium use mixer for $700 on credit to M. Bausenn and one for $750 on credit to D. Mein, a new customer.

(h) Sold one medium use mixer to L. Elanndes for $700. L. Elanndes paid $300 cash and owes the balance.

(i) Purchased on credit from Howard Machine Co. the following:

Two light use mixers at $600 each.

Two medium use mixers at $500 each.

(j) Placed advertising with the Daily Gazette for the month at a total cost of $150. Payment for this advertising is due June 15.

(k) Sold one light use mixer for $900 cash.

(l) Paid salaries to employees for the month of May totaling $3400 cash.

(m) Paid the Daily Gazette $260 for advertising that appeared during April.

(n) Determined that the miscellaneous inventory of parts, supplies, and accessories was $1800 at the end of May, compared to $2500 at the beginning of the month.

Determine and record the ending balance in each T-account. Prepare a balance sheet at May 31, 1995 and an income statement for May.

5.3 The following transactions occurred during the month of October, 1994 at the Peach Company. The balance sheet for the Peach Company at September 30, 1994 was as follows:

Balance Sheet

Assets		Liabilities	
Cash	$ 4,500	Accounts payable	$ 16,000
Accounts receivable	24,000	Notes payable	30,000
Supplies on hand	8,000	Wages and salaries payable	5,000
Equipment	51,000	Invested capital	50,000
Truck	20,000	Retained earnings	6,500
	$107,500		$107,500

The general ledger at Peach company includes the following accounts besides those listed in the balance sheet above:

Advertising expense

Bonus expense

Bonus payable

Decline in value of equipment (expense)

Decline in value of truck (expense)

Insurance expense

Interest expense

Prepaid insurance

Rent expense

Service revenue

Supplies expense

Utilities expense

Wages and salaries expense

Record the opening balances in the appropriate T-accounts, and then make the entries required to record the following:

(a) Mr. Peach, the owner, invested an additional $20,000 in the business.

(b) Rent in the amount of $7000 was paid in cash for the month of October.

(c) Supplies were purchased on credit at a cost of $3000.

(d) Credit customers were sent invoices totaling $23,000 for services rendered during the month.

(e) Cash customers paid $10,000 for services rendered to them during October. (Note: Total of credit and cash sales was $33,000.)

(f) Cash in the amount of $17,000 was received from customers for services rendered in previous months.

(g) A six-month insurance policy, with coverage beginning on October 1, 1994, was purchased for $3000 in cash.

(h) The invoice from the utility company in the amount of $3800 was received and paid.

(i) The accountant for Peach estimated that the truck declined in value by $1000 and that the equipment declined in valued by $2500 during October.

(j) Additional equipment to be used in the service activity was purchased on credit at a price of $7500.

(k) Wages and salaries earned by employees for the month totaled $13,000.

(l) Total cash payment of wages and salaries during the month was $12,000, including $5000 that was payable at the beginning of the month.

(m) Invoices from suppliers for supplies and equipment received in previous months were paid in the amount of $14,500.

(n) A count and valuation of supplies on hand at the end of the month revealed an end of month balance of $6500.

(o) Peach Company paid $5500 to the bank from which the company was borrowing: $5000 in principal repayment and $500 interest.

(p) Advertising for the month totaled $1750, paid in cash.

(q) In return for extra services that the general manager rendered to the company during October, Mr. Peach agreed that the company would pay a bonus to the general manager equal to 10 percent of October's sales; this bonus is to be paid on November 10.

Prepare an income statement for the month of October and a balance sheet as of October 31, 1994.

5.4 The balance sheet at December 31, 1996 and income statement for the calendar year 1996 for the Weingart Company are as follows:

Balance Sheet

Assets		Liabilities & Owners' Equity	
Cash	$ 27,700	Accounts payable	$ 47,100
Accounts receivable	68,300	Compensation payable	24,300
Inventory	73,900	Other liabilities	38,300
Prepaid expenses	14,800	Total current liabilities	109,700
Total current assets	184,700	Long-term liabilities	130,000
Property, plant and equipment	191,400	Owners' equity	136,400
Total	$376,100	Total	$376,100

Income Statement	
Sales revenue	$610,000
Cost of goods sold	407,500
Gross profit	202,500
Operating expenses	
Selling expenses	91,600
Administrative expenses	88,600
Total expenses	$180,200
Operating profit	$ 22,300

Consider the effects on these financial statements of applying the basic concepts indicated to the particular circumstances outlined. Recompute the two financial statements, incorporating any suggested modifications in valuation.

(a) Entity: Included within administrative expenses are $2500 for travel expenses for the president's spouse. The president has agreed to reimburse the company in early 1997 for this amount.

(b) Going-concern assumption: In late 1996, Weingart decided to abandon a particular line of business. This decision renders essentially useless $3500 of equipment shown on the balance sheet above.

(c) Conservatism: Weingart's auditors have suggested that $2000 of revenue shown in the 1996 total would be better deferred until next year as the associated work has not quite been completed by Weingart's staff, although the customer has been invoiced.

(d) Realization: The auditors have also suggested that $3700 received from Customer 186 for a software package to be delivered in February 1997 should not be included in revenue until the package is actually delivered.

(e) Accrual: The human resources manager has calculated that the amount of vacation time earned by employees but not yet used has a value of $4600. The accounting manager has now decided this amount should be accrued in 1996.

(f) Consistency: In years prior to 1996, Weingart treated bonuses as expenses in the month (typically January) when they were paid. Included in the Compensation Payable amount at December 31 are provisions for $6600 of bonuses to be paid early in 1997. The accounting manager has decided to revert to prior practice.

(g) Materiality: Included in the December 31 inventory valuation is $1100 of office supplies. The accounting manager has decided that these supplies should be expensed when received because of the excess time required each month to count, value, and account for the current status of these low-value inventory items.

___6
ACCOUNTING MECHANICS

We now turn to the mechanics of operating an accounting system, the procedures to assemble, organize, and present the vast stream of accounting data and thus turn it into useful financial information.

Bookkeeping is emphasized in most accounting courses and books. By contrast, this book assumes that you are or will be a user of accounting information—a manager or an investor, for example—not a practitioner of the accounting trade. You seek to be a proficient user, not a skilled bookkeeper. Nevertheless, you need to know something of the mechanics and jargon of bookkeeping, enough to communicate and to visualize the key activities of an accounting department. To be a proficient user of financial statements you need to know how an accounting system functions. This chapter provides that overview.

Everyone in an organization encounters and influences data that end up in the accounting department. Purchase orders, labor time records, invoices to customers, bills from vendors, checks received, and checks paid are all part of this data flow. Thus, you need a sense of the way these and other documents are utilized by the accounting department.

Recall the verbs in our definition of accounting: observe, measure, record, classify, and summarize. To this point we have concentrated on the first two of those verbs: observe and measure. Once measured and valued, assets, liabilities, revenues, and expenses must be recorded in the accounting system, classified in some useful manner, and summarized for interpretation.

CHART OF ACCOUNTS

Classification is key to bookkeeping. Consider the very many transactions, the huge volume of data generated in any large organization. Perhaps hundreds or thousands of sales take place each day, hundreds or thousands of bills are received, checks paid out, and checks received. Legions of employees earn wages and salaries, and many types of fixed assets are owned. Money is borrowed and repaid; tax obligations recorded and paid.

Accounting's task is to turn data into information. The accounting system must do more than simply collect and record the data; it must classify data in ways useful to management, creditors, shareholders, tax collectors, and other readers of financial statements.

The chart of accounts, introduced in Chapter 3, is a road map of the accounting system, listing all accounts available to the accountant for classifying assets owned, liabilities owed, revenues earned, and expenses incurred. The chart of accounts defines the accounting system's classification scheme. Drawing up a chart of accounts is the first step in designing an accounting system.

The type, size, and complexity of the business organization dictate the particular ledger accounts needed (recall that the T-account is shorthand for a general ledger account). For example, some companies classify sales extensively to provide management information for product line and pricing decisions; others sell only a single product or service and need only one sales account in the chart of accounts. An organization with many separate departments categorizes expenses not only by type of expense (for example, salary, telephone, travel, supplies, rent), but also by the department (machine shop, assembly shop, sales department, accounting department), since each departmental manager needs financial information relevant to his or her segment of the enterprise.

Bear in mind that information costs money, not only to prepare but also to assimilate and interpret. Resist the temptation to construct a very lengthy chart of accounts to provide elaborate data classification. Computerization makes this urge almost irresistible, since the computer can classify and reclassify data with great speed. To often, computer-generated accounting reports are so voluminous as to be both intimidating and not terribly useful.

You want the data summarized—*summarize* is the fifth and penultimate verb in the definition of accounting. The more detailed the classification, the less the data are summarized. You must make the cost versus benefit trade-offs: sufficient detail (classification) to be useful, and enough summarization so that financial reports can be prepared and interpreted efficiently. This trade-off is not easy to make; from time to time you should revise your chart of accounts to reflect changed conditions and informational needs.

Charts of accounts are numerically coded to facilitate data processing. Each digit of the account code has meaning in the account's classification. Figure 6-1 is a kind of table of contents for Perez Corporation's chart of accounts; Figure 6-2 shows detailed account names and numbers for certain account categories. Perez, a small company, does not need an elaborate or extensive chart of accounts—only about 100 general ledger accounts. A larger company with many product lines, departments, and offices might have 1000 or more accounts. Such a company might, for example, want not a single set of general and administrative (G&A) expense ac-

FIGURE 6-1 The Perez Corporation, Chart of Accounts—Table of Contents.

Account Number (Range)	Account Category
101–149	Current assets
150–199	Noncurrent assets
200–249	Current liabilities
250–259	Long-term liabilities
261–299	Ownership equity
300–349	Revenue (Sales)
350–399	Cost of goods sold
400–699	Operating expenses
400–499	Selling expenses
500–599	Research and Development (R&D) expenses
600–699	General and Administrative (G&A) expenses
700–799	Other income and expense

counts, but further classification to each of, say, seven departments comprising the G & A function.

Note in Figure 6-2 that the Perez Corporation uses 15 current asset accounts, including three categories of inventory, and a separation of receivables into a number of categories. The company has four classifications of sales: products A and B, special contracts, and the inevitable "other" category. The company's selling expenses are divided among 11 accounts, but more extensive categorization here might be useful. For example, field sales force salaries might be separated from office support staff salaries, and travel and entertainment expenses might be further divided into air travel, auto rental, hotel, meal, and entertainment expenses. The sales manager might desire this additional detail, or tax reporting requirements might demand it (for example, entertainment separated from other travel expenses).

THREE KEY ELEMENTS OF AN ACCOUNTING SYSTEM

Accounting systems are composed of three primary elements: **source documents, journals,** and **ledgers.** The flow of data is from source document to journal to ledger. While the physical appearance of these elements varies considerably depending upon the sophistication of the system, the elements are present in a simple accounting system maintained by a single bookkeeper as well as in elaborate, computerized systems.

Source Documents

As implied by the name, source documents are the original evidence of a transaction to be recorded. What are the primary, recurring transactions in a merchandising or manufacturing company? These are essentially only four: (1) sales to customers, (2)

FIGURE 6-2 The Perez Corporation, Excerpts from Chart of Accounts

Account Number	Account Name
101–149	Current Assets
101	Petty Cash
105	Cash (Checking)—First Bank
107	Cash (Savings)—Provident Savings and Loan
111	Accounts Receivable—Trade
112	Allowance for Doubtful Accounts—Trade
113	Accounts Receivable—Other
115	Notes Receivable—Trade
117	Notes Receivable—Other
118	Travel Advances—Employees
121	Inventory—Raw Material
125	Inventory—In-process
131	Inventory—Finished Goods
141	Prepaid Expenses
145	Other Current Assets
147	Freight Clearing
300–349	Revenue (Sales)
301	Sales—Product A
305	Sales—Product B
321	Sales—Special Contracts
329	Other Sales
345	Sales Returns and Allowances
347	Sales Price Discounts
400–499	Selling Expenses
401	Sales Commission Expense
411	Sales Salaries
413	Fringe Benefit Expenses—Sales
415	Travel and Entertainment Expenses
421	Advertising (Space) Expense
423	Promotional Literature Expense
425	Miscellaneous Supplies and Other Expenses
429	Miscellaneous Outside Services
431	Telecommunications Expenses
433	Occupancy Expense
435	Depreciation Expense

cash received from customers (concurrently with the sale in a cash-sale transaction), (3) incurrence of expense, and (4) cash disbursement, or the payment of cash (again, sometimes concurrent with the incurrence of expenses). Surely other transactions occur—money is burrowed and repaid, fixed assets are acquired and disposed of, and so forth—but the primary transactions that the accounting system must handle routinely are these four, as follows.

Sales. The primary evidence of a sale on credit is the **invoice** prepared for the customer. Typically, this invoice is prepared on a multi-part form and one or more copies of the invoice become the source document for the sale. Cash sales may be evidenced by a copy of a customer receipt or by a cash register tape (or equivalent in electronic or magnetic media).

The customer invoice must contain all information required to classify the sale, as well as simply to record it: the customer's name, the date, the amount of the sale, the type of product sold or service rendered, freight charges, sales tax, terms of payments, and so forth. The invoice may be coded by geographic region, or responsible salesperson, if the accounting system is to provide sales data classified by sales region or salesperson. (A computer-based accounting system is, of course, capable of multiple classifications.) Data processing is facilitated by assigning numerical codes to the various products, customers, regions, and so forth.

Cash Receipts. Most cash is received in the form of checks, rather than currency, and the check itself is a source document. Most organizations, however, are anxious to deposit checks without delay, and thus a satisfactory source document is either a copy of the check or the "voucher" attached to checks drawn by commercial or industrial organizations.

Just as the cash register tape or copy of the customer receipt evidences a sales transaction, it also evidences the cash received in that transaction.

Incurrence of Expenses. An invoice (or bill) received from a vendor is evidence of an expense incurred, just as a customer invoice is evidence of a sales transaction. The accrual concept requires timely recording of this expense, typically well in advance of when the bill is paid; thus, the vendor's invoice, not the company's subsequent payment, triggers the accounting entry to record the expense.

The vendor's invoice alone is not complete evidence of the amount and validity of the expense. It alone does not provide assurance that the merchandise or services received correspond in fact with those ordered or authorized by the company. Furthermore, it does not verify either that the merchandise has been received or that the prices charged are the agreed upon prices. Therefore, the accounting department collects and matches several documents to confirm that the vendor's invoice represents a bona fide expense to be recorded. A copy of the company's **purchase order** (forwarded from the purchasing department) confirms both the agreed upon price and the fact that the products or services were indeed ordered. The vendor's invoice should reference the appropriate purchase order. Evidence is still required that the merchandise was received by the company. This verification document typically is the **packing slip** (or **packing list**) that the vendor enclosed with the shipment, indicating quantities of each item shipped; the receiving clerk notes on the packing slip any discrepancies between the quantities shown and the quantities actually received and forwards it to accounting. By matching data on the packing slip and the original purchase order to the vendor's invoice data, the accounting clerk verifies that the expense is appropriate without any further contact with either the purchasing department or the receiving department.

Wages and salaries expenses are evidenced by specialized documents, typically **time cards,** showing not only the total hours an employee worked, but, when appropriate, the particular activity on which he or she worked. Time cards are usually signed by the individual's supervisor to provide independent accuracy verification.

Cash Disbursements. As most payments are made by check rather than in currency, a copy of the firm's check is the logical source document for cash disbursements (payments).

Commercial and industrial organizations typically use a multi-part check form, sending the original to the payee and retaining one or more (nonnegotiable) copies as a source document. In a simple (for example, personal) accounting system, the check stub serves as the source document. Payments in currency are made infrequently and typically from a petty cash fund. Individual vouchers prepared when cash is paid out from the fund serve as source documents in support of the checks drawn periodically to reimburse the petty cash fund.

The preceding discussion of the four most prevalent transactions describes "hard copy" (paper) source documents for each. As organizations move to "paperless" environments, source documents are increasingly made available to the accounting department in electronic form through the organization's networked computer system. The accounting procedures remain conceptually the same.

Journals

Journals are the accounting system's so-called books of original entry: data from source documents are recorded first in one of the journals. (The term **register** is often used interchangeably with journal.)

An accounting system could be operated with a single journal. All transactions would be listed in chronological order, referencing the appropriate source document. In an organization of even modest size, such a journal would be voluminous and not very useful. The initial step in classifying accounting data is accomplished through the use of specialized journals. While all accounting systems do maintain a **general journal** for the recording of nonroutine transactions, most use one or more specialized journals, often one for each category of source document: **sales journal, cash receipts journal, expense journal** (or **voucher register**), and **cash disbursements journal** (or **check register**). Even finer classification of transactions can be achieved with more specialized journals. For example, many companies utilize an expense journal and a cash payments journal for nonsalary expenses and payments, but also a specialized **payroll journal** for all wage and salary payments. These payments are unlike other transactions: they are circumscribed by numerous strict legal requirements and wage and salary expenses are typically recognized at the same time payroll checks are drawn.

Figures 6-3 through 6-5 show examples of two specialized journals and the general journal used by the Perez Corporation.

The sales journal shown in Figure 6-3 contains entries for the first several days of March. Note that the normal entry involves a debit entry to Accounts Receivable (account number 111) and a credit entry to one of the sales accounts (account numbers 301, 305, or 321). Essentially all debit entries to Accounts Receivable occur in this journal. Sales are classified by type, and at month end the summary totals in these three columns indicate total sales for the month, by product category.

This specialized journal also records certain ancillary transactions that are, by their nature, linked to the sales transactions. Perez pays commissions to sales agents on certain sales. Proper matching of expenses and revenues demands that the commission expense be recognized in the same accounting period as the related sale. While the commission expense could be recorded in the expense journal, a more convenient approach is to record commission expenses concurrently with the related sales transactions. Such a procedure is permitted by the specialized journal shown in Figure 6-3. A column has been provided here for account number 401, Commission Expense, and for account no. 225, Commission Payable. When a sales transaction on which an agent earns commission is recorded in the sales journal (for example, the sale on March 2 to General Mammoth), the appropriate debit to Commission Expense and credit to Commission Payable is recorded simultaneously. Careful design of specialized journals facilitates efficient bookkeeping.

Figure 6-4 illustrates a cash disbursements journal, often called a check register. Checks written by the Perez Corporation are listed sequentially as a control procedure (or double check) that all of the company's prenumbered checks have been used properly and none for unauthorized withdrawals of funds. The routine debit is to Accounts Payable and each transaction necessitates a credit to Cash; thus, columns are dedicated to each of these two accounts. In certain instances, cash discounts for prompt payment are earned (as discussed in a future chapter) and this information is also recorded in this special journal in a Cash Discounts Earned column on the credit side (see check numbers 263 and 264). In situations where expenses were not previously recognized in other journals, the debit entries are not to Account Payable; this specialized cash disbursements journal permits the bookkeeper to record the account number (as determined from the chart of accounts) and the amount of the debit. For example, check number 265 refunds $500 to a customer (debit to account number 111, Accounts Receivable—Trade) and check number 266 pays principal and interest on a loan from Security Bank (debit to account numbers 251 and 721, Bank Loan Payable and Interest Expense, respectively).

Figure 6-5 illustrates a form of general journal, the journal used to record all transactions and adjustments (including corrections) that do not fit any specialized journal. All accounting systems require a general journal, but the extent of its use depends upon the number and design of the system's specialized journals. Each

FIGURE 6-3 The Perez Corporation, Sales Journal

| | | Debit | Debit | Credit — Sales | Credit — Sales | Credit — Other | Credit — Other | Credit — Other |
| | | #401 Commission Expense | #111 Accounts Receivable | #301 Product A | #305 Product B | #321 Special Contracts | #147 Freight Clearing | #225 Commissions Payable |
Date	Customer Name							
Mar. 1	Cox Supply Co.		4050	4000			50	
Mar. 2	General Mammoth Corp.	150	3200		3200			150
Mar. 4	Mansfield Distributors		3160	2480	650		30	
Mar. 8	Foster Bros. Wholesalers	100	3900	2500	1400			100
Mar. 8	Willamette Supply Co.		2600	2600				

FIGURE 6-4 The Perez Corporation, Cash Disbursements Journal (Check Register)

			Debit			Credit	
Date	Payee	Check Number	Account Payable Amount	Other Accounts	Amount	Cash	Cash Discount Earned
March 10	Overland Freight	259		147	100	100	
March 10	VOID	260					
March 10	Kennedy Trucking	261		147	50	50	
March 10	Dean and Balmer	262		233	1000	1000	
March 10	Creative Publ.	263	2000			1950	20
March 10	Ajax Webbing	264	2500			2450	50
March 10	Moore Supply	265		111	500	500	
March 13	Security Bank	266		251	600	950	
				721	350		

FIGURE 6-5 The Perez Corporation, General Journal

Date		Account Name	Account Number	Debit	Credit
March	3	Cash	105	10,000	
		Short-term Bank			
		Borrowing	211		10,000
	8	Depreciation Expense	435	200	
		Accumulated Depreciation,			
		Office Equipment	167		200

entry in the general journal must show the account titles and numbers and the amount of both the debit and the credit. Of course, no classification is accomplished in this journal. The first entry in Figure 6-5 records the borrowing of $10,000 from the Security Bank on a short-term loan and the second records this month's depreciation expense on office equipment used by the sales department. Note that the second of these entries (to record depreciation) involved no transaction with an outside party. Perez's accountant simply recognized that some of the fixed asset's original cost should be recorded as an expense (that is, depreciation expense should be charged); all such recognitions, discussed at length in the next chapter, are typically recorded in the general journal.

General Ledger

The third step in the process is to transfer the categorized and summarized data from the journals to the general ledger, the fundamental books of the accounting system, containing all accounts listed in the chart of accounts. All accounting data ultimately find their way to the general ledger, and financial statements are prepared from the summarized data contained therein.

At the end of the accounting period (for example, a month) data from the journals are transferred to the general ledger:

(1) First, the journals are totaled and double-checked to be certain that they are in balance—the sum of all debits equals the sum of all credits.

(2) The totals of those columns in the specialized journals devoted to a single account are transferred to the corresponding general ledger account. Note that the detailed individual entries are not transferred, only the totals.

(3) Other entries that appear in the specialized journals (see, for example, the Other Debits in Figure 6-4) and all entries in the general journal are transferred to the appropriate general ledger account.

At this point, the general ledger should be in balance (debits equal credits). All data from the source documents have flowed through one of the journals and now appear in classified and summarized fashion in the general ledger. The format of the

FIGURE 6-6   The Perez Corporation, General Ledger Account

Account Number 423
Promotional Literature Expense

Date	Explanation	Debit	Date	Explanation	Credit
February 28	Balance	600	March 31	GJ2	100
March 12	CDJ 3	100			
March 21	CDJ 4	150			
March 31	EJ	400			

general ledger is analogous to the T-accounts: debits on the left and credits on the right. General ledgers provide space to record both the date of the entry and the journal (specialized or general) from which it came.

In summarizing and categorizing the data, the bookkeeper leaves a trail from the general ledger back through the journals to the source documents, so that, if required, the detail behind each general ledger entry can be examined and the resulting balance verified. This trail is needed both by the accounting staff and by the company's independent auditors. Suppose the sales manager or an auditor at Perez wishes to know just what caused the promotional literature expense to be so high during the month of March. The balance in account number 423 in the general ledger shown in Figure 6-6 on February 28 (that is, after the first two months of the year) was $600. The entries for March net to a debit of $550, and thus indeed the March expenses do seem high in relation to the expense for the previous two months. The entries in March are as follows:

(1) On March 12 at $100 debit entry was made from page 3 of the cash disbursements journal (CDJ 3).

(2) Similarly, on March 21 a $150 entry was made from page 4 of that journal.

(3) At the end of the month, the expense journal (EJ) was summarized, and the column total ($400) related to this expense was transferred to the general ledger.

(4) Also on March 31, a $100 credit entry is detailed on page two of the general ledger (GJ 2); this entry reduces the expense and is probably a correction.*

The accountant can now go back to the pages indicated in these three journals—the expense, cash disbursements, and general journals—and determine the individual transactions that comprised the total $550 expense for the month. The entries in the journals in turn reference the particular source documents, and, if the auditor or sales manager wants still more detail, these individual source documents can be retrieved from the files.

*Entries are not erased from either journals or ledgers; rather, corrections are made by reversing the original (incorrect) entry and then proceeding with the correct entry. A debit entry is reversed by an equal credit entry to the same account, and a credit entry is reversed by a debit to the same account.

Subsidiary Ledger

The general ledger provides insufficient detail for certain asset and liability accounts; often you need to know more about what is owned and who and what is owed. For example, the accounts receivable balance in the general ledger indicates the total amount owed by all customers, but does not tell you the amount owed by each customer. Your obviously need this customer-by-customer information; you want to pursue late-paying customers, and you want to cease selling to customers who are excessively delinquent.

Similarly, you need to know not only the total amount owing to vendors (total accounts payable) but also the detailed amount owing to each. Perez may wish to know the amount of sales commission owing to each agent, not simply the total amount of sales commissions payable shown in account number 225 in the general ledger.

The detailed backup data in support of a general ledger balance are maintained in a **subsidiary ledger**—a set of records that elaborates on a particular general ledger account and reconciles with its balance. The accounts receivable subsidiary ledger is the most common. It is organized by individual customer and records each sale as a debit, each payment as a credit, and any other adjustments. While most subsidiary ledgers are formal and automated, an informal but useful subsidiary accounts receivable ledger can be maintained simply by placing a copy of each customer invoice in a file identified with the customer's name and removing and destroying that copy as soon as payment is received from the customer. The file at all times contains that customer's unpaid invoices; the total of all invoices remaining in all customer files equals the accounts receivable balance in the general ledger.

Any asset or liability account may be the subject of a subsidiary ledger. While accounts receivable and accounts payable are the most common, some accounting systems provide subsidiary detail on inventory, fixed assets, and even cash (if the company maintains accounts in numerous banks). Computerized computer systems permit us to maintain subsidiary ledgers with very little additional work.

Entries are made to subsidiary ledgers at the time the related journal entries are made, utilizing data from the source documents. When at the end of the accounting period the data are transferred from journals to ledgers, accountants reconcile the resulting general ledger balances with the detail already in the subsidiary ledgers.

THE ACCOUNTING CYCLE

The bookkeeping just described goes on throughout the accounting period. Source documents arrive daily in the accounting department, and data contained therein are processed to the journals (both specialized and general). Also, all subsidiary ledgers are maintained on a current basis. However, no entries have been made in the general ledger during the course of the accounting period.

At the end of the accounting period, a good deal of work remains to get the accounting books in shape to construct financial statements for the period. Information from the journals now is transferred to the general ledger, as discussed earlier;

in accounting parlance, data from the journals are posted to the general ledger. A preliminary **trial balance,** a listing of all accounts in the general ledger and the debit or credit balance in each, is constructed. This preliminary trial balance allows the accountant to be certain that the ledger is in balance—the debits equal the credits. A balanced trial balance does not guarantee that all entries were made to the correct accounts, but simply that, in posting from source documents to journal and in posting from journal to ledger, debit entries have been balanced with equal credit entries. Of course, if the trial balance fails to balance, a hunt for the error or errors commences.

Also at this stage the accountant reconciles all subsidiary ledgers to their corresponding control accounts in the general ledger.

This first trial balance is referred to as preliminary because additional entries are necessary to complete the accounting for the period. These additional entries—referred to as adjusting entries or end-of-period adjustments—are discussed in the following chapter. Suffice to say here that adjusting entries are not triggered by transactions with parties outside the organization and therefore are not subject of typical source documents; rather, the entries, initiated by the accountant, are necessitated by certain events (including simply the passage of time) that alter values of assets or liabilities. For example, the accountant may learn that a certain customer will be unable to pay, and thus accounts receivable need to be adjusted, or that current borrowing will soon require an interest payment and thus current liabilities need to be adjusted. These adjusting entries are recorded in the general journal and then posted to the general ledger. After all adjusting entries have been made, the accountant is prepared to construct a final trial balance (a final check that debits equal credits) and the financial statements for the accounting period.

Remember that, in a sense, all income and expense accounts are a part of owners' equity. Thus, at the end of a fiscal year, all income and expenses are closed to the Retained Earnings account; that is, debit and credit entries are made in these accounts so as to drive their balances to zero, with the offsetting entries in Retained Earnings. These **closing entries** transfer net income for the year to retained earnings, and the income and expense accounts have a zero balance at the beginning of the new fiscal year.

Income and expense accounts could be closed monthly, thus transferring each month's profit to retained earnings. This procedure is not typical, nor is it necessary to determine monthly profit. When these accounts are closed only annually, the profit for a particular month is determined by deduction. For example, the profit for the sixth month is derived by (1) constructing an income statement from the income and expense account balances at the end of six months, (2) constructing the same statement from account balances at the end of five months, and (3) subtracting the five-month statement from the six-month statement.

SUMMARY

While this book emphasizes accounting concepts and interpretation of accounting data rather than bookkeeping, some knowledge of accounting mechanics is essential for all who must interact with and gain information from an accounting system.

The basic road map of the accounting system is the chart of accounts, a listing of all available accounts; the extent and nature of classifications are codified in this account listing. The accountant must balance costs and benefits in deciding the amount of detail to be maintained in the accounting books.

The basic flow of accounting data is from source document to journal to general ledger. While a wide variety of source documents are used, each typically evidences one of four basic transactions: sale, incurrence of expense, receipt of cash, or payment of cash. Specialized journals facilitate efficient processing of information, permitting similar transactions to be grouped. All accounting systems require also a general journal for recording both transactions that do not fit the specialized journals and various adjusting (end-of-period) entries.

At the end of the accounting period, data from the journals are posted to the general ledger and a preliminary trial balance is constructed. End-of-period entries are then recorded in the general journal and posted to the general ledger before a final trial balance is constructed and the financial statements—income statement and balance sheet—are drawn up.

NEW TERMS

Cash disbursements journal. A specialized journal to record cash payments. This journal is frequently referred to as a *check register,* as checks are typically recorded sequentially within the journal.

Cash receipts journal. A specialized journal to record cash receipts.

Check register. Another name for cash disbursements journal.

Closing entries. Those entries that transfer net income for the period to retained earnings, returning all income and expense accounts to zero balances for the new accounting period.

Expense journal. A specialized journal to record expenses.

General journal. The journal to record all transactions and recognitions that do not fit one of the specialized journals.

Invoice. The document issued by the seller specifying amounts owed by the buyer in connection with items provided or services rendered. Invoices are often referred to as bills.

Journals. Books of original entry where data from source documents are recorded before posting to the general ledger. Accounting systems typically utilize both specialized journals and a general journal.

Ledger. Refers to the general ledger, the fundamental accounting books of the organization. In an accounting system, data flow from source documents to journals to the general ledger.

Packing slip (or packing list). The document prepared by the seller and included with shipments to the buyer. The packing list details the quantity and description of all items included in the shipment.

Payroll journal. A specialized journal to record wages and salaries expenses, together with transactions related to payroll.

Purchase order. The document issued by the buyer to the seller specifying the particular item(s) or service(s) ordered, quantities, prices, terms of purchase, required delivery date, and so forth.

Register. Another name for a specialized journal. For example, the cash disbursements journal is sometimes referred to as the check register.

Sales journal. A specialized journal to record sales transactions.

Source documents. The evidence of transactions with other entities. These documents (for example, invoices and checks) provide the data required to record the transactions.

Subsidiary ledger. A set of records providing detail on the composition of a particular general ledger account. For example, an accounts receivable subsidiary ledger details amounts owed by individual customers; the sum of the balances in the subsidiary ledger agrees with the single balance in the Accounts Receivable account in the general ledger.

Time card. The document maintained by individual employees detailing the hours worked and, in many instances, the job, task, or project worked on. Time cards are the source documents for salaries and wages expenses.

Trial balance. A listing of all accounts in the general ledger and their balances.

DISCUSSION QUESTIONS

6.1 A payroll check stub typically includes information on the actual cash paid, as well as an itemized list of the deductions taken. Why is this necessary?

6.2 A phone bill contains information about routine charges and about non-routine charges, such as long distance phone calls. This information is itemized, usually sorted in order of date and time when the phone call took place. Do you think this itemization is adequate? Is there anything the phone company might do to improve its billing scheme?

6.3 If you had sent a check to pay your utility bill, and the company then indicated that you had not made a payment, what documents would you use to prove that you had indeed made the payment?

6.4 How do you record personal cash receipts? Do you record them on a cash or an accrual basis?

6.5 What is the role of journals in an accounting system? Why aren't data from the source documents recorded directly in the general ledger?

6.6 Describe the data and information that you would expect to find in an accounts payable subsidiary ledger for a janitorial service firm.

6.7   Why are general ledger accounts typically assigned both a number and a name rather than just a name?

6.8   Suppose that you just joined the accounting department of a hotel chain and wished to become familiar with its accounting system. What document or documents would you review first, and why? What if the company was an auto tire manufacturer?

6.9   To assure accurate payment of vendors' invoices, the accounting department (typically, the accounts payable clerk), needs to obtain information from several different documents. What are these documents and what information is obtained from each?

6.10   At the end of an accounting period, what simple check for accuracy should be performed on a set of subsidiary ledger accounts?

6.11   In what way or ways does the use of specialized journals increase the efficiency of the accounting function (that is, reduce the time required to complete the accounting cycle)?

6.12   Describe a simple form of accounts receivable subsidiary ledger that uses copies of the source documents. Why would such a system be important?

6.13   If a department manager suspected that the repair expenses charged to her department in a particular month were incorrect, what procedure would the company's accountant have to follow to determine exactly what charges had been included in the Repairs Expense account?

6.14   This book uses T-accounts to illustrate accounting entries. The set of T-accounts is equivalent to what part of the accounting records in a formal accounting system?

6.15   Describe and categorize the source document that would represent the original evidence of the following:

(a)   Wages expense for an inventory clerk

(b)   Sales revenue derived from merchandise shipped to a customer

(c)   Commission expense to be paid to one of the company's salespersons in connection with the sale described in (b)

(d)   Purchase of a fixed asset

(e)   Payment to a trade supplier for merchandise received in a previous accounting period

(f)   Payment received from a customer for merchandise shipped in a previous accounting period

(g)   Cash payment received from a retail customer for merchandise purchased in the store

(h)   Purchase of material for the company's inventory

6.16 The following questions relate to specialized journals:

    (a) In a check register, the credit entry is typically to what account?

    (b) Describe the types of accounts to which debit entries are typically made in a check register.

    (c) In a sales journal, what account is most frequently debited?

    (d) In a sales journal, to what other accounts might debit entries be made? Describe the circumstances that might give rise to these entries.

    (e) How can a sales journal be used to classify and summarize accounting information in ways that might be useful to management?

    (f) Why is a separate payroll journal frequently used, rather than including salary and wages expenses with other expenses in an expense journal?

    (g) What debit and credit entries predominate in a cash receipts journal?

PROBLEMS

6.1 Specialized journals are designed to facilitate recording similar transactions. For example, a company whose employees do a great deal of traveling might wish to design a specialized journal to record travel expenses. Design such a journal, indicating the information that you would expect to see in it.

6.2 The controller at an office supplies company wishes to establish a paperwork flow system that will permit the sales department to instruct the shipping department as to the exact items to be shipped to a customer and that will assure that the accounting department will accurately bill the customer for the merchandise shipped. Describe an appropriate paperwork system.

6.3 Suppose that you were asked to set up an accounting system for a restaurant that serves both lunch and dinner and operates a bar. Prepare a simple chart of accounts for such an operation. What specialized journals, if any, would you recommend that the restaurant use? Why?

6.4 Assume you own a small apartment building consisting of twelve rental units. Prepare a simple chart of accounts for the business. Would you use any specialized journals? Any subsidiary ledgers?

6.5 The following are entries appearing in a general journal. Describe the event or condition that probably caused the accountant to make each entry. (Note: In journal entries, Dr = debit and Cr = credit.)

(a)	Dr Bad debt expense	$300	
	Cr Accounts receivable		$300
(b)	Dr Cash	$5000	
	Cr Invested capital (owners' equity)		$5000

(c)	Dr Cash	$7000	
	Cr Marketable securities		$7000
(d)	Dr Customer down payments	$1000	
	Dr Cash	$2000	
	Dr Accounts receivable	$4000	
	Cr Sales		$7000
(e)	Dr Interest expense	$60	
	Dr Installment contract payable	$1400	
	Cr Cash		$1460
(f)	Dr Accounts payable	$250	
	Cr Office supplies expense		$250
(g)	Dr Retained earnings	$1100	
	Cr cash		$1100
(h)	Dr Purchases	$4000	
	Cr Accounts payable		$3600
	Cr Cash		$400

6.6 Record each of the following transactions or changed circumstances in general journal format (the format illustrated in the preceding question). Choose an appropriate name for each account you use and indicate for each whether it is an asset, liability, owners' equity, revenue, or expense account.

(a) Receive new production equipment (with an expected useful life of five years) having a value of $47,000. The company had previously provided the equipment supplier with an advance payment (down payment) of 20 percent, or $9400.

(b) Pay a $1000 bonus to a sales manager, withholding income taxes of $150 that will be paid to the Internal Revenue Service next month.

(c) Receive $2800 from a customer in full payment of a disputed invoice for $3000 in connection with a shipment of merchandise to the customer two months ago.

(d) Receive $1100 from an employee in partial repayment of a loan made by the company to the employee last year. $100 of this amount represents interest and the balance is principal.

(e) Receive a $1400 invoice from the utility company for gas, water, and electricity service from the 25th of last month to the 25th of this month.

(f) Ship merchandise valued at $8300 to a customer that had previously made a $1000 advance (down) payment.

6.7 Kline's, an ostrich ranch, has asked you to record in general journal format (see problem 6.5 for illustration of the appropriate format) the following transactions. Choose an appropriate name for each account you use and indicate for each whether it is an asset, liability, owners' equity, revenue, or expense account.

(a) Sold 25 fertilized ostrich eggs for $300 each, on account, to J. B. Costas.

(b) Purchased 1000 kg of feed on account from Seeds 'r' Us for a total bill of $2250.

(c) Paid last month's electric and gas bill, a total of $173.

(d) E. H. Brem paid for two adult ostriches purchased last month on account. The selling price was $7000 each.

(e) Sold a female adult ostrich to The Chicken Emporium for $7000. Since this is the first purchase for this customer, the sale was cash, with a 1 percent ($70) discount on the selling price.

(f) Sold three ostrich chicks for $1250 each to N. A. Lutz on account.

(g) E. K. Perry, a customer, paid $1000 on account.

(h) Paid the bank a monthly installment on an outstanding loan. The payment was $750 principal, and $50 interest.

(i) Processed payroll of $3800, as follows: $3000 paid in cash to employees, federal withholding taxes $500, and state withholding taxes $300, both taxes to be paid in a subsequent period.

(j) Purchased a feather cleaning machine from R. E. Hutz, equipment supplier, for $6000 on account.

(k) Sold 300 kg of ostrich meat to The African Queen restaurant for $19 per kg on account.

(l) Sold 6 kg of feathers to Hats & Costumes & Stuff for $215 per kg, on account.

(m) Received payment of $2400 from Le Petit Gourmet for purchases made last month.

(n) Purchased 1000 m of fencing wire at $0.25 per m at the local hardware store. Paid cash.

6.8 The Kallberg Company, a small electrical power supply manufacturer, uses a specialized sales journal with the following accounts:

> Debit: Accounts receivable
> Commissions expense
> Cash
> Other
>
> Credit: Sales, product P
> Sales, product S
> Sales commissions payable
> Sales tax payable
> Freight billed

Construct such a specialized journal and record the following transactions. When you have completed recording the transactions, check to be certain that the sum of the debit entries equals the sum of the credit entries.

(a) Ship to Ruthen Distributors 100 units of product P, invoiced at $45 per unit plus $75 in freight. No sales tax is charged on this sale, but a 10 percent commission is due to one of Kallberg's salespersons.

(b)   Ship to Yoshihara Electric 200 units of product S, invoiced at $60 per unit. The customer is also charged 5 percent state sales tax and $120 for freight. The sale is not commissionable.

(c)   Ship to Sprague Corporation 50 units of product P, invoiced at $50 per unit. Kallberg agrees to pay the freight on this shipment. A 5 percent commission is due to a Kallberg salesperson. A 5 percent sales tax is included in the invoice.

(d)   A representative of Lindblad Electrical Repair Co. purchases for cash and picks up two units of product P at $60 per unit plus 5 percent state sales tax. This sale is not commissionable.

(e)   Ship to Seltzer Instrument Company 100 units of product S, invoiced at $61 per unit plus $50 for freight. The sale is not taxable. A 5 percent commission is due to a Kallberg salesperson.

(f)   Ship 200 units of product P to Chan Distributors. To qualify for a special price of $43 per unit, Chan paid Kallberg a $1500 downpayment two months ago when the order was placed. Freight of $80 is also billed, but no state sales tax. A 5 percent commission is due to a Kallberg salesperson.

Identify the two subsidiary ledgers that would probably be used in connection with these transactions.

─────7
FURTHER REFINEMENTS IN VALUATION

The accounting concepts of accrual and conservatism press the accountant to consider further refinements in valuations of assets and liabilities, and thus expenses and revenues. These refinements, or adjustments, are typically recorded at the end of the accounting period. Frequently expenses and incomes need to be transferred from one accounting period to another in order to achieve a better match and to guard against overstating earnings or assets. These shifts trigger, of course, offsetting shifts in assets and liabilities to preserve the accounting equality (debits equal credits). The key concern is timing: when shall revenues and expenses be realized?

Remember that a firm's profitability on an interim basis (month, quarter, or year) can only be estimated. Total profitability can be determined with absolute certainty only after the affairs of the firm have been wound up, all assets converted to cash, and all liabilities paid. At that point, all remaining cash is the property of the shareholders and only then can they know the total return received from their investments. Of course, for most companies this day of reckoning—when the enterprise owns nothing but cash and has no obligations other than to stockholders—never arrives. Unless a company gets into financial trouble and is liquidated in bankruptcy proceedings, it continues to function—earning revenues, incurring expenses, owning assets, and owing liabilities. (The company may be sold as a going concern or merged, but these events do not cause the ultimate cash reckoning.)

Thus, to respond to the informational needs of stockholders, creditors, and (most importantly) managers, profitability must be estimated on an interim basis. Accordingly, accountants struggle at the end of each accounting period to adjust the general ledger for the proper timing of revenues, expenses, and changes in asset and liability values.

This chapter focuses on the most common adjustments, typically referred to as

end-of-period adjustments or simply **adjusting entries.** Note that transactions do not trigger these adjusting entries. Adjusting entries are initiated by the accountant and are typically recorded in the general journal.

PREPAIDS AND ACCRUALS

Recall that in accrual accounting cash inflows and outflows do not always coincide with the flow of revenues and expenses, respectively. (Review again Figure 4-3 on page 88.) When this timing difference spans accounting periods—when the cash transaction occurs in one period and the revenue/expense recognition in another—an asset or liability is created and must be recognized at the intervening period-end. These assets and liabilities then have to be adjusted or closed out in the appropriate future period.

The names of the balance sheet accounts affected by these timing differences are shown in Figure 7-1. There are four categories as follows.

Liabilities and Revenue

First, consider revenue. Most business in industrialized countries is conducted on a credit, rather than a cash, basis; we expect customers to pay for goods or services sometime following their delivery. When a sale is made, an asset, Accounts Receivable, is increased (debited) to balance the increase in revenue (credit to Sales). When the customer pays the invoice, the reduction in the asset account, Accounts Receivable, is matched by the increase in another asset account, Cash. Two transactions (delivery of merchandise or services and receipt of cash) trigger two sets of entries. No adjustments are required.

Now suppose the customer makes a partial or full payment in advance of delivery. For example, a customer of the O'Malley Company makes a down payment at the time it orders specialized merchandise to be manufactured by O'Malley. Here the cash flow precedes the revenue recognition, rather than following it. When O'Malley receives this payment, for example $3500, a debit to Cash is appropriate (increasing cash) but a credit to Sales is inappropriate: the realization concept requires that sales be recorded only when the goods or services are delivered.

FIGURE 7-1   Balance Sheet Accounts Affected by Timing Differences

	Revenue	Expense
Cash flow occurs before revenue/expense is to be recognized	Unearned Revenue (liability)	Prepaid Asset (asset)
Cash flow occurs after revenue/expense is recognized	Accrued Receivable (or Accounts Receivable) (asset)	Accrued Liability (or Accounts Payable) (liability)

O'Malley is now obligated to the customer either to deliver the specialized merchandise or to return the $3500. Thus, the appropriate credit entry is to a liability account entitled **Unearned Revenue:** Customer Down Payments (alternative names are **Deferred Income** or Deferred Revenue). The entry at the time the cash is received (in T-account format) is:

Cash	Unearned Revenue: Customer Down Payments
3500	3500

When O'Malley subsequently delivers the merchandise, this liability is eliminated. Suppose the full price of the merchandise is $14,000 and the customer will pay the balance on normal 30-day terms. Then the entry at the time of delivery, again in T-account format, is

Accounts Receivable	Unearned Revenue: Customer Down Payments		Sales
10,500	3500	Balance	14,000

The liability is thereby eliminated.

Another example of deferred income: assume O'Malley contracts to provide customers with preventive and emergency service in return for an annual fee. O'Malley must recognize revenue from the service contract month-by-month throughout the contract period, not all at once. Typically customers pay the annual service fee in advance, thus giving rise to another unearned revenue (liability) in O'Malley's general ledger. O'Malley's accountants must be careful to make the adjusting entry each month that will recognize both the service revenue earned that month and the corresponding decline in the liability.

Another example: suppose O'Malley subleases part of its space for $800 per month; the tenant makes quarterly payments in advance. Assume O'Malley receives a check for $2400 (three months, April through June, at $800 per month) on March 20, 1994. The debit is again to Cash, but O'Malley has not earned $2400 of rental income in March; the rental will actually be earned pro rata over the next three months. In the meantime, O'Malley has an obligation to the tenant to provide the space. Therefore, the appropriate entry at the time the cash is received is

Cash	Unearned Revenue: Rental Income
2400	2400

Now step forward to the end of April. What end-of-period adjustment is necessary to state correctly the company's revenues and expenses for the month of April? In April, O'Malley earns $800 rental income from the sublease even though no transaction occurred during the month. The following adjusting entry (shown in general journal format) must be made both to recognize the revenue and to reflect the reduction in the obligation to the tenant ($2400 less $800 benefit already received by the tenant):

Dr.	Unearned Revenue: Rental Income	$800	
	Cr. Rental Income		$800

Accrued Assets and Revenues

Alternatively, suppose the terms of the sublease are that the tenant pays at the end of each quarter for the use of the space during that quarter. Once again, O'Malley should recognize that in April it eared $800 of rent, even though payment will not be received for two more months. The appropriate April month-end adjusting entry is

Dr.	Accrued Rent Receivable	$800	
	Cr. Rental Income		$800

This entry recognizes that the tenant is obligated to O'Malley: O'Malley has an asset equal to the rent for the time that the tenant has already occupied the space. As similar adjustments are made at the end of May and June, the Accrued Rent Receivable will grow to $2400. When, at the end of June, the tenant pays $2400 rent for the previous three months, the Accrued Rent Receivable account will be credited and returned to a zero balance.

If a company such as O'Malley owns notes due from individuals or other firms, interest income on these notes will be similarly accounted. If interest payments are received in advance, O'Malley recognizes a liability that is then reduced as the interest is earned over time. If interest is received in arrears (at the end of the period), O'Malley recognizes an asset (accrued interest receivable) that builds over time until discharged by the borrower's payment.

Accrued Liabilities and Expenses

Concerns with timing of revenues are paralleled by concerns with the timing of expenses. If O'Malley's borrowing agreement with the bank provides for quarterly interest payments at the end of the quarter, O'Malley needs an adjusting entry in each month of the quarter to match the interest expense to the period and to recognize the company's liability to pay this interest one or two months hence; that is, O'Malley's accountant recognizes the **accrued liability.** Thus, if in October 1995 O'Malley's total bank borrowing is $40,000 and the interest rate is 9 percent per annum (0.75 of 1 percent per month), interest expense of $300 should be accrued for October by the following end-of-period entry:

Dr.	Interest Expense	$300	
	Cr. Accrued Interest Payable		$300

Prepaid Expense

If O'Malley pays in advance for goods and services to be received in subsequent accounting periods, a **Prepaid Expense** account is created. (Prepaid expenses are also referred to as **deferred expenses.**) This asset is then adjusted as the expense is matched to the appropriate accounting period. For example, O'Malley purchases a one-year property insurance policy, providing comprehensive coverage from July 1, 1995 through June 30, 1996. If the $6000 premium is paid in advance during June 1995, the reduction in cash must be accounted for, although no expense is then incurred. Thus, the asset, cash, is exchanged for another asset, a prepaid. The entry is

Cash		Prepaid Insurance Premium	
Balance	6000	6000	

Beginning in July 1995, O'Malley's accountant will recognize as an expense each month a pro rata portion of the insurance premium; the adjusting entry is

Dr.	Insurance Expense	$500	
	Cr. Prepaid Insurance Premiums		$500

With the final adjusting entry in June 1996, the prepaid asset created by the June 1995 payment will be reduced to zero.

REMINDER: CONCEPT OF MATERIALITY

Bear in mind the concept of materiality when considering adjusting entries. If the adjustment would make no material difference to expenses (or revenues) or to assets (or liabilities), then the adjustment should be ignored. Situations abound in which an adjusting entry is theoretically appropriate but practically unnecessary. If O'Malley pays $72 for an advertisement in the telephone directory classified section (the Yellow Pages) for the following year, it is theoretically correct to prorate this expenditure through the year, showing $6 per month for advertising expense. But for most companies such adjustments are so immaterial as to be unwarranted; the $72 payment is simply recorded as an expense in the particular accounting period when it is made.

Monthly billings for utility, telephone, and other services offer similar examples. The utility company's billing cycle may not coincide with a calendar month (for example, the cycle may be from the 14th day of one month through the 13th day of the following month); theoretically the bill should be split between the two months. However, if O'Malley's utility bill does not vary greatly from month to month, this refinement is unnecessary. As long as one utility bill is included in each month, utility expenses are adequately matched to the accounting period.

Salaries are the largest expense category for most companies and are typically paid weekly, biweekly, or semimonthly. Nevertheless, adjusting entries—debits to the Salary Expense account, offset by a credit to Salaries Payable—may be required at month-end to reflect earned but unpaid salaries that are quite material.

LIABILITIES CREATED BY TODAY'S OPERATIONS

Accountants need to be alert to obligations that a company generates routinely in today's operations, but that need not be met or discharged until months or years into the future. Noteworthy examples are employee pensions and product warranties. In both cases, the firm undertakes only a contingent obligation to perform: expenditures for warranty repair are required only if the product proves defective, and pension payments are required only when the conditions specified in the pension agreement (e.g., age of employee and length of service) have been met.

One might be inclined to ignore these contingent future liabilities, arguing that companies, after all, obligate themselves in a myriad of ways every day. For example, purchase orders imply a promise to pay; employment agreements with engineers or managers obligate the company to pay future salaries. These two obligations are not valued in an accounting sense, however, until, in the first case, the products or services are received and, in the second case, the engineers or managers actually perform services and thereby earn salaries.

How are pensions and warranties different from employment contracts? Employment agreements obligate a company to pay *future* salaries for (and at the time of) *future* services. In contrast, future warranty repair arises because of the past delivery of products or equipment. Thus, the future warranty provided to the customer is a part of the total cost of the products or equipment delivered. This warranty cost, then, should be matched to the period when the sale is made, since that is the period when all of the revenue is recognized, not to the period when the customer brings the defect to light.

The exact amount of the warranty obligation is, of course, not known in advance. Typically, companies must repair under warranty only a small percentage of the products they sell. Accountants exercise judgment to determine, in a probabilistic sense, the future warranty obligation that arises from today's shipments. If, for example, warranty expenditures have historically amounted to about 1 percent of sales, then in a month when sales total $850,000, the appropriate end-of-period adjusting entry is

Dr.	Warranty Expense	$8500	
	Cr. Allowance for Warranty		$8500
	(or Warranty Reserve)		

When the warranty work is performed sometime in the future, the associated expenditures are debited to the Allowance (or Reserve) for Warranty account (a liability account), and not an expense account; thus, the future period's profit is affected by the necessity to repair products shipped in earlier periods.

Accounting for pension obligations is similar. Although pension obligations are discharged in the future, they arise because of the past employment of the individual to whom the pension payments will be made. The exact dollar amount of the future pension obligation, however, may be even more difficult to predict than warranty obligations. Pension payments are typically made years, rather than months, after they are earned by (become the right of) the employee, and they are a function of the employee's length of service, age at retirement or death, and final salary at retirement or death. Nevertheless, if by working today an employee earns the right to a future pension, then the employer should recognize as an expense of the current period the obligation to pay that future pension.*

Other employee benefits require similar recognition of liabilities for future payments. For example, most companies carefully define vacation and sick-leave policies. A company that provides its employees with two weeks of paid vacation leave per year recognizes that an employee accrues $10/12$ of a day of vacation for each month of work. The wages or salary paid to a vacationing employee in August is not an expense of August, but rather an expense of the months during which the vacation leave was accrued. Proper matching requires that these obligations to pay vacation wages and salaries be recognized month-by-month by debiting Vacation Expense and crediting Vacation Wages and Salaries Payable. Then when an employee whose salary is $600 per week takes a two-week vacation, the vacation salary payment is recorded as follows:

Cash		Vacation Wages and Salaries Payable	
Balance	1200	1200	Balance

Proper accounting for another employee benefit illustrates the difficulty of accurate matching. Many companies make bonus or profit-sharing payments to key employees at year-end. Are these payments appropriately recognized as expenses of the final month of the year, or should they be recognized pro rata throughout the year? There is no right answer; the accountant must exercise judgment. On the one hand, if the accountant is relatively certain that bonuses will be paid at year-end, failure to spread the impact of these bonuses throughout the year results in an overstatement of profit in each of the first 11 months of the year, offset by a drastic understatement of profit in the 12th month. On the other hand, early in the year the accountant may not have a clear view of what bonuses, if any, will be paid at year-end, since bonuses are a function of the company's profits. The accountant faces a dilemma, and the resolution of that dilemma will almost surely not satisfy all audiences of the financial statements. Typically, if the profit-sharing payments or bonuses are highly predictable because of the company's size, stability and past practice in paying bonuses, such year-end payments are accrued throughout the year; by year-end the general ledger contains an amount in the Bonuses Payable liability account approximating the amount of the payments. In other situations the

*Many employers pay insurance companies to provide employees with pensions. By doing so, the employer is paying today to relieve itself of these future obligations by shifting the obligation to the insurance company. Pension expenses are thereby matched to the appropriate accounting periods.

accountant may have no practical alternative but to wait until year end to recognize the bonus expense.

DERIVING COST OF GOODS SOLD BY END-OF-PERIOD ADJUSTMENT

Some companies derive cost of goods sold expense only once per accounting period: by adjusting inventory values at the end of the period. (This approach eliminates the opportunity to maintain detailed, day-to-day inventory values in the accounting records.)

By now you are fully aware of the importance of matching Cost of Goods Sold to Sales in each accounting period so that the gross margin (or gross profit) indicates accurately the margin earned on the revenue of the period. Examples earlier in this book showed that a $4000 credit sale of equipment having a finished-goods inventory value of $2500 is accounted for as follows:

Dr.	Accounts Receivable	$4000	
Dr.	Cost of Goods Sold	2500	
	Cr. Sales		$4000
	Cr. Finished Goods Inventory		2500

Note that this method of determining Cost of Goods Sold, referred to as the **perpetual inventory method,** requires that an associated cost be identified for each sale. This requirement presents no problem in the illustration above: the equipment is of large dollar value and relatively few sales are made. Consider, alternatively, a variety store or supermarket grocery store that sells thousands (or tens of thousands) of items each day. Tracking the cost of each item would be an onerous chore. Moreover, the tracking costs might overshadow the worth of the information derived.*

An alternative method of determining cost of goods sold is to derive this expense only once per accounting period. One can reasonably assume that the cost of items sold in a particular period is equal to the amount purchased into inventory, adjusted for any increase or decrease in that inventory. Stated another way, the total value of merchandise available for sale in the period equals the amount in inventory at the beginning of the period plus the amount purchased during the period; this total is either sold or remains in inventory at period end. Or, equivalently, cost of goods sold equals

> Beginning inventory
> plus: net purchases
> less: ending inventory

---

*The advent of low-cost computers, universal product codes, and laser-based-code-reading devices makes it feasible to maintain perpetual inventory values in accounting records, but to date most such systems have been used to control physical inventory and not to maintain accounting records.

FIGURE 7-2   Tollini Company

Trial Balance at October 31, 1994

	Dr.	Cr.
Cash	$10,000	
Accounts receivable	30,000	
Inventory	19,600	
All other assets	33,400	
All liabilities		50,000
Total owners' equity		40,000
Sales		86,000
Cost of goods sold	—	
Purchases	58,000	
Purchase returns		3,000
All other expenses	28,000	
	$179,000	$179,000
Value of Inventory at October 31		$21,000
(This amount was determined		
by physically counting and		
valuing all items in inventory at		
October 31.)		
Cost of Goods Sold, October 1994:		
Beginning inventory	$19,600 (see trial balance above)	
plus: Purchases	58,000 (see trial balance above)	
less: Purchase returns	(3,000) (see trial balance above)	
less: Ending inventory	(21,000) (see note above)	
Cost of goods sold	$53,600	
End-of-Period Adjusting Entry:		
Dr. Inventory	$21,000	
Dr. Purchase Returns	3,000	
Dr. Cost of Goods Sold	53,600	
Cr. Inventory		$19,600
Cr. Purchases		58,000
	$77,600	$77,600

One cannot be certain that all items not in inventory at period end were, in fact, sold; some might have been lost, stolen, misplaced, or discarded for some reason. Such inventory shrinkages are typically small compared to the amount actually sold, but the end-of-period adjustment method of determining cost of goods sold does not allow such shrinkages to be isolated and valued.

The advantage of determining cost of goods sold this way is that it requires less accounting; cost of goods sold is determined only once each accounting period, rather than at the time of each sale. There are three disadvantages. First, the ability to determine the margin on individual sales is lost; only the aggregate margin for all sales during the period can be determined. Second, as just noted, inventory shrinkages cannot be isolated. Third, the method requires that the inventory be physically counted and valued at the end of each accounting period, a tedious and

FIGURE 7-3 Tollini Company: General Ledger with Adjusting Entry Recorded

Cash	Receivable	Inventory		All Other Assets
10,000	30,000	19,800	**19,800**	33,400
		21,000		

	All Liabilities	Owners' Equity	
	50,000		40,000

Sales	Cost of Goods Sold
86,000	**53,600**

Purchases		Purchase Returns		All Other Expenses
58,000	**58,000**	**3000**	3000	28,000

time-consuming job.* Note that the ending inventory for one accounting period becomes the beginning inventory for the following period.

This method of determining cost of goods sold is outlined for the Tollini Company in Figure 7-2. Throughout the month of October 1994 the Tollini Company recorded no entries in the Cost of Goods Sold account and debited to the Purchases account (rather than the Inventory account) all merchandise acquired. Think of the Purchases account as a temporary expense account—temporary in the sense that, after the end-of-period adjustment, it will have a zero balance. Note, too, that during the month Tollini returned to its suppliers items valued at $3000; this amount is in the Purchase Returns account. Net purchases for the month, therefore, were $55,000.

No entries to the Inventory account were made during October; merchandise acquired was debited to Purchases and no accounting has yet been made for merchandise sold. Thus, the amount in the Inventory account on the trial balance is the inventory value at the end of the last accounting period—that is, the value at the close of business on September 30, 1994. This is obviously also the inventory value at the start of business on October 1.

The accounting records do not reveal the inventory value at October 31. Rather, the Tollini personnel must physically count and value the inventory at that date. Assume this value is $21,000; then the value of merchandise sold must have been $19,600 + 58,000 − 3000 − 21,000 = $53,600.

Figure 7-2 shows both this cost-of-goods sold derivation and the required end-of-period adjusting entry. Note that this end-of-period adjustment reduces to zero both

*Even if the perpetual inventory method is used, physical inventories must be taken from time to time to determine the amount of inventory shrinkage due to breakage, pilferage, and similar causes. However, items may be counted on a rotating basis (referred to as cycle counting), and they need not all be counted at the end of each accounting period. Estimates of inventory shrinkage are typically adequate for interim financial statements.

the Purchases and Purchase Returns accounts (the temporary expense accounts) and revalues the Inventory account to the appropriate October 31 balance.

Since Tollini's inventory grew during October, had the accountant not made the end-of-period entry but rather simply treated net purchases as equal to cost of goods sold, the inventory values on Tollini's October 31 balance sheet would have been understated, with a corresponding understatement of profit.

Figure 7-3 illustrates the T-account entries to adjust the preliminary trial balance.

SUMMARY

This chapter reviews end-of-period entries required to record revenues and expenses in a timely manner and to adjust accordingly the asset and liability values. These entries are not triggered by transactions but are initiated by accountants as they apply the accrual concept. They are essential if we are to be faithful to the concept of conservatism: anticipating expenses and not accelerating revenues.

The precise matching of revenues and expenses is unattainable; judgment must be exercised. However, two other accounting concepts mitigate distortions that may arise from differences in judgment. First, the concept of materiality tells us to be concerned only with timing adjustments that have a material effect on profit or on the balance sheet. Second, the consistency concept, dictating that recurring timing problems be resolved consistently across accounting periods, assures that financial statements, even if not precisely accurate, are comparable from period to period.

To satisfactorily state revenues, expenses, assets and liabilities, various general ledger accounts must be adjusted to reflect changed conditions or simply the passage of time. These end-of-period adjustments are categorized as

(1) Adjusting unearned revenue (liability) accounts and prepaid asset accounts.
(2) Recognizing liabilities created by today's operations. Examples: allowances for warranty expenses and pensions and other employee benefits.

When perpetual inventory records are not maintained within the accounting system, cost of goods sold is determined by deduction and recorded as an end-of-period entry.

Chapter 8 focuses on end-of-period adjustments to a particular asset category, fixed assets, and still other end-of-period adjustments are illustrated in Chapter 9.

NEW TERMS

Accrued liability. An obligation that arises when an expense is recognized in one period and the cash outflow occurs in a subsequent period. Examples are accrued tax, interest, and rental liabilities.

Adjusting entries. An alternate name for end-of-period adjustments.

Deferred expense. An alternate name for prepaid expense.

Deferred income (or deferred revenue). A liability that arises when cash is received in an accounting period preceding the period when the corresponding income (revenue) is to be recognized.

End-of-period adjustments. Entries occurring at the end of the accounting period and initiated by the accountant (rather than being triggered by transactions); these entries are necessary to match revenues and expenses and, accordingly, to adjust asset and liability values.

Perpetual inventory method. A method of accounting for each inventory increase (receipt) or decrease (shipment) as it occurs. Alternatively, inventory values may be adjusted only at period-end as cost of goods sold for the full period are recorded.

Prepaid expense. An asset that arises when cash outflow occurs in an accounting period preceding the period when the corresponding expense is to be recognized.

Unearned revenue (or income). An alternative name for deferred income (or deferred revenue).

Warranty reserve. A liability account that arises when warranty expenses are matched to revenue at the time of shipment, although performance of warranty repair will occur in future periods. Expenditures for warranty reduce this liability and do not appear as expenses of those future periods.

DISCUSSION QUESTIONS

7.1   Why are end-of-period entries required?

7.2   Do you think companies' profits would typically be over-stated or under-stated if end-of-period entries were ignored? Why?

7.3   What accounting concept (or concepts) discussed in Chapter 5 require the use of the "Allowance for Warranty"?

7.4   For what types of companies would you choose the end-of-period adjustment method for determining cost of goods sold rather than the perpetual inventory method?

7.5   Many appliance and computer manufacturers offer extended warranties on the products they sell. Describe why and how entries are made to account for fulfillment of these warranty services.

7.6   Why don't companies simply consider every receipt of cash as revenue and every cash disbursement as expense?

7.7   Give three examples that illustrate situations where it is difficult to match revenues with expenses.

7.8   An insurance carrier specializes in 12-month fire insurance policies. All of its clients pay their policies in advance, in cash. How do the payments get recorded when they come in to the insurance company? What adjusting entries have to be made at the end of each month?

7.9   At Clark & Sons, salaries are always paid on the 15th and the last day of the month. If all financial statements are always prepared as of the end of the month, does Clark ever have to record salaries payable or accrued salaries expense? Why?

7.10   If the employees of Clark & Sons are granted vacation leave at the rate of 6 percent of the hours they work, how often would Clark record the increase in vacation liability? Why?

7.11   Do you think there are any manufacturers in the United States that should set up funds for future legal liabilities for the products they sell today? Which companies? Why might this accrual be necessary?

7.12   In some countries, sharing profit with the workers is mandatory, and profit-sharing payments are made after income tax returns are filed with the government. How would you set up a liability account for this expense? How often would you record an increase/decrease in the liability? Why?

7.13   What would be the effect on the net income of a firm of the following mistakes:

   (a)   No adjustment was made for accrued taxes of $700.

   (b)   Income of $1700 was recorded for services to be performed the following month, and was not adjusted.

7.14   A crack in the sidewalk in front of Compton Furniture caused a child to trip and break her hand. Her parents have filed a lawsuit against Compton for negligence, asking $40,000 in damages. Compton's lawyer, who originally stated that Compton would undoubtedly win the suit, now feels that Compton can probably settle out of court for about $2500, but that this settlement will not be reached for several months. As the accountant for Compton, would you make any accounting entries at this time? Why?

7.15   Clark & Sons purchased, by accident, enough pencils for five years. The total cost of the pencils was $57. What adjusting entries, if any, should Clark's accountants make at the end of the accounting period?

7.16   *Multiple choice:* Select those debit and credit entries (shown in general journal format) that you think best record the end-of-period entry described. (*Hint:* Develop your answer using T-accounts and then select the journal entries that correspond.)

   (a)   Singh Restaurant is planning to rent a billboard next to the highway to try to attract tourist business. Singh paid $3575 last month to the leasing company, and charged $3575 to Promotion Expense. The accountant notes that the $3575 rental is for a full year, commencing next month.

In order to correct the records, Singh's accountant must make which of the following entries:

1	Dr:	Loss/Gain account $3575
2	Dr:	Promotion expense $3575
3	Dr:	Accounts payable $3575
4	Dr:	Prepaid promotion expense $3575
5		Cr: Loss/Gain account $3575
6		Cr: Promotion expense $3575
7		Cr: Accrued promotion expense payable $3575
8		Cr: Prepaid promotion expense $3575

(b) Ceczen Textiles, an importer of fine European fabrics, determines cost of goods sold by the end-of-period adjustment method at the end of each month. During the month just ended, purchases totaled $27,000, inventory declined by $4500, and purchase returns to suppliers totaled $1500. Sales totaled $40,500 for the month, and sales returns totaled $3000. The entries required to record cost of goods sold at the end of the period are

1	Dr:	Purchases $27,000
2	Dr:	Cost of goods sold $30,000
3	Dr:	Cost of goods sold $25,500
4	Dr:	Cost of goods sold $12,000
5	Dr:	Sales $40,500
6	Dr:	Sales returns $3000
7	Dr:	Inventory $4500
8	Dr:	Purchase returns $1500
9		Cr: Sales returns $3000
10		Cr: Purchases $27,000
11		Cr: Loss/Gain account $7500
12		Cr: Loss/Gain account $12,000
13		Cr: Purchase returns $1500
14		Cr: Sales $40,500
15		Cr: Inventory $4500
16		Cr: Loss/Gain account $15,000

7.17 *Multiple Choice:* Select those debit and credit entries (shown in general journal format) that you think best record the end-of-period entry described. (*Hint:* Develop your answer using T-accounts and then select the journal entries that correspond.) The transactions described must be accounted for in light of adjusting entries made at the end of earlier accounting periods.

(a) After a very profitable year, Jonsson Corporation last month declared a dividend of $15,000 to be paid this month. If Jonsson closes its books monthly, which of the following entries would be appropriate to account for the payment of the dividends now?

1		No entry required at this time.
2	Dr:	Prepaid expense $15,000
3	Dr:	Dividend expense $15,000
4	Dr:	Retained earnings $15,000
5	Dr:	Dividends payable $15,000
6		Cr: Owners' equity $15,000
7		Cr: Cash $15,000
8		Cr: Prepaid expense $15,000

(b) The Costas Paper Co. pays on March 5 wages that had been accrued as of February 29. Of the total wages accrued, $12,780, net cash payments to the employees total $10,440. The remaining difference is made up of $1800 income tax withheld from salaries, and $540 in trade union dues withheld. Payments for the withheld amounts are made quarterly, with the next one due on April 15.

1	Dr:	Wages expenses $10,980
2	Dr:	Accrued wages payable $12,780
3	Dr:	Wages expense $12,780
4	Dr:	Cash $10,440
5	Dr:	Prepaid wages $12,780
6		Cr: Trade union dues expense $540
7		Cr: Cash $10,440
8		Cr: Cash $10,980
9		Cr: Income tax payable $1800
10		Cr: Trade union dues payable $540

(c) Sanders Co. is a provider of electric motors for industrial businesses. When a motor is sold, Sanders adds to the Allowance for Warranty account to provide for warranty expenditures that may be required in the future. To account for the shipment now of spare parts valued at $11,250 to one of its customers—half of the parts shipped are covered under warranty, and the other half are billed to the customer at $9000— Sanders should make the following entries:

1	Dr:	Inventory $11,250
2	Dr:	Warranty expense $5625
3	Dr:	Cost of parts sold $11,250
4	Dr:	Accounts receivable $9000
5	Dr:	Cost of parts sold $5625
6	Dr:	Accounts receivable $5625
7	Dr:	Allowance for warranty expense $5625
8	Dr:	Loss/Gain account $2250
9		Cr: Loss/Gain account $9000
10		Cr: Sales $11,250
11		Cr: Sales $9000

12	Cr: Loss/Gain account $3375
13	Cr: Allowance for warranty expense $5625
14	Cr: Warranty expense $5625
15	Cr: Inventory $11,250

PROBLEMS

7.1 When its inventory of office supplies was depleted, Stone Corporation purchased additional supplies for $2700, paid in cash, on October 15. At year's end, Stone's accountant is making adjusting entries and finds that office supplies valued at $1600 remain. Show the adjusting entry in journal entry format.

7.2 Of the items Horren, Inc. ships to its customers, on average, one percent are returned for repair during their warranty period. Each item is sold for $55 and the average warranty repair cost is $40 in labor and parts. Show the necessary end-of-period entry in T-account format to account for possible returns during a period when 1000 items were delivered to customers.

7.3 Marones, Inc. is a manufacturer of specialized heavy equipment. When an order for a piece of equipment is placed, Marones requires a nonrefundable 20 percent down payment with the balance of the sale price payable upon delivery.

(a) Al Smith placed in June an order for a $25,000 piece of equipment, with a $5000 down payment. How should this payment be recorded by Marones?

(b) Two months later, Smith receives the new piece of equipment and pays off the $20,000 balance of his order. How should these transactions be recorded by Marones, Inc.?

(c) How is this accounting different from the one that an auto dealer would follow in connection with selling a car with a $4000 down payment and $10,000 to be paid in monthly installments over 60 months?

7.4 Mosson, Inc. is required by agreement with the union to pay group health insurance for its employees in the amount of $281 per month per employee. Payment is required on the fifteenth of the following month for all employees who worked during the previous month. Assuming that 15 employees worked in February, show, in journal-entry format, what adjusting entries should be made at the end of February with respect to group health insurance.

7.5 As illustrated in Chapter 2, it is sometimes desirable to pay expenses in advance if a discount can be earned. Your rent is $100 per month ($1200 per year), and your landlord is willing to give you a discount of $100 if you pay the whole year in advance. If you were to agree to these terms, show the entries your landlord must make, in journal-entry form, to account for your payment.

7.6 The Wang Corporation purchased a one-year insurance policy for $12,000 in cash on January 1, 1996. If coverage under the policy is for the calendar year 1996 and Wang treats each month as an accounting period, show the adjusting entry, in journal-entry format, that should be made in August.

7.7 Scallin's, Inc. has just signed a contract with an advertising agency. The advertising agency is going to run a promotional campaign for Scallin's products over the next four months, from January to April, 1994. The total cost for the campaign will be $100,000, payable at the end of the campaign.

  (a) Show the entries, in journal-entry format, that Scallin's should make in each of these four months to recognize this expense.

  (b) What entry should Scallin's make in April, at the end of the campaign?

7.8 Manderlaw, a property management business, leases a building to the Huang Company for five years. The rental period begins at the first of this month, and the rental rate is $1200 per month. Manderlaw just received a check from Huang for $7200 covering a deposit (equivalent to three months rent) and advance rent for the first three months. As the accountant for Manderlaw, what accounting entries would you make when you receive the $7200 check?

7.9 Present and explain the end-of-period entries required to make the following adjustments for the monthly accounting period ending June 30.

  (a) Wages have been paid through June 26. Wages of $180 per day were incurred on June 27, 28, and 29. The business is closed on Sunday, June 30.

  (b) Comprehensive insurance for 12 months was purchased on January 1 for a total of $2400.

  (c) $450 in rent for the month of June from a sublease has not yet been received.

7.10 The following transactions occurred at Williams, Inc. during the month of May:

  (a) A sale to J. E. Bands was made for $6000.

  (b) A purchase was made from B. E. Smith for $22,000.

  (c) Freight was paid for the purchase in (b), $300 in cash.

  (d) A sale to A. S. Monden was made for $14,000.

  (e) Merchandise having an original sale price of $2000 was returned to B. E. Smith.

  (f) Received payment from J. E. Bands, $2000 on account.

  (g) Additional expenses of $6000 were incurred during the month.

Determine cost of goods sold for Williams, Inc., and prepare an income statement for the Month of May, assuming that inventory grew during the month from $12,000 to $18,000.

7.11   Show, in journal-entry format, any entries required to record:

   (a)   A $300 anticipated warranty liability in connection with products sold during this period.

   (b)   The signing of a $400,000, three-year employment contract with a scientist.

   Why are these two items treated differently?

7.12   Selected financial data for a commercial gardening service for the accounting years 1995 and 1996 are

	1995	1996
For the year:		
Total revenue	$300,000	$400,000
Gross margin	150,000	200,000
Net Profit	18,000	24,000
On December 31:		
Cash	20,000	20,000
Accounts receivable	30,000	40,000
Total assets	150,000	160,000
Accounts payable	10,000	10,000

These financial results were determined using accrual accounting. If the gardening service had used cash rather than accrual accounting, do you think its profits in 1996 would have been $24,000, more than $24,000 or less than $24,000? Why?

7.13   The Electronics Outlet, a television and electronics appliance store, starts the month with $137,000 in inventory. The following transactions take place during the month:

   (a)   Receives $21,230 worth of stereo equipment on account.

   (b)   Returns a $300 television to a supplier because it did not work.

   (c)   Purchases $130 in promotional materials for the store.

   (d)   Acquires (and receives) three used television sets for $90 per unit or a total of $270.

   (e)   Discovers that one of the three televisions purchased in (d) is defective and throws it in the trash.

   (f)   Merchandise sales during the month total $33,000.

   (g)   Determines that the month-end inventory at the store has a value of $132,000.

   What is the cost of goods sold for the month for The Electronics Outlet?

7.14 Determine the cost of goods sold for April by the end-of-period adjustment method using the following information. Record in T-account format; if you place existing balances in your T-accounts, circle them so that they will not be confused with entries required for this recognition.

Opening inventory balances, at April 1	$18,250
Purchases, during April	13,750
Purchase returns, during April	500
Closing inventory, at April 30	19,250

7.15 Refer again to problem 7.14 and assume that, after you made the required entries, you discovered additional inventory valued at $900 that you failed to include in your April 30 valuation. Make an appropriate correcting entry.

7.16 Determine and record in T-account format the appropriate entries to recognize cost of goods sold for January, using the end-of-period adjustment method. The general ledger at January 31 reveals the following balances:

Accounts payable	$54,000 Cr
Accounts receivable	93,000 Dr
Cash discounts allowed	300 Dr
Cost of goods sold	0
Inventory	88,800 Dr
Purchases	66,000 Dr
Purchase returns	1,500 Cr
Sales	63,000 Cr
Sales returns	3,000 Dr

Note: This is not a complete trial balance. Inventory increased during the month by $19,500.

7.17 The Rojas Grocery preliminary trial balance (before adjusting entries) at the end of March 1995 is shown below. Rojas closes its books monthly; thus, the balances in the income and expense accounts on the trial balance are applicable to March only.

	Preliminary Trial Balance (Before Adjustments) March 31, 1995	
Account	Dr.	Cr.
Cash	$11,000	
Merchandise inventory, March 1	12,000	
Prepaid insurance expense	1,250	
Prepaid rent expense	0	
Supplies inventory	1,320	
Store fixtures	19,800	
Accounts payable		$8,510

Bank loan payable		3,960
Wages payable		0
Payroll taxes payable		0
Partnership capital		25,300
Sales		167,200
Cost of goods sold	0	
Purchases	132,000	
Purchase returns		2,640
Wages expense	26,620	
Rent expense	1,650	
Insurance expense	0	
Interest expense	0	
Supplies expense	0	
Payroll tax expense	0	
Miscellaneous expense	1,870	
	$207,610	$207,610

The accountant for Rojas has gathered the following information as she considers possible month-end entries.

(a) The bank loan payable at February 28 was $2000, and the payment to the bank in March of $200 has been debited to the Bank Loan Payable account. In fact, the $200 payment included $20 of interest and $180 of principal repayment.

(b) Wages earned but unpaid at March 31 totaled $2860.

(c) Rojas paid rent to the landlord during March of $1650. Although this payment covered rent for both March and April, the full $1650 was charged as an expense in March.

(d) Supplies inventory was valued at $990 at March 31.

(e) Payroll taxes due on the tenth of April will be 5 percent of all wages earned during March.

(f) Rental for the telephone switch is $430 per month, but it is paid only every three months. The last payment was January 31 for the prior three months, and the next payment will be due April 30.

(g) On January 1, Rojas purchased for $1650 an insurance policy providing coverage for the entire year.

(h) A count and valuation of merchandise inventory at March 31 revealed a total on hand of $11,660.

Make adjusting entries in T-account format and determine cost of goods sold for the month of March. Also, construct an income statement and balance sheet in conventional format.

_____8
FIXED-ASSET ACCOUNTING

Fixed assets are fundamentally different from current assets. By definition, they have a useful life of more than one year. A company's purpose in owning fixed assets is to use them for a number of years and not to earn a profit in their purchase and resale.

The accrual concept requires that fixed assets be **capitalized** when acquired— that is, the expenditure is treated as an increase in an asset, not as an expense. While valuing a fixed asset when it is acquired is relatively straightforward, that initial valuation cannot remain unchanged over time, since a typical fixed asset declines in value over its life. To avoid distorting reporting income either at the acquisition date or when the asset is finally disposed of (probably for a fraction of its original cost), its value must somehow be reduced periodically and in steps throughout its life.

A retail store values purchased inventory at its acquisition cost throughout the weeks or months the inventory is owned, because the store expects to sell the inventory at a price higher than cost. The same store, however, cannot purchase a delivery truck, use it for several years, and expect to sell the truck for more than a fraction of its original cost. Thus, while the store need not record a decline over time in its merchandise inventory value, it does need to account systematically for the decline in the delivery truck's value.

The impact of fixed asset accounting is particularly great in firms that are fixed asset intensive. For example, electric power utilities invest far more in property, plant, and equipment (fixed assets) than in current assets (accounts receivable and inventory). The way they allocate as expenses over the years the decline in value of those fixed assets has a major impact on the utilities' year-to-year reported profits. By contrast, a professional service firm is a labor-intensive enterprise; since the firm owns few fixed assets and the primary expenses are personnel salaries and related expenses, fixed-asset accounting has little influence on profits or asset balances.

ALTERNATIVE VALUATION METHODS

Recall the three valuation methods: the time-adjusted value, the market value, and the cost value. The first two of these methods automatically recognize a decline in the value of fixed assets throughout their years of use. The time-adjusted value method recomputes the remaining stream of ownership benefits at the end of each accounting period. As the asset ages, the remaining benefit period shortens, and thus the time-adjusted value decreases. The market value method similarly redetermines the asset's then-current market value at the end of each accounting period. As the asset ages or wears, its market value typically declines. Under both of these methods, the decline in the value during each accounting period is recorded as an expense of that period. Appealing as these two methods of valuation are in concept, they are, you will recall, extremely difficult to implement.

We are left, then, with the cost valuation method, currently the only method acceptable for financial statement purposes in the United States. We must find some procedure to record the decline in the capitalized value of assets during their years of use. That is, we must allocate over the years of ownership the difference between original cost and the anticipated amount to be realized when the asset is ultimately sold or scrapped. This procedure is **depreciation accounting.**

Depreciation accounting is defined as the rational, equitable, and systematic allocation over the estimated years of use of the difference between an asset's acquisition cost and its estimated salvage value. Bear in mind that depreciation is a process of allocation, not valuation: the fixed asset's value on the firm's balance sheet (assuming depreciation has been properly recorded) bears no necessary relationship to the asset's market value. The presumption is that the owner will not sell the asset until the end of its useful life, and thus interim market values are irrelevant. The asset's estimated market value at the end of its useful life—its disposition value—is relevant to depreciation accounting; that value equals the salvage value used in the depreciation calculation.

IMPACT OF ACCOUNTING RULES AND CONCEPTS

Consider the impact on fixed-asset accounting procedures of the various accounting rules and concepts. If these rules are indeed useful in resolving accounting dilemmas, they should undergrid these procedures.

Accrual

It is the accrual concept, coupled with the requirement to use historical costs, that gives rise to the need for depreciation accounting. The expense associated with fixed-asset ownership must be matched to the periods when the benefits of ownership (use) are derived.

Typically, depreciation is calculated as a function of time, since the asset's estimated period of use is defined in terms of time—for example, eight or 15 years.

The usefulness of certain assets, however, is better defined in terms of units of work rather than time. For example, consider an injection molding tool capable of producing 10,000 parts before it is so corroded or worn that it must be replaced; the time period over which these 10,000 parts will be manufactured is a function of market demand. In this situation, the difference between the tool's acquisition cost and its scrap value after producing 10,000 parts is matched against parts production, rather than time; 1/10,000 of this difference is charged as an expense for each part manufactured.

Consistency

A rational, equitable, and systematic depreciation procedure must be consistent from accounting period to accounting period. However, depreciation methods may vary by class of assets: buildings may be depreciated using a different procedure from tools and fixtures, and transportation equipment may utilize a third procedure.

Conservatism

To lean in the direction of understating both profit and asset values, bear in mind that higher depreciation expenses recorded earlier in the asset's life result in more conservative financial statements. Thus, conservative depreciation expenses result from (1) assuming fewer years of use, (2) estimating lower disposition (salvage or scrap) values, and (3) recognizing more depreciation expense in the earlier years of ownership and less in the later years.

Materiality

Inexpensive assets such as hand tools, desktop staplers, and hand-held calculators provide benefits for more than a single accounting period, just as do high-priced buildings, trucks, computers, and machine tools. But not all long-lived assets need to be treated as fixed assets—that is, not all need to be capitalized and then depreciated. Assets with an acquisition cost below some threshold level (for example, $100 or $1000) are treated as expenses—in the jargon of accounting, they are expensed. This simplification reduces accounting costs, and no material distortion of reported profits or asset valuations results.

Thus, the capitalizing and depreciating procedure is reserved for assets having a material acquisition cost and useful life.

Going-Concern Assumption

Depreciation accounting pays no heed to interim market valuations of fixed assets, since we assume that for the estimated life of the asset the owner will continue both to be a going concern and to use the asset in its intended manner. If either of these assumptions should cease to be valid, the value of the asset must be reassessed, acknowledging the new circumstances.

Suppose an asset being depreciated over five years is rendered obsolete after two years by a technological advance. If the asset can no longer be used or sold, it has zero value to its present owner, and the accounting records should reflect this fact. The asset's remaining undepreciated value should be recorded as an expense of the period when the asset is recognized as obsolete. If the owner decides to dispose of the asset prematurely (that is, before the end of the useful life originally estimated), the owner should reflect that decision; the relevant accounting value now is estimated realizable value, a value that may necessitate that a substantial reduction in the asset's value be recorded, giving rise to a corresponding expense, in the accounting period when the decision is made.

CALCULATING DEPRECIATION EXPENSE

Depreciation accounting requires you to estimate (1) the acquisition cost of the asset—**initial cost,** (2) the years of use—**useful life,** (3) the asset's value at the end of its estimated useful life—**salvage value,** and (4) the rational, equitable, and systematic method of allocating this difference between acquisition cost and salvage value—depreciation method. The fourth factor, the depreciation method, requires the most discussion, but the first three factors also present some challenges.

Initial Cost

The initial cost includes, in addition to simply the asset's cash purchase price, any other outlays required to get the asset into a position and condition where it is productive. Thus, freight charges and installation costs are normally included in the initial cost of the asset, so that they are depreciated over the asset's life and not expensed in the accounting period when the asset is acquired.

Major overhauls or rebuilding of existing fixed assets should be treated as fixed asset expenditures if the result of the refurbishing is to substantially increase the asset's useful life. Thus, a major overhaul of a machine tool or the replacement of the factory roof is capitalized and depreciated.

Useful Life

What determines the period over which the asset will be depreciated, that is, its life? We are concerned only with its useful life, the period that it will be productive for its present owner. This useful life may be a good deal shorter than the asset's total life—that is, less than the total time from its initial creation until its final owner discards or demolishes it. A truck may have several owners during its total life, but the depreciable life for a particular owner is the time that owner uses the truck.

The life of an asset is typically dictated by wear, obsolescence, or change in requirements. A truck may truly wear out. The motor, transmission, and other mechanical parts may deteriorate to the point that the truck is no longer reliable or not worth repairing; if so, the owner ceases to use it and its useful life to the present owner terminates. A second owner—perhaps one more tolerant of breakdowns—may now purchase the truck, thus commencing a useful life for this second owner.

Unlike a truck, a computer seldom wears out, but is likely to obsolesce. It may be operable for 20 or 30 years, but its useful life may be only five years, after which technological improvements will give the owner strong motivation for replacing it.

The life of a specialized production tool may be determined by neither wear nor technological change, but by changes in demand for the end product or service produced. For example, the tooling required to make a child's toy that is heavily promoted by television advertising during one holiday season may have a relatively short useful life simply because the demand for the toy will evaporate when the promotional program ends. The tooling is neither worn nor technologically obsolete, but it is no longer required and therefore is no longer useful.

Income tax regulations provide guideline depreciable lives for certain classes of assets. Beware of routinely accepting these guidelines lives. While they govern income tax calculations, frequently shorter or longer lives are more appropriate for profit reporting, that is for the equitable distribution of the difference between original cost and salvage value. The income tax laws should not determine accounting policy. More on this subject later.

Salvage Value

If useful life is difficult to estimate, salvage value—the asset's probable market value at the end of that useful life—is that much more difficult. Fortunately, for most (but not all) assets, estimated salvage value is a small percentage of initial cost (for example, 10 percent or less) and estimation errors do not have a material effect on depreciation expense and asset valuation. When in doubt about salvage value, the accountant should remember that the lower the salvage value, the more conservative the depreciation accounting.

Salvage values are influenced by many unpredictable factors. The market value at the end of a commercial building's estimated 40-year useful life will depend not only on the condition of the building itself but the condition of its neighborhood. If the building happens to be in a part of the city that has developed into a high-rent, retail–commercial area, the building may have a market value well in excess of its initial cost. (Remember that the cost value method prohibits using an estimated salvage value greater than the asset's initial cost.) On the other hand, in 40 years the building's undesirable location may drive away prospective buyers.

Rates of inflation (or deflation) also influence salvage values. The next chapter discusses the effect of price level changes on fixed-asset accounting.

In many situations zero salvage value is the only sensible assumption. A specialized asset, useful to its present owner but unlikely to be useful to others, should carry a zero salvage value. **Leasehold improvements**—that is, lighting, electrical equipment, and other improvements installed in rented facilities—normally are fully depreciated (i.e., zero salvage value) over the term of the lease, as the leasee will derive no continuing benefit from the improvements after moving out of the facility.

Depreciation Method

The depreciation method selected determines how the total depreciation expense is spread among the accounting periods that comprise the asset's useful life. The three fundamental methods are **straight-line, units of production,** and **accelerated.**

The straight-line method is explained by its name: the value of the asset is reduced from initial cost to estimated salvage value in a straight-line manner over the asset's estimated useful life. If the asset has a 10-year life, depreciation expense during each year of life is $1/10$ of the depreciable value (or 1/120th during each month of life).

The unit-of-production method assigns depreciation expense in proportion to actual usage. The asset's life is defined in usage terms—for example, estimated hours of operation of the machine, units produced by the equipment, or miles traveled by the vehicle. The amount of depreciation expense in any accounting period is a function of usage during that period. For example, if a particular tool's life is defined as the production of 450,000 units, depreciation expense on this asset during a year when 75,000 units are produced is 16.7 percent (75,000 divided by 450,000 = 16.7 percent) of the difference between the asset's initial cost and estimated salvage value. The unit-of-production method of depreciation is not widely used.

Accelerated methods assign greater depreciation expenses to the asset's early years, and lower expenses to later years. Consider now the arguments for accelerated depreciation.

Arguments for Accelerated Depreciation. Straight-line depreciation is both simple and apparently equitable. What are the arguments for accelerated depreciation? Recall the objective: allocate rationally and systematically over the asset's life the difference between initial cost and estimated salvage value. To reflect the asset's declining market value is not an objective. Although accelerated depreciation frequently comes closer than straight-line depreciation to approximating market values, this cannot be an argument for its use when that is not the objective.

There are, however, two rational arguments for accelerated depreciation. First, the asset may well be more useful during its early life, before wear and technological obsolescence have taken their toll. Toward the end of its life, the asset may serve only a standby role, with the primary productive load assumed by newer, technologically superior assets. A second argument is that maintenance expenses are likely to increase over the asset's life. The total cost of owning and operating an asset (including both depreciation and maintenance) may be spread more equitably if more depreciation is recognized early in the asset's life and less later when maintenance expenditures are likely to be greater.

Moreover, accelerated depreciation is conservative. If the company is growing and thus continually adding to its stock of fixed assets, accelerated depreciation results in conservatively stated profits throughout the growth phase of the company.

Accelerated depreciation is widely used, and two common conventions are **sum-of-the-years' digits** and **declining balance.**

Sum-of-the-Years' Digits (SOYD). Under this clever (contrived?) convention, depreciation expense each year is a decreasing fraction of the difference between initial cost and salvage value. The numerator of the fraction is the remaining years of life (including the current year) and the denominator is the sum of all the digits in the asset's life. For example, an asset with a seven-year estimated life will be depreciated during its first two years using the following fractions:

$$\text{Year 1:} \quad \frac{7}{7 + 6 + 5 + 4 + 3 + 2 + 1} = \frac{7}{28}$$

$$\text{Year 2:} \quad \frac{6}{28}$$

Declining Balance. While the sum-of-the-years' digits convention reduces the fraction each year, the declining-balance convention holds the fraction constant but reduces the base to which the fraction is applied. The base each year is the initial cost less depreciation accumulated to date—that is, the remaining book value of the asset. The fraction is set by reference to the straight-line method: the double-declining-balance method sets the fraction at twice (double) the straight-line rate.

Thus, an asset with a 10-year estimated life is depreciated $1/10$ per year under the straight-line method and $2/10$ ($1/5$) under the double-declining-balance convention. However, the depreciation expense declines year by year because the one-fifth fraction is applied to the current book value, a declining amount. For example, depreciation expenses for an asset with an initial cost of $8000 and a useful life of 10 years, assuming double-declining-balance depreciations are

Year 1: $1/5$ ($8000) = $1600
Year 2: $1/5$ ($8000 − $1600) = $1/5$ ($6400) = $1280
Year 3: $1/5$ ($8000 − $1600 − $1280) = $1/5$ (5120) = $1024

Two additional refinements to this convention should be noted. First, since the unswerving application of the declining-balance convention precludes an asset being depreciated to zero, we switch from the declining-balance convention to the straight-line method during that year when the straight-line method would result in greater depreciation expense, and the remaining book value is depreciated accordingly over the remaining life.

Second, estimated salvage values are ignored when determining depreciation expense under the declining-balance convention. When the switch is made to the straight-line method, however, the asset is then depreciated to its anticipated salvage value.

Figure 8-1 illustrates the straight-line depreciation method and the two common accelerated depreciation conventions for an asset having an initial cost of $26,000, a 10-year estimated useful life, and an estimated salvage value at the end of its useful life of $2000. Total depreciation over the asset's life is, of course, the same under all three methods—$24,000, the difference between initial cost and estimated salvage

FIGURE 8-1   Illustration of Alternative Depreciation Methods

Initial Cost of Asset:	$26,000 (includes freight and installation)	
Useful Life:	10 years	
Estimated Salvage value:	$2,000	

	Year	Depreciation Calculation	Annual Depreciation Expense	End-of-Year Book Value
Straight-Line	1	1/10(26,000 − 2,000)	$ 2,400	$23,600
Depreciation	2	1/10(26,000 − 2,000)	2,400	21,200
	3	1/10(26,000 − 2,000)	2,400	18,800
	4	1/10(26,000 − 2,000)	2,400	16,400
	5	1/10(26,000 − 2,000)	2,400	14,000
	6	1/10(26,000 − 2,000)	2,400	11,600
	7	1/10(26,000 − 2,000)	2,400	9,200
	8	1/10(26,000 − 2,000)	2,400	6,800
	9	1/10(26,000 − 2,000)	2,400	4,400
	10	1/10(26,000 − 2,000)	2,400	2,000
		TOTAL	$24,000	
Sum-of-Years'	1	10/55(26,000 − 2,000)	$ 4,364	$21,636
Digits	2	9/55(26,000 − 2,000)	3,927	17,709
	3	8/55(26,000 − 2,000)	3,491	14,218
	4	7/55(26,000 − 2,000)	3,054	11,163
	5	6/55(26,000 − 2,000)	2,618	8,545
	6	5/55(26,000 − 2,000)	2,182	6,363
	7	4/55(26,000 − 2,000)	1,745	4,618
	8	3/55(26,000 − 2,000)	1,309	3,308
	9	2/55(26,000 − 2,000)	873	2,435
	10	1/55(26,000 − 2,000)	435	2,000
		TOTAL	$24,000	
Double-Declining	1	2/10(26,000)	$ 5,200	$20,800
Balance	2	2/10(20,800)	4,160	16,640
	3	2/10(16,640)	3,328	13,312
	4	2/10(13,312)	2,662	10,650
	5	2/10(10,650)	2,130	8,520
	6	2/10(8,520)	1,704	6,816
	7	2/10(6,816)	1,363	5,452
	8[a]	1/3(5,452 − 2,000)	1,151	4,301
	9	1/3(5,452 − 2,000)	1,151	3,150
	10	1/3(5,452 − 2,000)	1,151	2,000
		TOTAL	$24,000	

[a] Change to straight-line method and depreciate to estimated salvage value over remaining life.

value. Thus, once again the difference among the alternative accounting methods is solely in the timing of expenses.

CONTRA ACCOUNT: ALLOWANCE FOR DEPRECIATION

So much for calculating depreciation expense for each year of the asset's life. What are the accounting entries to record the expense and the corresponding decline in the asset's book value?

The procedure could parallel the accounting for Prepaid Assets, discussed in Chapter 7. That is, debit Depreciation Expense and credit the Fixed Asset account. If so, however, the general ledger will no longer carry information as to the initial cost of the fixed asset. The Fixed Asset account will show book value: initial cost less all depreciation recorded to date.

To preserve in the general ledger the unadjusted original value of assets (or, indeed, of liabilities), we use a **contra account.** Contra accounts permit values of assets (or liabilities) to be adjusted in a separate, but related, account and without disturbing the existing asset (liability) balance. Contra accounts appear in charts of accounts and general ledgers just after the associated account being adjusted, and they carry balances of the opposite sign: Contra asset accounts carry credit balances, and contra liability accounts carry debit balances.

Depreciation is thus accumulated in the contra account, **Allowance for Depreciation.** How should depreciation for the third year of the asset that is the subject of Figure 8-1 be recorded, assuming double-declining balance depreciation? In journal entry format:

Dr. Depreciation Expense $3328
     Cr.   Allowance for Depreciation $3328

After this entry is made, the general ledger balances with respect to this asset (in T-account format) are

| | Allowance for |
Fixed Asset	Depreciation
26,000	12,688

The Allowance account balance is the sum of the first three years' depreciation expenses and the difference between these accounts balances, $13,312, is the book value of the asset, as shown in Figure 8-1.

When the company's balance sheet is constructed, it may contain both amounts or simply the net of the two accounts. Thus, the balance sheet of the company that owns only the fixed asset illustrated in Figure 8-1 could indicate the value of fixed assets either as

Fixed Assets, net $13,312

or

| Fixed Assets | $26,000 | |
| less: Allowance for Depreciation | 12,688 | $13,312 |

The second construction provides the financial statement reader with more information: what the company paid for the asset and how much has been depreciated.

The contra account Allowance for Depreciation is sometimes incorrectly referred to as **Reserve for Depreciation.** Obviously, the balance in this contra account is not a reserve in the sense of cash available for the purchase of a replacement asset. The purpose of the contra account is simply to adjust (or offset) the corresponding asset valuation.

Note that this entry is not triggered by a transaction. Rather, it is one of the adjusting or end-of-period entries that accountants must initiate to state properly the accounting period profit and period-end asset values.

Many people erroneously refer to depreciation expense as a source of cash; it is not. Cash is paid out when the asset is originally acquired. Depreciation, an expense, does not consume cash as most expenses do, and thus is a so-called **noncash charge** or expense. Profit is a source of cash; that is, to the extent sales exceed expenses, cash is generated by the business, ignoring for the moment changes in the balances of accounts receivable, accounts payable, and other working capital elements. However, cash generated by business operations typically exceeds operating profit by the amount of noncash expenses. Total cash flow from operations, then, may be viewed as operating profit plus noncash expenses. In this sense only can depreciation be considered a source of cash. More on this in Chapter 11.

ADJUSTING OTHER LONG-TERM ASSETS

A company may own other assets, aside from fixed assets, that diminish in value over time. For example, suppose Glen Partners purchases a patent from an inventor for $45,000. Since a patent by U.S. law has a 17-year life, the new owner, Glen Partners, should recognize a decline in the patent's value over its estimated useful life, a period that might be shorter than, but certainly not longer than, its 17-year legal life. Assume that Glen Partners, after assessing the rate of technological change in its industry, determines that the patent's probable useful life is five years, or 60 months. Glen Partners should then **amortize** the value of the patent, month-by-month, again utilizing a contra account. The month-end adjusting entry to recognize patent amortization is

Dr. Amortization expense, patents $750
    Cr. Allowance for amortization, patents $750

ACCOUNTING FOR THE DISPOSITION OF FIXED ASSETS

Seldom does actual ownership of an asset conform exactly to estimates of life and salvage value. What accounting entries need to be made when the original life and salvage value assumptions do not work out precisely?

Sometimes an asset is owned for longer than its estimated life. When the asset has been fully depreciated—that is, when the allowance for depreciation is built up to the point that the asset's book value equals its estimated salvage value (or, if zero salvage value is assumed, until the allowance equals the initial cost)—no additional depreciation expense is recognized. The balances in both the asset and the contra accounts simply remain unaltered so long as the company owns and uses the asset.

Refer again to the example in Figure 8-1. The asset was depreciated over 10 years to a $2000 estimated salvage value. If after 12 years it is finally salvaged for $2000, the accounting entry is

Dr.	Cash	$ 2,000	
Dr.	Allowance for Depreciation	24,000	
	Cr. Fixed Asset		$26,000

These entries will exactly offset the initial cost and accumulated depreciation balances contained in the fixed asset and contra accounts; the income statement (and thus owners' equity) is unaffected by these entries.

Frequently an asset is sold prior the end of its estimated useful life. A change in the company's business may eliminate the need for the asset or technological changes may cause the company to reequip with a more up-to-date asset. Suppose a cattle rancher owns a piece of ranching equipment with useful life and initial and salvage values conforming to the assumptions in Figure 8-1. Now, suppose that the rancher sells this equipment after six years. Sales of productive assets are fundamentally different from sales of the ranch's products. The cattle rancher is in the business of selling cattle, not buying and selling the ranching equipment used by the ranch. Thus, when the ranching equipment is sold, the sale is viewed as an occasional sale, not in the normal course of business, and is not recorded as a sale of cattle would be. Almost inevitably, the sale occurs at a price above or below the asset's current book value; thus, typically the owner must recognize some gain (profit) or loss upon disposing of the asset.

Gain (Loss) on Disposition of Fixed Assets

Assume that the equipment in Figure 8-1 is sold after six years for $8000. The owner incurs a loss on this sale, if straight-line basis depreciation was used, but a gain if either of the accelerated depreciation conventions was used, since the book values after six years are

If depreciated straight line	$11,600
If depreciated sum-of-years' digits	6,363
If depreciated double-declining balance	6,816

Any gain or loss is recorded in an account entitled Gain (or Loss) on Disposition of Fixed Assets. Assuming straight-line depreciation was used the appropriate entry in journal entry format is

Dr. Cash	$ 8,000	
Dr. Allowance for Depreciation	14,400	
Dr. Loss on Disposition of Fixed Asset	3,600	
Cr. Fixed Asset		$26,000
Total	$26,000	$26,000

If the double-declining-balance depreciation convention was used, the entry is

Dr. Cash	$ 8,000	
Dr. Allowance for Depreciation	19,184	
Cr. Gain on Disposition of Fixed Asset		$1,184
Cr. Fixed Asset		$26,000
Total	$27,184	$27,184

Note that the balances (with respect to this one asset) in both the Fixed Asset and Allowance for Depreciation accounts are driven to zero by appropriate credit and debit entries. Also note that neither the Sales nor the Cost of Goods Sold accounts is used. Gain (or loss) on disposition of fixed assets is nonoperating revenue or expense, and accordingly is typically shown below the operating profit line on the company's income statement.

Trade-In

The accounting entry to reflect the sale of an asset for cash is straightforward. Complications arise when the disposition is part of a barter transaction, for example, when one asset is traded in on another—that is, when part of the payment is the transfer of the old asset to the seller of the new asset.

Suppose that a restaurant trades in a piece of equipment having an initial cost of $13,000 and a current book value of $5000 on a new piece of restaurant equipment having a list price of $21,000. After much negotiation, the equipment dealer agrees to accept the restaurant's old equipment plus $14,000 in cash. Apparently the dealer is ascribing a $7000 value to this trade-in, the difference between the list price of the new equipment and the cash balance to be paid by the restaurant. If so, the restaurant has realized a $2000 gain on the disposition of the old asset, as the book value of this asset is only $5000.

But, assume further that, in the absence of any trade-in, the restaurant could have negotiated a discount off the $21,000 list price. If so, was the equipment dealer really ascribing a value of $7000 to the trade-in or was the $7000 difference between list price and cash to be paid the sum of a price discount and the trade-in value? The restaurant's accountant must separate these two effects in order to record this transaction. For example, assume the restaurant believes the dealer would have accepted $19,500 in cash and no trade-in; if so, the dealer actually valued the trade-in at only $5500, and the restaurant realized a correspondingly smaller gain on the trade-in of the old equipment. These assumptions lead to the following entries:

Dr. Fixed Asset (new equipment)	$19,500	
Dr. Allowance for Depreciation		
(old equipment)	8,000	
Cr. Fixed Asset (old equipment)		$13,000
Cr. Gain on Disposition of Fixed Assets		500
Cr. Cash		14,000
Total	$27,500	$27,500

Note that the new equipment is recorded at its equivalent cash purchase price, somewhat less than its list price. The gain on disposition is now substantially lower. The basic accounting concept of conservatism is better served by factoring into the accounting entries the apparent cash discount, since doing so values both assets and profits more conservatively.

Timing in the Recognition of a Loss

When an asset is no longer useful to its owner, the asset's value should be adjusted accordingly. Suppose, for example, that in 1989 the Cody Company purchased computer equipment for $85,000, and has been depreciating this equipment over a 10-year estimated useful life. Five years later, in 1994, Cody upgrades its computer network so that the 1989 computer is no longer used; Cody's management, after determining that only a very nominal amount could be realized by selling this now-obsolete computer, decides to retain it in storage. Without debating the wisdom of this decision, consider what accounting entry, if any, should now be made. Depreciating this computer in the normal fashion is inappropriate as the computer is no longer productive; with respect to this particular asset, the going-concern assumption no longer applies. If the computer has no market value (or scrap value) its remaining book value should be written off—that is, expensed. The conservative approach is to recognize the expense at the time the network is revamped, for it was that event that rendered the 1989 computer valueless to Cody.

INCOME TAX CONSIDERATIONS

Tax laws in the United States contain certain incentives to spur investment in fixed assets. Thus, tax considerations are important in decisions regarding the acquisition, depreciation, and disposition of fixed assets. While you should understand these considerations, you also need to recognize that the tax laws should not dictate a company's accounting policy, as frequently tax law provisions are inconsistent with sound accounting practice. Tax laws are enacted to generate tax revenue consistent with overall government economic policy. They are not meant to dictate how companies should account for fixed assets.

As a result the accounting for fixed assets in reports of company performance directed to shareholders and creditors (financial accounting) may be quite different from fixed-asset accounting in the company's income tax returns (tax accounting). Most companies end up maintaining two sets of books—appropriately, legally, and openly.

Recall the objective of depreciation accounting: to allocate in a rational, systematic, and equitable manner the difference between initial cost and estimated salvage value over the estimated life of the asset. When determining the depreciation expense deduction for income taxes, the objective is quite different: to minimize tax payments and postpone them as long as possible. Every taxpayer—individual or corporate—is expected to use all opportunities to minimize income tax payments. To do otherwise is both foolish and inconsistent with management's obligations to corporate shareholders. Further, the deferral of tax payments is always desirable, as the money can be used during the period of postponement; remember that money has a time value.

Therefore, for tax purposes a company typically seeks to accelerate depreciation to the extent possible, thereby decreasing its taxable income (by increasing expenses) and decreasing its tax liability. Remember that depreciation expense is a noncash expense; therefore, an increase in depreciation expense has no cash cost; instead, it produces a cash savings by reducing income taxes. Thus, we speak of depreciation as a **tax shield**—higher depreciation expenses shield more of the corporations' earnings from taxation.

Understandably, therefore, the income tax laws and regulations are filled with provisions limiting the extent to which depreciation can be accelerated and proscribing the accounting for fixed-asset acquisition and disposition.

Income-Tax Laws

These tax laws and regulations are too complex to discuss in detail. The purpose here is simply to indicate the types of provisions you can expect to encounter.

First, the law requires that assets that meet certain tests be capitalized and depreciated, not expensed—that is, accounted for as fixed assets. The law requires that freight, installation, and similar expenditures also be capitalized. Inevitably, disputes arise: taxing authorities argue for capitalization, the company argues that the expenditure should be deductible immediately.

Second, the law establishes guideline useful lives for various classes of assets. While the company seeks as short a depreciable life as possible in order to maximize and to accelerate in time the depreciation tax shield, tax authorities expect careful justification for use of a life shorter than the guidelines provide.

The specific tax provisions fill many volumes and apply to a broad range of new and used assets in various industries and under alternative circumstances. It is critical that management obtain sound tax advice regarding these issues.

Deferred Income Taxes

When corporations use one depreciation method in financial accounting and another in tax accounting, timing differences in expense recognition are the result. These differences give rise to so-called **deferred income taxes.**

Suppose that the Wong Corporation uses straight-line depreciation for financial reporting purposes and double-declining balance for tax purposes. In 1992, its depreciation expense using straight line is $250,000; its double-declining balance depreciation expense is $360,000; its operating profit before depreciation and income tax expenses is $780,000; and its effective income tax rate is 40 percent.

Under these assumptions, Wong's reported net income (financial accounting) and related income tax expense are

Operating profit before depreciation and taxes	$780,000
less: Depreciation expense	250,000
Taxable income (internal reporting purposes)	530,000
less: Income tax expense (at 40 percent)	212,000
Net Income	$318,000

But, is Wong liable currently for $212,000 of income tax payments? No; using the double-declining-balance depreciation method for tax purposes, its income tax currently payable (tax accounting) is calculated as follows:

Operating profit before depreciation and taxes	$780,000
less: Depreciation (double-declining balance)	360,000
Taxable income (tax reporting purposes)	420,000
Income tax currently payable (at 40 percent)	$168,000

This difference is obviously in Wong's interest: the company has postponed the cash payment of $44,000 ($212,000 less $168,000.) How should this discrepancy—this postponement of taxes—be handled in Wong's accounting records? For financial reporting purposes the proper income tax expense is $212,000; of this amount, $168,000 is currently payable (a current liability) and the balance, $44,000, is a deferred income tax (a long-term liability). In journal entry format:

Dr.	Income tax expense	$212,000	
	Cr. Income tax payable		$168,000
	Cr. Deferred income taxes		44,000

If Wong acquires no new or replacement assets (an unlikely prospect unless the company falls on sustained hard times), eventually the deferred income taxes will become payable when, late in the assets' lives, straight-line depreciation expenses exceed those calculated by the double-declining-balance method. Then, cash payments for income taxes will be greater than the income tax expense reported on Wong's income statement, and the deferred tax liability will be reduced. Remember that the differences here are solely in timing; the full difference between initial cost and estimated salvage value of the fixed assets will ultimately be depreciated by both methods.

Interestingly, if a company grows and periodically adds fixed assets, the amount of its deferred income taxes will typically continue to grow. As a result, many growing companies view deferred income taxes as permanently deferred; although they are accounted for as long-term liabilities, the company does not anticipate having to pay them in the foreseeable future.

Timing differences between financial and tax recognition of expenses (and revenues) can also run the other way, resulting in prepaid rather than deferred income taxes. For example, warranty expenses are typically not allowable deductions for tax purposes until the actual expenditures occur, although for financial reporting purposes the company accrues an allowance for warranty (with a corresponding warranty expense) at the time of delivery.

Investment Tax Credit

The U.S. income-tax laws from time to time provide for **investment tax credits** to spur investments in fixed assets, presumably to stimulate the U.S. economy and to make U.S. industry more competitive in world markets. These provisions permit a firm that acquires certain productive fixed assets to deduct from its tax liability a percentage of the initial cost. For example, an industrial firm acquiring a new machine tool at an initial cost of $15,000 and entitled to a 10 percent investment tax credit can reduce its income tax liability by $1500 (10 percent of $15,000) in the year the asset is acquired. Note that the $1500 does not simply reduce taxable income as $1500 of depreciation expense would; rather, it is a direct reduction of taxes and is correspondingly more valuable to the firm.

Investment tax credits do not affect future depreciation expenses for the asset. In the example, the industrial firm is able to depreciate the full difference between the $15,000 acquisition cost and the estimated salvage value over the asset's life, in addition to availing itself of the one-time investment tax credit.

Limitations on Deductions and Tax Credits

Tax laws and regulations are replete with provisions, including some that are quite obscure, to limit the deductible expenses and tax credits available to individuals and corporate taxpayers. Careful tax planning is required to be certain that anticipated tax savings are in fact realized.

Keep in mind one more limitation. Tax shields and tax credits are of no value to an individual or corporation who, in the absence of shields or credits, would not be required to pay tax. Thus, accelerated depreciation is no benefit to an unprofitable corporation. A tax deduction or tax credit is only of value if and when the deduction or credit reduces actual cash tax payments.

The U.S. tax law does, however, permit most taxpayers to carry back and carry forward any taxable losses for a limited number of years. For example, if a company incurs a $1 million pretax loss in the current year after several years of large pretax profits, the company can carry back and apply for a refund of some income taxes paid previously. If these pretax profits did not total $1 million, the company could then carry forward the loss and apply it against future years' profits, reducing income tax payments in those future years.

SUMMARY

While the time-adjusted and market value methods account routinely for the decline in value of a fixed asset over its life, the historical cost method requires that some arbitrary but systematic procedure allocate over the asset's life the difference between the initial cost of the asset and its estimated salvage value. Depreciation accounting does not attempt to reflect in the accounting records the market values of assets, but seeks simply to make rational, systematic, and equitable allocations of the costs of owning the fixed assets.

Depreciation accounting requires the estimation (in some instances with potential for substantial error) of (1) initial cost, (2) estimated useful life, (3) estimated salvage value at the end of the useful life, and (4) the depreciation (or allocation) method. Three alternative methods of depreciation are straight line, accelerated, and units of production. The most common conventions for accelerating depreciation are sum-of-the-years' digits and declining balance. Depreciation is accumulated in a contra account so as to preserve information in the accounting records regarding the asset's initial cost.

At the time of disposition, any difference between the amount realized in the sale (or scrapping) of the asset and the asset's book value (initial cost less accumulated depreciation) is recorded as other income and expense, typically in an account entitled Gain (or Loss) on Disposition of Fixed Assets.

Because depreciation expense is a noncash but deductible expense for income tax purposes (that is, a tax shield), taxpayers seek to maximize and accelerate depreciation for tax purposes, while taxing authorities limit the use of this tax shield. As a result, tax laws in the United States are replete with provisions regarding the capitalization, depreciation, and disposition of fixed assets. The use of straight-line depreciation for financial reporting purposes and accelerated depreciation for tax reporting gives rise to deferred income taxes.

NEW TERMS

Accelerated depreciation. Methods of depreciation that result in greater depreciation expenses in the early years of the asset's useful life and lower depreciation expenses in later years. The two common methods of accelerated depreciation are declining balance and sum-of-the-years' digits.

Allowance for depreciation. The contra account to fixed assets reflecting the cumulative depreciation of the assets to date.

Amortization (amortize). The accounting process to reduce systematically the book value of a long-term asset with a finite life (other than fixed assets) to zero or the appropriate terminal value at the end of its predicted life.

Capitalization (capitalize). The accounting process to record an expenditure as an asset (to be subsequently depreciated or amortized) rather than as an expense.

Declining-balance. A method of accelerated depreciation that results in a depreciation expense equal to a specified fraction of the book value (initial cost less accumulated depreciation to date) of the asset, an amount which declines each year.

Deferred income taxes. An income tax liability, not payable currently, typically resulting from differences in accounting procedures for financial reporting and for tax reporting.

Depreciation accounting. The rational, equitable, and systematic allocation over the years an asset is expected to be owned of the difference between the asset's cost of acquisition and its estimated salvage value.

Initial cost. An amount that includes the purchase price of the asset and all ancillary costs required to get the asset into a position and condition where it is productive.

Investment tax credit. A provision of the U.S. tax law permitting the acquirer of certain fixed assets to reduce its income-tax expense by a specified percentage of the initial cost of the assets.

Leasehold improvements. Those fixed assets that arise when a lessee invests in lighting, partitions, or other building improvements within a facility (typically a building) that is leased and not owned. These improvements are owned by the lessee and not the lessor.

Noncash charge (or noncash expense). An expense, such as depreciation or amortization, that does not involve an expenditure of cash.

Reserve for depreciation. An alternative, but somewhat inappropriate, name for Allowance for Depreciation, a contra account to fixed assets.

Salvage value. The value of an asset at the end of its useful life; the amount received by the present owner from the sale to a subsequent owner or from scrapping the asset.

Straight-line depreciation. A method of depreciation that results in equal depreciation expense in each accounting period of the asset's estimated useful life.

Sum-of-the-years' digits (SOYD). A method of accelerated depreciation resulting in depreciation expense equal to a fraction of the difference between initial cost and estimated salvage value, where the numerator of the fraction is the asset's remaining life and the denominator is the sum of all of the digits representing the years of estimated useful life.

Tax shield. A noncash expense (or charge) that is deductible for income-tax purposes. Such an expense does not consume cash but rather, because it is deductible, reduces cash outlays for income taxes.

Units-of-production depreciation. Methods of depreciation that result in depreciation expense being a function of usage of the asset during the particular accounting period.

Useful life. The period of time during which an asset is useful to and used by its present owner; useful life is often only a portion of the total life of the asset.

DISCUSSION QUESTIONS

8.1 What is the objective of depreciation accounting? Is that objective consistent with the cost value, market value, and time-adjusted value methods discussed in Chapter 2?

8.2 Under what circumstances is the useful life of a depreciable asset shorter than the asset's full life?

8.3 Under what circumstance would you choose the units-of-production method of depreciation instead of a method based on the passage of time?

8.4 Why are the proceeds from the sale of a fixed asset not considered as sales revenue to the selling corporation?

8.5 Why is land not depreciated? Can you think of other fixed assets that might be owned by a corporation that also should not be depreciated?

8.6 Consider whether each of the following accounting concepts, considered separately, argues for the use of straight-line or accelerated depreciation:

(a) matching

(b) going concern

(c) conservatism

(d) consistency

8.7 What is meant by the book value of a fixed asset?

8.8 Would you expect the market value to be above or below the book value for each of the following assets? Explain your answers.

(a) A three-year-old personal computer

(b) A one-year-old machine tool that was supplied by a manufacturer now quoting a two-year wait for delivery of the same machine tool to new customers

(c) A seven-year-old asset owned in a country that has experienced a high rate of inflation for the past decade

(d) A four-year-old truck during a period of rapid inflation

(e) A ten-year-old commercial office building that is fully leased to financially-strong tenants

(f) Leasehold improvements installed two years ago and being depreciated over eight years (the remaining term of the lease at installation)

8.9 How would you estimate the useful life of a patent (that is, the number of years over which you would amortize the patent) acquired by your company from an inventor?

8.10 Why are depreciation and amortization expenses considered to be a different category of expense than, for example, salaries, rent, and utilities expense?

8.11 Explain the nature of the dispute that is likely to arise between a government taxing agency and a taxpayer regarding:

(a) what expenditures to capitalize in connection with the installation and start-up of a new, technologically-sophisticated fixed asset.

(b) the estimated useful life of the fixed asset.

(c) the salvage value of the fixed asset estimated for depreciation purposes.

8.12 Explain briefly how deferred income taxes arise in depreciation accounting.

8.13 Why would a country pass tax legislation providing for an investment tax credit?

8.14 The managements of some companies seek to maximize depreciation expenses while managements of other companies seek to minimize them. Is it possible that they are each acting rationally? Explain.

8.15 Why is a tax credit more valuable to a tax-paying company than a so-called tax shield?

8.16 Under what circumstances does a tax shield provide no current benefit to the owner of an asset?

PROBLEMS

8.1 Calculate the depreciation expense for the second year of the life on an asset having a $12,000 original cost, zero estimated salvage value, and an estimated five-year life, using:

(a) Straight-line depreciation method

(b) Double-declining balance depreciation method

(c) Sum-of-the-years'-digits depreciation method

8.2 In problem 8.1 above, what would be the depreciation expense in the second year using the declining balance method at the 150 percent rate?

8.3 Calculate the depreciation expense for the fourth year of the life of an asset having a $70,000 original cost, 10 percent estimated salvage value, and an estimated eight-year life, assuming:

(a) Straight-line depreciation method

(b) Double-declining balance method

(c) Units-of-production method where the fourth year will account for 17 percent of the asset's lifetime production

8.4 The Leland Company sells for $5000 cash an asset that had an original cost of $13,500, and accumulated depreciation of $9300. Account for this transaction in T-account format.

8.5 The Weiner Corporation sells for $2000 cash an asset that has a current book value of $2800. The asset is six years old and its annual depreciation, determined on a straight-line basis, has been $1100. Account for this transaction in T-account format.

8.6 Palm Enterprise trades in a five-year-old tourist bus on a new model. The old bus had an original cost of $37,000 and its current book value is $16,000. Palm pays $23,000 in addition to the trade-in for a new bus having a list price of $40,000. Account for this transaction in T-account format.

8.7 Refer again to problem 8.6. If Palm's accountant felt that the company could have negotiated a five percent discount on the bus's list price if Palm had not traded-in the old bus, would you account differently for this transaction? Explain.

8.8 A ten-year-old, fully-depreciated asset (assuming zero salvage value) is given away by the corporation to a charity. If the asset originally cost $7000, show the accounting entry, if any is required, that the corporation should make at the time of the gift.

8.9 In what year should a company switch from double-declining balance depreciation to straight-line depreciation for an asset with a ten-year estimated useful life and zero estimated salvage value? Show your work.

8.10 If a company owns an asset having a $1 million initial cost, an eight-year estimated useful life, and zero estimated salvage, how much more cash will the company have at the end of the third year of the life of the asset if it uses sum-of-years'-digits rather than straight-line depreciation, assuming the company is profitable and pays income tax at a 40 percent rate?

8.11 Record in T-account format for Warren Corporation the following transaction: Warren sold a piece of production equipment that it has used for three years to Tam, Inc. Tam has agreed to pay Warren $1600 next month and $1600 at the end of six months. Warren will incur a $150 expenditure in removing the equipment from its plant. The original price of the equipment was $10,000 and it has been depreciated on the sum-of-the-years'-digits method, assuming a five-year useful life and $1000 salvage value.

8.12 Record in T-account format the following transaction: The Lyzenga Corporation receives delivery of a large punch press purchased for $9300, payable in 30 days. The company pays $800 in cash to the trucking company for delivery of the press and $1100 in cash to riggers and electricians for installation of the equipment.

8.13   The Blueridge Corporation uses straight-line depreciation for financial accounting and sum-of-the-years'-digits depreciation for tax accounting. If the corporation acquires machinery having an original cost of $40,000, an eight-year estimated life, and a 10 percent estimated salvage value, what will be the balance in the deferred income tax account attributable to this asset after two years? Assume Blueridge's incremental tax rate is 35 percent.

8.14   The following transactions and events occurred at the Dym Foundry Corporation in July 1995. During this month, Dym moved from its old facility to a new plant that was constructed to the company's specifications on a nearby site. The move also signaled a substantial increase in capacity for Dym. Prepare T-account entries to record the events and transactions.

(a)   The old facility was sold for $198,000. The land on which the old facility was located had been purchased many years before at a cost of $20,000. The building had an original cost of $80,000, and depreciation in the amount of $46,000 had been accumulated against the building. The purchaser of the old facility gave Dym $155,000 in cash and a second mortgage note on the facility in the amount of $43,000.

(b)   Certain equipment used in the old facility but not appropriate for the new facility was sold for $36,000 in cash. This equipment appeared on the company's records at an original cost of $70,000 less accumulated depreciation of $31,000.

(c)   A new furnace was purchased for the newly constructed plant at a cost of $90,000. Dym paid freight expense of $6,000 and installation expense of $15,000. All payments were in cash.

(d)   A forklift truck that had been owned by the company for three years was sent out for a major overhaul. The forklift had an original cost of $8000; it had been depreciated on a straight-line basis for three years, assuming a four-year life and a 20 percent salvage value. The overhaul, which cost $2800 (paid in cash), was expected to extend the life of the forklift for an additional two years.

(e)   Because the configuration of the new plant was different from that of the old facility, the company's material-handling equipment had to be modified and portions had to be replaced. Certain conveying equipment that originally had been purchased for $5000 and had accumulated depreciation of $2300 had been traded in on other new conveying equipment. The vendor of the conveying equipment allowed Dym a trade-in value on the old equipment of $3000 against the $9000 purchase price of the new equipment. Dym's plant engineer estimated that the old equipment could have been sold to a secondhand dealer or another industrial concern for about $2000. Record both the purchase of the new equipment (payment due in 30 days) and disposition of the old equipment.

(f) The installation of the conveying equipment was accomplished by Dym's own work force. A total of 100 hours was accumulated by the work force against this task. These workers earned an hourly wage of $11.50; normal fringe benefits, including payroll taxes and group insurance, totaled another $2.75 per hour. Typically, the time of these same workers was charged to customers at the rate of $22.00 per hour.

(g) The landscape contractor with whom Dym contracted for landscaping the new facility at a fixed price of $10,000 offered to accept only $9200 for the work if Dym agreed to pay at the completion of the work rather than 60 days following completion, as had been specified by the contract. Dym accepted this offer and made the $9200 cash payment.

(h) A large grinder installed at the old facility cold not be used in the new plant, and Dym sold the grinder for $5,000 in cash under the condition that Dym deliver the grinder to the purchaser. The grinder, which the company had purchased many years ago for $6000, was fully depreciated with no allowance for salvage value. Dym paid $350 in cash for the removal of the grinder from the old plant and $600 for transport to the purchaser's plant.

(i) Costs of the new facility were the following: land, $68,000; improvements to the land, including drainage and sewers, as required by the city ordinances, $14,000; building, $317,000; building improvements, including air conditioning, some movable partitions, and electrical bus ducts, $46,500. The entire project (cost totalling $445,500) was financed with a $350,000 first mortgage, and the balance of $95,500 was paid in cash by Dym.

____9
MORE CHOICES IN ACCOUNTING PROCEDURES

By now you are aware that accountants face many choices:

- What changes in conditions should be valued and recorded?
- Should values be determined by the time-adjusted, market, or cost value methods?
- Should the accounting records incorporate specialized journals and subsidiary ledgers?
- Should depreciation be straight line or accelerated?
- Should perpetual inventory records be maintained or cost of goods sold determined by end-of-period adjustment?
- What future obligations should be accrued as liabilities, and what past expenditures should be reflected as future expenses by use of a prepaid asset account?

This chapter outlines several more choices. While the possibilities are by means exhausted in this short discussion, some common procedural choices are included here to illustrate the wide range of issues and dilemmas that the accountant must resolve. Note, however, that they *all* relate to the valuation of assets and liabilities and thus to the *timing* of expense and revenue (and thus profit) recognition.

ACCOUNTING FOR ACCOUNTS RECEIVABLE

Discounts for Prompt Payment

Standard terms of sale or purchase frequently provide that the buyer may deduct a small percentage of the invoice amount if the invoice is paid within a specified number of days; the discount is a reward for paying quickly. For example, the **cash discount** terms "2 percent, 10 days/net, 30 days" mean that the invoice may be discounted by 2 percent if payment is made within 10 days of the invoice date and, alternatively, the full amount of the invoice is due in 30 days.

The timing of the recognition of revenues and expenses is affected by the handling of discounts allowed or earned because of prompt payment. When shall the discount be reflected: at the time of purchase/sale or when payment is finally made or received? The accountant is guided by when he or she *expects* payment to occur.

A buyer who fails to take a cash discount is, in essence, borrowing from the supplier for a period of days in return for giving up the discount. Thus, a buyer who does not promptly pay an invoice subject to "3 percent, 10 days/net, 30 days" terms is paying 3 percent to borrow the invoice amount for an additional 20 days—from the tenth to the thirtieth day. As there are approximately eighteen 20-day periods in a year, paying 3 percent for 20 days of borrowing is equivalent to a 54 percent (18 × 3 percent) annual interest rate. Obviously, passing up such discounts is a very costly financial policy; accordingly, we can expect that a large majority of buyers will raise sufficient funds through other borrowing or sale of equity stock to take advantage of such very attractive cash discount terms.

Since a company that offers its customers a 3 percent discount for paying within 10 days can expect most customers to avail themselves of this attractive discount, it should assume that in normal circumstances it will receive only 97 percent of the invoice amount. Under these conditions, the so-called **net method** of accounting for discounts allowed should be used, as illustrated in Figure 9-1.

However, not all cash discounts are attractive. Suppose the discount terms offered to customers are "1/2%, 10 days/net, 30 days"—equivalent to annual interest cost of about 9 percent. Under these circumstance, few customers will pay within 10

FIGURE 9-1   Net Method of Accounting for Cash Discounts

Sale: $1000   Terms: 3 percent, 10 days/net, 30 days

(1)   Recording the sale:

A/R		Sales	
970			970

(2a)   Recording the receipt of cash, if discount is taken:

A/R		Cash	
	970	970	

(2b)   Recording the receipt of cash, if discount is not taken:

A/R		Cash		Other Income	
	970	1000			30

days and take the 0.5 percent discount and thus the **gross method** of accounting for sales should be utilized: Any discounts taken by a customer are recorded only when the customer's payment is in fact received. The gross method of accounting for cash discount terms in illustrated in Figure 9-2.

Note that the gross method presumes that cash discounts will typically not be taken; discounts taken are expenses of the period when the cash is received or are debited to a contra account to Sales. The net method, on the other hand, never records as a sale that portion of the invoice typically discounted (in this illustration, $30); thus, the net method is conservative in the recognition of revenue. If, finally, the customer does not take advantage of the discount, then in that future period when the payment is received the $30 is recognized as income.

Accounting for cash discounts for prompt payment on *purchases* of goods or services is exactly parallel. If the cash discount available is so attractive that the company will typically pay promptly, then the company should use the net method of recording these purchases or expenses. Otherwise, the gross method is more appropriate. Note that, while the *net* method of recording *sales* is more conservative, the *gross* method of recording *purchases* (*expenses*) is more conservative, since the benefit of the discount is deferred until the accounting period when the payment is finally made.

The cash-discount dilemma is another illustration of the timing problem. Interim financial results are affected by how such dilemmas are resolved. However, the *consistency* accounting rule significantly reduces the problem. Note that the profit for a particular month will be virtually identical for both the gross and net methods so long as no change in methods is undertaken during the period and the aggregate value of transactions doesn't vary between periods. If the net method is used, the

FIGURE 9-2 Gross Method of Accounting for Cash Discounts

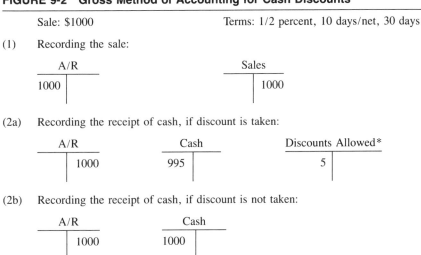

| Sale: $1000 | Terms: 1/2 percent, 10 days/net, 30 days |

(1) Recording the sale:

A/R	Sales
1000	1000

(2a) Recording the receipt of cash, if discount is taken:

A/R	Cash	Discounts Allowed*
1000	995	5

(2b) Recording the receipt of cash, if discount is not taken:

A/R	Cash
1000	1000

*An expense account or a contra account to sales.

amount recorded as sales will be less than under the gross method but will approximate the difference between (1) sales that would have been recorded using the gross method and (2) the discounts allowed (an offset to sales) using that method.

Allowance for Doubtful Accounts

A prevalent end-of-period entry for companies selling predominantly on credit (rather than for cash) adjusts the value of accounts receivable to allow for probable uncollectible accounts, or bad debts. Extending credit to customers almost inevitably exposes a company to bad-debt losses. The extent of those losses depends upon the nature of the customer group, the care with which the company screens its customers for creditworthiness, and the diligence and tenacity with which it pursues slow-paying customers.

The accrual and conservatism concepts suggest that the expense (or loss) on accounts that ultimately prove to be uncollectible should be matched to (included in the accounting period of) the original sale. Of course, a seller who knew in advance that a certain customer wouldn't pay would not extend credit to that customer; the customer would be required to pay cash or would simply be turned away. Thus, we cannot identify in advance exactly *which* accounts will prove uncollectible, and yet, on a probabilistic basis, we know that *some* accounts receivable will never be collected. With this knowledge, we can adjust the Accounts Receivable balance. Failure to do so overstates an asset.

Again the accountant is called upon to exercise judgment in developing some decision rule for this adjustment. The company's history of bad-debt losses is a useful guide, but this historical pattern should be tempered with such considerations as the state of the economy, changes in credit-granting policies of the firm, and changes in the mix of customers.

Suppose the accountant determines that a conservative estimate of bad-debt losses is 0.5 of 1 percent of credit sales for the period. Then, if credit sales for February 1994 are $460,000, the value of those receivables that will ultimately prove uncollectible is estimated to be (0.005 × 460,000) $2300, and the end-of-period adjusting entry is

Dr.	Bad Debt Expense	$2300	
	Cr. Allowance for Doubtful Accounts		$2300

Note again the use of a contra account, **Allowance for Doubtful Accounts** (see Chapter 8) so as to preserve the gross value of all accounts receivable in the accounting records. This adjustment has no effect on the accounts receivable subsidiary ledger, which continues to reconcile with the general ledger account. The allowance for doubtful accounts is a pooled, or overall, adjustment, not an adjustment of amounts owed by particular customers. Note, too, that the effect of this adjustment is to include a bad-debt expense in February 1994 that is a function of that month's credit sales, even though the company won't know which of the credit sales proved uncollectible until months later.

If bad-debt losses are estimated conservatively high, the credit balance in the contra account, Allowance for Doubtful Accounts, could grow to unreasonable levels. Therefore, decision rules regarding bad-debt adjustments typically provide that the total balance in the Allowance account not exceed a certain percentage of the Accounts Receivable balance. The complete decision rule might read as follows:

> The Allowance for Doubtful Accounts shall be increased each month by 0.5 of 1 percent of the credit sales for the month, provided, however, that the increase in the Allowance account shall not result in the total Allowance exceeding 5 percent of outstanding accounts receivable.

Now, how is the balance in the contra account reduced? What triggers debit entries? Recognition that an amount is uncollectible. Suppose that you learn in February that a customer who had purchased $1700 of merchandise late in the previous year (that is, several months previously) has encountered financial difficulties and probably will never pay the $1700 account currently outstanding. The customer's promise to pay is therefore valueless and should be eliminated from assets. The entry to recognize this write-off is

Dr.	Allowance for Doubtful Accounts	$2300	
	Cr. Accounts Receivable		$2300

Note two facts about this entry: (1) the *net* value of the Accounts Receivable in your general ledger (the gross amount less the Allowance for Doubtful Accounts) is unaffected; and (2) no expense account is debited in this entry, since both the debit and credit are to asset accounts (one of them a contra asset account). Thus, the profit in February is not reduced by the current discovery that a particular receivable created in an earlier period is a bad debt.

Occasionally, a customer whose account was previously written off does, in time, pay. Obviously, the payment will be accepted, but what account should be credited to balance the debit to Cash? Typically, the credit is to the Allowance account, but one can reasonably argue that the credit should be to the Bad Debt Expense account.

ACCOUNTING FOR INVENTORY

Inventory accounting also presents some interesting dilemmas for accountants. Just as accounts receivable values are adjusted to allow for probable noncollection in the future, so inventory values may be adjusted for spoilage, shrinkage, obsolescence, and similar phenomena that affect value.

Consider the cost of obsolescence, one of the inevitable costs of carrying inventory. The proper matching of expenses to accounting periods suggests that, when the risk of obsolescence is high, some inventory obsolescence expense should be included in each accounting period, even though you can't verify exactly which items are obsolete until some time in the future. As in the case of Allowance for Doubtful Accounts, a contra account, perhaps entitled Allowance for Obsolete Inventory, is created. This account is built up by employing a decision rule that relates this period's obsolete inventory expense to the level of purchases during this period and to inventory balances. (This decision rule should provide for larger increases in the Allowance when the firm decides to replace one product line with another or when it anticipates that some other event will increase the risk of obsolescence.) When in a future accounting period particular inventory items are determined to be obsolete, the Inventory account and the contra account, Allowance for Obsolete Inventory, are both adjusted with no effect on the firm's profitability during that period.

Conventions to Handle Price Fluctuations

A specific set of conventions widely followed in the valuation of inventory makes alternative assumptions as to the flow of historical costs through the accounting system. The issue is straightforward: identical inventory items were purchased at different times and at different prices (because of price-level changes, or quantities purchased, or other reasons). The cost value method is used but we are faced with more than one cost; when the item is sold, what value should be used to credit Inventory and debit Cost of Goods Sold?

The **first-in, first-out** (or **FIFO**) convention assumes that those historical costs first arriving in inventory (that is, the oldest costs) are the first to flow to cost of goods sold; the corollary assumption is that the last prices (the most recent prices) remain in inventory. The **last-in, first-out** (or **LIFO**) convention assumes just the opposite: the most recent (last-in) prices appear first in cost of goods sold, and the oldest (first-in) prices remain in inventory.

In inflationary periods, the increasing prices will be reflected sooner in cost of good sold if the LIFO convention is used. Thus, the costs of goods sold are better matched to sales by the LIFO convention, since the cost-of-goods-sold value more closely approximates the replacement, or current, cost of the inventory being sold. This improved matching is advantageous in making various production, investment, and marketing decisions, particularly pricing. Also, the LIFO convention states profits more conservatively in times of inflation than does the FIFO convention.

High inflation rates encourage the use of the LIFO convention. As just mentioned, LIFO values cost of goods sold more currently, while FIFO values inventory more currently; management typically relies more on profit-and-loss data than balance-sheet data in making operating decisions. Second, LIFO leads to lower profits, lower income tax expense, and thus higher cash flow in periods of inflation. Bear in mind that the conventions have the opposite effect on profits and taxes in periods of deflation (declining prices).

These conventions do not abandon the use of historical costs: both FIFO and LIFO use only historical costs to value both inventory and cost of goods sold. The difference between them is simply the assumption about the flow of these costs. Note too that the convention refers only to the monetary flow, not to the physical flow of inventory items. Good inventory management practice requires that the older inventory be used up before the newer inventory; thus, for example, when retail store shelves are stocked, the older merchandise is moved to the front and the new merchandise is placed at the back of the shelf. The physical flow of inventory, then, is generally first-in, first-out, but we still have the choice of using either FIFO or LIFO to account for the monetary flows.

Chapter 7 discussed the two basic methods of accounting for cost of good sold and inventory: (1) end-of-period adjustment and (2) perpetual inventory records. FIFO and LIFO conventions can be used with both methods, as illustrated in Figures 9-3 and 9-4. These figures illustrate values of a single inventory item that is experiencing very rapid inflation—its price increases from $1.00 to $1.12 per unit during the course of a single month. Assume that opening inventory was 300 units

FIGURE 9-3 FIFO and LIFO Conventions: Cost of Goods Sold Determined by End-of-Period Adjustment (July)

	Purchases			Sales	
Date	Quantity (Units)	Price/Unit	Purchase Value	Date	Units
7/2	200	$1.00	$ 200	7/3	80
				7/5	120
7/14	300	$1.05	315	7/9	160
				7/13	100
7/21	200	$1.10	220	7/17	100
				7/18	80
7/27	250	$1.12	280	7/22	100
	950		$1015	7/26	80
				7/29	100
					920

Valuation of Ending Inventory*

FIFO			LIFO		
Units	Price/Unit	Value	Units	Price/Unit	Value
250	$1.12	$280	300	$0.95	$285
80	1.10	88	30	1.00	30
330		$365	330		$315

Valuation of Cost of Goods Sold*

	FIFO	LIFO
Opening Inventory	$285	$285
plus: Purchases	1015	1015
less: Ending inventory	368	315
Cost of goods sold	$ 932	$ 985

*Assumes opening inventory was 300 units a $0.95 per unit or $285.

FIGURE 9-4 FIFO and LIFO Conventions: Cost of Goods Sold Determined by Perpetual Inventory (July)

| | | Cost of Good Sold | | | | | |
| | | FIFO | | | LIFO | | |
Date	Units	Source of price	Price/Unit	COGS Value	Source of price	Price/Unit	COGS Value
7/3	80	Opening inventory	$0.95	$ 76	Purchase on 7/2	$1.00	$ 80
7/5	120	Opening inventory	0.95	114	Purchase on 7/2	1.00	120
7/9	160	Opening inventory	0.95	95	Opening inventory	0.95	152
	(100)	Purchase on 7/2	1.00	60			
	(60)						
7/13	100	Purchase on 7/2	1.00	100	Opening inventory	0.95	95
7/17	100	Purchase on 7/2	1.00	40	Purchase on 7/14	1.05	105
	(40)	Purchase on 7/14	1.05	63			
	(60)						
7/18	80	Purchase on 7/14	1.05	84	Purchase on 7/14	1.05	84
7/22	100	Purchase on 7/14	1.05	105	Purchase on 7/21	1.10	110
7/26	80	Purchase on 7/14	1.05	63	Purchase on 7/21	1.10	88
	(60)	Purchase on 7/21	1.10	22			
	(20)						
7/29	100	Purchase on 7/21	1.10	110	Purchase on 7/27	1.12	112
				$932			$946
Ending Inventory	300	Purchase on 7/21	$1.10	$ 88	Opening inventory	$0.95	$ 38
	(80)				(40) Purchase on 7/14	1.05	126
		Purchase on 7/27	1.12	280	(120) Purchase on 7/21	1.10	22
	(250)				(20) Purchase on 7/27	1.12	168
	(330)			$368	(150)		$354
					(330)		

Note: Assumes opening inventory of 300 units at $.95 per unit or $285. See Figure 9-3 for information on purchases for the month.

valued at $0.95 per unit (total value = $285) and that the purchase and sale transactions shown on Figure 9-3 occurred in July.

Note in Figure 9-3 that FIFO values the ending inventory at the most recent prices, since the older prices flowed to cost of goods sold. The opposite occurs in LIFO valuation of ending inventory: the oldest prices (including the full value of opening inventory) are in inventory, as the most recent prices flowed to cost of goods sold. The cost of goods sold under LIFO is indeed higher by $53 ($985 versus $932). The difference in ending inventory values is, of course, exactly the same $53, since opening inventory values and purchases were the same. Again, the only difference is timing, here of cost-of-goods-sold expense.

Figure 9-4 applies the conventions to a perpetual-inventory situation. Each sale is matched with cost of goods sold determined from the most recent or oldest purchase price. Once again, LIFO results in higher cost of goods sold—higher by $14; and, once again, $14 also is the difference in ending inventory values.

The accounting profession's generally accepted accounting principles permit the use of either the FIFO or LIFO convention. You should be aware of the convention used, as specified in the financial statement footnotes, when interpreting financial results, particularly during periods of rapidly changing prices.

The current U.S. income tax laws also permit either the FIFO or LIFO convention but with restrictions. First, a company may not switch freely between the two conventions in an attempt to take advantage of periods of increasing and periods of decreasing prices. Second, a company that uses the LIFO convention for income-tax purposes must use the same convention for reporting profits to shareholders. This requirement that tax and financial accounting be the same is unusual. In virtually all other instances, one is free to select tax accounting methods that will minimize tax obligations consistent with the tax laws and to select alternative accounting methods for public reporting. Some managers forego tax savings (in actuality, a postponement of taxes, rather than an outright savings) associated with the LIFO convention because they are unwilling to report the lower profits that LIFO yields in inflationary times.

ACCOUNTING FOR PRICE LEVEL CHANGES

The terms inflation and deflation refer to increases and decreases in general price levels in an economy. In periods of inflation or deflation, the price of specific assets or liabilities also typically increase or decrease, although often at widely varying rates. The historical cost method of valuation takes no account of these general or specific price changes. When the rate of inflation or deflation in an economy is low—say, 1 or 2 percent per year, the rate in the United States for many decades prior to about 1960—valuation distortions are minor. In recent decades, however, rates of inflation in countries around the world have varied widely, sometimes reaching very high levels. The inflation problem, once thought to be unique to less-developed and unstable economies, has become a periodic or perpetual problem for most countries. As a result, the inadequacies of historical cost valuations have become more apparent.

Distortion arising from price-level changes is potentially most significant for those assets and liabilities that are held for a considerable time—fixed assets, long-term liabilities, and, to a lesser extend, inventory. The distortion affects not only the balance sheet but also the income statement, as described below.

(1) If inflation has been high since an inventory item was purchased some months ago, the balance sheet value of the asset (inventory) is now low in relation to current purchase prices. When the item is sold, its price to the customer reflects the intervening inflation but its cost does not: today's sale price is matched to the historical purchase cost. The company's reported gross margin is higher than the difference between today's sale price and the replacement cost of the inventory, a value far more relevant to managers. The use of historical costs, then, understates the amount of inventory and overstates profits during periods of rapid inflation. (The problem is mitigated but not eliminated by the use of LIFO in preference to FIFO.)

(2) A similar situation pertains to fixed assets. Historical costs understate the asset on the balance sheet; depreciation based upon these historical costs is less than depreciation based upon replacement costs. Arguably, then, in periods of inflation depreciation expenses are understated and accordingly profits are overstated.

(3) Long-term liabilities are affected in the opposite manner. In periods of rapid inflation, the purchasing power of specified repayments on long-term lia-bilities declines each year. In effect, the obligation becomes progressively less painful to the borrower as inflation occurs. The lender is harmed by the effects of inflation, but the borrower benefits. The financial statements of neither borrower nor lender reflect these changes.

Accounting for price-level changes is a very complex subject the detailed discus-sion of which is beyond the scope of this book. The fact that high inflation occurs in some years and in some economies, however, demands some limited discussion of two approaches to price-level accounting: (1) **specific-price adjustments**—that is, adjusting for specific price changes of inventory and fixed assets; and (2) **general-price-level adjustments** that attempt to reflect in the financial statements the effects of inflation on equivalent purchasing power, without concern for changes in prices of individual assets and liabilities.

Over the past two decades, much debate concerning the most effective method of allowing for inflation in accounting valuations has resulted in no consensus as to the best choice between these two approaches. Inflation-adjusted accounting reports have in some instances been provided as supplementary information, but the prima-ry financial reports continue to be those prepared on the basis of historical costs. The cost method is unlikely to be abandoned as the primary basis for day-to-day accounting.

Specific-Price Adjustments (SPA)

This approach requires that specific nonmonetary assets be revalued. Cash and accounts receivable—both monetary assets—are unaffected, and adjustments are typically limited to inventory and fixed assets (property, plant, and equipment). Making specific-price adjustments appears easier than it is.

The time-adjusted value method discussed in Chapter 2 provides just such a specific adjustment. If the stream of net benefits of ownership are expressed in today's dollars and the benefit stream is adjusted for time, the result is an inflation-adjusted value. Recall, however, that this valuation method is unreliable and subject to bias because the expected future ownership benefits are so difficult to estimate.

The market value method also offers some possibilities. For example, an item in inventory that cost one dollar but whose replacement would now cost $1.25 could be adjusted to its current price, $1.25. For certain other assets, particularly fixed assets, price indices may be available to inflate historical costs to a reliable current value.

But how would one value assets, particularly aging equipment, that would not be replaced in kind? If technological improvements have occurred since the original acquisition, the owner would take advantage of the improvements at the time of replacement. Thus, the appropriate specific-price adjustment would not necessarily reflect the current cost of duplicating the exact physical asset now owned. Determining equivalent productive capacity is frequently difficult, time-consuming, unreliable, and subject to bias. For example, consider the task of determining the appropriate specific-price adjustment for a three-year-old mainframe computer that would probably now be replaced by a network of work stations.

Assuming that satisfactory specific-price adjustments for inventory and fixed assets can be determined, these adjustments can be reflected in balance sheet valuations. Then, however, we face the dilemma of how these revaluations—gains or losses from owning the inventory and fixed assets—should be reflected in the income statement. If the application of specific-price adjustment (SPA) accounting results in higher inventory and fixed assets values, as it normally will in periods of inflation, owners' equity also increases. Is this increase a profit? Yes, but a profit that arises from inflation and not from operation. Proponents of SPA accounting feel that a clear separation of these two elements of profit—operating profit and inflationary gains arising from holding assets—is of significant benefit to management, shareholders, prospective investors, and other readers of financial statements. If the problems associated with making the specific price adjustments could be overcome, the SPA approach would improve the matching of revenues and expenses.

Specific-price adjustment accounting has not been enthusiastically embraced by managers who find the task of compiling the data onerous and expensive. Moreover, managers tend to question both the validity of the data, particularly in light of the assumptions that lie behind the estimates, and the usefulness of the data to readers of their financial statements.

Moreover, because auditors have difficulty verifying SPA values, they favor approaches that are more objective and free from potential bias. For this reason, the general price-level adjustment approach is typically preferred by auditors.

General-Price-Level Adjustments (GPLA)

A prime objective of financial accounting is to provide comparable data for successive accounting periods in order that financial trends can be observed and comparisons can be struck. Our emphasis on consistency arises from this objective. In times of rapid changes, however, the monetary unit used to measure assets and liabilities does not remain consistent. In periods of inflation the purchasing power per monetary unit declines. An asset purchased for $1000 five years ago is not comparable to an asset purchased for $1000 today, as more purchasing power was spent to acquire the five-year-old asset than to acquire the new one. Or, viewed in another way, if the five-year-old asset were to be replaced today at the same cost in purchasing power, its cost would be substantially more than $1000. Some argue that financial statements ought to be expressed in terms of equivalent purchasing power.

The general-price-level adjustment (GPLA) approach recomputes financial statements in equivalent monetary units (in the United States, in constant dollars). Adjustments are not restricted solely to inventory and fixed assets, but are made to all assets and liabilities and to revenues and expenses. The adjustments can take the form of restating prior years' financial statements in today's dollar value, or restating the current financial statements in the value of the dollar in some base year.

The index used to make the price adjustments is a general one, such as the Gross National Product price deflator or the Consumer Price Index, rather than an index relevant to the specific asset or liability being adjusted. The purpose of the adjustment is not to reflect changes in cost, market, or replacement values of individual assets and liabilities. Historical costs continue to be the basis for the valuation; they are simply adjusted to reflect changed purchasing power of the monetary unit (dollars, yen, marks, francs, etc.). **General price indices** are readily available and generally reliable. Their application to the revaluation of an asset or liability is straightforward, objective, verifiable, and essentially free from bias. As a result, auditors tend to be more comfortable with this approach to accounting for inflation and deflation than with the various specific price adjustment methods.

Figure 9-5 indicates how a plant site (nondepreciable asset) might be valued in constant purchasing power. Assume the site was acquired four years ago for $2 million. The firm's financial statements continue to carry this asset at its original, historical cost. If inflation progressed as shown on the second line of Figure 9-5, a general price level index for the economy would be approximately as shown in the following line, increasing from a base of 100 in the year of acquisition to 145 today. The plant site can be revalued either in today's purchasing power or in purchasing power at some other date, for example the year of acquisition; the trend information is the same. Remember that the market value or resale value of this plant site is not reflected in these adjustments; the adjustment has been applied to the historical cost without reference to current values. The market value of the plant site might be

**FIGURE 9-5   Illustration of Revaluation of an Asset in Constant
Purchasing Power**

	Current Year	Year 3	Year 2	Year 1	Year 0
Plant site valued at historical cost ($000)	$2000	$2000	$2000	$2000	$2000
Approximate annual inflation	9%	10%	12%	8%	—
General price index	145	133	121	108	100
Revalued plant site in constant purchasing power					
in current dollars	$2000	$1834	$1669	$1490	$1379
in year 0 dollars	$2900	$2660	$2420	$2160	$2000

affected by a host of factors other than simply inflation, principally the pattern of industrial land development in the surrounding area.

In practice, readers of financial statements are often more confused than enlightened by inflation-adjusted statements, whether adjusted by SPA or GPLA. The accounting profession (the FASB, the SEC, and the AICPA), after a flurry of activity in the decade of the 1970s when inflation was high, has more recently shown less interest in the subject of inflation accounting, although research and debate over preferred methods continue.

ACCOUNTING FOR CURRENCY FLUCTUATIONS

Another problem related to, and in effect arising from, price-level change is that of accounting for currency exchange-rate fluctuations. The rate of exchange between two currencies typically changes when the rates of inflation in the two countries are different. If country A is experiencing 5 percent inflation while inflation in country B is 10 percent per year, the currency of country B is likely to lose value (become devalued) in terms of country A's currency.

All multinational firms, and many smaller companies, have operations—or at least own assets and liabilities—in countries other than their home country. If a multi-national company operates a foreign subsidiary, the foreign government insists that the subsidiary's financial statements be maintained in the foreign currency. Yet such companies maintain consolidated financial records in the currency of a single country, typically their home country. Thus, assets, liabilities, incomes, and expenses (and therefore owners' equity) denominated in another currency must be translated into the home-country currency for purposes of consolidated financial reporting of the worldwide operations.

Over the last several decades international currencies have fluctuated widely. Companies based in countries with strong currencies, such as Switzerland, have seen their foreign assets (denominated in the foreign currency) lose substantial value in terms of the Swiss franc, even while the assets have maintained their value in terms of the local currency.

Suppose your company is located in a strong currency country (call this country SCC) and sells machinery to a customer in a weak currency country (WCC), with one-year credit terms. At the time of the sale the exchange rate between SCC and WCC is 1:3—that is, one unit of SCC currency purchases three units of WCC currency. The customer receivable is denominated as 30,000 units of WCC currency, which translates to a value of 10,000 units of SCC currency. Stepping forward a year to the time when the customer pays, suppose that the prevailing exchange rate is then 1:4—that is, the currency of WCC has devalued vis-à-vis that of SCC. One unit of SCC currency now purchases four units of WCC currency. The customer pays the outstanding receivable: 30,000 units of WCC currency. When this payment is converted into SCC currency, your company receives only (30,000/4) = 7500 units of SCC currency. Thus, during the course of the year, this account receivable has declined in value from 10,000 to 7500 in terms of SCC currency, although to the customer the account payable continued to be 30,000 units of WCC currency.

Alternatively, suppose your company located in SCC, had borrowed 150,000 units of WCC currency (when the exchange rate was 1:3), promising to repay at the end of one year. The loan proceeds are converted into SCC currency immediately (50,000 units) and the funds are used productively. A year later, when your company repays and the exchange rate is 1:4, it needs to convert only 37,500 units of SCC currency into WCC currency to repay the loan: 37,500 units × 4 = 150,000 of WCC currency. Your company has fared very well on this transaction, while losing on the receivable transaction described in the previous paragraph.

These two brief examples illustrate one way to hedge foreign-currency positions—that is, minimize the financial impact of currency fluctuations: owe as much in the foreign currency as you own. This hedging strategy is followed by many companies. Highly organized foreign-exchange futures markets permit still other approaches to hedging. Nevertheless, many companies experience exchange-rate gains and losses that must be accounted for.

Accounting for currency fluctuations continues to be a controversial area. Exactly what exchange rates should be used in translating particular assets and liabilities? And when should the gains or losses be recognized in the income statement? In the illustrations above, the loss on the receivable and the gain on the borrowing transaction must be completely accounted for by the end of the year. Should a portion of the gain or loss be accounted for during the year as the exchange rate moves from 1:3 to 1:4—that is, before the gain or loss is finally realized through the receipt or payment of cash? Or should the recognition of gain or loss be postponed until the entire transaction is closed out? When nonmonetary assets and liabilities, such as fixed assets, owned in a foreign country are translated into the home currency for the purposes of consolidated financial reporting, should they be translated at the exchange rate prevailing at the time of their purchase or at the exchange rate today?

EXCEPTIONS TO ACCRUAL AND REALIZATION CONCEPTS

While generally accepted accounting principles require accrual accounting rather than cash-basis accounting, certain businesses, particularly small businesses and professional service firms, do utilize the cash-basis method. Recall that this method recognizes sales or revenue only when cash is received, regardless of when merchandise was delivered or service rendered, and recognizes expenses only when cash is paid out. Firms for which cash-basis accounting is appropriate have few fixed assets and little inventory, and they typically do not have public shareholders to whom they must report. The method is simple and, although it is conservative in recognizing profit, it is permissible for income tax reporting under certain circumstances. While emphasis in this book is on the accrual concept, remember that the cash-basis method is appropriately used by certain types of enterprises.

Still other businesses find the realization concept not applicable to their circumstances. Recall that the realization concept requires that revenue be recognized on the date when the particular goods or services are delivered or furnished. Some businesses, such as heavy construction, encounter very long in-process time. A large concrete dam is only delivered once: when complete, although the construction project may proceed over several years. The primary contractor on such a job typically employs a **percentage-of-completion method** of accounting. Rather than recognizing revenue only at the end of the project—and then recognizing an enormous amount of revenue—the contractor recognizes a portion of the revenue in each of the accounting periods throughout the project. The great challenge here is to match expenses to revenue as it is being recognized, and do so accurately and without bias.

Some businesses operate under *cost-plus contracts;* that is, the amount charged to the customer is a function of the costs incurred, typically cost plus a fixed fee or cost plus a percentage of cost. Consulting firms, auditing firms, law firms, research centers, and defense contractors frequently have cost-plus contracts with their customers. In these circumstances, revenue for interim accounting periods while the contract is in process is relatively easy to determine. The recognition of revenue, therefore, is typically not delayed until the end of the contract, but is recognized period-by-period, as the costs are incurred.

SUMMARY

As further evidence that accounting is an imprecise science requiring judgment, this chapter illustrates several issues requiring choices among acceptable accounting procedures. All such choices—only a small sample is discussed here—relate to timing of expense and revenue, and thus profit.

Cash discounts for prompt payment of invoices—whether applicable to sales to customers or purchases from vendors—can be accounted for by the net or gross method. The choice is driven largely by whether the cash discounts are typically taken; if they are, the net method is preferable. The net method of accounting for sales is more conservative than the gross method, while just the opposite is true of cash discounts for purchases.

A provision for bad-debt losses on credit sales is accrued so as to match the bad-debt expense (on a probabilistic basis) to the time period when the credit sale occurs. The account Allowance for Doubtful Accounts is contra to the Accounts Receivable account. When in a subsequent period an individual account is found to be uncollectible, the reduction in Accounts Receivable is offset with a debit entry to the contra account rather than to an expense account.

Similarly, inventory contra accounts are often used to accrue provisions for obsolescence, spoilage, and other hazards associated with holding inventory.

Accounting for inventory and cost of goods sold in the typical situation where prices for physically identical items vary over time requires the choice between FIFO (first-in, first-out) and LIFO (last-in, first-out) conventions, procedures that incorporate opposite assumptions about the flow of monetary values from inventory to cost of goods sold. In inflationary periods, FIFO leads to higher reported profits and higher values for inventory, while LIFO, the more conservative convention, provides more useful data for operating decisions and also minimizes income tax expenses. LIFO is the convention preferred by most managers.

As the world has experienced higher inflation rates in recent decades, the dilemma of accounting for these price-level changes has taken on added importance. Matching expenses with revenues is difficult when inventory and fixed assets are purchased in one period and used in a subsequent period when price levels are sharply lower or, more typically, higher. Comparability among financial statements from different years is weakened when the monetary unit is unadjusted for changed price levels. While consensus has not developed on the best method for effecting these adjustments, the two primary methods are specific-price adjustments (SPA) and general-price-level adjustments (GPLA). The first seeks to reflect specific price changes in assets such as inventory and fixed assets and to account separately for profits arising from operations and for inflationary (and deflationary) gains (and losses). The second seeks to reflect in the financial statements the changed purchasing power of the monetary unit by adjusting historical costs through the use of broad indices such as the Consumer Price Index. Unadjusted historical costs are likely to continue to be the primary form of reporting, with price-level adjusted statements no more than supplementary information.

Varying rates of price-level changes among countries lead to changes in currency exchange rates, in turn presenting problems in valuing assets and liabilities denominated in other than a company's home-country currency. Controversy persists over the preferred method and timing of recognizing gains and losses from these currency fluctuations as a company translates the financial statement of foreign operations into units of home-country currency for the purposes of worldwide financial reporting.

Even such fundamental accounting principles as the accrual and realization concepts are subject to exceptions. Certain companies should use cash-basis rather than accrual-basis accounting, and both the percentage-of-completion and cost-plus-contract methods of accounting for revenue (and associated costs of revenue) are logical and appropriate exceptions to the realization rule for certain types of companies.

NEW TERMS

Allowance for doubtful accounts. A contra account to adjust the value of the asset account, Accounts Receivable, for the probability that receivables from some customers will prove uncollectible.

Cash discounts (or discounts for prompt payment). Small discounts (typically 2 percent or less) allowed by some suppliers to customers who pay invoices within a prescribed number of days of the invoice date.

Cost-plus contract. A contract providing that the price charged is a function of the cost of performing the contact—cost plus a fixed fee or cost plus a percentage of cost; revenues and costs on such contracts are typically recognized in each accounting period rather than the full amount only at the completion of the contract.

First-in, first-out (FIFO). A convention that values inventory and cost of goods sold by assuming that the oldest purchase prices included in inventory are the first prices reflected in costs of goods sold.

General price indices. Indices such as the Consumer Price Index or the Gross National Product price deflator that are designed to reflect the impact of inflation and deflation on general price levels; these indices are used in general-price-level adjustments (GPLA) accounting.

General-price-level adjustments (GPLA). A method of accounting for price-level changes (inflation and deflation) by reflecting in the valuation of assets and liabilities the changed purchasing power of the monetary unit (e.g., dollars).

Gross method (of accounting for cash discounts). In contrast to the net method, this method recognizes sales or purchases at their face (or full) value, accounting for any cash discounts allowed or earned in the period when cash is finally received or paid out.

Last-in, first-out (LIFO). A convention that values inventory and cost of goods sold by assuming that the most recent purchase prices included in inventory are the first prices reflected in costs of goods sold.

Net method (of accounting for cash discounts). In contrast to the gross method, this method recognizes sales or purchases at their net value (i.e., net of available cash discount) with any discount not taken by customers or foregone on purchases accounted for in the period when cash is finally received or paid out.

Percentage-of-completion method. A method of recognizing sales (or revenue) on an extended contract (e.g., research or construction) in proportion to the percentage of the contract completed, rather than recognizing the full amount only at the completion of the contract.

Specific-price adjustments (SPA). A method of accounting for price-level changes (inflation and deflation) by reflecting the changed prices of individual assets.

DISCUSSION QUESTIONS

9.1 Most accounting dilemmas turn on the question of timing. Explain what is meant by this statement.

9.2 Contrast the business situation where you would use the net method of accounting for cash discounts with the situation where you think the gross method would be more appropriate.

9.3 Which method of accounting for cash discounts (earned by customers for prompt payment)—the gross method or the net method—is more conservative?

9.4 Should all businesses account for bad debts of customers by use of the contra account Allowance for Doubtful Accounts? Why or why not?

9.5 Explain how you would determine for a particular accounting period the appropriate value for:

    (a) Warranty expense, assuming the company accrues an Allowance for Warranty.

    (b) Bad debt expense, assuming the company accrues an Allowance for Doubtful Accounts.

    (c) Pension expense, assuming the company accrues a Pension Liability.

9.6 Which of LIFO and FIFO inventory valuation methods is more conservative? Which is more accurate?

9.7 Assuming you were an advisor to a high-technology manufacturing company, would you advise the company to use the LIFO or the FIFO method of inventory valuation? Why?

9.8 *True/False:* A legislator interested in maximizing corporate income tax collection might be inclined to pass tax laws that would:

T	F	(a)	Insist on the use of FIFO rather than LIFO inventory valuation.
T	F	(b)	Insist on the accrual of an allowance for doubtful accounts.
T	F	(c)	Insist on the use of high salvage values in calculating depreciation of fixed assets.
T	F	(d)	Insist on suppliers using the gross method of accounting for prompt-payment discounts taken by their customers.
T	F	(e)	Press for the use of percentage-of-completion method in accounting for revenues on large contracts.

9.9 If a company is considering the choice between FIFO and LIFO inventory valuation methods in a period of continuing inflation, which method will:

    (a) Minimize income tax expense?

    (b) Provide more useful information to management for pricing decisions?

    (c) Provide more useful information regarding valuation of inventories?

9.10 Describe how you would develop SPA data for the following assets owned by an automotive manufacturing company. Indicate what difficulties you might encounter.

(a) Sheet aluminum used for certain parts of the automobile and purchased three months ago.

(b) A fuel pump manufactured three years ago and maintained in inventory to fill spare parts orders, although the pump is no longer used on current models.

(c) The final 2000 automobiles of last year's model that should be sold over the next two months.

(d) A word processing typewriter system purchased five years ago for the sales department; substantial improvements in speed and capacity have been incorporated in similar devices available now.

(e) A building in Princeville built 35 years ago and now housing one of the company's foundries.

(f) A forklift truck purchased two years ago.

(g) An automatic warehouse system custom-built and installed for the company three years ago.

(h) The land in midtown New York City purchased 25 years ago and now the site of the corporate headquarters building.

9.11 State briefly the difference between SPA and GPLA accounting. Which method of accounting for price-level changes do you think would be easier to implement?

9.12 Is LIFO a form of SPA accounting for inventory? Explain.

9.13 Accounting for price-level changes was a major issue among accountants in this country from about 1975 to 1985. The issue has assumed less importance since about 1985. Why?

9.14 Explain how an international company can hedge against gains and losses arising from fluctuations in currency values by borrowing and lending funds.

9.15 A company that builds a product in a strong-currency country, country S, and sells it to a customer in a weak-currency country, country W, has the choice of billing the customer in the currency of either S or W. Which currency should it choose?

9.16 The exchange rate between country G currency and country H currency is 3:1. If this exchange rate moves over time to 5:1, has G currency appreciated or depreciated with respect to H currency?

9.17 For the past several decades, both the construction price index and the higher-education price index have increased faster than the consumer price index. What relevance might that information have to accountants and financial officers?

9.18 Published balance sheets often show in the asset section a line labeled "Accounts receivable, net." In this context, what does the term net mean?

9.19 Is SPA accounting likely to have major or limited impact on the financial statements of the following firms? Explain.

  (a) A large legal partnership founded 75 years ago.

  (b) An electric public utility, whose generating capacity was constructed 20 years or more ago.

  (c) An electric public utility in a rapidly growing geographic area whose generating capacity has been constructed in the past 10 years.

  (d) A retailing firm whose store facilities are all rented.

  (e) A retailing firm whose store facilities are all owned.

  (f) A motor manufacturer whose plant facilities are all rented (compare to (d) above).

  (g) A machine tool manufacturer whose plant facilities are all owned (compare to (e) and (f) above).

9.20 If the exchange rate between currency A and currency B changes from 2 units of A = 1 unit of B to 2.5 units of A = 1 unit of B:

  (a) Will a borrower located in country A and borrowing currency B be helped or hurt by this change?

  (b) Will a company located in country A and owning a deposit in a bank in country B and denominated in currency B be helped or hurt by this change?

  (c) How can a company located in country B protect (hedge) the value of its accounts receivable denominated in currency A?

PROBLEMS

9.1 In October the Hamilton Corporation sold on credit merchandise valued at $138,000. The company's preliminary trial balance (before adjusting entries) shows the following balances:

Accounts receivable	$296,000	Dr
Allowance for doubtful accounts	7,400	Cr

Hamilton's accounting guidelines state that the monthly addition to Allowance for Doubtful Accounts should be 1 percent of the month's credit sales, provided that the balance in the Allowance account does not exceed 3 percent of the accounts receivable outstanding. Show in journal-entry format the adjusting entry you would make at the end of October, if any.

9.2 Refer again to Problem 9.1. Would your answer be different if you knew that Hamilton wrote off $1975 of bad debts in the month of October?

9.3 The Ascot Corporation learns that a customer who owes Ascot $23,500 has gone bankrupt. Show in T-account format the accounting entry, if any, that Ascot should make upon learning this information, assuming Ascot uses an Allowance for Doubtful Accounts.

9.4 Suppose one of your customers who owes you $5000 gets into financial difficulty and liquidates his business. In this liquidation, all creditors, including your company, are sent checks in amounts equal to 40 percent of their valid claims and are told to expect no further payments from this failed company. Show in T-account format the entries you would make at this time, assuming you use an Allowance for Doubtful Accounts.

9.5 Refer again to problem 9.4. If your company had previously written off this $5000 receivable, what entry would you now make to record receipt of the partial payment check?

9.6 The Hulbert Science Company receives from customer B $550 in full payment of a receivable that Hulbert wrote off as uncollectible three months ago. Record this transaction in T-account format:

(a) Assuming Hulbert does not use an Allowance for Doubtful Accounts.

(b) Assuming Hulbert does use an Allowance for Doubtful Accounts.

9.7 The Baum Corporation uses the net method of accounting for cash discounts allowed to its customers. Record in T-account format:

(a) An invoice for $3000 issued to customer 47 with payment terms of 2 percent, 10 days, net 30.

(b) Receipt of $1200 from customer 73 in full payment of her invoice; customer 73 did not take the 2 percent cash discount as she did not pay promptly.

(c) Receipt of $990 from customer 14 in full payment of a $1000 invoice subject to payment terms of 1 percent, 10 days, net 30.

9.8 Refer again to problem 9.7. Show the entries in T-account format assuming the gross method of accounting for cash discounts on sales.

9.9 Tanenbaum Men's Store accounts for cash discounts on its purchases of men's furnishings on the net method. Record in T-account format:

(a) Receipt of $7200 of merchandise subject to a 5 percent cash discount if paid within 15 days.

(b) Payment of $3500 to a supplier in full payment of an invoice; Tanenbaum did not pay in time to earn the 3 percent cash discount. (The merchandise was received in a previous accounting period.)

(c) Payment of $2280 to a supplier in full payment of a $2400 invoice subject to payment terms of 5 percent, 15 days, net 45. (The merchandise was received in a previous accounting period.)

9.10   Refer again to problem 9.9. Show the entries for Tanenbaum in T-account format assuming the gross method of accounting for cash discounts on purchases.

9.11   Given the following data on purchases into and shipments out of inventory for the month of April for McIntosh Enterprises, calculate the value of cost of goods sold for April and inventory at April 30 under the following alternative assumptions:

(a)   FIFO, perpetual inventory.

(b)   FIFO, cost of goods sold determined by end-of-period adjustment.

(c)   LIFO, perpetual inventory.

(d)   LIFO, cost of goods sold determined by end-of-period adjustment.

Opening inventory at April 1 was 150 units, each valued at $3.00.

Transaction	Date	Number of units	Value of purchase
purchase	4/2	50	$155
sale	4/5	60	
sale	4/8	40	
purchase	4/11	100	310
purchase	4/16	50	160
sale	4/18	70	
sale	4/23	30	
purchase	4/28	100	320
sale	4/29	70	

9.12   If opening inventory is zero for a particular product and you are told the following:

$$\text{cost of goods sold, FIFO} = \$4500$$
$$\text{cost of goods sold, LIFO} = \$4700$$
$$\text{closing inventory value, FIFO} = \$3100$$

Determine the value of closing (end-of-period) inventory determined by the LIFO method.

9.13   You are asked to provide an inflation-adjusted valuation today of a commercial building that was built 10 years ago for $2.5 million. The building is being depreciated on a straight-line basis assuming a 40-year life and zero salvage value. Use the two methods discussed in this chapter and assume:

(a)   The construction price index for commercial building in this geographic region ten years ago was 120 and today is 230.

(b)   The consumer price index in the country was:

$$10 \text{ years ago} = 100$$
$$\text{today} = 157$$

9.14 Emmet Consulting is based in country S but performs consulting services in many countries, including country T. For work performed in February for a client in country T, Emmet invoices the customer 10,000 units of country T currency. This customer pays the invoice five months later, in July. Currency exchange rates in the two months are:

> February: 0.5 units of currency S = 1 unit of currency T
> July: 0.7 units of currency S = 1 unit of currency T

Show in T-account format (assuming Emmet maintains its financial records in currency S):

(a) the revenue earned in February.

(b) the cash received in July.

9.15 Yang, Inc., a company headquartered in country K, borrows $5 million from a U.S. bank at a time when the currency exchange rate was $1 U.S. = 5 units of currency K. A year later, before any of the principal on the bank loan has been repaid, the exchange rate has moved to $1 U.S. = 4 units of currency K. Should Yang revalue this bank loan liability? If so, show in journal-entry format the appropriate adjustment.

9.16 The Madden Company maintains its books in U.S. dollars but has an account receivable expressed in hycas (a hypothetical foreign currency). The value of the receivable is 1000 hycas, and the sale occurred when the exchange rate was four hycas per dollar.

(a) Record in T-account format the sale and the account receivable in dollars.

(b) Assume that in a subsequent period the receivable is still outstanding but the exchange rate has now changed to five hycas per dollar. What entry, if any, should be made in Madden's general ledger at this time?

———10
FINANCIAL STATEMENT ANALYSIS

The financial statements that have been our focus to this point—the balance sheet and income statement—must offer more than data; they must provide useful information to the firm's various audiences, particularly managers, shareholders, and creditors. This chapter discusses the various techniques used to extract from the statements meaningful observations and conclusions about an enterprise's financial health and operating results.

Readers of financial statements are concerned primarily with the company's progress in satisfying the dual objectives of (1) earning profits and (2) maintaining a sound financial position. One reader may put more emphasis on profitability, with less concern for financial position, while another may emphasize financial stability and security, with less concern for current profitability. But all readers and all companies must be interested in both corporate objectives. If financial soundness is ignored, the company's risk of failure escalates; if the firm's profitability is ignored, its financial soundness will eventually become impaired.

We learn about a company by drawing comparisons among financial data. It is relationships among amounts on the income statement and balance sheet that convey information, much more so than isolated totals plucked from either statement. If you are told that a particular company has $1 million of assets, you know that the sum of its liabilities and owners' equity is also $1 million, but you learn nothing about its financial condition or profitability. If you are also told that this company's owners' equity (or net worth) totals $500,000, you can deduce the relationship among equity, liabilities, and assets: one-half of the company's assets have been financed by borrowing; you have learned something about the company's financial position. If you are also told that the company earned $75,000 profit in the year just ended, you learn something about profitability: the 7.5 percent return on the $1 million asset investment.

Suppose you are told that another company has $800,000 of accounts receivable. That number alone means little. If you are also told that sales in the most recent year were $10 million, you can calculate that accounts receivable are about 8 percent of annual sales, and thus you can estimate the average time the company's customers take to pay their bills. Again, the comparison, not the absolute number, is essential for the analysis.

RATIO ANALYSIS

Therefore, the fundamental method of analyzing financial statements is by ratio analysis. This chapter discusses the most common ratios and categorizes them by type of information revealed.

Actually, ratio analysis is not an entirely new subject for you. In the discussion of the balance sheet Chapter 3 defines *current assets* and *current liabilities* in a parallel manner. This parallelism was purposeful, since the resulting ratio of current assets to current liabilities is meaningful. In Chapter 4, *gross margin* is defined; the ratio between gross margin and sales—the gross margin percentage—is another relevant ratio. Chapter 7 stressed the consistent valuation of inventory and cost of goods sold; the ratio between these two values indicates the rate at which a company is using, or turning over, its inventory.

Analysts of financial statements learn to think in ratios. Current assets are instinctively compared to current liabilities. Cost of goods sold is automatically compared to total sales to measure gross profitability, and to total inventory to judge the rate of inventory usage.

Calculation of ratios is straightforward. Their interpretation, however, requires judgment, and judgment is sharpened by experience. An analyst who has studied a variety of financial statements—statements of companies in different industries and in both prosperous and recession periods—is able to glean more reliable conclusions from a particular set of statements than is an inexperienced analyst. This chapter provides a first step in gaining that experience.

CATEGORIZATION OF RATIOS

There are about as many financial ratios as there are analysts calculating them. Here we will deal with only the most commonly employed ratios. The four primary categories of information that they provide are:

(1) Liquidity: How able is the company to meet its near-term obligations?
(2) Working capital utilization: How efficiently is the company using the various components of its current assets and current liabilities?
(3) Capital structure: What are the company's sources of capital?
(4) Profitability: How profitable is the company in light of both its sales and its invested capital?

To illustrate both the calculation and meaning of the various ratios, this chapter analyzes the financial statements of the Hewlett-Packard Company (HP) for the fiscal years ending October 31, 1992 and 1993. The HP income statements (statements of earnings) and balance sheets for these two years and the income statement for 1991) are shown in Figures 10-1 and 10-2, but the financial notes accompanying these statements have been omitted.

Hewlett-Packard is a large and growing company that describes itself in the company's 1993 Annual Report as follows: "Hewlett-Packard designs, manufactures and services electronic products and systems for measurement, computation and communications. . . . The company's products are used in industry, business,

Figure 10-1   Hewlett-Packard's Consolidated Statement of Earnings for 1991, 1992, and 1993

For the years ended October 31 In millions except per share amounts	1993	1992	1991
Net revenue:			
Equipment	$15,533	$12,354	$11,019
Services	4,784	4,056	3,475
	20,317	16,410	14,494
Costs and expenses:			
Cost of equipment sold	8,929	6,625	5,634
Cost of services	3,194	2,533	2,224
Research and development	1,761	1,620	1,463
Selling, general and administrative	4,554	4,228	3,963
	18,438	15,006	13,284
Earnings from operations	1,879	1,404	1,210
Interest income and other income (expense)	25	17	47
Interest expense	121	96	130
Earnings before taxes and effect of 1992 accounting change	1,783	1,325	1,127
Provision for taxes	606	444	372
Earnings before effect of 1992 accounting change	1,177	881	755
Transition effect of 1992 accounting change, net of taxes	–	332	–
Net earnings	$ 1,177	$ 549	$ 755
Earnings per share before effect of 1992 accounting change	$ 4.65	$ 3.49	$ 3.02
Transition effect per share of 1992 accounting change, net of taxes	–	1.31	–
Net earnings per share	$ 4.65	$ 2.18	$ 3.02

Reprinted with permission from Hewlett-Packard.

Figure 10-2   Hewlett-Packard's Consolidated Balance Sheet for 1992 and 1993

October 31 In millions except par value and number of shares	1993	1992
Assets		
Current assets:		
Cash and cash equivalents	$ 889	$ 641
Short-term investments	755	394
Accounts and notes receivable	4,208	3,497
Inventories:		
Finished goods	2,121	1,271
Purchased parts and fabricated assemblies	1,570	1,334
Other current assets	693	542
Total current assets	10,236	7,679
Property, plant and equipment:		
Land	514	402
Buildings and leasehold improvements	3,254	2,994
Machinery and equipment	3,759	3,196
	7,527	6,592
Accumulated depreciation	(3,347)	(2,943)
	4,180	3,649
Long-term receivables and other assets	2,320	2,372
	$16,736	$13,700
Liabilities and shareholders' equity		
Current liabilities:		
Notes payable and short-term borrowings	$ 2,190	$ 1,384
Accounts payable	1,223	925
Employee compensation and benefits	1,048	913
Taxes on earnings	922	490
Deferred revenues	507	449
Other accrued liabilities	978	933
Total current liabilities	6,868	5,094
Long-term debt	667	425
Other liabilities	659	633
Deferred taxes on earnings	31	49
Shareholders' equity:		
Preferred stock, $1 par value (authorized: 300,000,000 shares; issued: none)	–	–
Common stock and capital in excess of $1 par value (authorized: 600,000,000 shares; issued and outstanding: 252,713,000 in 1993 and 250,824,000 in 1992)	937	874
Retained earnings	7,574	6,625
Total shareholders' equity	8,511	7,499
	$16,736	$13,700

Reprinted with permission of Hewlett-Packard.

engineering, science, medicine and education in approximately 110 countries."* Founded in the late 1930s, HP has been one of the brightest high-technology success stories, having grown so rapidly that by 1993 it was ranked by Fortune magazine as the 24th largest industrial company in the United States. The company has an enviable financial record: strong growth rate, excellent profitability, and sound financial position.

The ratios discussed here are particularly applicable to manufacturing enterprises. Companies engaged in different industries find some of these ratios irrelevant; other ratios, not discussed here, may be highly relevant to them. For example,

*1993 Hewlett-Packard Company Annual Report, inside front cover.

a commercial bank is concerned with the ratio between loans outstanding and customer deposits—the loan-to-deposit ratio—since customer deposits provide the funds that the bank lends to its borrowers.

Liquidity

A company unable to meet its obligations as they come due runs the risk of bankruptcy. Trade suppliers and employees must be paid on time; interest and principal payments on borrowed money must be made when due. A company that has substantial liquid assets in relationship to its near-term obligations has strong **liquidity,** is very liquid. Note that a company might be very nonliquid, and thus risk failure, even while making substantial profits. Liquidity is only a measure of financial position or condition.

Current Ratio. The most widely quoted financial ratio is the **current ratio:**

$$\text{Current ratio} = \text{current assets} \div \text{current liabilities}$$

Recall that current assets are those assets that are either presently the equivalent of cash or within the next 12 months will be turned into cash. Cash, accounts receivable, and inventory are the primary current assets, listed in order of decreasing liquidity. Current liabilities are obligations that must be met within the following 12 months, including primarily accounts payable, wages and salaries payable, short-term bank borrowing, current portion of long-term debt, and miscellaneous accruals.

The higher the current ratio, the greater the margin of safety—that is, the more likely the company is to have sufficient liquid assets to meet its obligations as they come due.

Note that current assets do not include all the cash that the company will receive during the next 12 months, nor do the current liabilities include all obligations that must be met over the next 12 months. Sales occurring tomorrow, next week, and next month will result in cash receipts well before a year from now, and over the coming weeks and months employees and vendors will have to be paid amounts not now included in current liabilities.Thus, the current ratio does not define comprehensively the ability of the company to meet all near-term obligations; it is only an indicator, albeit the most important one.

Hewlett-Packard's current ratio at the end of its 1993 fiscal year was

$$\text{Current ratio} = 10{,}236 \div 6868 = 1.5$$

Acid-Test (or Quick) Ratio. Another liquidity measure is the **quick ratio,** often referred to as the **acid-test ratio:**

$$\text{Quick ratio} = (\text{cash} + \text{marketable securities} + \text{accounts receivable})$$
$$\div \text{ current liabilities}$$

Note that the denominator here is the same as for the current ratio: current liabilities. The numerator, however, includes only the most liquid of the company's current assets. No asset can be more liquid than cash! In addition, many companies own assets that are **cash equivalents:** short-term investments of temporary or permanent cash reserves. These investments in U.S. Treasury securities or other interest-bearing instruments or accounts are highly marketable—they can be converted into cash on a moment's notice. Thus, **marketable securities** are considered part of the company's quick assets.* Accounts receivable are also quick assets, since they will normally be collected (converted to cash) soon, typically within 90 days.

The primary difference between the numerators of the current and quick ratios is inventory; inventory is excluded from the quick ratio. A service company that holds little or no inventory might therefore have a quick ratio that approximates its current ratio. Also, a company that sells primarily for cash (for example, certain retail stores), has few (or no) accounts receivable in comparison to another that sells on credit. Typically, the sale-for-cash company has a lower quick ratio, but this fact does not necessarily mean it is illiquid. Recall the earlier admonition: financial ratios must be interpreted in light of the company's particular business and circumstances.

The quick (or acid-test) ratio at HP at October 31, 1993 was

$$\text{Quick ratio} = (889 + 755 + 4,208) \div 6868 = 0.85$$

Working Capital Utilization

Current assets, particularly accounts receivable and inventory, are major investments for many companies. At HP, current assets at October 31, 1993 represented 61 percent of total assets. The more efficiently the company uses its current assets— that is, the faster it collects from customers and the less inventory it requires to accomplish its sales—the less capital the company will require.

Recall that working capital is the difference between current assets and current liabilities. The following ratios indicate how efficiently the company is using the primary elements of working capital.

Accounts Receivable Collection Period. Most manufacturing companies extend customer credit. The longer customers take to pay their bills the more the manufacturer must invest in accounts receivable. A comparison of sales volume with outstanding accounts receivable indicates how promptly customers are paying—the **accounts receivable collection period** ratio:

$$\text{Collection period (in days)} = \frac{\text{accounts receivable}}{\text{average sales per day}}$$

*The company may own other marketable securities that are not cash equivalent. For example, when company A purchases on the open market shares of company B's stock, company A is presumably making a long-term investment in company B; thus, this asset is not included in company A's current assets.

where

$$\text{Average sales per day} = \text{annual sales} \div 365$$

The collection period is the number of days of sales remaining uncollected (and therefore in accounts receivable) at the end of the accounting period. Stated another way, the ratio equals the average number of days between the customer invoice date and the date that payment is received. Actual time between invoice dates and collection dates vary widely by customer; some pay very promptly and others take a distressingly long time to pay. The mean of a frequency distribution of days from invoice date to payment date approximates the collection period expressed in days.

Observe several cautions as you interpret the accounts receivable collection period. First, annual sales should include only credit sales; if the company has substantial cash sales, adjust the sales data accordingly. Second, the formula utilizes annual sales. Sales for shorter periods (for example, fiscal quarters) can be used with only minor and obvious adjustments to the formula; however, if a business is seasonal, the collection period ratio is substantially distorted at certain times of the year. For example, suppose that the ratio is calculated just after the conclusion of the company's busiest season. Average sales per day are higher during this busy season than for the year as a whole; moreover, the recent high rate of sales causes a high accounts receivable balance at the end of the period.

Seasonal distortion of the collection period is illustrated in Figure 10-3. Note that each quarter's collection period, based upon sales for just that quarter, is consistent at 45.6 days. However, the year-end accounts receivable is inflated by high sales in the final quarter; when this balance is compared to the average sales per day for the year (5.48), the resulting collection period is quite misleading.

A similar distortion results when a company is growing rapidly. The accounts receivable collection period is the first (but not last) ratio we encounter that utilizes data from both the income statement and the balance sheet. Recall that the income statement is for a period, while the balance sheet is a snapshot at the end of a period. The balance sheet therefore is a function of the activity level at the end of an accounting period while the income statement records performance throughout the period. Consider the hypothetical company illustrated in Figure 10-4. It grew in sales volume by $3000 per month—from $100,000 last December to $136,000 this

FIGURE 10-3   Effect of Seasonality on Accounts Receivable Collection Period

Fiscal Period	Sales	Average Sales per Day	Accounts Receivable at End of Period	Collection Period*
Quarter 1	$ 400	4.38	$200	45.6 days
Quarter 2	400	4.38	200	45.6 days
Quarter 3	400	4.38	200	45.6 days
Quarter 4	800	8.77	400	45.6 days
Full Year	$2000	5.48	400	73.0 days

*Accounts Receivable ÷ Average Sales per day.

FIGURE 10-4 Effect of Growth on Accounts Receivable Collection Period

Month	Sales ($000)
December (1994)	$ 100
January (1995)	$ 103
February	106
March	109
April	112
May	115
June	118
July	121
August	124
September	127
October	130
November	133
December	136
Total: 1995	$1434

Accounts receivable balances:
  December 31, 1994 $100
  December 31, 1995   136

Collection period, based upon year-end A/R = $\dfrac{136}{1434 / 365}$ = 34.6 days.

Collection period, based upon average A/R = $\dfrac{(100 + 136) \div 2}{1434 / 365}$ = 30 days.

December. The accounts receivable balance at each month end was just equal to sales in the most recent month; the average collection period was obviously one month, or about 30 days. However, a comparison of average sales per day for the entire year with the year-end accounts receivable balance results in a collection period that overstates the true situation: the collection period appears to be 34.6 days instead of 30 days. A simple adjustment compensates adequately for the effect of steady growth: use an average accounts receivable balance, instead of the year-end balance. If you have the balance sheet for the previous year-end as well as the current balance sheet, as we do for HP, an average can be struck between these two numbers. Thus, the better formulation of the accounts receivable collection period ratio is

$$\text{Collection period} = \frac{(\text{opening A/R} + \text{ending A/R}) \div 2}{\text{annual sales} \div 365}$$

An even more accurate average is obtained by averaging the 13 month-end accounts receivable balances from December 1991 through December 1992, but these data are seldom available in published statements.

In 1993, HP grew by 24 percent in sales, and thus the two calculations of collection period are considerably different.

Ratio based on year-end A/R:

$$\text{A/R collection period} = \frac{\text{accounts receivable}}{\text{annual sales} \div 365}$$

$$= \frac{4208}{20,317 \div 365} = \frac{4208}{55.66} = 76 \text{ days}$$

Ratio based on average A/R:

$$\text{A/R collection period} = \frac{(\text{opening A/R} + \text{ending A/R}) \div 2}{\text{annual sales} \div 365}$$

$$= \frac{(4208 + 3497) \div 2}{20,317 \div 365} = \frac{3853}{55.66} = 69 \text{ days}$$

Inventory Turnover. Most manufacturing and merchandising companies invest substantial amounts in inventory in order to serve customers and assure the uninterrupted flow of manufacturing processes. Carrying inventory is expensive, when one includes the costs of storage, insurance, risk of obsolescence, and the tied-up capital. Thus, in deciding on inventory levels, every company trades off (explicitly or implicitly) the costs with the benefits of carrying inventory.

When inventory is sold, inventory values are reduced and a charge is made to Cost of Goods Sold. A comparison of inventory and cost of goods sold, then, indicates the rate at which inventory is used—that is, the speed with which inventory is moving from receipt to final sale.

This **inventory turnover** ratio parallels the accounts receivable collection period: the collection period ratio compares sales and accounts receivable, both valued at sales prices, while the inventory turnover ratio compares cost of goods sold and inventory, both valued at cost values.

The inventory turnover ratio is typically expressed in times-per-year, but an alternate form of the ratio is the **inventory flow period** ratio, expressed in number-of-days. The ratio in times-per-year is

$$\text{Inventory turnover} = \frac{\text{cost of goods sold}}{\text{inventory}}$$

and in number-of-days, the ratio is

$$\text{Inventory flow period} = \frac{\text{inventory}}{\text{cost of goods sold} \div 365} \quad \text{or} \quad \frac{365}{\text{inventory tunover}}$$

The inventory turnover ratio is subject to the same distortions from seasonality and growth as the accounts receivable collection period. A retail store enjoying substantial holiday trade builds inventories in the fall with the anticipation of high sales in November and December. Its apparent rate of inventory usage at the end of October is very different from an inventory turnover calculated on January 31 when inventories are depleted. Growth in sales typically necessitates an increasing investment in inventory; for a growing company inventory turnovers should thus be calculated with average inventory balances, rather than year-end balances.

Hewlett-Packard separately classifies its revenue and cost of goods sold for equipment and for services. If we assume its inventories are related solely to equipment manufacturing (an imperfect assumption), we can relate average inventory to equipment revenues in 1993 as follows:

$$\text{Inventory turnover} = \frac{\text{cost of equipment sold}}{(\text{opening inventory} + \text{ending inventory}) \div 2}$$

$$= \frac{8929}{(2121 + 1570 + 1271 + 1334) \div 2}$$

$$= \frac{8929}{3148} = 2.84 \text{ times per year}$$

$$\text{Inventory flow period} = \frac{(\text{opening inventory} + \text{ending inventory}) \div 2}{\text{cost of equipment sold} \div 365}$$

$$= \frac{(2121 + 1570 + 1271 + 1334) \div 2}{8929 \div 365}$$

$$= \frac{3148}{24.46} = 129 \text{ days}$$

Interpreting inventory turnover is difficult because the nature of the particular business affects so greatly the inventory flow. At one extreme, a dairy had better have a very rapid turnover of inventory if its milk, butter, and cheese are to remain fresh until purchased by the consumer. At the other extreme, a shipbuilding firm requiring a year or two to complete the fabrication and assembly of a large ship necessarily has very large inventories in relationship to its annual sales.

Some published financial statements do not separate product and period costs. If cost-of-goods-sold data are unavailable, the inventory turnover ratio can be calculated using sales, rather than cost of goods sold, in the numerator. The numerator and denominator are now not expressed in comparable terms: the numerator in sales prices, including the company's gross margin, the denominator (the inventory) in cost values. While the resulting ratio does not, in fact, indicate inventory turns in times per year, a comparison of this ratio over a number of years may be useful in assessing trends in inventory flow over time. (Bear in mind that changes in gross profit margins will also affect the ratio.)

Accounts Payable Payment Period. A major determinant of working capital is the amount of trade or vendor credit utilized. Just as a comparison of sales and accounts receivable reveals the collection period, a comparison of credit purchases and accounts payable yields the **accounts payable payment period**—the average time a company takes to pay its suppliers. This payment period compared to the normal terms of purchase assesses how well the company is meeting its obligations to suppliers.

Unfortunately, total credit purchases seldom are either revealed in published financial statements or readily available even within the company. However, a proxy for credit purchases may be used—that is, another value, more readily available, that tends to increase or decrease coincident with credit purchases. Cost of goods sold is a reasonable proxy, if the large majority of credit purchases is goods and merchandise for resale.

We do not have data on HP's credit purchases in 1992 and 1993, and we know that cost of goods sold includes production and service labor and overhead in addition to materials purchased on credit. Thus, here cost of goods sold is quite an imperfect proxy for credit purchases. Nevertheless, based upon year-end Accounts Payable totals and costs of both equipment and services, HP's payment period is

$$\text{A/P payment period} = \frac{\text{accounts payable}}{\text{cost of sales} \div 365}$$

$$\text{A/P payment period (1992)} = \frac{925}{(6625 + 2533) \div 365} = 37 \text{ days}$$

$$\text{A/P payment period (1993)} = \frac{1223}{(8929 + 3194) \div 365} = 37 \text{ days}$$

For many companies, borrowing from trade creditors (that is, accounts payable) is a major source of capital. While there are practical limits to this source, the more this noninterest-bearing source is used, the less the company must obtain from sources to whom it must pay a return. Thus, many companies will seek to stretch their A/P payment period.

Working Capital Turnover. The **working capital turnover** ratio summarizes the efficiency with which the company is using its net investment in current assets less current liabilities.

$$\text{Working capital turnover} = \frac{\text{sales}}{\text{average working capital}}$$

This ratio, typically expressed in times-per-year, shows the dollars of sales achieved per dollar of working capital invested. If the ratio decreases, the company is investing more in working capital per dollar of sales; if the ratio increases, the company is making more efficient use of its working capital. Again, this ratio is subject to the same distortions from seasonality and growth that plague all ratios that draw data from both the balance sheet and the income statement.

In 1993 Hewlett-Packard's working capital turnover was

Working capital turnover

$$= \frac{\text{sales}}{(\text{opening working capital} + \text{ending working capital}) \div 2}$$

$$= \frac{20{,}317}{[(10{,}236 - 6868) + (7679 - 5094)] \div 2} = \frac{20{,}317}{2977} = 6.8 \text{ times per year}$$

Other Asset Turnover Measures. Still other asset turnover measures are sometimes useful. A comparison of sales and fixed asset investment indicates the number of dollars of annual sales realized from the company's investment in productive assets. The higher the **fixed asset turnover** ratio, the more effectively the company is utilizing its fixed assets. The most global measure of asset utilization is the **total asset turnover** ratio—the relationship between sales and total assets. These two ratios, although unrelated to working capital, are mentioned here because we will use them later in discussing the linkage among ratios.

For Hewlett-Packard in 1993 these ratios were

$$\text{Fixed asset turnover} = \frac{\text{sales}}{\text{average net fixed assets}}$$

$$= \frac{20{,}317}{(4180 + 3649) \div 2} = \frac{20{,}317}{3915} = 5.2 \text{ times/year}$$

$$\text{Total asset turnover} = \frac{\text{sales}}{\text{average total assets}}$$

$$= \frac{20{,}317}{(16{,}736 + 13{,}700) \div 2} = \frac{20{,}317}{15{,}218} = 1.3 \text{ times/year}$$

The total asset turnover ratio at HP has remained quite constant in recent years at about 1.2 to 1.3, indicating that, as this company grows, its investment in assets grows apace. If the ratio continues to hold in future years, HP can expect to have to invest 77 cents (1/1.3) in assets for every one dollar increase in annual sales volume.

Capital Structure Ratios

Capital structure ratios help to evaluate the liabilities + owners' equity side of the balance sheet—that is, how the company is financed. These ratios assess the financial riskiness of the business as well as the potential for improved returns through the judicious use of debt.

When a company borrows money, it undertakes a firm, ironclad obligation to pay interest and principal repayments on schedule. Failure to make these various payments when due (that is, default on the provisions of the loan agreement) subjects the company to the risk of bankruptcy. For any particular company the higher the debt, the greater the risk. If the company's operating performance is erratic or encounters difficulties, the company may not be able to comply with its borrowing agreements. By contrast, when a corporation obtains additional funds by the sale of new capital stock, it undertakes no such firm obligation to its new shareholders; these shareholders will receive dividends only if and when declared by the corporation's board of directors. Failure to pay dividends does not constitute default and does not subject the company to the risk of failure, although it may subject the management to other pressures. Thus, from the point of view of the corporation, common stock financing is much less risky than borrowing.

However, the judicious use of borrowing benefits shareholders. If a company can borrow funds at an interest rate equal to x percent and invest those funds to earn consistently at a rate greater than x percent, then this incremental return results in a higher return on shareholders' invested capital. We will return to this phenomenon, known as **debt leverage,** later in the chapter.

For now, bear in mind that the use of borrowed funds is inherently neither good nor bad. The greater the use of borrowed funds—that is, the greater the use of debt leverage—the greater the financial risk to which the company is exposed, but also the greater the potential return to shareholders. Decisions on the amount of debt to be utilized by a corporation—that is, capital structure decisions—are a matter of judgment to be exercised by the corporation's board of directors and management.

Total Debt to Owners' Equity Ratio. The debt of most corporations is composed of both current and long-term liabilities; owners' equity consists of both capital invested by the owners and earnings retained in the business. The ratio between the two sums indicates the relative contribution of creditors and owners to the company's financing. For HP, the **total debt to owners' equity** ratio in 1992 and 1993 was

$$\text{Total debt to owners' equity} = \frac{\text{current liabilities} + \text{long-term liabilities}}{\text{total shareholders' equity}}$$

$$(1992) = \frac{5094 + 425 + 633}{7499} = 82\%$$

$$(1993) = \frac{6868 + 667 + 659}{8,511} = 96\%$$

Total Debt to Total Assets Ratio. A closely related ratio compares total debt to total assets owned by the company, thus indicating the percentage of total assets represented by liabilities. Since assets are equal to the sum of liabilities and owners' equity, the **total debt to total assets** ratio provides only information that was inherent in the total debt to owners' equity ratio. For HP, this ratio in 1992 and 1993 was

$$\text{Total debt to total assets} = \frac{\text{current liabilities} + \text{long-term liabilities}}{\text{total shareholders' equity}}$$

$$(1992) = \frac{5094 + 425 + 633}{13,700} = 45\%$$

$$(1993) = \frac{6868 + 667 + 659}{16,736} = 49\%$$

The remainder of HP's assets (51 percent in 1993) were financed by owners' equity (ignoring the minor amount of deferred taxes).

Long-Term Debt to Total Capitalization Ratio. This ratio requires careful definition of both the numerator and denominator. Long-term debt is that portion of total borrowings having a maturity longer than one year (and therefore not included in current liabilities). **Total capitalization** is defined as the total permanent capital. Current liabilities are not a permanent source of capital, since they arise spontaneously from operations; amounts owing to trade creditors and employees and miscellaneous accruals would not be present if the company were not actively engaged in trade. Total capitalization, then, is defined as long-term debt plus owners' equity. This ratio indicates the percentage that permanent, or long-term, borrowed funds are of total permanently invested capital. For HP in 1992 and 1993, this ratio was

$$\text{Logn-term debt to total capitalization} = \frac{\text{long-term debt}}{\text{long-term debt} + \text{owners' equity}}$$

$$(1992) = \frac{425}{425 + 13,700} = 3.0\%$$

$$(1993) = \frac{667}{667 + 16,736} = 3.8\%$$

Hewlett-Packard obtains virtually all of its permanent financing from owners' equity, in accordance with a corporate policy to minimize the use of long-term debt.

Recall from Chapter 8 that deferred taxes typically appear on the balance sheet between long-term debt and owners' equity. Some analysts include deferred taxes in total capitalization and others omit them entirely. Since most deferred taxes will not require payment in the foreseeable future, deferred taxes have been omitted here, as have the amounts labelled Other Liabilities.

Times Interest Earned. The ability of a corporate borrower to service its debt—that is, to pay interest when due—is indicated by comparing the company's annual interest expense with its earnings before the payment of interest or income taxes.

The ratio assumes that **earnings before interest and taxes** (often abbreviated EBIT) approximate the company's cash flow available for debt service, an assumption which for any of a number of reasons may not be accurate. (Note that pretax operating profit is used since current U.S. tax law permits interest to be deducted in computing taxable income.) The higher this ratio, the greater the safety margin, and the lower the risk that the company will be unable to service its debt. As this ratio declines, the greater the risk that some untoward event such as an economic recession will cause the company to be unable to meet its interest payment obligations. Hewlett-Packard utilizes very little borrowed funds and thus its **times interest earned** ratio is very, very high (almost 16 times in 1993). Public utilities such as telephone or gas and electric companies by their nature rely heavily on borrowed capital, and this ratio is very relevant in judging the financial risk inherent in the capital structures of these companies. For example, in 1992, Pacific Gas and Electric Company had EBIT of $1957 million and net interest payments of $739 million, and thus its times interest earned ratio was

$$\text{Times interest earned} = \frac{\text{earnings before interest and taxes}}{\text{annual interest expense}} = \frac{1957}{739} = 2.65$$

Profitability

The ratios dealing with liquidity, working capital utilization, and capital structure focus primarily on the company's financial position. By contrast, the profitability ratios measure the company's performance, the rate at which it is earning financial returns.

Two types of profitability ratios are useful. The first measures profit in relation to sales levels and is obtained by comparing data solely within the income statement; the second measures profit in relation to investment and involves comparisons of income statement and balance sheet data.

Percentage Relationships on Income Statement. The ratio of net income to total sales is a useful indicator of the company's profitability. In addition, the percentage that each line item on the income statement is of total revenue, or sales, also provides useful insights. For example, the gross margin percentage shows the relationship between sales revenue and product cost. Sales expense as a percentage of sales revenue shows what percent of the sales dollar the company spends on selling and marketing activities.

Figure 10-5 analyzes HP's income statements for 1992 and 1993. Note the consistency between the two years. The company's gross margin—the difference between sales and costs of goods sold—declined some in the most recent year, for both equipment and services, but still represents a healthy gross margin; this change in gross margin may be the result of decreased prices, increased costs, a change in the mix of products and services sold, or some combination of these three effects. (The narrative in the report mentions significant price pressure in 1993.) Selling, general and administrative expenses were sharply lower as a percent of sales; the

FIGURE 10-5   Percentage Analysis of Income Statement, Hewlett-Packard Co., 1992 and 1993

	1993	1992
Net revenue		
Equipment	76%	75%
Services	24	25
Total	100%	100%
Costs and expenses		
Cost of equipment sold	57*	54*
Cost of services	67*	62*
Research and development	9	10
Selling, general and administrative	22	26
	91	91
Earnings from operations	9	9
Interest and other income and expenses	—	1
Earnings before taxes	9	8
Provision for taxes	3	3
Net earnings	6%	5%**

*Percentages are of associated revenue; thus, cost column does not sum.
**Ignoring 1992 accounting change.

report indicates "ongoing efforts to adjust expense(s)."* Because of the nature of its technical products, the company spends heavily both on research and development—9 percent in the most recent year. Net earnings at 5 to 6 percent of sales ranks HP above average among manufacturing companies.

These percentages vary greatly by industry. Consider the probable percentages for a large food retailer: cost of goods sold is a very high percentage of sales, research and development expenses are essentially nonexistent, and net earnings as a percentage of sales are very small, typically 1 to 2 percent. Thus, the admonition is repeated: Comparisons between companies engaged in dissimilar businesses can be very misleading.

Return on Sales. Note particularly the last of these percentage relationships, net income to total sales, or **return on sales (ROS).**

Return on Equity. Turn now to profitability related to investment. The most fundamental ratio is net income to total owners' equity, the so-called **return on equity (ROE).** To compensate for growth, the ratio compares earnings for the year to average equity, or

$$\text{Return on equity} = \frac{\text{net income}}{(\text{opening equity} + \text{ending equity}) \div 2}$$

*Hewlett-Packard 1993 Annual Report, p. 26.

Hewlett-Packard's return on equity in 1993 was

$$\text{Return on equity} = \frac{1177}{(8511 + 7499) \div 2} = \frac{1177}{8005} = 14.7\%$$

The ROE ratio compares net income, after payment of all expenses including interest and taxes, with the total book value of the shareholders' investment, including both invested capital and earnings retained by the business. Since all shareholders invest for a return, ROE is one ratio that can be compared across different industries.

Return on equity does not, however, indicate the degree of risk inherent in the return. Shareholders are typically willing to accept a lower ROE in exchange for a lower risk. Later in this chapter we will see how the use of greater debt leverage leads to both higher risk and potentially higher ROE.

Note also that this ratio compares net income to book shareholders' equity. An investor typically has to pay more or less than equivalent book value for a share of stock, as market values of securities bear no necessary relationship to book values. Thus, the ROE generally does not indicate for a particular investor the rate of return on an actual securities investment.

Return on Assets. The return on equity for a company is influenced by its capital structure, as explained later in this chapter. A company employing high debt leverage is typically subject to wider swings in ROE than another company obtaining its permanent capital primarily through shareholders' equity. To factor out the influence of capital structure when appraising the company's earnings on investment, total assets can be used as the measure of investment—the total amount owned by the company, whether financed through debt or owners' equity.

The **return on assets (ROA)** ratio compares earnings to total assets. However, net income is inappropriate as the numerator, since net income is profit after payment of interest, and the amount of interest is a function of the capital structure. Thus, again we use earnings before interest and taxes (EBIT) in calculating return on assets:

$$\text{Return on assets} = \frac{\text{earnings before interest and taxes}}{(\text{opening assets} + \text{ending assets}) \div 2}$$

At HP in 1993, return on assets was

$$\text{Return on assets} = \frac{1783 + 121*}{(16,736 + 13,700) \div 2} = \frac{1904}{15,218} = 13\%$$

*Earnings before taxes on income plus interest expense.

Bear in mind that the return on assets percentage and the return on equity percentage are not comparable, since ROA is a before-tax percentage and ROE is an after-tax percentage.

INTERPRETING RATIOS

Experienced financial statement analysts instinctively observe ratios as they review financial statements. You will learn to think in ratios as you scan financial statements, searching for strengths and weaknesses in the company's financial condition and operating performance. Bear in mind that not every ratio provides useful information in every situation. For example, if you observe that a particular company's current ratio conforms to typical industry averages, you may conclude that liquidity is neither a problem nor a strength. Further analysis may reveal a relatively long collection period. If the company is encountering problems in obtaining prompt payment from customers—and a relatively low total debt to owners' equity ratio—the company has low financial risk and low debt leverage. These observations are useful and suggest areas for further inquiry: Why are customers paying slowly? Could the company benefit from further debt leverage?

Ratios should be calculated accurately, but not with undue precision. A collection period calculated to the nearest whole day, rather than to the second decimal point, is quite adequate to suggest customer payment patterns. Since income statement and balance sheet values are affected by a host of variables such as seasonality, price-level changes, and random events occurring just prior to the balance sheet date, don't attribute unwarranted significance to minor changes in ratios.

No Absolute Standards

By now, you undoubtedly wonder: what should be the value of these various ratios? What represents an appropriate current ratio, or total debt to total assets ratio, or collection period, or return on equity?

Unfortunately, your questions cannot be answered. Adequate liquidity or appropriate debt leverage is a function of industry characteristics, the company's stage of development, philosophy of the management and owners, and many other factors. While conventional wisdoms do exist—such as, a manufacturing company should have a current ratio of 2.0 and a quick ratio of 1.0—these wisdoms are dangerous. Some companies (including HP) enjoy very adequate liquidity with a current ratio less than 2.0—for example, service companies with low inventories or companies that sell for cash and thus have no accounts receivable. Other companies need a current ratio well in excess of 2.0 to assure adequate liquidity—for example, companies whose manufacturing processes require large inventories.

Not only will you be frustrated in seeking absolute standards for the various ratios; in addition for most ratios you cannot conclude that *the higher the better* or *the lower the better*. You might be inclined to think that the higher the current ratio, the more sound the company's financial condition. While a high current ratio indicates strong liquidity, an excessively high current ratio suggests inefficient use of the current assets. Or, you may be inclined to conclude that the shorter the collection period, the better. However, if a company achieves rapid collection by refusing to sell to any but the most creditworthy customers and then by harassing customers to pay quickly, the company may suffer loss of sales volume as a result of its collection policies. Or, you may be inclined to feel that the lower the total debt to total assets ratio, the healthier the business. Low debt leverage does indicate low financial risk, but many companies can and should avail themselves of the benefits of debt leverage; for them very low debt ratios may point up financial policies that are unnecessarily timid.

In short, judging the appropriateness of a particular ratio is not easy. An analyst's judgment is aided by two techniques, however: reviewing trends over time, and comparing the ratios with those of similar companies in the same industry.

Trends

Suppose that companies A and B now both have current ratios of 2.0; they apparently have equivalent liquidity. Now, suppose that the current ratios for these two companies over the past three years have been

	Two Years Ago	One Year Ago	This Year
Company A	1.4	1.8	2.0
Company B	2.6	2.2	2.0

Now, Company A seems to be building somewhat more comfortable liquidity (its current ratio has strengthened over recent years), while company B's liquidity has deteriorated. Trend information shapes your conclusion.

Figure 10-6 shows the trend in selected HP ratios over a recent five-year period. While all are quite stable—and that observation itself is meaningful—the ratios reveal a few trends. Debt leverage has increased nearly one-third in the most recent two years. Profitability trended downward and then recovered over the past two years. Liquidity, collection periods and inventory turnover have bounced around a little, but the variations in the ratios are not more than 5 percent from the means (except liquidity in 1991), and no trends are discernable.

Analyses of other companies reveal more dramatic trends. Figure 10-7 shows the trend in the long-term debt to total capitalization ratio for the Chrysler Corporation, a company that encountered such severe financial problems in the early 1980s that a governmental guarantee of the company's debt was required to reduce the risk of financial failure. Note the sharp reduction in debt leverage over the five-year period, from the time in 1981 and 1982 when the company had negative net worth (a debt-to capitalization ratio of more than 100 percent).

FIGURE 10-6 Trends in Financial Ratios, Hewlett-Packard Co., 1988–1993

	1989	1990	1991	1992	1993
Liquidity					
Current Ratio	1.53	1.47	1.65	1.51	1.49
Working Capital Utilization					
A/R Collection Period* (days)	76.5	79.5	74.9	77.8	75.6
Inventory Turnover* (X per year)	2.32	2.42	2.48	2.54	2.42
Capital Structure					
Total Debt to Total Assets	43.5	41.9	37.3	44.9	49.0
Profitability					
Return on Sales	7.0	5.6	5.2	5.4**	5.8
Return on Equity*	15.2	11.6	10.4	11.7**	13.8

*Based on year-end (not average) values.
**Ignoring the 1992 accounting change.

Comparison with Similar Companies

A company's ratios must be interpreted in light of its particular industry. A comparison of HP to an electric power utility is irrelevant. Utilities typically have high fixed assets and little working capital; their fixed asset and total asset turnovers are low, but they employ substantial debt leverage to earn competitive returns on equity. Light manufacturing companies, such as HP, have substantially greater investment in current assets than in fixed assets and HP has eschewed debt financing.

But a comparison of HP to other companies of comparable size whose business is closely related to "electronic products and systems for measurement, computation and communication" is revealing. Comparisons among direct competitors may be particularly useful, but comparisons with industry averages may be even more revealing. These comparisons are facilitated by many industry (trade) associations that collect from their members, typically on a confidential basis, detailed information regarding financial ratios, and then compile, categorize, and publish these data for the benefit of those members. Certain government agencies and some banks provide similar industry financial ratio data. Such data can prove invaluable as a benchmark for comparisons.

The American Electronics Association (AEA) periodically surveys its members

FIGURE 10-7 Trends in Capital Structure Ratio, Chrysler Corporation, 1981–1985

Year	Ratio of Long-Term Debt to Total Capitalization
1981	135%
1982	118%
1983	49%
1984	19%
1985	36%

FIGURE 10-8   Industry Comparative Ratios

	HP	Industry*
Current ratio	1.5	2.6
A/R Collection period (days)**	69	58
Inventory turnover (times per year)**	2.84	3.11
Working capital turnover (times per year)**	6.80	2.67
Gross margin	40.3%	58.3%
Return on assets**	13.0%	6.7%
Return on equity**	14.7%	9.4%

*Includes data from 9 companies, each in the computers and office equipment segment of the electronics industry and each with sales in excess of $75 million per year. Data shown are medians for 1992.
**Based on average (not year-end) values.

Source: 1993 Electronics Industry Operating Ratios Survey, American Electronics Association, Santa Clara, California.

for financial ratio information and publishes the results for participating members. Some useful comparative data for HP are shown in Figure 10-8. Despite HP's lower liquidity (current ratio), the company has high current assets compared to the industry median: note its slower collections and lower inventory turnover. Because of relatively high current liabilities, HP's working capital turnover is high for the industry. And, despite a lower gross margin, HP's bottom-line return on investment (ROA and ROE) substantially exceeds the industry median.

LINKAGE AMONG FINANCIAL RATIOS

By now, you probably surmise that some interesting linkages may exist among ratios, particularly among asset utilization, capital structure, and profitability. For example, a company that can achieve higher total asset turnover can reduce its total investment in assets, thus requiring less capital; if this condition results in lower total owners' equity, then return on equity is enhanced. A capital structure employing higher debt leverage results in higher return on equity. Also, a company that can improve its return on sales without changing total asset turnover or capital structure earns higher returns on equity.

These interrelationships or linkages are expressed by the product of three ratios:

$$\text{Return on equity} = \frac{\text{net income}}{\text{total sales}} \times \frac{\text{total sales}}{\text{total assets}} \times \frac{\text{total assets}}{\text{total equity}}$$

The first ratio is return on sales (ROS); the second is total asset turnover; and the third is a debt-leverage ratio. (Since the difference between the numerator and denominator of this third ratio equals total liabilities, the higher this ratio, the greater the level of debt, and therefore the higher the company's debt leverage.) This entire expression must be true, since by the rules of algebra total sales and total assets cancel out of the equation and the ratio of net income to total equity—the definition of return on equity (ROE)—remains.

Focus on this expression for two reasons: (1) return on equity is the fundamental measure of how well the company earns on the shareholders' funds, and (2) the three individual ratios, or fractions, suggest three distinct approaches for improving return on equity. This second point deserves further elaboration.

The first fraction indicates that ROE is improved if ROS increases, that is, if the company earns more profit per dollar of sales. The second fraction focuses on asset management: if the company achieves the same sales with lower asset investment, the right-hand side of the balance sheet equation is reduced (i.e., less debt and equity capital is required); this phenomenon also improves ROE. Finally, if the company substitutes debt for equity in its capital structure—that is, if it takes on greater debt leverage—ROE is increased. (Remember, however, that this last action also increases the company's risk of failure.)

Hewlett-Packard's ROE for 1993, based on year-end equity, is 13.8 percent. This value is the product of the three fractions just described:

$$\text{ROE} = \frac{1177}{20{,}317} \times \frac{20{,}317}{16{,}736} \times \frac{16{,}736}{8511}$$

$$= 5.79 \times 1.21 \times 1.97$$

$$= 13.8\%$$

Suppose HP could improve its net profitability in relationship to sales to 9 percent; this change would improve the company's ROE from 13.8 to 21.5 percent. Or, suppose the company could, by careful control of assets, improve its asset turnover from 1.21 to 1.40; if this reduction in asset investment were reflected by proportionate decreases in both debt and equity so that the company's debt leverage remained unchanged, ROE would be improved from 13.8 to 16.0 percent. Finally, if management had elected to assume greater financing risk by increasing debt leverage so that the ratio of assets to equity was 2.5 instead of 1.97, ROE would increase to 17.5 percent. And if all of these changes were undertaken simultaneously, ROE would grow to 31.5 percent. For a variety of reasons these changes may be impractical or undesirable, but the linkage equation focuses attention on the importance of

Return on sales
Asset utilization
Debt leverage

in the company's fundamental measure of profitability, return on equity.

FINANCIAL OR DEBT LEVERAGE

Debt leverage has been mentioned repeatedly in this chapter, and particularly the effect of debt leverage on ROE. This concept is so fundamental—and so widely applicable to both corporate and personal financial structures—that it warrants further illustration.

To recap: The greater the use of debt in the company's capital structure, the more leveraged is the company, a condition that in certain circumstances benefits the shareholders and in other circumstances leads to financial failure. If on a consistent basis a company is able to earn a return on its investments in excess of the interest rate it must pay on borrowed funds, this incremental return over the cost of the borrowed funds benefits the company's shareholders. Leverage has worked positively for the shareholders. On the other hand, if the company's poor operating performance renders it unable to comply with its borrowing agreements—that is, the company defaults on its loan agreements—the company may suffer financial ruin.

To illustrate both the benefits and risks of debt leverage, Figure 10-9 details the capital structure of two hypothetical companies, identical in all respects except that company R has minimized debt leverage by borrowing no long-term funds and company S has chosen to borrow one-half of its permanent capital. Company S is more highly leveraged than company R.

Figures 10-10 and 10-11 show the effects of leverage in periods of strong operating performance (periods of prosperity) and in down periods (periods of recession). In prosperous times, return on assets is 20 percent for both companies, well in excess of the interest rate paid by company S on borrowed funds. As a result, the more-leveraged company S produces higher shareholder returns (ROE of 21 versus 12.5 percent), even though its total dollar profit is lower than that of company R.

FIGURE 10-9   Alternative Capital Structures: Companies R and S

	Company R	Company S
Assets		
Current assets	$ 5,000,000	$ 5,000,000
All other assets	5,000,000	5,000,000
Total assets	$10,000,000	$10,000,000
Liabilities and Owner's Equity		
Current liabilities	$ 2,000,000	$ 2,000,000
Long-term debt (interest at 8%)	0	4,000,000
Owner's equity	8,000,000	4,000,000
Total liabilities + owners' equity	$10,000,000	$10,000,000
Ratios		
Current ratio	2.5	2.5
Total debt to owners' equity	25%	150%
Total debt to total assets	20%	60%
Long-term debt to total capitalization	0	50%

**FIGURE 10-10 Effects on Debt Leverage
in Periods of Prosperity**

	Company R	Company S
Sales	$22,000,000	$22,000,000
Total operating expenses	20,000,000	20,000,000
Operating profit	$ 2,000,000	$ 2,000,000
Interest expense	0	320,000
Profit before taxes	2,000,000	1,680,000
Income taxes (50% tax rate)	1,000,000	840,000
Net Income	$ 1,000,000	$ 840,000

Ratios

Return on assets	$\frac{2,000,000}{10,000,000}$	$\frac{2,000,000}{10,000,000}$
	= 20%	= 20%
Return on equity	$\frac{1,000,000}{8,000,000}$	$\frac{840,000}{4,000,000}$
	= 12.5%	= 21.0%

Thus, debt leverage has worked to the benefit of company S's shareholders in prosperous times.

In mild recessionary times illustrated at the top of Figure 10-11, both companies earn 5 percent return on assets, a rate below the cost of (interest rate on) borrowed funds, and thus company S's return on equity suffers by comparison with company R (2.25 versus 3.13 percent). Debt leverage has in this case worked to the detriment of company S's shareholders.

If both companies follow a policy of paying 50 percent of net income as cash dividends on common stock, company S's dividend payments will be affected favorably when conditions described in Figure 10-10 prevail and unfavorably under conditions described in Figure 10-11.

If the mild recession turns into a deep recession or depression, as illustrated in the lower part of Figure 10-11, both companies incur operating losses. This eventually is a good bit more serious for company S than for company R. Not only are its losses greater, but also Company S must make substantial interest payments on its borrowed funds each year, and these obligations are absolute. Failure to make these payments may result in company S's bankruptcy. Company R, facing no requirements for the payment of interest, is exposed to less risk of financial failure.

INVESTMENT RATIOS

Thus far this chapter has focused solely on ratios utilizing data from the company's financial statements. Investors, and therefore necessarily management as well, are also interested in the relationship between the company's financial results and the market price for its common stock.

**FIGURE 10-11   Effects of Debt Leverage
in Periods of Recession**

	Company R	Company S
Mild Recession		
Sales	$16,000,000	$16,000,000
Total operating expenses	15,500,000	15,500,000
Operating profit	500,000	500,000
Interest expense	0	320,000
Profit before taxes	500,000	180,000
Income taxes (50% tax rate)	250,000	90,000
Net income	$ 250,000	$ 90,000
Ratios		
Return on assets	$\dfrac{500,000}{10,000,000}$	$\dfrac{500,000}{10,000,000}$
	= 5%	= 5%
Return on equity	$\dfrac{250,000}{8,000,000}$	$\dfrac{90,000}{4,000,000}$
	= 3.13%	= 2.25%
Severe Recession		
Sales	$13,000,000	$13,000,000
Total operating expenses	13,500,000	13,500,000
Operating profit (loss)	(500,000)	(500,000)
Interest expense	0	320,000
Profit (loss) before taxes	$ (500,000)	$ (820,000)

Common stock market prices are determined by the actions of buyers and sellers. The shares of larger companies are traded on organized auction exchanges, such as the New York or London Stock Exchanges, while the shares of smaller companies trade in other formal and informal manners. In all cases, market prices reflect what potential investors are willing to pay and what present stockholders are willing to accept for shares. The market price bears no necessary relationship to the data that appear in the company's accounting records.

Market prices for common stocks are quoted in per-share amounts. To make comparisons between accounting data and market prices, certain accounting data need to be translated to a per-share basis.

Earnings per Share

Published financial statements provide data on **earnings per share (EPS)**—that is, net income attributable to each share of common stock.

$$\text{Earnings per share} = \frac{\text{net income}}{\text{number of shares of common stock}}$$

If the number of shares outstanding increased or decreased during the year, an average number of shares should be used in the denominator.

In 1993 HP earned net income of $1177 million and at year-end had outstanding 252,713,000 shares (see balance sheet, Figure 10-2).

$$\text{Earnings per share} = \frac{\$1,177,000,000}{252,713,000} = \$4.66$$

This figure appears at the bottom of the income statement in Figure 10-1.

This EPS calculation is somewhat more complex for companies that are under contract to issue additional common shares under certain circumstances; such contracts grant rights to certain investors or executives to purchase common shares at set prices. These rights, typically called stock options, warrants, or convertible securities, may permit purchases at per-share prices significantly below current market prices; large price differences are particularly prevalent when the company has prospered since the time these rights were granted. As investors or executives exercise these rights, the to-be-issued shares will participate in the future earnings and dividends of the company. Accountants have devised a rather complex method for calculating EPS, giving effect to these additional shares that will eventually be issued; the resulting EPS value is labeled **earnings per common and common equivalent share.** Because HP has some stock options and similar instruments outstanding, the company's earnings per share shown at the bottom of the income statement in Figure 10-1 ($4.65) is slightly lower than the calculation shown above.

Book Value per Share

A company's **book value per share** is simply shareholders' equity divided by the number of shares outstanding. For HP at the end of 1993:

$$\text{Book value per share} = \frac{\text{total shareholders' equity}}{\text{number of shares outstanding}}$$

$$= \frac{\$8,511,000,000}{252,713,000}$$

$$= \$33.68$$

A share's market price is frequently very different from its book value per share, either above or below; as with most well-regarded, successful companies, HP's stock trades well above its book value—it averaged over $70 per share in 1993. Thus, a comparison between market price and book value can be revealing.

Dividends per Share

Dividends are declared by a company's board of directors if, as, and when the board feels that such a payment is in the best interests of the company and its shareholders.

Dividends are declared in per-share amounts. In 1993 HP paid total dividends of 90 cents per share.

Payout Ratio

A company's **payout ratio,** the ratio of dividends per share to earnings per share, indicates the percentage of the firm's earnings being paid out as dividends. That portion not paid as dividends is, of course, retained and reinvested in the business. A company's **earnings retention ratio** is simply (100 percent − payout ratio). HP's payout ratio in 1993 was

$$\text{Payout ratio} = \frac{\text{dividends per share}}{\text{earnings per share}}$$

$$= \frac{0.90}{4.65} = 19.4\%$$

Hewlett-Packard's payout ratio is low; the company retains most of its earnings (80.6 percent) to finance its high rate of growth.

Price/Earnings Ratio

The **price/earnings (P/E) ratio,** or **earnings multiple** as it is sometimes called, is the ratio of market price per share to earnings per share. For HP's stock, which is traded on the New York Stock Exchange, the average of the highest and lowest trading prices throughout the 1993 fiscal year was $71.44. Using this average market price, the company's price/earnings ratio was

$$\text{Price/earnings ratio} = \frac{\text{market price}}{\text{earnings per share}}$$

$$= \frac{71.44}{4.65}$$

$$= 15.4$$

Market prices are not valid indicators of relative stock value among companies, since the number of shares currently outstanding is a function of (1) the prices at which the company sold shares in earlier years and (2) additional shares that it may have granted to shareholders (typically in the form of stock splits or stock dividends). Suppose companies A and B are identical in all respects except that A has twice as many shares outstanding as B. You would expect the market price of A to be one-half B's market price. Since the earnings-per-share of A would also be one-half that of B, the price/earnings ratios of the two companies would be identical. Thus, stocks can be compared in terms of price/earnings ratios, while they cannot be compared in terms of absolute market prices.

A high P/E ratio evidences that investors are willing to pay a high multiple of current earnings to participate as shareholders in the company's future. Investors are willing to bid up the price of the shares because they feel that the company's prospects for growth in sales, earnings, and dividends are above average.

Yield

A common stock's **yield** is the ratio of dividends per share and market price. HP's yield in 1993 was

$$\text{Yield} = \frac{\text{dividends per share}}{\text{market price per share}}$$

$$= \frac{\$0.90}{71.44} = 1.3\%$$

Hewlett-Packard's yield is low. Obviously, individuals invest in HP not with a view to current cash return but with a view to future company growth, growth that they believe will be reflected in higher market prices in the future. Note that part of the reason that HP's yield is low is that its market price is high.

INTERPRETING INVESTMENT RATIOS

Price/earnings ratios and yields do not determine market prices of common stocks; the reverse is the case: they are determined by and calculated from the market prices. Therefore one should not decide to buy or sell particular securities solely on the basis of these ratios. Investment decisions—purchases and sales—are based upon investors' expectations about the future. The world's stock exchanges are amazingly efficient in quickly reflecting in securities prices any changes in the collective expectations of investors.

Ratios assist investors in assessing the future and formulating their expectations but, since financial statements are historical documents, all ratios discussed here are historical. Because these ratios alone do not reliably predict the future, they should not be used mechanistically to make investment decisions.

A stock with a high P/E and a low yield will be a good investment if the company grows and prospers and its share price appreciates. On the other hand, it will prove to be a poor investment if investor expectations of growth and profits are not realized and its share price declines (or appreciates only modestly); in the latter case the P/E ratio will probably decline over time.

Conversely, a stock with a low P/E will be a good investment if (and only if) the company's future performance exceeds the modest investor expectations reflected in today's low P/E. Moreover an investor attracted by a current high yield will be disappointed if the company's future operations do not permit the present dividend rate to be maintained; if the dividend is reduced, the stock's yield may remain unchanged but only because the share price has fallen—an unfavorable outcome for the investor.

SUMMARY

The fundamental tool used to extract useful information from financial statements is ratio analysis. Comparisons between amounts appearing on the financial statements, rather than their absolute levels, provide insight into the two key questions: how sound is the company's financial position, and how well is the company performing in earning returns on the capital employed?

Many different ratios are in active use. Ratios that are highly relevant to certain industries or companies may be of marginal or no interest in other circumstances. The most common ratios, grouped into the four categories discussed in this chapter, are as follows:

Liquidity
  Current ratio
  Acid-test ratio (or Quick ratio)
Working capital utilization
  Accounts receivable collection period
  Inventory turnover
  Accounts payable payment period
  Working capital turnover
Capital structure
  Total debt to owners' equity
  Total debt to total assets
  Long-term debt to total capitalization
  Times interest earned
Profitability
  Percentage relationships on income statement
  Return on sales (ROS)
  Return on equity (ROE)
  Return on assets (ROA)

A number of caveats apply to the interpretation of ratios. Ratios that compare data from the income statement with data from the balance sheet (for example, the working-capital-utilization ratios) can be significantly distorted by seasonality and by high growth (or decline) rates. No absolute standards exist for ratios; indeed, with respect to most ratios one cannot even conclude that the higher the better, or the lower the better. Judgment is required to ascertain when a particular ratio is providing a danger signal or revealing a particular strength about a company.

Trends in ratios typically reveal additional information about a company, particularly trends in the liquidity and capital structure ratios. Comparisons between similar companies in like industries are also helpful. However, bear in mind that the optimum level of a ratio depends very much on the nature of the particular company's business, as well as, for example, on the company's future plans, management policies, and access to additional capital.

Some ratios discussed in this chapter are interrelated, or linked. Return on equity can be viewed as the product of (1) return on sales, (2) total asset turnover, and (3) leverage.

Debt leverage benefits shareholders when returns on investments exceed the cost of borrowed funds, but it also exposes the company to greater risk of failure when business turns down.

A company's financial performance can also be related to the company's stock market price, which is established in turn by the actions of potential buyers and sellers of the company's shares. Two important investment ratios are price/earnings (P/E) ratio and yield.

NEW TERMS

Accounts payable payment period.   The average number of days from receipt of merchandise or service to cash payment of the associated invoice. It is calculated as follows:

$$\frac{\text{Average accounts payable}}{\text{Average credit purchases per day}}$$

Accounts receivable collection period. The average number of days from invoice date to cash collection date. It is calculated as follows:

$$\frac{\text{Average accounts receivable}}{\text{Average sales per day}}$$

Acid-test ratio. The ratio of the sum of cash, cash equivalents (including marketable securities), and accounts receivable to current liabilities. An alternative name is quick ratio. The ratio measures liquidity.

Book value per share. The amount of shareholders' equity attributable to each share of common stock. It is calculated as follows:

$$\frac{\text{Total shareholders' equity}}{\text{Number of shares of common stock outstanding}}$$

Capital structure. The composition of the capital employed in the business.

Cash equivalents. Short-term investments that are highly marketable and can be quickly converted to cash.

Current ratio. The ratio of current assets to current liabilities. The ratio measures liquidity.

Debt leverage. The extent to which the company relies upon borrowed funds (debt) for financing. Companies with high debt leverage are exposed to greater financial risk but also enjoy the potential of greater returns to shareholders.

Earnings before interest and taxes (EBIT). A company's earnings before the payment of (1) interest on borrowed funds and (2) income taxes. EBIT is used to calculate the times-interest-earned ratio and the return-on-assets ratio.

Earnings multiple. Another name for price/earnings ratio.

Earnings per common and common equivalent share. A variant of earnings-per-share (EPS) that gives effect to the company's contractual obligations to issue additional shares of common stock to certain investors or executives.

Earnings per share (EPS). The net income attributable to each share of common stock. It is calculated as follows:

$$\frac{\text{Net income}}{\text{Average number of shares of common stock outstanding}}$$

Earnings retention ratio. The percentage of the company's earnings reinvested in the business and not paid out as dividends. It is calculated as follows:

$$\frac{(\text{Earnings per share}) - (\text{dividends per share})}{\text{Earnings per share}}$$

or 100 percent − payout ratio.

Fixed-asset turnover. A measure of the efficiency with which the company is using its net investment in fixed assets. It is calculated (in times per year) as follows:

$$\frac{\text{Sales}}{\text{Average net fixed assets}}$$

Inventory flow period. The average number of days from receipt of inventory to its shipment to customers. It is calculated as follows:

$$\frac{\text{Average inventory}}{\text{Average cost of goods sold per day}} \quad \text{or} \quad \frac{365}{\text{Inventory Turnover}}$$

Inventory turnover. The number of times per year that the firm's inventory turns over. It is calculated as follows:

$$\frac{\text{Cost of goods sold}}{\text{Average inventory}} \quad \text{or} \quad \frac{365}{\text{Inventory Flow Period}}$$

Liquidity. The extent to which a company has funds available to meet its near-term obligations as they come due. The most popular liquidity ratios are the current and quick (acid-test) ratios; the higher these ratios, the more liquid the company.

Long-term debt to total capitalization. A financial ratio that measures debt leverage. It is calculated as follows:

$$\frac{\text{Long-term debt}}{\text{Total capitalization}}$$

Marketable securities. Those investment securities for which a ready market exists. U.S. Treasury securities and certain other interest-bearing short-term investments are marketable securities that are cash equivalents.

Payout ratio. The ratio of dividends per share to earnings per share. This ratio indicates the percentage of the company's earnings paid out in dividends.

Price/earnings (P/E) ratio: The ratio of market price per share to earnings per share. This ratio is also referred to as the earnings multiple that investors are willing to pay for the company's common shares.

Quick ratio. An alternative name for the acid-test ratio.

Return on assets (ROA). A measure of the company's return on investment that is independent of the company's capital structure. It is calculated as follows:

$$\frac{\text{Earnings before interest and taxes}}{\text{Average total assets}}$$

Return on equity (ROE). A measure of the company's return on shareholders' investment. It is calculated as follows:

$$\frac{\text{Net income}}{\text{Average shareholders' equity}}$$

Return on sales (ROS). A measure of the company's rate of profitability on sales. It is calculated as follows:

$$\frac{\text{Net income}}{\text{Total sales}}$$

Times interest earned. A financial ratio that measures a company's ability to meet its interest payment obligations. It is calculated as follows:

$$\frac{\text{Earnings before interest and taxes}}{\text{Annual interest expense}}$$

Total-asset turnover. An assessment of the efficiency with which the company is using its total investment in assets. It is calculated (in times per year) as follows:

$$\frac{\text{Sales}}{\text{Average total assets}}$$

Total capitalization. The total of permanent sources of capital within the business; it is nominally equal to long-term debt plus total shareholders' equity.

Total debt to owners' equity. A financial ratio that measures debt leverage. It is calculated as follows:

$$\frac{\text{Current liabilities} + \text{long-term debt}}{\text{Total shareholders' equity}}$$

Total debt to total assets. A financial ratio that measures debt leverage. It is calculated as follows:

$$\frac{\text{Current liabilities} + \text{long-term debt}}{\text{Total assets}}$$

Working capital turnover. A measure of the efficiency with which the company is using its net investment in current assets less current liabilities. It is calculated (in times per year) as follows:

$$\frac{\text{Sales}}{\text{Average working capital}}$$

Yield. The ratio of dividends-per-share to market price per share.

DISCUSSION QUESTIONS

10.1 What are the primary categories of ratios?

10.2 Among the most common ratios, which ratios require data from both the income statement and the balance sheet?

10.3 What is the essential difference between the Current Ratio and the Acid Test (or Quick) ratio?

10.4 In calculating the Accounts Receivable Collection Period, under what conditions is it advisable to use the average accounts receivable rather than the year-end accounts receivable balance?

10.5 Both the Return on Assets and the Return on Equity ratios provide a view of the returns a company earns on its investments. What are the essential differences between these two ratios?

10.6 Does a company's current liabilities contain all the cash obligations of the company for the next 12 months? Explain your answer and its relevance to the liquidity ratios discussed in this chapter.

10.7 Why is the Accounts Payable Payment Period a difficult ratio to calculate, particularly for those financial analysts external to the company?

10.8 What factors should a corporation consider in deciding what its Payout Ratio should be?

10.9 Explain the difference between Yield and Price-Earnings Ratio for a corporation's common stock.

10.10 Explain two differences in circumstances that might cause Company A to choose higher debt leverage than Company B.

10.11 Is the Current Ratio a liquidity ratio, a leverage ratio, neither, or both? Explain your answer.

10.12 Are investors in common stocks more attracted to stocks with high price-earnings ratios or to those with low price-earnings ratios? Explain your answer.

10.13 Are investors in common stocks more attracted to stocks with high yield or to those with low yield? Explain your answer.

10.14 In evaluating a company's Return on Equity, why is it also necessary to consider that company's debt leverage?

10.15 Identify an industry where companies are likely to have relatively
   (a) High debt leverage
   (b) High inventory turnover
   (c) High current ratios
   (d) High asset turnover

Explain your answers by identifying the characteristic(s) of the industry that affect the particular ratio.

10.16 Would you expect a high-technology company to have a higher or lower gross margin than a company competing in an industry where technology leadership is less critical? Explain.

10.17 Define the term Total Capitalization.

10.18 In general would you expect companies operating in an industry requiring high asset investments (and thus low asset turnover ratios) to have higher or lower operating margins than the average for all companies? Explain your answer.

10.19 Explain the circumstances that might lead to
   (a) Company M having a current ratio judged to be too high.
   (b) Company N having an accounts receivable collection period judged to be too low.
   (c) Company O having a debt/equity ratio judged to be too low.
   (d) Company P having a yield judged to be too high.

10.20 If a company could get its customers to make large down payments (advance payments) with their orders, would the company thereby improve its Current Ratio? Under what circumstances?

10.21 Explain why price/earnings (P/E) ratios are a better measure of the relative value of common stock securities than are the absolute prices of the securities.

10.22 What effect does the action of declaring and paying cash dividends on common stock have on the current ratio and the total debt to owners' equity ratio of the company?

10.23 If the ratio of net income to total assets for a company is approximately the same as its return on equity, what can you conclude about the composition of the company's balance sheet?

10.24 As you review the trend of ratios for a company, would you conclude that the riskiness of the company is increasing or decreasing if you observed that

   (a) the current ratio is increasing?

   (b) the inventory flow period (in days) is increasing?

   (c) the debt/equity ratio is increasing?

   (d) the payout ratio is increasing?

10.25 If the Alvarez Corporation's board of directors votes a 2-for-1 stock split, each shareholder will receive one additional share for each share then owned.

   (a) What effect would you expect this action to have on the market price of the company's common stock?

   (b) What accounting entries would you make to reflect this action?

   (c) What effect would you expect this action to have on the P/E ratio of the company's common stock?

PROBLEMS

10.1 If a company has a ratio of net income to total assets of 10 percent and a total debt to equity ratio of 1.0, what is the company's return on equity?

10.2 If a company has an ROS (return on sales) of 5 percent, a total asset turnover of 1.2 and a total debt to equity ratio of 1.0, what is the company's return on equity?

10.3 If a company's common stock has a P/E (price/earnings ratio) of 15 and a yield of 4 percent, what is the company's (dividend) payout ratio?

10.4 The Wong Corporation achieved sales of $5.3 million during 1995 and had an accounts receivable balance at the end of 1995 of $2.1 million. If that accounts receivable balance grew by 20 percent during the course of the year, what was Wong Corporation's average accounts receivable collection period for 1995?

10.5   If a company's total debt to equity ratio is 1.3, its long-term debt to total capitalization ratio is 1.0, and its total assets are $13.7 million, what is the value of the company's owners' equity?

10.6   If a company has a current ratio of 1.6, no long-term liabilities, a total debt to equity ratio of 1.0, and owners' equity of $5.1 million, what is the value of the company noncurrent assets?

10.7   A financial analyst for the Aquilar Company has available the following information for fiscal year 1994:

> Pretax return on assets: 10 percent
> Total debt to total assets: 65 percent
> Accounts receivable collection period: 65 days
> Pretax return on sales: 15 percent
> Total assets: $3.6 million
> Working capital: $800,000

Determine:
(a) Accounts receivable balance (in dollars).
(b) Pretax return on shareholders' equity.
(c) Current ratio, if current assets equal noncurrent assets.
(d) Long-term debt (in dollars).

10.8   Given the following information for the Li and Higgins Corporation, prepare an income statement for the year in as much detail as possible.

> Times interest earned: 7 times
> Return on owners equity: 18 percent
> Average accounts receivable collection period: 50 days
> Average inventory turnover: 4 times
> Total accounts receivable (average): $0.8 million
> Total inventory (average): $0.9 million
> Total average debt (assume interest rate of 8 percent): $1.5 million
> Total owners' equity: $1.8 million

10.9   Construct a balance sheet for the Linelli Corporation as of December 31, 1995 in as much detail as possible, utilizing the following information. Make estimates as required, and state any assumptions you make.

> Current ratio: 3.2
> Acid-test ratio: 2.0
> Accounts receivable collection period (year-end A/R): 55 days

Return on equity: 17.6 percent

Yield on common stock: 4 percent

Total debt to total equity ratio: 1.2

Net (after-tax) income to total sales: 10 percent

Net (after-tax) income to total assets: 8 percent

Sales for the year ended December 31, 1995: $24.0 million

Cash (including marketable securities at 12/31/95): $1.4 million

10.10 The condensed, audited financial statements for the fiscal year ended June 30, 1995 for the Marvin Machinery Corporation are as follows (in $ thousands):

Balance Sheet, June 30, 1995

Assets	
Cash	$ 16,400
Accounts receivable, net	25,590
Inventory, net	36,930
Other current assets	16,110
Total current assets	95,030
Fixed assets, net	48,580
Total assets	$143,610
Liabilities and Owner's equity	
Accounts payable	$ 21,370
Bank loan payable (interest at 8 percent)	15,000
Other current liabilities	21,690
Total current liabilities	58,060
Long-term debt (interest at 10 percent)	20,000
Capital stock	12,000
Retained earnings	53,550
Total liabilities & owners' equity)	$143,610

Income Statement, year ended June 30, 1995

Sales	$163,700
Cost of goods sold	96,610
Gross margin	67,090
Operating expenses	38,220
Operating profit	28,870
less: Interest expense	3,810
Profit before taxes	25,060
less: Income taxes	9,770
Net income	$ 15,290

Calculate the following ratios:

(a) Times interest earned

(b) Accounts receivable collection period (year-end)

(c) Inventory flow period (year-end)

(d) Current and acid-test ratios

(e) ROA (return on assets)

(f) ROS (return on sales)

(g) ROE (return on equity)

(h) Long-term debt to total capitalization

(i) Total asset turnover

(j) Effective income tax rate

10.11 Refer to the financial statements for the Marvin Machinery Company shown in problem 10.10 above. The company belongs to an industry association that collects financial information from its members and provides to its members average financial ratios by industry segment. The executives at Marvin Machinery Company have received the following industry data for 1995:

Ratio	Industry Average
Current ratio	1.85
Inventory turnover	3.6 times per year
Accounts receivable	
collection period	63 days
Total asset turnover	1.15
Total debt ÷ total assets	61 percent
Times interest earned	4.7 times
Return on sales	6.6 percent
Return on equity	16.3 percent

Write a brief report to the company's managers comparing Marvin to the industry in terms of both 1995 operating performance and year-end financial position.

10.12 Refer to the financial statements for the Marvin Machinery Company shown in problem 10.10 above. Answer the following questions.

(a) If the company's retained earnings were $44,930 at June 30, 1994, estimate the amount of dividends the company paid to its shareholders in fiscal year 1995.

(b) On balance, did Marvin assume additional interest-bearing debt or repay some of that debt in fiscal year 1995? How can you tell?

(c) If Marvin had just prior to year-end used $10,000 of its cash balance to pay down its bank loan, how would that action have affected its

    (i)   Current ratio?

    (ii)   Acid-test ratio?

(d) If the P/E ratio of the company's common stock is 18, what is the ratio of its total market value to its book value?

(e) If the company at the beginning of the fiscal year had sold $10,000 of additional common stock and used the proceeds to pay down its long-term debt, what would be the value of the following ratios at June 30, 1995?

    (i)   ROS

    (ii)   ROE

    (iii)   Long-term debt to total capitalization

(f) If in the course of the year-end audit inventory valued at $5,000 had been determined to be obsolete and had been "written off," how much would this action have changed

    (i)   The company's net income for fiscal 1995?

    (ii)   The company's inventory turnover at June 30, 1995?

    (iii)   The company's current ratio at June 30, 1995?

(g) If the company had switched from the cost value to the market value method of valuing its fixed assets, its fixed asset value at June 30, 1995 would have been $12,000 higher and its accumulated depreciation would have been $4,000 higher. What would be the effect of this switch on the company's

    (i)   Working capital at June 30, 1995?

    (ii)   Ratio of total debt to total equity at June 30, 1995?

    (iii)   Total asset turnover for fiscal year 1995?

____11
CASH FLOW STATEMENT

The first 10 chapters focus on the two principal statements produced by a company's financial accounting system: the income statement and the balance sheet. A third statement, called the **cash flow statement,** is a requirement in all annual reports of publicly owned companies. It is audited just as are the income statement and balance sheet. The official name for the statement is *statement of cash flows*. Former names, and colloquial but descriptive labels, are *funds flow statement, statement of changes in financial position, sources and uses of funds* and *where got, where gone*. These names suggest the purpose of the statement: to explain the source of cash that was used to invest in new assets of the business or to repay the obligations of the business.

The cash flow statement, like the income statement, relates to a specified time period; but unlike the income statement, it focuses only on events that affect cash. Cash is critical to every operation, the life blood of business. Running out of cash—cash insolvency—is a crisis, and often the fatal blow for a failing business. While cash insolvency is most frequently precipitated by persistently unprofitable operations, a profitable, growing business can also run out of cash simply because it pays out more cash than it receives. Such a cash crisis can lead to business failure in spite of strong signs of vigor and growth, particularly within the income statement. Conversely, a sick, declining business may withstand years of unprofitable operations if, through a variety of actions, it maintains an adequate cash flow.

WHY A CASH FLOW STATEMENT?

Why is a third statement necessary? Since the income statement and the balance sheet contain all of the balances from the general ledger, why are they not sufficient for both internal management and external audiences?

Chapter 4 distinguishes between cash-basis and accrual-basis accounting and emphasizes the importance of the accrual basis for companies that sell goods and purchase supplies on credit, and own substantial assets. The accrual method of accounting provides essential information on operating performance and financial condition. At the same time, it obscures information regarding cash flow. Think of the cash flow statement as a recasting or translation of the accrual basis statements to a cash basis.

If cash-basis statements are so useful, why has this book emphasized for 10 chapters the importance of accrual statements? The point is that both are useful. If you want to assess current profitability of the business, the accrual-basis income statement is essential. If you want to assess what the company owns and owes, the accrual-based balance sheet provides just that information. What these accrual-based statements do not provide is a good view of the flow of cash in and out of the business.

The cash flow statement summarizes the primary sources of cash—typically transactions with customers and various external financing sources—and the primary uses of funds—typically investments in working capital and fixed assets, debt repayment, and dividend payments. It helps evaluate such questions as: how important to the company is external financing? What portion of the company's cash needs (uses) are derived from internal rather than external sources? Are the company's needs (uses) dominated by investments in working capital or fixed assets, or payments to creditors or shareholders? Did the company experience unusual cash needs during the year? And, were extraordinary cash sources tapped during the year?

SOURCES OF CASH

Where does a company obtain its cash? Our early discussion of the balance sheet and the fundamental accounting equation emphasized that the right side of the accounting equation defines where financial resources are obtained to invest in the assets shown on the left side. Two important sources are creditors and investors in newly issued common stock of the company. Thus, if the bank lends your company additional money or a trade supplier extends new credit, the resulting bank loan or account payable is a source of investable funds in the period when the credit is extended. The sale of new shares of the company's securities during the accounting period is another source, one represented by an increase in the invested capital account, part of owner's equity.

Of course, customers also provide cash. Little of that cash, however, "sticks" with the company since most of it must be quickly paid out to employees (as salaries) and to trade suppliers for goods and services. How much does stick? As a first approximation, it is the cash from customers that is retained by the business—the amount of profit earned, the difference between revenue and expense. But this is only an approximation: not all revenue brings immediate cash receipts since some cash may have been received as a down payment and some may not be due for several months; and not all expenses consume cash, for example, depreciation and amortization.

Summarizing, then, the primary sources of cash in any period are (1) increases in liabilities during the period; (2) increases in invested capital during the period; and (3) profits for the period. Note that both sources (2) and (3) increase owners' equity. So, again as a first approximation, any increase in a liabilities or owners' equity account in the general ledger represents a source of investable funds.

What other sources of cash might a company tap? Suppose it sold assets or in some other way decreased its asset investments—the left side of the accounting equation? These decreases also represent sources of cash. For example, if the company sells a truck, a piece of real estate, or some other fixed asset it owns, cash is realized. Another important example: suppose you are able, through careful asset management, to reduce your investment in inventory by increasing inventory turnover, or to reduce accounts receivable balances by persuading customers to pay more quickly (reducing the collection period). You realize cash to the extent (1) accounts receivable balances are reduced by receiving more cash from customers than you extend in new credit; or (2) inventory is reduced by shipping more from inventory than you replenish. Thus, the definition of sources must be expanded to include both increases in liabilities and owners' equity, and decreases in assets.

USES OF CASH

What are uses of cash? The possible uses now should be obvious. Just as an increase in a liability is a source, so an increase in an asset is a use, whether the increase occurs in the cash account, or in accounts receivable, or inventory, or fixed assets.

Is a decrease in a liability a use of cash? Of course. If during a period you repay a bank loan, or reduce your accounts payable by paying vendors more than the amount of new credit they extend to you, liability balances are reduced. Cash is used to effect this reduction. (Incidentally, a loan might also be repaid by issuing to the creditor new shares of common stock; such a transaction is equivalent to selling stock to the creditor for cash and immediately using the cash to pay the loan.)

Recall that to the extent revenue exceeds expenses, the company earns a profit and achieves a source of cash equal to the profit. To the extent that expenses exceed revenue, the company incurs a loss and that loss consumes cash. Are there other ways in which owners' equity might be reduced, thus consuming funds? Two such events occur, one frequently and the other infrequently. Cash dividend payments—a frequent occurrence in successful companies—consumes cash; the cash is paid out to shareholders and the owners' equity is reduced correspondingly. The infrequent transaction that also reduces owners' equity is the repurchase of the company's outstanding equity securities. If a company purchases its own stock from one or more shareholders, cash flows out of the company to the selling shareholders and owners' equity is reduced by that amount.

In summary, then, a use of cash is created by an increase in an asset account or decrease in a liability or owners' equity account. It is also obvious, but worth repeating, that for each period, sources must equal uses. Otherwise the fundamental accounting equation—assets equal liabilities plus owners' equity—will not be satisfied.

ANOTHER VIEW OF THE CASH FLOW STATEMENT

Thus far, the cash flow statement appears to be principally a refinement of the balance sheet. Now view it for a moment as a refinement of the income statement.

This view places profit as the primary source of cash, the excess of customer revenues over expenses of employees' salaries and goods and services received from suppliers. As a company grows, it may need to supplement this basic cash source through external, permanent financing, either borrowing long-term or selling additional equity securities. These sources do not appear on the income statement, and thus they must be considered separately. And we have seen that, as a company grows and sales increase, it typically needs to invest in additional long-term assets, principally equipment and facilities; these periodic asset investments are not reflected in the income statement when the cash is expended, that is, when they are acquired, although of course over time they lead to depreciation expenses. So, again, a use of cash must be considered separately: the cost of new long-term assets (less any associated depreciation expense for the current period). Finally, recall that debt repayment or the repurchase of equity securities uses cash, and the sale of fixed assets generates cash; these sources and uses must also be considered separately.

This income-statement view of cash flow has thus far ignored working capital: current assets and current liabilities. Working capital can be ignored if—but only if—(1) all revenues are received immediately in cash and all expenses are paid immediately in cash; or (2) the company's accounts receivable, inventory, and accounts payable balances are unchanged for the accounting period.

While either of these sets of conditions results in unchanged working capital, neither is met frequently in industry. Most buying and selling transactions are for credit, not immediate cash. Companies grow, and sometimes shrink; customers lag payments or accelerate them; inventory turns over more rapidly or accumulates; payments to vendors are stretched or brought more current; expenses are prepaid, or accrued and postpaid; and short-term borrowing is incurred and repaid. Cash balances fluctuate to compensate for all of these timing differences.

Note that as a company grows it invests cash in increased accounts receivable and inventory—a use of cash; this use is typically partially offset by increased balances in current liability accounts, particularly accounts payable—a source of cash. The net use of cash is the increase in working capital.

In practice, these working-capital fluctuations are important and are just the kind of dynamic change that is better revealed by a cash flow statement than by either the income statement or the balance sheet. Thus, our discussion comes full circle to the earlier view of the cash flow statement: the primary sources are profit earned, liabilities increased, or new equity securities sold; the primary uses are increases in assets, decreases in liabilities, and payments of cash dividends.

EXAMPLE: MEASUREX CORPORATION'S CASH FLOW

Before refining these definitions, let's apply these first approximation definitions to Measurex Corporation. The income statements and balance sheets for this company for the years 1992 and 1993 appear in Figures 11-1 and 11-2. Figure 11-3 shows the first-step cash flow statement, simply the difference between the balance sheet data at the end of the two successive years, 1992 and 1993. Obviously the same general ledger accounts are used here as in the balance sheets, and thus a cash flow statement simply recasts the data from the general ledger to provide useful additional information to managers and other readers.

Figure 11-3, then, contains a simple cash flow statement for Measurex Corporation for a single year, 1993. Cash flow statements, like income statements, can be constructed for longer or shorter periods—a month, a quarter, two years. Like an income statement, a cash flow statement, to be meaningful, must indicate the period over which the flows are analyzed.

What does Figure 11-3 reveal about Measurex in 1993?

The company neither grew nor shrank, as measured by both revenues and total assets. It returned to profitability (operating profits were negative in 1992), yet shareholders' equity declined by $6.6 million, or 3 percent; the company paid dividends and repurchased its common stock. Modest investments in receivables, inventories, and contracts receivable (receivables due more than one year in the future) are offset by the sale of marketable securities and by reduction in property, plant and equipment and service parts, presumably as a result of depreciation. Additional long-term borrowing (note both the current portion and the long-term portion) totaled over $20 million, offset by reductions in accrued expenses and deferred income taxes. In sum, the primary sources were decreases in marketable securities investments and increases in long-term borrowing, while the primary uses were decreases in liabilities—accrued expenses and deferred taxes—increases in contracts receivables, and modest increases in current assets.

Figure 11-3 is, in fact, too simple to reveal the complexity of events—operational, financing and investing—affecting cash flows and balances at Measurex in 1993. These events can be separated, and are in the more formal statement of cash flows, into three categories:

Cash flows from operating activities,
Cash flows from investing activities, and
Cash flows from financing activities.

SOME REFINEMENTS

A bit more work can yield a cash flow statement that is far more useful. For example, although you know that retained earnings decreased a bit at Measurex in 1993, this number, $0.9 million, is really the net of a source (net income) and a use

FIGURE 11-1   Measurex Corporation

MEASUREX | Consolidated Balance Sheets

November 28, 1993 and November 29, 1992 (Dollar amounts in thousands except per share data)

	1993	1992
ASSETS		
Current assets:		
Cash and cash equivalents	$ 76,040	$ 74,368
Marketable securities and short-term investments	35,371	40,237
Accounts receivable	55,126	53,886
Inventories	35,697	34,790
Prepaid and other	11,473	14,809
Total current assets	213,707	218,090
Contracts receivable	26,651	21,793
Service parts, net	3,178	5,699
Property, plant and equipment, net	53,161	55,493
Other assets	21,619	21,809
Total assets	$318,316	$322,884
LIABILITIES AND SHAREHOLDERS' EQUITY		
Current liabilities:		
Current portion of long-term debt	$ 4,516	$ 49
Accounts payable	6,732	5,816
Accrued expenses	62,594	77,189
Income taxes payable	2,145	1,731
Total current liabilities	75,987	84,785
Long-term debt	16,783	842
Deferred income taxes	13,682	18,804
Commitments and contingencies		
Shareholders' equity:		
Preferred stock, $.01 par value; authorized: 10,000,000 shares; issued and outstanding; none		
Common stock, $.01 par value; authorized: 50,000,000 shares; outstanding 1993 – 19,036,948 shares, 1992 – 19,036,948 shares	190	190
Additional capital	75,202	75,181
Retained earnings	167,211	168,098
Cumulative translation adjustments	(5,707)	(2,019)
Less: Treasury stock at cost: 1993 – 1,192,726 shares, 1992 - 1,009,229 shares	(25,032)	(22,997)
Total shareholders' equity	211,864	218,453
Total liabilities and shareholders' equity	$318,316	$322,884

The accompanying notes are an integral part of the financial statements.

FIGURE 11-2   Measurex Corporation

MEASUREX	Consolidated Statements of Income			
		1993	1992	1991
	Three years ended November 28, 1993 (Dollar amounts in thousands except per share data)			
REVENUES	Systems	$152,839	$148,367	$148,249
	Service and other	101,158	104,220	105,730
	Total revenues	253,997	252,587	253,979
OPERATING COSTS AND EXPENSES	Systems	99,728	99,244	93,715
	Service and other	64,501	67,814	72,418
	Product development	21,146	20,612	22,999
	Selling and administrative	61,122	63,695	61,600
	Restructuring charges	–	8,974	11,695
	Total operating costs and expenses	246,497	260,339	262,427
	Earnings (loss) from operations	7,500	(7,752)	(8,448)
OTHER INCOME (EXPENSE)	Interest expense	(948)	(810)	(834)
	Interest income and other	6,127	7,831	9,801
	Gain on sale of technology and assets	–	2,409	–
	Total other income, net	5,179	9,430	8,967
	Income before income taxes and extraordinary credit	12,679	1,678	519
	Provision for income taxes	4,464	964	130
	Income before extraordinary credit	8,215	714	389
	Extraordinary credit from utilization of tax loss carryforwards	–	911	–
	Net income	$ 8,215	$ 1,625	$ 389
	Net income per share:			
	Income before extraordinary credit	$ .46	$ .04	$ .02
	Extraordinary credit	–	.05	–
	Net income per share	$ .46	$ .09	$ .02
	Dividends per share	$ .44	$ .44	$ .44
	Average number of common and common equivalent shares (thousands)	18,051	18,296	18,213

The accompanying notes are an integral part of the financial statements.

(dividends paid). Separating these provides more information. Also, Figure 11-3 lists as a source the net decrease in investment in property, plant, and equipment. This net figure is the difference between new investment in fixed assets during the year and additions to the accumulated depreciation account. Again, a separation can better inform readers of Measurex's financial statements. Moreover, it acknowledges that depreciation expense is simply an allocation of a portion of a past expenditure; it does not consume cash as do most other expenses.

Thus, important refinements to the cash flow statement shown in Figure 11-3 are (1) decompose the change in retained earnings into its two primary elements: profits earned and cash dividends paid; (2) recognize that **noncash expenses** do not consume cash, and thus the profit for the period typically understates the cash flow generated from transactions with customers, suppliers, and employees; and (3) factor the change in fixed assets into its three primary elements: acquisition of new fixed assets, disposition of old fixed assets, and additions to the allowance for depreciation.

The data required to effect these refinements are not usually available on either the income statement or balance sheet. Dividends paid, since not an expense, do not appear on the income statement. Depreciation expense appears aggregated with other expenses, principally in the Cost of Goods Sold account, but in other expense

FIGURE 11-3   Simplified Cash Flow Statement, Measurex Corporation ($ millions)

	Balance Sheets as of November 30		1993 Cash Flow Statement	
	1993	1992	Sources	Uses
ASSETS				
Current assets				
Cash & cash equivalents	$ 76.0	$ 74.4		$ 1.6
Marketable securities and short-term investments	35.4	40.2	$ 4.8	
Accounts receivable	55.1	53.9		1.2
Inventories	35.7	34.8		0.9
Prepaid and other	11.5	14.8	3.3	
Total current assets	213.7	218.1	8.1	3.7
Contracts receivable	26.6	21.8		4.8
Service parts, net	3.2	5.7	2.5	
Property, plant & equipment, net	53.2	55.5	2.3	
Other assets	21.6	21.8	0.2	
	$318.3	$322.9	$13.1	$ 8.5
LIABILITIES AND SHAREHOLDERS' EQUITY				
Current liabilities				
Current portion of long-term debt	4.5	—	4.5	
Accounts payable	6.7	5.8	0.9	
Accrued expenses	62.6	77.2		14.6
Income taxes payable	2.2	1.8	0.4	
Total current liabilities	76.0	84.8	5.8	14.6
Long-term debt	16.8	0.8	16.0	
Deferred income taxes	13.7	18.8		5.1
Shareholders' equity				
Common stock	75.4	75.4	0	
Retained earnings	167.2	168.1		0.9
Cumulative translation adjustments*	(5.7)	(2.0)		3.7
Less: treasury stock	(25.0)	(23.0)		2.0
	211.9	218.5	0	6.6
	$318.3	$322.9	$21.8	$26.3

*Valuation adjustment of certain assets and liabilities denominated in foreign currencies.

categories as well. The same is true of other noncash expenses such as amortization of intangibles and provisions for doubtful accounts. These data are, of course, available in the general ledger and most, but probably not all, are typically included in the notes that accompany the published financial statements.

For Measurex in 1993 the data needed to incorporate these refinements into the simplified cash flow statement are

(1) Total dividends paid: $7.9 million.

(2) Total depreciation and amortization expense: $15 million. Notes to financial

statements explain the depreciation procedures used by the company (for example, the depreciation method, estimated useful life by class of asset, and amount of the depreciation expense). In addition to depreciating its fixed assets, Measurex depreciates its service parts inventory (a noncurrent asset) and amortizes its capitalized software.

(3) Other income statement items that did not affect cash were increases in the inventory reserve (a noncash expense), and currency translation gains and decreases in deferred income taxes (the latter two representing uses.)

One further word of explanation: The accepted format for cash flow statements nets the sources and uses to a single line item "Increases (decreases) in cash and cash equivalents."

Figure 11-4 shows Measurex's Consolidated Statement of Cash Flows (the formal name of the funds flow statement) in the conventional format (with cash outflows, uses of cash, shown in parentheses) and reveals a great deal. While the net change in cash (inflow of $1,672,000, or 2 percent of the opening balance) was minor, and operations were approximately break-even in a cash sense (a use of $136,000), during the year much occurred worthy of note.

From operating activities, noncash items were far more significant than net income in generating cash and virtually all of this cash (more than $21,000,000) was used to build working capital: about half of it in increases in receivables and inventory and the other half in reductions to current liabilities.

Measurex is a major investor in short-term and marketable securities, but decreased those investments by nearly $5 million (net purchases less matured securities) in 1993. These freed-up funds offset the quite modest investments in new plant ($8.3 million, just over half of the annual depreciation), the acquisition of a small subsidiary, and the capitalization of software ($1.7 million). If Measurex had sold a material value of fixed assets or tangible assets, these would have appeared as sources in this section of the cash flow statement.

In terms of financing, Measurex borrowed an additional $20 million on a long-term basis, paid dividends very nearly equal to its net income for the year, sold a modest amount of common stock to its employees, and purchased over $5 million of its own stock in the open market (stock that it did not retire but rather is holding in its treasury).

A final comment: the concept of depreciation (and other noncash expenses) as a source of cash may confuse you. Think of the Allowance for Depreciation accounts—here the contra accounts to fixed assets and to service parts, as both of these categories of long-term assets are depreciated—as a negative asset. This may help you see that an increase in this Allowance must be a source, since an increase in an asset is a use. Or, you may think of adding a kind of correction to the net income figure, correcting it from an accrual to a cash basis. Chapter 8 stressed that the Allowance for Depreciation is not a pool of cash; it is instead simply a valuation adjustment. But, because an addition to this Allowance (depreciation expense) reduces net income while not consuming cash, it is a source of cash.

FIGURE 11-4   Statement of Cash Flows, Measurex Corporation, for the Year Ending November 28, 1993 ($000)

Cash flow from operating activities:	
Net income	$ 8,215
Noncash items included in net income	
Depreciation and amortization	14,987
Deferred income taxes	(2,307)
Inventory reserves	3,473
Translation (gain) loss	(2,921)
Net (increase) decrease in:	
Accounts and contracts receivable	(7,420)
Inventories	(3,912)
Prepaid and other	273
Net increase (decrease) in:	
Accounts payable and accrued expenses	(11,814)
Income taxes payable	468
Other, net	822
Net cash provided (used) by operations	(136)
Cash flows from investing activities:	
Purchase of short-term investments and marketable securities, net	(40,310)
Maturities of short-term investments	45,176
Acquisition of property, plant and equipment	(8,329)
Acquisition of subsidiary, net of cash acquired	(1,668)
Capitalized software	(1,725)
Net cash used in investing	(6,856)
Cash flows from financing activities:	
Additions to long-term debt, net	19,780
Dividends	(7,886)
Stock issued under employee stock purchase and stock option plans	1,930
Payment for treasury stock	(5,160)
Net cash provided by investing	8,664
Net increase in cash and cash equivalents	1,672
Cash and cash equivalents at beginning of year	74,368
Cash and cash equivalents at end of year	$76,040

OTHER EXAMPLES

Cash flow statements particularly help in understanding financial condition and performance of companies that are expanding or contracting rapidly, or undergoing sharp changes in their financial structures. Here are two simplified examples.

Figure 11-5 shows the cash flow statement for Consolidated Industries, Inc., a large company undergoing substantial structural changes. First, note that earnings are quite modest in relationship both to total cash needs ($271 million) and to dividends paid (twice 1995 earnings). The sale of fixed assets is the largest source of cash, but the uses of cash are dominated by investment in new property, plant, and equipment; apparently, the company is redeploying its assets away from some activities and in favor of others. The source of cash from working capital reduction is explained either by improved asset management (all of cash, accounts receivables, inventories, and accounts payable declined) or, more likely, by a decline in the company's business activity in 1995. Why did Consolidated Industries have to incur $65 million more long-term debt? About one-third of this borrowing was used to repay short-term notes payable ($22 million), but the balance funded substantial investments in property, plant, and equipment; these investments in production facilities could not be funded by internal sources (earnings plus noncash expenses) of $68 million and the sale of other fixed assets. Obviously, two conditions revealed in this cash flow statement cannot persist for Consolidated Industries: dividend payments in excess of earnings, and increased long-term debt in a business that is apparently not growing.

Figure 11-6, the cash flow statement for Comptronics, Inc., presents quite a different picture. Comptronics, a much smaller company, is apparently growing. It pays no common stock dividends and has this year succeeded in selling $20 million

FIGURE 11-5   Cash Flow Statement, Consolidated Industries, Inc., for 1995

	$ Millions
Cash flows from operating activities	
Net earnings	$25
Adjustments for noncash expenses	
Depreciation and amortization	33
Other, net	10
Net (increase) decrease in:	
Accounts and notes receivable	53
Inventories	33
Net increase (decrease) in:	
Accounts payable and accrued liabilities	(42)
	112
Cash flows from investing activities	
Investments in property, plant and equipment	(221)
Sale of property, plant and equipment	109
	(112)
Cash flows from financing activities	
Increase in long-term debt	65
Increase (decrease) in notes payable	(22)
Dividends	(50)
	(7)
Increase (decrease) in cash and cash equivalents	($7)

FIGURE 11-6 Cash Flow Statement, Consolidated Industries, Inc., for 1991

	$ Millions
Cash flows from operating activities	
Net earnings	$6
Noncash expenses:	
Depreciation and amortization	3
Other, net	1
(Increase) decrease in:	
Accounts receivable	(11)
Inventories	(5)
Increase (decrease) in accounts payable and accrued liabilities	6
	0
Cash flows from investment activities	
Investment in property, plant, and equipment	(9)
Other, net	2
	(7)
Cash flows from financing activities	
Proceeds from sale of common stock	20
Repayment of long-term debt	(10)
	10
Increase (decrease) in cash and cash equivalents	$3

of additional common stock. The proceeds from this stock sale were used to repay $10 million of long-term debt and the balance, combined with internally generated cash, funded investments in new plant and equipment and in increased working capital necessitated by the company's growth. The cash inflow from operations (including noncash expenses) plus the increase in accounts payable just balanced the increases in accounts receivables and inventories. This cash flow statement reveals the kind of dynamic financing and investing typical of growth companies.

SUMMARY

The cash flow statement—formally called the Statement of Cash Flows—is a third financial statement that supplements the income statement and balance sheet. Recasting the income statement on a cash basis, the cash flow statement also incorporates the cash effect of financing and investment activities during the period. The primary sources of cash are typically internal operations, including noncash expenses, and external financing, while the primary uses of cash are investments in fixed assets and other long-term assets, payments of dividends, and repayment of debt. Both a company's own management and its external audiences, particularly investors and creditors, require knowledge of the company's cash flow position— all the more when the company is undergoing rapid change.

NEW TERMS

Cash flow statement (or statement of cash flows). The financial statement, supplementing the income statement and balance sheet, that details for a specified period the primary sources of cash (typically, operations and additional financing) and uses of cash (typically, investments in fixed assets and working capital, repayment of debt and payment of dividends).

Noncash expenses. Expenses included on the income statement, and thus in the determination of profit, that do not consume cash.

DISCUSSION QUESTIONS

11.1 What are two common, alternative names for the Cash Flow Statement?

11.2 For a company that operates its accounting system on a cash basis, rather than an accrual basis, is its income statement approximately equivalent to its cash flow statement?

11.3 Name two noncash expenses: expenditures that appear as expenses on the income statement but do not involve the use (outflow) of cash.

11.4 Name two expenditures that involve the outflow (use) of cash but do not appear on the income statement as expenses.

11.5 Name two inflows (sources) of cash that do not appear as revenue on the income statement.

11.6 Explain in simple terms why an increase in accounts receivable balances between two dates represents a use of cash during the interval, and why a decrease in inventory balances between two dates represents a source of cash during the interval.

11.7 What are the two primary external (coming from outside the corporation) sources of cash for a corporation?

11.8 Is an increase in the balance of deferred taxes a source or use of cash?

11.9 As a company expands, its working capital typically increases, thereby using cash. To balance that use of cash, what are the primary sources of cash for such a growing company?

11.10 What set of company circumstances would cause the executives of the company to focus more attention on the Cash Flow Statement than on the Income Statement of the company?

PROBLEMS

11.1 The Miranda Company acquired new fixed assets in 1994 valued at $133,000, retired no fixed assets, and showed an increase of $107,000 in net fixed assets on its year-end balance sheet. Show the detailed sources and uses of cash for the year as related to fixed assets.

11.2   The Josephson Corporation acquired new fixed assets in 1995 valued at $54,000, realized a $4000 gain on the sale of fixed assets (which had an original cost of $16,000 and a net book value at the time of sale of $7000), and showed an increase of $27,000 in net fixed assets on its year-end balance sheet. Show the detail of sources and uses of cash for the year as related to fixed assets.

11.3   The Madrid Mercantile Company sold $10 million of common stock in 1996, repurchased for $4 million stock that was owned by the estate of its late founder, incurred an after-tax loss of $1 million and paid $2 million in dividends. Show the detailed sources and uses of cash for the year as related to shareholders' equity. By how much did total shareholders' equity increase or decrease for the year?

11.4   The Bjorn Corporation's balance sheets at the end of the most recent two fiscal years are shown below. For fiscal year 1995 Bjorn recorded $2,300,000 in depreciation expense and paid dividends totaling $1,150,000. Construct a Cash Flow Statement in as much detail as possible.

Fiscal Years Ended Sept. 30

Balance Sheet	1995	1994
Assets	($000)	
Cash	$ 2,351	$ 2,498
Accounts receivable	14,610	12,106
Inventory	7,552	6,623
Other current assets	2,986	3,671
Total current assets	27,499	24,898
Fixed assets, at cost	26,411	22,541
less: Accumulated depreciation	(9,188)	(7,416)
Net fixed assets	17,223	15,125
Total Assets	$44,722	$40,023
Liabilities and Owners' Equity		
Accounts payable	$ 7,792	$ 6,183
Other current liabilities	10,060	9,113
Total current liabilities	17,852	15,296
Long-term debt	6,000	5,000
Capital stock	10,000	10,000
Retained earnings	10,870	9,727
Total liability and owners' equity	$44,722	$40,023

11.5   Fletcher Fiber Company's Cash Flow Statement for 1996 is shown below.

Cash flow from operations

Net income	$ 837
Depreciation	776
Increase in working capital	(522)
	1,091

Cash flow from investing

Investment in fixed assets	(1,732)
Disposition of fixed assets	102
	(1,630)

Cash flow from financing

Sale of common stock	1,200
Reduction in long-term debt	(400)
Dividends	(261)
	539
Net change in cash and cash equivalents	$ 0

Fletcher's 1995 year-end balance sheet revealed the following summary balances:

Working capital	$ 6,063
Fixed assets, net	8,911
	$14,974
Long-term liabilities	$ 4,200
Shareholders' equity	$10,774
	$14,974

Questions:

   (a) Did Fletcher's debt leverage increase or decrease in 1996? Explain your answer.

   (b) What is the value of Fletcher's net fixed assets at December 31, 1996?

   (c) What is Fletcher's Payout Ratio in 1996?

   (d) What is the value of Fletcher's shareholders' equity at December 31, 1996?

   (e) What evidence from the Cash Flow Statement indicates that Fletcher's sales volume grew in 1996 compared to 1995?

   (f) If Fletcher's current ratio at December 31, 1996 is 1.7, what is the value of its current assets at that date?

11.6 The Complete Cabinet Works' (a partnership) balance sheets at September 30, 1993 and 1994 are shown below in summary form. Construct a Cash Flow Statement for fiscal year 1994, assuming no change in cash invested by partners; one-half of net income paid out to the partners; no fixed assets sold; and $125,000 of new fixed assets acquired.

| | September 30 | |
	1994	1993
Current assets	$381,000	$406,000
Fixed assets, net	493,000	493,000
	$874,000	$899,000
Current liabilities	$266,000	$234,000
Long-term debt	90,000	180,000
Partnership capital	518,000	485,000
	$874,000	$899,000

___12
BUDGETING AND ANALYSIS OF PERFORMANCE

Every person and every organization operates to a plan, whether explicitly or implicitly. Well-managed enterprises operate to a documented, explicit financial plan: a **budget.** The best-managed operations—businesses, schools, governmental units, social organizations—also generate detailed reports to compare actual financial performance to their budgets. This chapter focuses on the budgeting process and on the role budgets can plan in analyzing performance.

Estimates of (or standards for) costs and expenses—manufacturing costs, selling, marketing, administration expenses, and so forth—provide a base or yardstick against which to compare actual expenditures. The process of setting these standards or benchmarks is called *budgeting*. Comparing actual financial results with budget expectations—budget analysis—highlights deviations from plan and can help signal appropriate corrective action.

MANAGERIAL ACCOUNTING

The use of accounting data to inform operating decisions is referred to as **managerial accounting,** the subject of the balance of this book. Since budgeting and budget analysis are key tools for operating managers, this first chapter on managerial accounting, and the next, focus on how operating plans, or budgets, are set and then on how they are used to ascertain whether operations are on plan or require remedial steps to return to plan. Chapter 14 introduces cost accounting, the process to develop detailed information on the cost of manufacturing a product or delivering a service. Chapters 15 through 17 then review the key techniques for analyzing these so-called production costs. Concluding the book, Chapter 18 guides you in selecting, compiling, and analyzing accounting data to make better operating decisions in such realms as pricing products or services, investing in new productive assets, and adding, deleting or redesigning products.

GUIDELINES FOR BUDGETING

One is tempted to dive right into the details of budgets and budgeting. How much should we spend on salaries in department X? How should salary levels be set? How much should we spend on advertising and promotion, and how should that relate to the company's present size or future growth? But the critical first step in budgeting is the same as for most complex tasks: establishing the objectives. If you don't know where you're trying to go, you can't plan how to get there!

Setting Objectives

In a profit-seeking enterprise, management typically has in mind some profit objective. The profit objective may be set in terms of return on equity or return on assets. Alternatively, it may be set in terms of profits of previous years—for example, increase profit 10 percent from last year, return to the record profitability of three years ago, or hold profit decline to only 15 percent in the coming recession.

Managements typically have other financial objectives as well; profit may not be the overriding one. The company may currently be geared more to revenue growth or to market-share improvements. For a fledgling company, the objective may be simply to break even this year, that is, avoid a loss. Or, financial objectives may be framed in light of commitments to repay $X to creditors or pay dividends to shareholders of $Y per share.

In a nonprofit organization, the objective on which the financial budget focuses is often simply to achieve equilibrium of cash inflow and cash expenditures, or to generate a specified surplus of inflow over outflow, or, for example, to increase revenue by 10 percent to permit an expansion of services, or to reduce expenditures by 7 percent in the face of declining membership. In recent years the budgeting struggle for certain national governments, including the United States, has been to limit government's operating deficit, the prospect of a balanced budget or surplus being so remote as to provide no realistic budgeting target.

The point is that you need to have in mind as you begin the budgeting process a set of target financial objectives. In turn, these are a distillation in financial terms of the myriad qualitative and quantitative objectives to which the organization is committed.

Budgeting: One Element of Planning

Chapter 1 emphasized that financial statements cannot provide a full and complete history. Much goes on in any operation that cannot be immediately reduced to monetary terms: personnel are hired or leave, stubborn technical problems are encountered or solved, the firm's reputation with customers is enhanced or eroded.

Financial statements are to history what budgets are to the future. Operating budgets simply state explicitly management's estimate of future income statements. Thus, just as financial statements do not completely record history, neither do budgets provide complete plans for the future. Budgeting is just one element of the planning process. Budgets describe only the monetary consequences of the plans.

Budgeting can neither precede detailed operational planning, nor follow it. Financial budgets don't dictate plans—although operating plans are often tempered by financial realities revealed by the budgets—nor should plans be finalized without a careful review of their budgetary implications. Thus, budgeting must be integrated into the planning process. Planning is iterative: Some planning must be completed to provide a basis for financial budgeting, but some replanning is typically required to adjust plans to budget constraints. Sometimes several rounds of replanning and rebudgeting are necessary before both operating plans and financial budgets become compatible with the organization's overall purposes, objectives, and available resources.

"Bottom Up" versus "Top Down"

Who sets the budget for the organization? How is an acceptable operating budget finally assembled? Just as one person cannot do all of the planning (except in the smallest of organizations), neither can one person establish budgets. Everyone responsible for developing and refining operating plans must also be party to developing and refining budgets.

Some top-level managers are inclined to impose detailed budgets and budgetary constraints on their organizations. Once established, they expect their subordinates to live within these budgets. At the same time, these top-level managers expect their subordinates to accept responsibility for their respective operating units, to make and revise plans, to be decisive, and to implement actions as required. These two views are incompatible. You cannot ask a manager at any level to accept responsibility for living within budgets that he or she had no hand in setting. Managers cannot be expected to take operating but not financial responsibility for their business segments. Therefore, an important budgeting guideline is that each manager should play a strong role in setting the budget for his or her operating segment. The budget of the entire organization is then built up from segment budgets. That is, the total budget is not established and then divided up among the operating segments. Just the reverse: The most useful budgets are developed from the bottom up rather than from the top down.

To illustrate, consider the process of developing the annual selling expense budget for the Reynolds Company, a manufacturer of specialty chemicals. The national sales manager, with offices at the Chicago headquarters, may be tempted to dictate to the regional sales managers budgets for both sales (or incoming orders) and for selling expenses for the regions for the coming year. Suppose you are the regional sales manager in Dallas, Texas. You are more knowledgeable than the national sales manager about the Texas market, about such matters as the relative positions of Reynolds and its competitors in the Dallas market; the need for additional training for the Dallas sales force; and the amount of travel, entertainment, and telephone expenses to be incurred by the Dallas office during the coming year. Moreover, the national sales manager undoubtedly wants to hold you, the Dallas regional manager, responsible for both sales and expense levels in the coming year. If so, you want to have a say in establishing sales and expenses targets for your region.

The nationwide sales and expenses budgets are, of course, the responsibility of the Chicago-based national sales manager. These budgets will be both more realistic and more useful if built up from the budgets established in and by each of the regions. Of course, you in Dallas must work with the national sales manager and others as you develop and refine your budget; while you are particularly knowledgeable about conditions in the Texas market and the Dallas office, others must provide you with planning information on new products, national sales promotions in the coming year, expected actions by competitors, and, most importantly, the company's overall objectives and financial constraints. The process, then, of establishing the Dallas regional budget is a joint one.

Most large organizations have a budget department within the financial function, a department headed by a person with a title such as Manager of Budgeting. While, unfortunately, too many managers of budgeting attempt to impose budgets on their organizations, the budgeting department's appropriate role is that of facilitator and consolidator: articulating budgeting guidelines that are consistent with the organization's goals, assisting individual managers at all levels to develop realistic budgets consistent with those guidelines, and assembling the organization's total budget from the segment budgets.

The Cornerstone: The Sales Forecast

The cornerstone of the budget is the forecast or budget of revenue for the coming period. In a profit-seeking company, the forecast of sales becomes the critical first step in the budgeting process. A nonprofit organization estimates revenue from dues, gifts, services, and all other sources. A governmental unit estimates tax revenues, fee revenues, and revenues from the sale of services.

Since most operations must incur expenses to generate revenue, and revenue provides the wherewithal to pay the expenses, neither the sales budget (or forecast) nor the expense budget can be set independently of the other. This situation leads to chicken-first/egg-first arguments. As the Dallas regional sales manager, you are reluctant to commit to a certain incoming order level for the coming year without a reciprocal expense budget commitment that determines the sales effort for the coming year. At the same time, the national sales manager is reluctant to commit to you permissible expense levels for the year without a reliable estimate from you of the region's sales.

But sales revenue is the place to start. The tentative sales forecast provides the basis for expense level guidelines. Necessarily, the first sales forecast must be considered tentative. Once the entire budget is compiled, Reynolds may discover that resources will be available to invest, for example, in opening several new sales offices or in launching a long-delayed new product; these investments may cause an upward revision in the tentative sales forecast. Or, Reynolds may discover that a decision to reduce promotional expenses and increase spending on research and development will make the tentative sales forecast difficult to achieve. In either case the tentative sales forecast needs to be modified, and in turn this revision may necessitate still another revision in the expense budgets. To repeat, budgeting is an iterative process.

Many companies develop both a sales target and a sales budget. The target, somewhat higher than the budget, represents a goal toward which the sales organization will strive, but one to which the company's management assigns, say, a 50 percent or lower probability of achieving. Management is unwilling to commit itself to expense levels based upon such a low-probability sales estimate. The lower sales budget—the sales forecast upon which the expense budget is based—is at a level that management is perhaps 80 percent confident can be met or exceeded. Such multilevel forecasting can be useful.

History as Prologue

The budgeting process relies heavily on historical financial data. Since an operating budget is simply an estimate of the income statement for a future period, past operating statements are obviously useful guides. Frequently, budget levels for the coming year are established simply by incrementing last year's actual expenditures up or down. In any case, a manager needs a detailed understanding of current expenditure levels as he or she considers appropriate budget levels for a future period. If you know that telephone expenses in the Dallas sales office have been running about $700 per month this year, you will consider factors that could affect this expense item next year: for example, telephone rates are expected to increase by 5 percent, one more salesperson will join the office early in the new year, or the staff now has fewer reasons to call the Chicago headquarters office. All factors considered, you may decide that an appropriate budget level for next year is about 7 percent above current levels, or about $750 per month.

This incrementing of historical expenses to set a budget has the unfortunate tendency to confirm present expenditure levels as appropriate and necessary. For example, you may not question whether your Dallas office really needs to spend $700 per month on telephones. Perhaps the sales force would be just as efficient with less use of the telephone, or, on the other hand, perhaps you should encourage greater use of the telephone to increase sales or decrease travel expenses. While the national sales manager may encourage you to ponder these questions, the inevitable tendency is to rely on present expense levels as the best indicator of what will be, or must be, spent in the future period.

A budgeting technique referred to as **zero-base budgeting** deemphasizes the use of historical data as the basis for budgeting. The technique, originally introduced in certain agencies of the U.S. federal government but now popular in the private sector as well, requires that each manager justify every dollar spent, not solely the budget increment. That is, the manager must justify from a zero base the need for each staff member and each expenditure for supplies, telephones, travel, maintenance, computer time, and so forth. Under zero-base budgeting you would need to build up the Dallas office telephone expense budget for the coming year by justifying the number of telephone lines coming into your office, the number of telephone sets, the number and duration of long-distance telephone calls, and so forth. The advantage of such a procedure is that you may thereby determine that, for example, a special leased line connecting the Dallas and Chicago offices would reduce long-distance telephone charges; or that the office could get along with fewer telephone sets since the salespersons spend most of their time traveling away from the office. Zero-base budgeting is time-consuming and often frustrating, but the benefits in terms of more efficient use of resources—reducing expenditures in some areas and increasing them with good effect in others—can far outweigh the costs. Even when pursued only informally, zero-base budgeting can lead you to some productive lines of inquiry.

Commitment

The effectiveness of budgets and the budgeting process varies widely among organizations. In some, budgeting is a meaningful planning step and budgets become working documents that are both useful and used. In others, budgeting is simply a required but perfunctory exercise that is accorded little time and less thought; the resulting budgets are filed away and seldom, if ever, referred to again. The difference in effectiveness is a function of the commitment made to the budgeting process, commitment not just by the manager of budgeting but by managers at all levels and particularly by senior managers.

If the head of the organization—president, chairman of the trustees, principal, or whoever—is serious about budgeting, the remainder of the management group will also take the process seriously. If the chief executive takes time to articulate meaningful objectives and budget guidelines, to review and analyze budget requests, to require rebudgeting until an acceptable overall budget is achieved, and to compare actual operating results to the budget, then lower levels of management will also devote the time required to develop, and redevelop, meaningful budgets and to use them in operating their departments.

On the other hand, where top management sees budgeting as a necessary evil—simply a translation of already agreed-upon plans to monetary terms, an activity for the clerical staff in the budgeting department—lower levels of management find little time for budgeting and pay no attention to budgets as they operate their departments.

Bottom-up budgeting requires the deep involvement of all management levels. Each manager must understand that organization-wide financial results depend upon each segment meeting budget, in terms of both revenue generation and expense control. Each manager negotiates his or her department budget with the next manager up the management hierarchy. Once agreed to, the budget becomes a commitment, a kind of contract, between the two individuals: the department manager commits to operate the department in conformance with the budget, thereby helping to assure on-budget results for the total company; and in turn, the supervisor commits resources to the department manager in accordance with the budget. Where budgeting is effective, these commitments are taken seriously.

Budgeting Nonfinancial Parameters

Recall that while budgeting is an integral part of the planning process, it is only a part. Plans contain much that cannot be reduced to financial terms. Just as managers rely on more than financial reports to monitor a company's operations, so also managers need, as part of budgeting, to estimate certain nonfinancial parameters.

For example, a detailed labor forecast or budget, expressed in number of people (perhaps by job classification) rather than wages and salaries, is a useful adjunct to financial budgeting. So also might be detailed estimates of the number of new customers, square feet of warehouse required, process yield, average price discounts allowed, average markup, number of sales calls per day per salesperson, percentage of late deliveries, employee turnover rate, and rate of absenteeism. Indeed, to do a competent and realistic job of financial budgeting requires the budgeting of these and many other operating parameters.

Frequency of Revision

Most organizations undertake a major budgeting exercise just prior to the beginning of each fiscal year. However, many also require interim rebudgeting as well, perhaps semiannually or even quarterly. The more volatile and unpredictable the operation, the more frequent and extensive must be the budget revisions. Revisions should not be so frequent—for example, monthly—that the budget, always in a state of flux, cannot serve as a guide; moreover, managers should not devote unwarranted amounts of time to budgeting. But neither should rebudgeting be so infrequent that the operating budget becomes unrelated to changed operating conditions facing the company.

RESPONSIBILITY ACCOUNTING

Central to the concepts of both bottom-up budgeting and management commitment is segmenting the operation in terms of **responsibility centers,** subdividing into departments, segments, or units for which a single manager is responsible. Most businesses operate in a manner quite consistent with responsibility centers: managers are assigned specific responsibilities and are delegated the authority to carry them out. That is, the first-line supervisor is responsible for a relatively small segment of the business—perhaps only several employees and a few expenses—while managers farther up the management hierarchy have responsibility for whole functions, divisions, or groups that are in turn composed of a number of small segments. Finally, the organization's chief executive has the ultimate responsibility for all operations.

Again assume you are a middle-level manager at Reynolds, manager of the company's Dallas office; you head a responsibility center that includes all of the company's activities in Texas. Reporting to you are several managers, each in turn heading a responsibility center—for example, the service manager responsible for the service force, their travel, and associated expenses; the office supervisor responsible for the secretarial and clerical staff, janitorial services, and the cost of supplies; and two area sales managers, each responsible for the activities and expenses of several salespersons. You report to the national sales manager who has responsibility for overseeing regional offices throughout the country.

As managers move up the management hierarchy, they become responsible for broader segments of the total enterprise and can, by their decisions, have greater impact on its financial health and success. The first-level supervisor in manufacturing is responsible for only a modest set of resources and has little direct impact on the company's revenues or on its assets and liabilities. At the other extreme, the decisions of the chief executive affect the revenues, expenses, assets, liabilities, and all other matters within the organization.

Responsibility centers are categorized in terms of the extent of control exercised by the responsible manager. A segment of the business for which the manager has responsibility only for expenses is referred to as a **cost center.** Where the manager is responsible for both expenses and revenue, but not for the investment of long-term resources, the center is referred to as a **profit center.** Finally, if the manager is accountable for the company's investment in the particular center, as well as for near-term revenues and expenses, the center is referred to as an **investment center.** The measure of performance is different for each of the cost, profit, and investment centers.

Cost Center

At a minimum, a manager is responsible only for expenses. An important measure of a manager's effectiveness is ability to operate the department within budget. Good performance requires that the manager develop and obtain approval for a realistic budget, and then control expenditures to that budget. In the example of the Dallas regional office, the office supervisor responsible for the secretarial and clerical staff is in charge of a cost center. The supervisor is not directly accountable for revenue and does not have the authority to commit the office to additional assets (such as office machines).

Profit Center

A manager accountable for both revenue generation and expense control is responsible for a profit center. He or she is expected to make operating decisions with the profit of the business segment in mind, not concentrating on just revenues or solely expenses. The Dallas regional office is a profit center; you are responsible both for the sales volume generated and the region's selling expenses. Your performance can be judged in terms of the profitability of the Dallas region. If the region is very successful in generating sales but at the sacrifice of very high selling expenses, the region's profit will be below budget and your performance must be judged accordingly. If you are frugal and incur expenses 10 percent below budget, your performance cannot be applauded if this frugality leads to sales that are substantially below budgeted levels.

Investment Center

A manager who combines the responsibility for revenues generated and expenses incurred with the authority for committing investment resources manages an investment center. Autonomous divisions of large companies are investment centers; the division manager is held accountable for both the assets at his or her command and the profits generated by those assets. In Dallas, you are not operating an investment center, nor presumably is your boss, the national sales manager; the division manager to whom the national sales manager reports, however, is in charge of an investment center. The financial performance of that division is evaluated in terms of return on assets, or a similar measure of the effectiveness with which the division's assets are being utilized. It is not enough that the division manager control expenditures to budget or even that the profit target for the division be realized; it is also important that the profit be realized with a reasonable investment of resources. The successful division manager must focus on the efficient management of assets as well as on profits.

RECAP: REASONS TO BUDGET

Before turning to the use of budgets in analyzing performance, let's recap the primary benefits of a well-managed budgeting process, well-managed in terms both of setting budgets and of utilizing those budgets as working documents.

The single most important benefit is to cause explicit planning. Operating plans have a tendency to be vague until their financial implications are reduced to budgets. As the Dallas regional manager, you may be inclined to talk about increasing the company's market share in Texas, or utilizing more efficiently the sales force's travel time, or making initial contact with 200 new customers. However, when you turn to setting next year's budget for incoming orders and selling expenses, you must become very explicit in planning: how many salespersons will be employed, how long will they be trained, who will make the contacts with new customers, how many cars will be leased and how many airplane trips will be taken, how much will telephone expense increase if the amount of travel is to be reduced. Since you need to do this planning to make sensible staffing and other operating decisions, the benefits of detailed and explicit planning extend well beyond simply setting budgets.

This explicit planning is neither easy nor comfortable. Most of us do not enjoy budgeting because we do not enjoy detailed planning and the myriad small decisions that it requires. Moreover, once we commit plans to writing, we are less free to change our plans and we are increasingly accountable for them. Commitment and accountability are important parts of the budgeting process.

A second important benefit of budgeting is communication. Once plans are translated, to the extent possible, into monetary terms, they are more easily communicated. As Dallas regional manager, you communicate in part by budget, as well as orally and in writing, with the national sales manager. You also communicate with others working in the Dallas office; they understand the commitment that you, their supervisor, has made to headquarters for orders to be generated during the coming year and expense levels to be met. Your Dallas regional budget also communicates to other groups within the company: the training department learns how much training support Dallas will need and the local advertising plans for the Texas market are communicated to the advertising department. Similarly, you learn about plans in other company departments by referring to their budgets.

Finally, budgets serve as a basis for comparing actual results. It is this third benefit of budgets that is most widely recognized and discussed, and the one to which we now turn.

VARIANCES AND MANAGEMENT BY EXCEPTION

Good managers recognize that the business areas requiring their attention are not those operating in accordance with plans, but rather those operating at odds with plans. Referred to as **management by exception,** this technique requires that the company's accounting system differentiate between those business segments that are "on-plan" and those that are not. Moreover, the accounting system must be able to highlight the magnitude and probable cause or causes of deviations from plan.

The differences between actual and planned results are referred to as **variances,** here budget variances: the difference between actual and budgeted costs and revenues.*

ANALYZING PERFORMANCE: BUDGET VERSUS ACTUAL

Figure 12-1 shows an operating report for the Dallas regional office that you received early in August. This report, prepared by the home-office accounting staff, was forwarded to you and to others at Reynolds, including the national sales manag-

---

*In companies that do not develop explicit budgets, management is operating on some type of implicit plan. This implicit plan is often simply to repeat last year's actual results. The managers of a mature company operating in a stable market may view last year's actual results as the best guide to this year's operation. If so, last year's actual results are a reasonable yardstick for judging this year's performance, even if management seeks some improvement in revenue or cost performance this year. In this situation variance reports can usefully highlight differences between this year and last year, so that managers can focus attention only on those business segments showing significant variations between the two years. Thus, variances may highlight differences between current actual costs and actual costs during a previous accounting period, typically the corresponding period of the previous year.

FIGURE 12-1 Operating Report: Actual Versus Budget, Dallas Region, July ($000)

	July			Seven Months Year-To-Date		
	Budget	Actual	Variance	Budget	Actual	Variance
Sales	$1,250	$1,370	$120	$8,600	$8,450	($150)
Region expenses						
Salaries	40.0	41.1	(1.1)	280.0	282.5	(2.5)
Sales commissions	25.0	27.4	(2.4)	172.0	169.0	3.0
Discounts and freight allowed	5.0	5.4	(0.4)	34.4	33.5	0.9
Travel and entertainment	16.0	19.0	(3.0)	112.0	110.5	1.5
Telephone	4.0	3.8	0.2	28.0	29.0	(1.0)
Advertising	8.5	8.0	0.5	59.5	57.0	2.5
Rent and other occupancy	3.5	4.6	(1.1)	24.5	24.3	0.2
	$ 102.0	$ 109.3	($ 7.3)	$ 710.4	$ 705.8	$ 4.6
Allocated Expenses						
Headquarters sales expense	20.0	20.5	(0.5)	140.0	142.5	(2.5)
National advertising	17.5	16.5	1.0	105.0	101.0	4.0
Trade shows	11.0	9.0	2.0	35.0	34.0	1.0
	$ 48.5	$ 46.0	$ 2.5	$ 280.0	$ 277.5	$ 2.5

er. It shows actual financial results for July, as well as for the first seven months of the company's fiscal year, and compares those results to the corresponding budgets.

Figure 12-1 and the following discussion of variances follows the normal convention of enclosing in parentheses variance amounts that reduce profit. Thus, for expense variances, when current actual expenditures are in excess of plan, the amount is enclosed in parentheses. Parentheses around sales or revenue variances indicate revenue below budget or plan. Thus, variances in parentheses are equivalent to debit balances; those that increase profits are credits.

The report's revenue section indicates that the Dallas region was for July over budget in shipments by $120,000—a favorable condition—but continued to be under budget for the year to date by $150,000. (The region must therefore have been $270,000 under budget after six months, that is at the beginning of the month.) July was a good month for sales.

In expenses, the region was over budget for the month—an unfavorable condition—but under budget for the seven-month period. In the next chapter we'll consider the possibility that the over-budget condition in expenses was caused by the strong July sales.

Note that the report contains two categories of expenses: regional expenses and allocated expenses. You, the regional manager, are in charge of a responsibility (profit) center and accountable for those expenses over which you have control. You cannot logically be held accountable or responsible for expenses over which you exercise no control. Presumably you do control salaries, travel, telephone, and the other regional expenses. On the other hand, you don't control the allocated expenses. You don't decide the staffing at headquarters, the national advertising campaign plans, or the trade-show schedule, and therefore you cannot be held responsible for these expenses, not even the portion allocated to your region. The national sales manager or someone else in the organization, not the Dallas regional manager, is responsible for these expenses. Thus, when judging your expense control performance, attention should be focused on the regional expenses alone.

A number of expense categories have unfavorable variances for July and favorable variances for the seven-month period. The reverse is true for telephone expenses. Since some randomness in monthly expenditures is inevitable, year-to-date data are useful, as well as the monthly data. The under-budget condition for telephone expense in July might be explained simply by several salespersons being on vacation or it might be the result of improved management of telephone expenses. Similarly, rent and other occupancy expenses are very high for the month—almost 30 percent over budget. Perhaps some major maintenance or repair expense was incurred in July; if the reason for the over-budget condition in July can be pinpointed, you can take comfort in the fact that the region's occupancy expenses are about on budget for the seven-month period. Thus, the year-to-date data help in judging whether an over- or under-budget condition is persisting or whether a particular month's variance is simply a random event.

INTERPRETING VARIANCE BALANCES

In the paragraphs above the terms favorable and unfavorable appear several times to describe variances which increase and decrease profit. Variance balances enclosed in parentheses are popularly referred to as **negative** (or **unfavorable**) **variances**— negative in the sense that they reduce profit. Similarly, variances that add to profit are popularly called **positive** (or **favorable**) **variances.** This nomenclature is both understandable and unfortunate. So-called negative and positive variances, or unfavorable and favorable variances, simply indicate actual expenditures at variance from plan. They do not necessarily indicate good or poor performance.

Note, for example, that the Dallas region was under budget in advertising expense for July and for the seven-month period as well. Is this a favorable variance? Yes, in that it added to this year's profit but it may not be favorable that the region is doing less advertising than originally planned. Is the reduced advertising level contributing to the lower-than-anticipated year-to-date sales? Advertising is a discretionary expenditure, requiring management judgment. The precisely correct amount of advertising for the Texas market is difficult, probably impossible, to ascertain. You, the Dallas regional manager, can be commended if you are carrying out the planned advertising campaigns at reduced cost; however, if you are achieving the under-budget condition by reducing total advertising exposure, this may or may not be a favorable situation, particularly over the intermediate and long term.

Consider your possible motivations. If you are under great pressure from (that is, if you feel threatened or coerced by) the national sales manager to live within your monthly budget, there is much you could have done to avoid July's $7,300 over-budget situation. You could have reduced advertising, dismissed one salesperson, or foregone the repair of the facility. Each of these actions would yield short-term financial benefits—and reduced the threat of your boss disciplining you—but they might not have been consistent with the company's long-term health.

Deterministic versus Discretionary Expenses

As you think about all the various expenses a company incurs, some probably strike you as easier to evaluate than others. About some you are willing to say "the lower the better," and therefore a credit variance balance is indeed a favorable event. About others you are far less certain: You recognize that a good deal of management judgment went into setting the budget, and a credit variance balance is not necessarily favorable.

The first type of expense is a **deterministic expense** and the second a **discretionary expense.** Now, in fact, almost no expense is wholly deterministic or discretionary; expenses fall along a spectrum from quite deterministic to quite discretionary.

In the Dallas region's budget, rent and other occupancy is at the deterministic end of that spectrum. Given a certain office size and location, to the extent that you, as the Dallas regional manager, can reduce occupancy expenses, including power, janitorial, insurance and similar costs, you are pleased. But you can go too far; if you cut back on janitorial or maintenance costs, you may save money in the short run only to end up with a deteriorating office, deferred maintenance that must someday be met, and unhappy employees. Thus, even this expense has some discretionary elements to it.

At the far end of the deterministic–discretionary spectrum is the donations budget (not shown as a separate line item on the exhibits). To be a good business citizen, the Dallas regional office needs to make certain contributions to local causes, but the amounts can hardly be determined in any objective, systematic way. They are entirely at management's discretion.

The advertising budget is also highly discretionary. It has some short-term benefits, but more longer-term benefits. You would be hard pressed to prove a strong linkage between this month's advertising and current sales volume. Nevertheless, you have confidence that, at some level, advertising is a necessary and desirable expense for the long-term health of your region. To determine the right level requires your best judgment.

Of course, it is just possible that advertising in the Dallas regional office is highly targeted direct-mail advertising, the type that experience says will generate X percent responses and Y percent actual sales. Under these circumstances you can determine what mailing lists are most productive and thus just how broadly you want to run your direct-mail advertising campaign. Advertising expense now becomes much more a deterministic expense than a discretionary one, but again it is a mix of both.

Why make this distinction? Variance interpretation is necessarily affected by where on the deterministic–discretionary spectrum the particular expense lies. If you are convinced that the expense is heavily deterministic, then you can say that debit balances are unfavorable and credit balances favorable, and take management action accordingly. If the expense is heavily discretionary, variance balances simply indicate deviation from plan. While all deviations are worth investigating, debit variances for discretionary expenses are not necessarily unfavorable, nor credit variances favorable.

As you interpret variance reports, be particularly alert to the possibility that expenses that are heavily discretionary are being inappropriately cut in order to *make* the budget. That's a great temptation! Ask the sales managers and R & D managers of the world; they will tell you that, when times are tight and budgets must be cut, the first budgets to be attacked are all too frequently the advertising budgets—particularly for so-called image advertising, the most discretionary advertising—and research budgets, particularly for work on programs or products that won't reach the market for years.

Some of this management behavior—cut discretionary expenses before you cut deterministic expenses—is appropriate. After all, the benefits of discretionary expenses tend to be more long term than short term, and the long term is irrelevant if the company doesn't survive the short term. But too much of this behavior is clearly inappropriate. It is the type of behavior for which U.S. managements have been strongly criticized, particularly in comparison to their long-term oriented Japanese competitors.

Materiality of the Variance

The concept of materiality certainly applies to variance analysis. Some variance is almost bound to occur for virtually all expenses in almost all accounting periods. If the magnitude of the variance is small (immaterial as a percent of the budgeted expenses), ascribe little significance to the variance. For example, in Figure 12-1, the favorable $200 variance in rent and other occupancy costs for the seven months is hardly material in relationship to the $24,500 budget; for this cost element we can conclude that the Dallas region is about on plan for the year to date.

Timeliness

Finally, note that the usefulness of the Figure 12-1 report depends very much on the timeliness with which you receive it. You are interested in seeing how your operation is performing relative to the plan to which you are committed. If the operation is off plan, you are anxious to take corrective action. If you receive this report by, say, August 10, you can still recall the July events reflected here in monetary terms. For example, you may recall why building maintenance and repairs were unusually large in July, and thus can quickly and accurately interpret the rent and other occupancy variance and decide that no corrective action is necessary. By contrast, you may be startled to see that travel expenses were well over budget; not recalling any unusual circumstances occasioning extra travel in July, you may want to take immediate corrective action. The longer the delay in obtaining financial feedback, the longer an out-of-control condition may persist and the more difficulty a manager has in correlating the events of the accounting period with the period's financial report. For these reasons, accounting departments should attach high priority to the timely reporting to operating managers of budget-versus-actual information.

HUMAN BEHAVIOR CONSIDERATIONS

The budgeting process, and particularly variance interpretation, is ripe with human behavior complexities. Human motivations infuse both the setting of budgets and the subsequent living with budgets. Many of the words used in this discussion elicit visceral reactions: commitment, responsibility, control, negotiation, unfavorable, discipline, positive and negative, and performance evaluation. These strong words suggest personal interaction and even confrontation. While we frequently speak of an organization in impersonal terms—set standards, exercise control, and alter direction—in fact, of course, an organization is not a machine to be controlled or changed as one might a television set. It is neither more nor less than a collection of individuals, some of whom are designated as managers. Control is exercised by managers with respect to other employees, and if the organization is to change direction or correct problems, then individuals have to take action.

Goal Congruency

A truism of human behavior is that people take action, in their professional lives as in their personal lives, only because they are motivated to do so. That motivation derives from a desire to satisfy some need, and each of us has a set of needs that we strive to satisfy. Budgets and budgeting create very personal needs. To satisfy these needs, employees are motivated to take actions; some of these actions may be beneficial to the organization, and others detrimental. In any case, human behaviorists assure us that, whatever needs are evoked for the managers, they will inevitably take action that they believe will help fulfill those needs.

If an individual manager's needs are closely aligned with those of the organization as a whole, then that manager's actions will benefit the organization's goals. Conversely, if the individual's needs deviate from those of the organization, the actions to which the manager is motivated will not be in the organization's best interests. Obviously **goal congruency**—that is, good alignment between the manager's goals and those of the organization—is desirable, although absolute and complete goal congruency is an ideal that is seldom achievable.

What actions is a manager motivated to take because of the existence of budgets? The manager is expected to participate in setting the budgets, yet the manager's subsequent performance will be judged in part by reference to the budgets: expense control for the cost center manager, profits for the profit center manager, and return on investment for the investment center manager. Motivations depend very much on top management's attitudes towards budgets and performance analysis.

The Pessimistic View

Suppose top management decides to use budgets in a threatening manner, indicating implicitly or explicitly that if managers fail to meet budget (expense, profit, or return on investment)—that is, if negative variances prevail—they will be disciplined and perhaps lose their jobs. Note that this top management attitude implies a quite pessimistic and demeaning view of middle managers. In essence, top management is saying, "Middle managers are interested in just getting by, not in doing a good job. They are somewhat incompetent and generally lazy. They can't be trusted to make decisions in the best interest of the company. Therefore, we must impose tight budgets and coerce the managers into meeting these budgets." In such an environment middle-level managers are motivated to avoid discipline and to retain their jobs, whatever actions that may require.

As budgets are established, the middle-level manager is motivated to "sandbag" top management, to attempt to negotiate a budget that can be easily met. The profit center manager who thinks that a $1.5 million profit can be realized next year will negotiate for a budgeted profit of perhaps $1.3 million or $1.4 million. In turn, the manager's boss, suspecting sandbagging, reacts by pressing for a profit budget of greater than $1.5 million. While some tension in budget negotiations between two levels of management is both inevitable and healthy, carried to an extreme it leads to much loss of time, poor communication, mutual suspicion, and an unrealistic budget.

Continuing the assumption that top management views budgeting as a device to threaten or coerce managers, what motivations will the middle-level managers have as they live with the budget? Financial reports, particularly those that compare actual results with the budget, are viewed as top management tools, not as information aids to help middle managers. The accounting department is viewed as a spying operation for top management, reporting financial data to permit top management to coerce, dominate, and discipline. Middle-level managers will take actions to cause their operations to appear to fit the budget, to minimize negative variances and maximize positive variances. These actions may or may not be in the best long-term interests of the company. The middle manager may be tempted to charge certain expenses to the wrong account, to defer certain discretionary expenses such as maintenance or training, to shift expenses to another profit center, or to speed up the recognition of income. All these actions merely improve the *appearance* of the profit center's financial results; the company's fundamental economic position remains unchanged. These actions are less than honest and moreover are simply wasted motion: the company as a whole and over the long run is not better off for them. If threatened sufficiently, moreover, most people will go to even great lengths to doctor up financial results and a few will succumb to illegal actions.

The Optimistic View

Alternatively, suppose top management views budgets and internal financial reports primarily as tools to aid managers at all levels in doing a better job of managing their particular operations. This view is built on the more optimistic top management assumption that all employees are competent, are motivated to do a good job, and will respond positively when they have information that suggests corrective action. Coercion is not required to cause managers to take appropriate actions. Rather, the assumption is that the organization's goals and those of the individual are sufficiently congruent that middle-level managers will, by seeking to satisfy their personal needs, take actions that also satisfy the organization's needs.

As budgets are negotiated, middle-level managers in this more optimistic and supportive environment are willing to discuss openly the problems and opportunities facing the operation; they are confident that top management seeks realistic budgets. With the threat of discipline greatly lessened, managers are willing to take actions that are in the company's long-run best interests, even if these actions lead to negative expense or revenue variances in the short term. They welcome accurate financial reports from the accounting department, particularly those that compare budget and actual amounts, because such reports help make better decisions. They are confident that higher levels of management are willing to hear explanations of variances (but not excuses) and will support actions that reflect negatively on the profit center's short-term financial results but positively on the company's future. The possibility is acknowledged that budgets may be unrealistic or accounting data inaccurate. All this communication takes place in an atmosphere free of threats or suspicion. The assumption is that middle-level managers want to do a good job, are trying to do a good job, and will be assisted in these efforts by senior management.

In summary, then, budgets and variance analyses can be used by top management as a blunt club to force middle managers to take action, the motivation being the avoidance of discipline. On the other hand, they can be viewed as tools to facilitate communication and assist managers in running their operations, the manager's motivations simply being the desire to do a good job.* Most middle-level managers prefer to operate in the second environment. In addition, there is good evidence that the budgeting process is much more efficient and useful when the management environment is supportive.

OTHER TYPES OF BUDGETS

This chapter has focused on operating budgets as established for individual months and for the accounting year. Operating budgets are analogous to income statements: the budget is prospective, while the financial statement is historical. Just as there are other financial reports, so there are other types of budgets, some of which are analogous to the other financial reports.

Long-Term Budgets

While discussion here has centered on budgets for one year and portions of a year, most companies also devote much attention to longer-term operating budgets. As part of the annual budgeting procedure, companies often develop budgets for each of the next three or five years, although typically in less detail than next year's budget. Focusing solely on a one-year budget, without considering the longer-term financial consequences of the year's operating decisions, can be dangerous. A five-year budget guards against this danger by causing some explicit thinking about the longer term. This exercise may reveal the need for additional facilities having a long construction lead time, or for additional equity or debt capital that may or may not be obtainable, or for a substantial increase in the sales force, or for the introduction of new products to replace those nearing the end of their life cycles.

Of course, a budget established now for a period beginning four years hence will be tentative at best. However, the budget will become firmer as it is revised in the course of each of the intervening annual budgeting cycles.

Pro Forma Balance Sheets

An operating budget is a **pro forma** (estimated in advance) **financial statement.** Pro forma, or estimated, balance sheets are also vital to the financial management of the company. Most companies develop pro forma balance sheets as of various dates in the future, particularly at the end of the year and perhaps at critical dates during the coming year. These pro forma balance sheets permit management (1) to consider

---

*Students of human (or organizational) behavior will recognize that the first approach is consistent with the so-called theory X management style and the second with theory Y management style.

the need for increases or decreases in inventory, accounts receivable, accounts payable, and other working capital items; (2) to judge the adequacy of the company's liquidity at these future dates; and (3) to decide whether to undertake additional short-term borrowing or perhaps repay existing loans. Thus, the ability of the company to finance its projected operations is revealed by pro forma balance sheets.

Cash Budgets

Operating budgets, being analogous to income statements, are prepared on an accrual basis. Yet every operation needs to keep a careful watch on the inflows and outflows of cash to (1) protect, on the one hand, against cash insolvency and (2) anticipate, on the other hand, cash surpluses that might be profitably invested. A cash budget is primarily a translation of the operating budget from an accrual basis to a cash basis of accounting (see Chapter 3 for a discussion of cash-basis accounting) and is related to the cash flow statement discussed in Chapter 11.

A seasonal business—for example, a toy manufacturer—must pay particular attention to the cash budget, as the inflows and outflows of cash throughout the year are very irregular, with most of the cash outflow occurring before and during the busy season and most of the inflows occurring at the end of and following that season. Remember that an operation can appear to be very profitable but still fail because it ran out of cash.

Capital Budgets

The capital budget focuses on the longer-term need for and generation of investment capital. Capital budgets should be developed for several years, typically five and in some cases 10, in order to provide plenty of advance warning of capital shortages or excesses. Both the raising of additional capital and the judicious deployment of extra resources require considerable planning, and once commitments are made they cannot easily be changed. The capital budget takes into account not only the forecasted operating results for the company but also the many other decisions that do not immediately affect profit and loss, for example, the investment in or disposition of plant and equipment, the build-up or reduction in working capital as operations grow or shrink, the payment of dividends and the scheduled repayment of borrowings, and anticipated changes in the capital structure of the operation.

SUMMARY

Budgets, an integral part of the planning process, provide a road map in financial terms. They facilitate the process of managing by exception.

Key guidelines for establishing and using budgets are:

(1) Objectives, generally both quantitative and qualitative, must be set before budgets are established.

(2) Budgeting is only one element of planning. Much important planning cannot be translated into monetary terms. Planning, including budgeting, is typically an iterative process; successive revisions occur until the plans and budgets are mutually consistent and are compatible with both the objectives and resources of the organization.

(3) Budgets for an operation should be built from the bottom up—that is, from segment budgets—and not imposed from the top down.

(4) While the setting of revenue and expense budgets must go hand in hand, typically the cornerstone of the process is the sales or revenue forecast.

(5) Historical accounting data provide a basis for budgets. Nevertheless, past expenditure levels should not simply be incremented to arrive at budgets. Zero-base budgeting is a useful technique.

(6) The budgeting process involves negotiation among levels of management. The important end result of these negotiations should be commitment on the part of each manager.

Budgets are organized by responsibility center. Typically, as a manager ascends the management hierarchy, he or she takes on broader responsibility centers—from cost centers to profit centers and finally, at the division manager level, to investment centers.

The three primary reasons to budget are (1) to cause explicit planning, (2) to communicate plans, and (3) to provide a basis for comparing actual and planned results.

Management by exception—that is, focusing attention on areas of the business requiring corrective action—is facilitated by developing and analyzing variances. A variance provides a systematic comparison between budgeted (planned) and actual results.

Analysis of budget-versus-actual expense reports must be conditioned by knowledge of where each expense lies along the deterministic–discretionary expense spectrum.

The establishment and use of budgets is replete with human behavior considerations. Enlightened and supportive managements view budgets, and subsequent performance reporting, as tools to permit managers at all levels to do a better job, rather than as devices to coerce, control, and discipline lower-level managers.

In addition to near-term operating budgets, several other types of budgets are useful planning documents: (1) operating budgets covering longer periods, say three to five years, (2) pro forma (or estimated in the future) balance sheets, (3) cash budgets that focus on the flow of cash rather than the flow of profit, and (4) capital budgets.

NEW TERMS

Budget. A description in monetary terms of the organization's plans.

Cost center. A responsibility center whose manager is accountable for the control of expenses but not revenues or investments.

Deterministic expense. An expense for which a budget can be set objectively and about which one can say "the lower the better."

Discretionary expense. An expense for which a budget can be set only with artful judgment and one that typically has more long-term than short-term benefits to the company.

Favorable (unfavorable) variances. Credit (debit) balances in variance accounts. The value judgments implied by these terms can be misleading.

Goal congruency. The alignment of the goals (objectives) of the individual manager with those of the overall organization.

Investment center. A responsibility center whose manager is accountable for investment in assets as well as for profit (revenues and expenses).

Management by exception. A practice of focusing management attention primarily on those segments of an operation that are not proceeding in accordance with plan.

Managerial accounting. The use of accounting data to assist management in making operating decisions.

Negative (positive) variances. Alternative names for unfavorable or debit (favorable or credit) balances in variance accounts. The value judgments implied by these terms can be misleading.

Pro forma financial statements. Financial statements that are projected, or estimated in advance. An operating budget is a pro forma income statement.

Profit center. A responsibility center whose manager is accountable for both revenues and expenses, and therefore for profit, but not for investments.

Responsibility center. A segment of a business or other organization for which a single manager can be held accountable.

Variance. An account wherein actual results (expenses or revenues) are compared to planned results.

Zero-base budgeting. A budgeting technique that requires justification for each dollar to be spent, rather than simply justification for expenditure increases or decreases from the previous period.

DISCUSSION QUESTIONS

12.1 Why is budgeting generally an iterative process, requiring several rounds of rebudgeting?

12.2 What are the two primary reasons why "bottom up" budgeting is more effective than "top down" budgeting?

12.3 Why do some companies revise their operating budgets more frequently than other companies? What are the company characteristics that lead to more frequent budgeting?

12.4 For each of the following units within a larger organization, indicate whether you think the unit should be considered a cost center, a profit center, or an investment center.

(a) The sales and service operation located in France of a U.S. manufacturing company

(b) The Taiwan manufacturing subsidiary of a Japanese electronics company

(c) The department responsible for the operation of the truck fleet for the local electric utility

(d) The service department within the local Ford automobile dealership

(e) The papermaking division of a large and diversified forest products company

(f) The shipping department in a plant manufacturing electronic integrated circuits

(g) The police department within a local city government

(h) The shoe department within a downtown department store

12.5 Explain the meaning of the term *goal congruence* as it relates to budgeting.

12.6 What are the three primary reasons for budgeting?

12.7 If you were designing the budgeting and financial reporting system for a large university, indicate which of the following units or segments you would classify as cost, profit, and investment centers:

(a) The Mathematics department

(b) The student union

(c) The university-owned bookstore

(d) The copy center that charges other units for reproduction work it performs

(e) The campus security force (campus police)

(f) The ticket office (box office) within the student union

(g) The intercollegiate athletics department

(h) The office in charge of fund raising (soliciting charitable gifts from individuals, foundations and corporations)

12.8 Discuss situations in which each of the following managers might respond to budgetary pressures in a dysfunctional manner—that is, might take actions that, while helpful in meeting budgets, are contrary to the best long-term interests of the organization:

(a) The engineering department manager whose engineering staff is working concurrently on several carefully budgeted and important projects

(b) The regional sales manager for a large paper distributor

(c) The superintendent of the local public schools

(d) The manager of the catering (kitchen) operations in a community hospital

(e) The production manager responsible for meeting monthly product shipment targets

(f) The manager in charge of the vehicle pool (the fleet of cars and trucks) for an electric power utility

12.9 Why do many companies need both a cash budget and an operating budget (the latter prepared on an accrual basis)?

12.10 For a particular fiscal quarter, the budget variance for the marketing department of the Pittsburgh Products Company showed a 10 percent credit variance. As the president of the company, what questions would you ask the marketing vice president in assessing whether this variance is positive or negative?

12.11 What is meant by the phrase "management by exception" and how does variance analysis contribute to that process?

12.12 Recognizing that few expenses are entirely deterministic or discretionary, characterize the following expenses as primarily deterministic or primarily discretionary:

(a) Travel expenses for the field service engineers

(b) Advertising for a new product line

(c) Electric power expense

(d) Travel expenses for design engineers to attend professional meetings

(e) Annual contribution to the Red Cross

(f) The expense of redecorating the office lobby

PROBLEMS

12.1 Shown below are the actual expenses and the budget for the engineering design department of Mancini Electronics, Inc. for the third fiscal quarter (in $ millions).

	Actual	Budget
Salaries	$14.3	$14.7
Fringe benefits	3.7	3.9
Supplies	4.8	4.3
Rent and other occupancy	2.9	2.3
Consulting services	3.3	3.3
Professional development	1.7	1.9
Travel expense	2.1	2.7
Telephone and computer	1.9	1.8
Total	$34.7	$34.9

(a) Develop a variance report by expense category.

(b) Which of these expense variances do you think would be the most useful to you (consider management by exception)?

(c) What are possible explanations for the large variance in travel expense? Which of these explanations do you think is most likely to be relevant?

(d) The variance in Rent and Other Occupancy is sizable. What actions might the engineering department manager take to meet budget in this expense category in the coming months?

(e) In order to interpret the Salaries expense variance, what other information would you need to have?

12.2 Carmen's Bakery is a specialty bakery that does a large share of its business around the holidays. During the busiest season, the bakery occasionally runs short of cash, and therefore the company's controller has asked you to assist in developing a cash budget for the coming three-month period, October through December. Historically, about 30 percent of the sales for the month are paid for in that month; another 55 percent of the receivables generated in one month are collected in the following month, and the final 15 percent are collected in the second month after sale. Bad debt risks are minimal. Sales results and projections are as follows:

Month	Sales $
August	$207,000 actual
September	256,000 actual
October	275,000 budget
November	375,000 budget
December	445,000 budget

(a) Estimate cash receipts for Carmen's bakery by month for the final three months of the year.

(b) What will be the accounts receivable balance at December 31?

(c) If Carmen's expects that monthly cash outflows (for salary payments, payments to vendors, and other purposes) will be $350,000, how large a cash balance will Carmen's need as of October 1 to be certain that the company does not run out of cash during its busy season?

12.3 Sidney Costello is manager of a small fast foods operation that experienced a considerable profit variance in the most recent month. The store's variance report, as prepared by the outside accountant retained by Sidney, is:

	Actual	Variance
Sales	$107,000	($23,000)
Cost of materials used	72,000	14,300

	Actual	Variance
Salaries and wages	22,000	700
Utilities and occupancy	8,500	(200)
Advertising	1,500	200
Miscellaneous	3,700	300
Operating profit (loss)	($ 700)	($ 7,700)

(a) How much was Sidney expecting to make in profit for the month?

(b) Which of the variance amounts should Sidney pay particular attention to?

(c) Obviously Sidney's sales fell well below budget, but expenditures on materials and salaries and wages also fell. Does the credit variance on Cost of Materials Used indicate a favorable condition? Can you determine how well Sidney controlled the use of materials during the month?

(d) What conclusions might you draw from the small credit (favorable) variance in Salaries and Wages for the month, particularly in light of the fact that sales were so far below budget?

(e) How serious is the debit (unfavorable) balance in Utilities and Occupancy expense?

(f) Where should Sidney focus his attention in improving his store's profitability?

12.4 Refer to problem 12.3. Assume that a careful analysis of Sidney's fast-food operation indicates that, with diligent management, the cost of materials used should equal 66 percent of sales and salaries and wages should equal $9700 per month plus 10 percent of sales. With this information determine what Sidney should have spent last month on (a) materials used, and (b) salaries and wages, and with that information determine how successful he was in controlling these two most important cost categories. If those expense categories had met the target percentages just outlined, how profitable would the fast food operation have been for the month?

──13

ANALYZING FIXED AND VARIABLE EXPENSES

Chapter 12 drew a distinction between deterministic and discretionary expenses. Another important distinction is between **fixed** and **variable expenses** (or costs), that is, between those expenses that increase or decrease proportionally with increases or decreases in volume of activity and those expenses that are independent of changes in volume. This fixed–variable distinction is important to both budget variance analysis and to our subsequent discussion of cost accounting, and thus is accorded its own chapter.

DEFINING FIXED AND VARIABLE

In the budget report for the Dallas regional office (Figure 12-1), recall that sales for the month of June were in excess of budget—a credit (positive) variance—while the subtotal of regional expenses, $7300 in excess of budget, showed a debit (negative) variance. Might these two conditions be linked? That is, are the higher expenses caused by the higher sales revenue? One recognizes quickly that some expenses are linked to the Dallas region's volume of business, while other expenses, such as rent and allocated expenses, are independent of the volume of the region's sales this year. Thus, expenses are composed both of those unaffected by changes in volume of activity—fixed expenses—and of those that can be expected to vary directly with activity—variable expenses. Explicitly recognizing this difference leads to a more insightful analysis of cost and expense variances.

The discussion of budgeting in Chapter 12 focused on setting budgets in absolute dollars for a subsequent accounting period. Figure 12-1 shows that the Dallas regional office budgeted $112,000 for travel expenses for its first seven months of the year 1994 and $25,000 for sales commissions for July. These budgeted expenses take no note of the fact that certain expenses vary with volume of sales. Sales commission expense will always appear below budget if sales revenue is below budget, and over budget, or unfavorable, if sales are above budget. By contrast, rent expense this year in 1994 is wholly unaffected by the year's sales revenue.

To repeat, a useful distinction can be drawn between those expenses that are variable with volume and those that are fixed regardless of volume. For example, in a manufacturing operation, as volume of production (total output) is increased within relatively narrow limits, some costs necessarily increase, while other costs are uninfluenced by modest changes in manufacturing volume (i.e., they remain fixed over the short run, measured typically in months, not years). The classic example of a variable cost is direct material: The amount of material required is a direct function of the volume of units manufactured. The classic example of a fixed cost is rent or depreciation: The rent expenditure is independent of the volume of units manufactured; even if managers wanted to they could not quickly expand the factory to accommodate a modest production increase.

Variability with Volume of Activity

Bear in mind that the terms variable and fixed as used in this context refer only to the behavior of costs with changes in *volume*. Costs vary for many other reasons, such as the passage of time, the rate of inflation or deflation, the number of persons employed, or the size of the production facility. However, as the terms are used in accounting, the variability is solely with respect to volume of activity.

Why is this distinction between fixed and variable costs important? While subsequent chapters will deal further with this question, two quick examples will foreshadow a more complete answer. Sometimes it is appropriate to omit the fixed and variable costs when addressing the question "What does a particular product cost?" For example, in weak economic times if a factory is operating at well below capacity, the company may be wise to accept a contract even if the price is below total costs—the sum of fixed and variable—so long as the price is above variable costs. Also, many financial analyses, including analyses of capital investment proposals, require information on differences in costs and revenue among the alternatives being studied; frequently fixed costs are irrelevant to these analyses. Chapter 18 discusses these and other operating decisions requiring information on variable product costs. Finally, effective budgeting depends on a clear separation of variable and fixed expenses.

It is tempting to argue that all Dallas region expenses are variable with volume—salaries, travel expenses, and so forth. In reality, however, these expenses may vary with sales *effort* but not directly with sales revenue realized. Salaries, travel expenses, and telephone expenses will vary as the Dallas region increases or decreases the sales power in the region; this change in sales power may ultimately result in changes in sales revenue, but at best there will be a time lag between effort expended and sales realized, and at worst there may be no relationship at all. Thus, these expenses are altered by management's discretionary decisions—for example, the number of salespersons in the field—but they do not vary with volume of sales. In Figure 12-1 the only expense category besides sales commissions that is variable is discounts and freight allowed.

Extent of Variability

How variable are the cost elements in a manufacturing environment? Chapter 14 returns to this question in discussing alternative definitions of product costs, for it is in that context that the separation of variable and fixed expenses is particularly critical. Product (or manufacturing) costs are traditionally comprised of direct labor, direct material and indirect production costs (frequently referred to as factory overhead). Direct material is typically, but not always, wholly a variable cost. That is, the amount of material utilized in or on the product is variable directly in proportion to the volume of production. Direct labor, too, is generally assumed to vary directly with production volume. However, this assumption implies that the production organization will add or remove persons from the direct labor force in direct proportion to volume, or that the production workers will be paid on a piece-rate basis (a certain amount per unit produced). While some production operations fit these assumptions, most do not, since skilled members of the direct labor force are considered indispensable; volume would have to decline dramatically before they would be laid off. In such cases, a large portion of direct labor costs may in fact be fixed.

Indirect production costs (factory overhead) are in most instances composed of both variable and fixed elements. As mentioned above, rent or depreciation on the factory space is typically a fixed cost. So too is the production superintendent's salary, depreciation on the production equipment, and perhaps expenses of the production control department. At the other end of the spectrum, production supplies such as lubricants, coolants, and shop rags are generally variable with the volume of production—the greater the output, the more supplies will be consumed. Often power consumption, equipment maintenance, and costs of operating the stockroom are also directly variable with production volume.

It has already occurred to you that in all environments—manufacturing as well as selling—many expenses are really semivariable with volume: they are neither entirely fixed nor do they vary in direct proportion to volume. Some may change in a step function. For example, the factory stockroom force may be able to handle a modest increase in volume, but when the increase exceeds this modest amount, another person must be hired. In the case of production equipment maintenance, a certain amount must be performed simply to take care of the ravages of time, but as volume increases, so too typically does the need for maintenance. Similarly, office salaries in the Dallas region office are probably semivariable: As sales increase, some clerical staffs may be augmented to handle increased invoicing, order acknowledgment, and other functions related to individual orders.

FLEXIBLE BUDGETING

How can the separation of variable and fixed expenses improve the quality of the budgeting process? Figure 13-1 recasts the July operating expense budget for the Dallas region to separate variable and fixed expense elements. The exhibit also shows the percentage that each expense element is of budgeted sales volume for the month. The key budget data for the variable expenses are the percentage figures; if sales for the month turn out to be other than $1.25 million, then the sales commissions budget should not be $25,000 but it should still be two percent of whatever sales turn out to be. On the other hand, the $8500 advertising budget for the month is independent of the sales realized for the month; there is no reason that advertising expenditures should be driven off plan by the fact that this month's sales revenue is different than plan. Thus, while the percentage figures in Figure 13-1 relating the fixed expenses to budgeted sales may be interesting, they are not really germane to the budgeting process. The budget for fixed expenses should be stated in absolute dollar amounts.

The month's budget, compromising both variable and fixed expense, is best stated as a **flexible budget:** variable expenses in percentages and fixed expenses in absolute dollars. The flexible budget for the Dallas region, according to Figure 12-1, is

$$\text{Budget} = 2.4\% \text{ of sales} + \$72,000$$

FIGURE 13-1   Recast Expense Budget: Flexible Budget, Dallas Region, July

	July Budget	
	$000	%
Sales	$1,250.0	100%
Regional expenses		
Variable		
Sales commissions	25.0	2.0
Discounts and freight allowed	5.0	0.4
	30.0	2.4
Fixed		
Salaries	40.0	3.2
Travel and entertainment	16.0	1.3
Telephone	4.0	0.3
Advertising	8.5	0.7
Rent and other occupancy	3.5	0.3
	72.0	5.8
Total	$ 102.0	8.2%

FIGURE 13-2 Operating Report: Actual versus Volume-Adjusted Budget, Dallas Region, July ($000)

	July			Seven Months Year-to-Date		
	Volume-Adjusted Budget	Actual	Variance	Volume-Adjusted Budget	Actual	Variance
Sales	$1,370	$1,370		$8,450	$8,450	
Regional expenses						
Variable						
Sales commissions (2.0%)	27.4	27.4		169.0	169.0	
Discounts and freight allowed (0.4%)	5.5	5.4	0.1	33.8	33.5	0.3
	32.9	32.8	0.1	202.8	202.5	0.3
Fixed						
Salaries	40.0	41.1	(1.1)	280.0	282.5	(2.5)
Travel and Entertainment	16.0	19.0	(3.0)	112.0	110.5	1.5
Telephone	4.0	3.8	0.2	28.0	29.0	(1.0)
Advertising	8.5	8.0	0.5	59.5	57.0	2.5
Rent and other occupancy	3.5	4.6	(1.1)	24.5	24.3	0.2
	72.0	76.5	(4.5)	504.0	503.3	0.7
Total	$ 104.9	$ 109.3	($4.4)	$ 706.8	$ 705.8	$ 1.0

Volume-Adjusted Budgets

This flexible budget allows us to construct for the Dallas region a **volume-adjusted budget,** giving effect to the impact that changes in sales volume have on budgeted expenses. The comparison of actual results for July (and the year to date) to the volume-adjusted budget provides the most useful information for analyzing the Dallas region's performance.

Figure 13-2 is a reconstruction of Figure 12-2, comparing actual results to volume-adjusted budgets. A comparison of these two exhibits reveals the following.

(1) For the month, sales commissions are just equal to the volume-adjusted budget, although Figure 12-1 indicated that they were $2400 over budget. That over-budget condition was fully explainable by the fact that actual sales exceeded budgeted sales.

(2) Discounts and freight allowed were closer to plan for both the month and year to date than suggested by Figure 12-1. That exhibit shows a $400 unfavorable variance for July, but on a volume-adjusted basis this variance changes to $100 favorable.

(3) Overall for the month, regional expenses were $4400 over the volume-adjusted budget—much closer to plan than indicated by the $7300 unfavorable variance shown in Figure 12-1.

(4) On the other hand, the $4600 under-budget condition in total expenses year to date as shown in Figure 12-1 was misleading. The bulk of this under-budget condition was the result of lower than expected sales volumes, not effective control of expenses. As compared to the volume-adjusted budget for the year to date, actual expenses have been only $1000 under budget.

This book argues strongly for clearly identifying and separating variable and fixed costs. Such a separation is paramount to an accurate assessment of performance for virtually any enterprise, profit-seeking or nonprofit. The procedure for developing and utilizing a volume-adjusted budget is further emphasized by the following example.

EXAMPLE: A SOCIAL OR RESIDENCE CLUB

Suppose Noel Reilly is the president of a social or residence club on a university campus—for example, a sorority or a fraternity. The club employs a finance manager, but Noel Reilly is ultimately responsible for controlling the operations of the club and overseeing its financial well-being. Noel receives monthly financial statements from the finance manager. Moreover, as a competent and progressive manager, Noel has worked out, in cooperation with the finance manager, the social chairperson, the manager of the dining room, and others, a detailed month-by-month budget for the club. The finance manager prepares statements comparing each month's financial results with the corresponding monthly budget. Statements for two months are shown in Figure 13-3.

Figure 13-3 seems to send Noel, as president, conflicting messages. In October the club developed a $220 surplus, when break-even operations were budgeted, but control of expenses appears to be poor, as the expense budget was overspent by $400. While noting that the revenue was well ahead of budget, Noel's key concern is whether the club's managers are doing a good job of controlling costs. Is the club operating in accordance with the plan worked out with the management team?

The November report in Figure 13-3 offers more conflicting evidence: The club incurred a deficit, but expenses were held to $200 below budget. Again, are expenses being well controlled in November?

The key is that in October revenue—presumably a function of membership—was well above budget, while in November it was below budget. If each member is charged $150 per month, the club must have included 44 members in October (44 times $150 equals the $6600 revenue from members) in contrast to the 40 planned (40 times $150 equals the budgeted $6000 revenue) and only 38 members in November (38 times $150 equals $5700). Obviously, certain expenses vary directly with number of members (and therefore with revenue from members). But these data still do not answer Noel's key question: Is the management doing a good job of controlling expenses? A clear separation of variable and fixed expenses—those expenses that vary with number of members separated from those expenses that are independent of membership—leads to a more useful management control report.

Assume that food is a fully variable expense—the more members the club has, the more it must spend on food. On the other hand, assume that the number of persons employed is constant, as are the club's obligations to pay rent. Utilities probably vary slightly with the number of members living in the house, taking showers and turning on lights, but the major utility expense is associated with

FIGURE 13-3 Campus Residence Club, Operating Report: Actual versus Budget, October and November

	October			November		
	Budget	Actual	Variance	Budget	Actual	Variance
Revenue						
Revenue from members	$6,000	$6,600	$600	$6,000	$5,700	($300)
Other revenue	400	420	20	400	420	20
	6,400	7,020	620	6,400	6,120	(280)
Expenses						
Food	3,000	3,200	(200)	3,000	2,800	200
Wages and salaries	1,100	1,150	(50)	1,100	1,100	0
Supplies	600	650	(50)	600	650	(50)
Utilities	500	500	0	500	500	0
Occupancy	1,200	1,300	(100)	1,200	1,150	50
Total	6,400	6,800	(400)	6,400	6,200	200
Surplus (Deficit)	0	$ 220	$220	0	($80)	($80)

operating the kitchen and heating the space. Thus, assume that wages and salaries, utilities, and occupancy are fixed. Supplies are probably semivariable; certain supplies, such as those used in the kitchen, are independent of the number of members, while other supplies, such as linen, soap, and toilet paper, vary directly with membership. The supplies expense can be divided into fixed and variable components—say, $200 per month fixed plus $10 per member per month. Because the budget shown in Figure 13-3 was predicated on membership of 40, supplies expense was budgeted at $600 per month: $200 fixed plus $400 variable (40 times $10). These assumptions and data are sufficient to develop a volume-adjusted budget for each of October and November.

In Figure 13-4 actual financial results for October and November are compared to budgets adjusted to reflect the actual number of club members. Operations were in fact close to volume-adjusted budgets for both months. Given the composition of fixed and variable costs and the fact that membership exceeded expectations in October, the club should have generated $260 surplus for the month; this figure appears at the bottom of October's volume-adjusted budget column. In fact, the surplus was only $220; the $60 unfavorable expense variance was only partly offset by the favorable variance in other revenue. Similarly, given the club's expense structure and the fact that membership in November fell below expectations, the club should have generated a $130 deficit that month; because of good expense control ($30 favorable variance) and a favorable variance in other revenue, the realized deficit was only $80.

As president of the club, Noel can reasonably conclude that expenses are under quite good control. The club's problem appears to be much more one of variation in membership than control of expenses. Looking at the individual expense categories, Noel might conclude that the food operation is under particularly good control: actual expenditures were below the volume-adjusted budget level for both months. However, financial results don't tell the whole story; Noel needs also to consider member satisfaction with the quality, quantity, and variety of the food served. Supplies, on the other hand, may deserve additional attention, as the club was over budget both months. The other expense categories appear to be in good control; the variation, for example, in the Occupancy account from month to month is not unusual and Noel may want to consult year-to-date data to ascertain whether this expense category is under control.

Note that flexible budgeting can also help the club in establishing its membership fees or dues. If the club can anticipate total membership in excess of 40, it should be able to reduce its fees from the present $150-per-month level, assuming that the financial objective of the club is to generate neither a surplus nor a deficit. On the other hand, if membership will persist at the November level of 38, the club will have to increase membership dues, as the total fixed expenses of the club will have to be spread over fewer members.

THE PERVASIVENESS OF MIXED COSTS

This book devotes an entire chapter to the subject of fixed and variable costs for two reasons. First, virtually any set of costs or expenses that one encounters in business,

FIGURE 13-4 Campus Residence Club, Operating Report: Actual versus Volume-Adjusted Budget

	Data for Volume-Adjusted Budget	October			November		
		Volume-Adjusted Budget*	Actual	Variance	Volume-Adjusted Budget†	Actual	Variance
Revenue							
Revenue from members	$150/member/month	$6,600	$6,600	0	$5,700	$5,700	0
Other revenue	$400/month	400	420	$20	400	420	$20
		7,000	7,020	20	6,100	6,120	20
Expenses							
Food	$75/member/month	3,300	3,200	100	2,850	2,800	50
Supplies	$10/member/month plus $200/month	640	650	(10)	580	650	(70)
Wages and salaries	$1,100/month	1,100	1,150	(50)	1,100	1,100	0
Utilities	$500/month	500	500	0	500	500	0
Occupancy	$1,200/month	1,200	1,300	(100)	1,200	1,150	50
		6,740	6,800	(60)	6,230	6,200	30
Surplus (Deficit)		$ 260	$ 220	($40)	($ 130)	($ 80)	$50

*44 members.
†38 members.

in government units, in nonprofit enterprises, or elsewhere is comprised of fixed, semivariable and variable elements. Second, those charged with interpreting financial performance of these entities tend to forget or ignore that fact; rather, they are disposed to make the implicit but erroneous assumption that all costs are variable.

We know from reading the public press that, when revenues fall by 20 percent in a particular company, profits typically decline by a much greater percentage. Why is this so? Because, while variable costs may decline by 20 percent, fixed costs are sticky: they do not decline automatically, but only as a result of explicit management action. Even alert and aggressive managers, however, find it difficult to reduce fixed costs as fast as, and in proportion with, short-term declines in volume.

This fixed-cost stickiness is hardly surprising. Recall that rent, occupancy costs and depreciation of fixed assets are important cost elements in most operations, and they are all fixed costs. Management simply cannot resize its operations—either up or down—in response to short-term fluctuations in revenue. Another important element of fixed costs is salaries of managers, technical and sales personnel and other individuals whose experience and personal relationships are critical to the long-term health of their companies. One does not lightly dismiss such employees to reduce expenses in periods of reduced sales volume, particularly if the revenue reduction is expected to be only temporary.

Conversely, a sudden surge in revenues will typically result in a substantially larger surge in profits, because, while variable costs will increase proportionally to the revenue increase, fixed costs will be sticky on the upside. Even if management scrambles to increase plant capacity and to augment the ranks of salespersons, development engineers and managers, these actions cannot be implemented immediately. It takes time to build or acquire facilities and equipment as well as to hire and train personnel, and thus the corresponding fixed costs will be slow to build.

A school, church, or temple has a cost structure that is dominated by fixed costs. That is, relatively few of its expenses are dependent upon short-term swings in enrollment or membership. A public school that suffers a 10 percent decline in enrollment is expected by many taxpayers and legislators to reduce its expenses by a corresponding 10 percent. Have some sympathy with the principal as he or she struggles to "resize" the institution. Ten percent fewer pupils spread among all classes may not permit the cancellation of a single class or the dismissal of a single teacher or any reduction in the school facility. The costs of operating the facility and paying the teachers are fixed. Classroom supplies usage probably is variable with enrollment (a measure of activity)—perhaps one of the only truly variable expenses—but obviously the expenses associated with classroom supplies are a trivial portion of the school's overall expenditures. In spite of the concentration of fixed costs in school operations, notice that schools are typically funded by state legislatures on the basis of average daily attendance; this basis of funding seems to imply that schools can adjust their expenditures directly and proportionally with changes in enrollment.

If book borrowing from the city library declines by 20 percent, the head librarian is going to have a tough time cutting expenses. The expenses associated with acquiring books and periodicals and staffing the reference and check-out desks are largely fixed.

At the other extreme is the flower stand in the local shopping mall. The primary expense item is the acquisition of flowers, a fully variable expense if we ignore spoilage and pilferage. The operator incurs essentially no heat, power, and other occupancy expenses, and even the rental paid to the mall may be a percentage of the stand's revenue, and thus fully variable. If the stand owner hires the salespersons on a commission basis, even the stand's labor costs are variable with volume.

But it should be obvious to you that few businesses and almost no public agencies or nonprofit entities have cost structures like the flower stand. More typically fixed costs are substantially greater than variable costs. The flexible-budgeting procedure permits us to acknowledge explicitly the relative importance of fixed and variable expenses and to interpret budget versus actual reports accordingly.

INTERRELATIONSHIP OF VOLUME, PRICE, COST, AND PROFIT

Business is a complex financial system. Decisions interact and opportunities for trade-offs are abundant. Changes in prices affect volume of sales and profits; changes in volume alone affect variable costs immediately and fixed costs over time; these changes affect profit; changes in cost may necessitate changes in price, which in turn affect volume and profit; changes in cost (for example, increased marketing effort) may lead to increased volume along with or instead of higher prices. These interrelationships and trade-offs lead managers to ask a broad variety of what-if questions:

(1) What if prices are increased by 5 percent, causing a 3 percent decline in volume; is the company better off? (The answer will depend on the mix of fixed and variable expenses.)

(2) What if commission rates paid to agents are increased by two percent (increased selling costs) and the agents' increased efforts result in a 5 percent increase in sales; will the company's profits be enhanced? (Again, the mix of fixed and variable expenses is relevant, but so also is the gross margin on products.)

(3) What if higher-cost materials are used to produce a higher-quality product that commands a higher market price; will profits be improved?

(4) What if marketing expenses are increased 7 percent to increase sales volume by 4 percent; if resulting economies of scale cause a 5 percent reduction in variable production costs, and no change in fixed costs, will profits improve?

(5) What if automation is enhanced, thus adding $40,000 to annual fixed expenses and reducing variable manufacturing costs by 5 percent; will profits suffer if volume drops 3 percent? If volume increases 3 percent?

(6) What if the rental agreement on retail facilities provided for a lower monthly fixed rent in exchange for a percentage of sales, thus turning a fixed expense into a variable expense; under what conditions would this be better for a retailer than continuing under the current fixed-rental plan?

Endless questions of this type might be asked.

The interrelationship of volume, price, cost, and profit for an engineering services firm, Tamaki Engineering Co., is pictured in Figure 13-5. This graph of operating results displays service volume along the *x* axis and dollars (both revenue and cost) along the *y* axis. The straight revenue line begins at the origin; its slope equals price. Costs are layered: first the fixed costs of selling and administration and of operations, represented by horizontal lines, and then the variable costs represented by upwardly sloping lines. The difference between the revenue line and the total expense line is operating profit; at the lower left of the graph, the negative difference represents operating loss. This graph is highly simplified and useful primarily in thinking conceptually about the interrelationships among volumes, prices, costs, and profits. Expenses do not in fact follow straight lines as volume changes; fixed costs tend to change in step functions and the slopes of the variable cost lines are different at different volumes. Nevertheless a manager's primary concern is with modest changes in costs, prices, and volumes around the company's present, or normal, operating point (*N* on the graph). While fixed costs do not remain absolutely fixed as volume goes from, say, zero to 120 percent of capacity, one can reasonably assume that they are fixed for short-term swings of, say, 10 or 20 percent around normal volume. Similar assumptions apply to variable costs and revenue.

This graph illustrates the four fundamental ways a company's profits can be changed: (1) increase or decrease prices, thus tilting up or down the revenue line; (2) increase or decrease activity (volume), thus moving to the right or left on the *x* axis; (3) reduce or increase variable costs, thus tilting down or up the total cost curve (although its origin remains at the same point on the *y* axis); and (4) reduce or increase fixed costs, thus shifting down or up on the *y* axis the origin of the total cost curve. Simple enough. However, each of these actions, as just pointed out, has second-order effects.

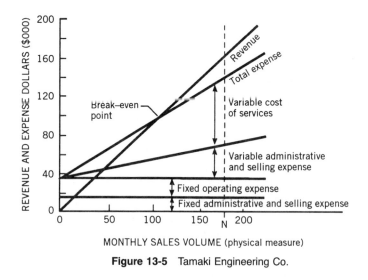

MONTHLY SALES VOLUME (physical measure)

Figure 13-5 Tamaki Engineering Co.

Figure 13-6 is a so-called **contribution statement** that displays financial data for Tamaki at normal volume; the cost–volume–profit relationships are those shown graphically in Figure 13-5. **Contribution** is defined as the difference between revenue and variable costs and a contribution statement is designed to highlight contribution by aggregating the variable costs above the contribution margin line and aggregating the fixed costs below that line. Note that *gross margin* is not shown in Figure 13-6, but *contribution*—revenue minus variable costs—is. The contribution at normal sales volume ($170,000 per month) is $68,000, and more importantly the **contribution margin** is 40 percent of revenue. One sees immediately that a $10,000 increase in monthly sales leads to a $4000 (40 percent of $10,000) increase in contribution, and, if fixed costs truly remain fixed with this volume increase, operating profit also increases by $4000.

Algebraically, these relationships are

$$\text{Operating profit} = \text{CM} \times \text{revenue} - \text{FC}$$

where

$$\text{CM} = \text{contribution margin}$$
$$\text{FC} = \text{fixed cost in dollars}$$

At normal volume, N, as shown in Figures 13-5 and 13-6:

$$\text{Operating profit} = 0.4\,(170) - 46 = \$22$$

Now with these data consider some simplified what-if scenarios for Tamaki. The calculations are detailed in Figure 13-7.

(1) Suppose Tamaki's managers believe that an increase of 1 percent in salespersons' commission (from 3.5 to 4.5 percent of sales) could substitute for

FIGURE 13-6   Tamaki Engineering Co., Monthly Contribution Statement—Normal Operations

	$000		% of Sales
Revenue		$170	$100.0%
Variable expenses			
Cost of services	$80		47.1%
Selling and administrative expenses	22		12.9
Subtotal		102	60.0
Contribution margin		68	40.0%
Fixed expenses			
Operating expenses	28		
Selling and administrative expenses	18		
Subtotal		46	
Operating profit		$ 22	

FIGURE 13-7 Tamaki Engineering Co., What-if Scenarios

1. Increase salespersons' commission from 3.5% to 4.5%; decrease advertising (fixed selling expense) by $2,000.

Revenue =	$170
Contribution margin (40 − 1%) =	39%
Contribution $(0.39 × 170) =	66.3
Fixed expenses (46 − 2) =	44.0
Operating profit =	$ 22.3

2. Increase salespersons' commission from 3.5% to 5%; no change in advertising; increase revenues by 5%.

New revenue volume ($170 × 1.05) =	$178.5
Contribution margin (40 − 1.5) =	38.5%
Contribution $(0.385 × 178.5) =	$ 68.7
Fixed expenses (unchanged) =	46.0
Operating profit	$ 22.7

3. Increase prices 5%; decrease volume 7%

New volume at old price (0.93 × 170) =	$158.1
New volume at higher prices (158.1 × 1.05) =	166.0
Variable expenses (0.6 × new volume at old price) =	94.9
Fixed expenses (unchanged) =	46.0
Operating profit =	$ 25.1

4. Decrease price 3%; increase volume 5%

New volume at old price (1.05 × 170) =	$178.5
New volume at lower prices (178.5 × 0.97) =	173.2
Variable expenses (0.6 × new volume at old price) =	107.1
Fixed expenses (unchanged) =	46.0
Operating profit =	$ 20.1

5. Renegotiate laboratory contract from $5,000 and 5% of revenue to $12,000 and 0% of revenue

Revenue =	$170
Contribution margin (40 + 5%) =	45%
Contribution $(0.45 × 170) =	76.5
Fixed expenses (46 + 7)	53.0
Operating profit =	$ 23.5

6. Increase advertising (fixed selling expense) by $5,000 per month and sales commissions from 3.5% to 5.0%; lease additional equipment at $4,000 per month; increase volume by 20%; achieve economies of scale to reduce variable operating expenses by 1.1 percentage points.

New revenues (170 × 1.2) =	$204.0
Contribution margin (40 + 1.1 − 1.5) =	39.6%
Contribution $(0.396 × 204) =	$ 80.8
Fixed expenses (46 + 5 + 4) =	55.0
Operating profit =	$ 25.8

$2000 of advertising without affecting total revenue volume. Contribution margin would be reduced to 39 percent, but fixed expenses would also be reduced.

$$\text{Operating profit} = (0.39 \times 170) - 44 = \$22.3$$

A modest increase in operating profit from $22,000 to $22,300 would result

(2) Because additional marketing effort seems productive, suppose the salespersons' commissions are increased still more—now by 1.5 percent—and advertising is not cut. Management feels that sales will then increase by 5 percent. The contribution margin is decreased, but sales volume is increased.

$$\text{Operating profit} = (0.385 \times 170 \times 1.05) - 46 = \$22.7$$

The result: a modest increase in operating profit. Note that if a lesser increase in volume (say 3.5 percent) is stimulated by increased commissions, the action would be unwise.

$$\text{Operating profit} = (0.385 \times 170 \times 1.035) - 46 = \$21.7$$

(3) Suppose service prices are changed, resulting inevitably in volume changes. Managers forecast that a 5 percent increase will bring about only a 7 percent decrease in volume. Now the former contribution margin no longer applies to the new revenue volume figured at new prices; the changed pricing assumption requires new contribution margin calculations. Service activity is expected to decrease by 7 percent to revenue of $158,100, stated in terms of the former prices; the old variable cost percentage, 60 percent, can be applied to this figure to determine the total variable cost. The new contribution margin is substantially higher than before (42.9 percent) because prices have been increased without any increase in the cost of services rendered. This price increase appears attractive: operating profit increases from $22,000 to $25,100.

(4) A price decrease of 3 percent would stimulate revenues. If this decrease leads to only a 5 percent increase in volume, the operating profit at Tamaki will suffer, as indicated in Figure 13-7. Again, the former contribution margin cannot be used directly.

(5) Tamaki now contracts for certain laboratory services at $5000 per month plus 5 percent of revenue. Alternatively, it could offer its laboratory vendor a fixed amount per month regardless of activity volume, say $12,000 per month. (Tamaki would thereby turn a variable expense into a fixed expense; the implications of this conversion are discussed in a moment.) Tamaki's contribution margin will increase to 45 percent, more than enough to compensate for the increase in fixed expenses, and therefore the company's operating profit is improved by $1500 per month.

$$\text{Operating profit} = [(0.40 + 0.05)170] - (46 + 7) = \$23.5$$

(6) The last what-if scenario contemplates more far ranging and ambitious changes. Suppose Tamaki feels that increasing volume is the key to improved profits; to get the volume, management considers increasing sales commissions to 5 percent and simultaneously also increasing advertising expenditures by $5000 per month. To service the added volume, additional space and equipment will have to be rented at an incremental fixed-rental cost of $4000. Management believes these changes can lead to a 20 percent increase in unit volume, with no changes in price, and the higher volume in turn can permit Tamaki to achieve some economies of scale in providing services, with the result that variable operating costs will decrease from 47.1 percent of revenue to 46.0 percent. The result: an erosion in contribution margin and somewhat higher fixed expenses are more than compensated by the increased volume.

$$\text{Operating Profit} = (0.400 + 0.011 - 0.015)\,(170 \times 1.2)$$
$$-(46 + 5 + 4) = \$25.8$$

Operating profit as a percentage of sales is reduced from 12.9 to 12.6 percent by this set of changes. And one can quickly calculate that if volume expands by only 10 percent, rather than the forecasted 20 percent, operating profit will be only $19,100, a $2900 reduction from present levels. Remember too that Tamaki may well have to invest somewhat more in accounts receivable and perhaps inventory (that is, invest more in working capital) to finance this expansion. Management needs to look at return on assets under this final scenario.

Similar what-if questions could be asked with respect to adding sales personnel, changing the mix of services offered, extending more liberal credit terms to customers, and so forth.

Modeling an Operation

The graph in Figure 13-5 is a simple model of a company. It assumes a single product or service, sold at a single price, complete linearity in all costs and expenses, and a direct relationship between variable expenses and dollars of revenue. In fact, of course, most businesses and other institutions are much more complex. Fortunately, it is increasingly possible to model these complexities, but the resulting model requires a computer, not a two-dimensional graph. Computers can develop, store, and use a sophisticated model of an operation, including multiple products at multiple prices, step functions in expenses, and variability of expenses in terms of parameters other than sales volume. With this useful model managers can consider a variety of what-if scenarios. Increasingly, managers use computer-based financial models of operations to test the financial consequences of alternative actions.

Backing into the Answer

Forecasting the specific changes in sales or margins that were used in the analyses above can be very difficult. The interrelationship among volume, price, cost, and profit is indisputable, but determining the extent of interdependency and exact dollar effects is quite another matter. To avoid single-point or discrete estimates, consider performing analyses in terms of probability distributions.

Another possibility is to rephrase the questions in terms of an indifference point. To illustrate, consider scenario (2) above. The original question was phrased as follows: Should Tamaki increase salespersons' commissions by 1.5 percent if such an increase will lead to 5 percent more sales? Because the precise increase in revenue—here estimated at 5 percent—is difficult to forecast, one might restate the question: By how much would sales have to be stimulated by a 1.5 percent commission increase in order for that increase to be warranted? The contribution dollars must be sufficient to cover fixed expenses and current profits.

$$\text{Revenue} = \frac{FC + \text{current profit}}{CM}$$

$$\text{Revenue} = \frac{44 + 22}{(0.40 - 0.015)} = \$176.6$$

Thus, revenue must increase from the normal rate of $170,000 by $6600, or 3.9 percent. From a profit standpoint, Tamaki is indifferent as to whether it continues the present commission rate and $170,000 per month of revenue, or increases the commission rate by 1.5 percent and achieves revenue of $176,600. One can now focus on the simple go–no go question: Are sales likely to be stimulated beyond this indifference point? Tamaki won't require 100 percent assurance before raising rates, but will certainly want a better than even chance that sales will exceed this indifference volume. In probability terms, the expected value of the distribution of possible revenue levels should exceed this indifference point.

Any of the other scenarios discussed above could be recast in terms of an indifference point. Scenario (4) might be recast to ask: By how much will revenues have to increase to offset the margin erosion from a 3 percent price decrease? Or, alternatively: How much of a price decrease could Tamaki withstand (i.e., operating profit to remain at present level) in return for a 5 percent volume increase? Decision makers often find it easier to make a go–no go judgment with respect to the single indifference point than to make single-point estimates regarding sales, prices, margins, volumes, competitor reactions, and so forth.

Break-Even Point

In Figure 13-5 the intersection of the total revenue line and the total expense line is labeled the **break-even** point. At that break-even point, Tamaki's sales revenue is just sufficient to cover all expenses with no profit or loss. Or, rephrased, at break-even revenue volume the contribution earned is just sufficient to cover the fixed expenses with no contribution to profit. The company's contribution margin is 40 percent, as shown in Figure 13-6. Therefore, the break-even point is

$$\text{Revenue} = \frac{\text{Fixed costs}}{\text{Contribution margin}} = \frac{FC}{CM} = \frac{46}{0.40} = \$115,000$$

In any month that the company's revenue drops below this point, the company incurs a loss. For example, at a revenue volume of $100,000:

Sales	$100,000
Variable expenses	60,000 (60% of sales)
Contribution	40,000
Fixed expenses	46,000
Operating profit (loss)	($ 6,000)

or

$$\text{Operating profit} = (CM) \times \text{Revenue}) - FC$$
$$= (0.40 \times 100) - 46 = \$6000 \text{ loss}$$

Stated another way, the loss equals the contribution margin times the amount by which revenue fell below the break-even volume:

$$(115,000 - 100,000) \times 0.40 = \$6000 \text{ loss}$$

New companies and inadequately financed companies need particularly to focus on break-even volumes. A company consistently operating below break-even will ultimately run out of financial resources and fail; it is marching a steady path to bankruptcy.

Two refinements of this break-even analysis are frequently useful. First, note that this break-even point is in terms of reported profits, measured on the accrual basis. Of even more criticality to a company is reaching *cash* break-even. A company with large noncash expenses (primarily depreciation) can operate for a long time below profit break-even so long as it is operating above cash break-even. If included among Tamaki's $46,000 fixed expenses are $10,000 of depreciation and amortization, the company's cash break-even is

Cash fixed expenses = $36,000
Contribution margin = 40%
Revenues required to break even = $36,000 ÷ 0.40 = $90,000

A second refinement considers points other than the zero-profit point. Many companies have obligations beyond just meeting their expenses. For example, suppose Tamaki's five-year term loan agreement requires monthly principal payments of $10,000. Tamaki needs to earn sufficient after-tax income to fund these payments; if the company's income-tax rate is 40 percent, it needs $16,667 per month in pretax profit to realize $10,000 in net income. The company's break-even for this profit requirement is

Contribution required = fixed cost plus required profit
= $46,000 + $16,667 = $62,667

Contribution margin = 40%
Revenues required to service debt obligations = $62,667 ÷ 0.40
$$= \$156,667$$

Other companies feel strongly about maintaining a certain dividend policy or funding a certain employee bonus plan or providing resources for a capital investment program; a break-even type analysis is useful in assessing the companies' risks in achieving these goals.

OPERATING LEVERAGE

This discussion of break-even makes clear that the higher a company's break-even point the greater its risk of operating at a loss. A high break-even point typically implies high fixed costs, costs that do not automatically reduce if the expected revenue volume fails to materialize.

On the other hand, the high contribution margin that generally accompanies high fixed expenses provides an opportunity for handsome profits if actual revenue exceeds the expected volume. That is, if most expenses are fixed, total expenses increase only modestly as revenues increase; much of the increased sales volume is then reflected in higher profits.

The mix of fixed and variable expenses defines a company's **operating leverage.** A company with high fixed costs—with attendant high risk of loss and opportunity for profit—has high operating leverage. To the extent that most of a company's expenses are variable, it has relatively low risk of loss (expenses decline as sales decline) and relatively low opportunity for extraordinary profits (expenses increase as sales increase); such a company has low operating leverage. The conditions of high and low operating leverage are shown in Figure 13-8. Leverage effects on profit and loss are demonstrated in Figure 13-9.

Recall the discussion of debt leverage in Chapter 10. A company has high debt

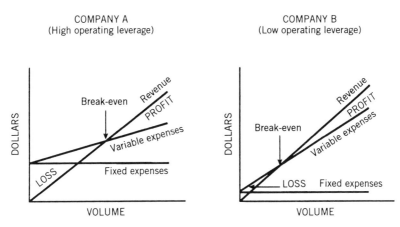

Figure 13-8   Illustration of operating leverage.

FIGURE 13-9   Effect of Operating Leverage

	Company A (High Operating Leverage)	Company B (Low Operating Leverage)
Normal Operations		
Sales	$1,000,000	$1,000,000
Expenses		
Variable	250,000 (25%)	600,000 (60%)
Fixed	600,000	250,000
	850,000	850,000
Operating profit	$ 150,000	$ 150,000
Break-even sales volume	$ 800,000	$ 625,000
Recession Conditions		
Sales	$ 750,000	$ 750,000
Expenses		
Variable	181,000 (25%)	450,000 (60%)
Fixed	600,000	250,000
	758,000	700,000
Operating profit (loss)	($ 31,000)	$ 50,000
Strong Economy Conditions		
Sales	$1,200,000	$1,200,000
Expenses		
Variable	300,000 (25%)	720,000 (60%)
Fixed	600,000	250,000
	900,000	970,000
Operating profit	$ 300,000	$ 230,000

leverage if a large proportion of its total capital is obtained from borrowings on which it is obligated to pay interest. A company has low debt leverage when most of its capital is obtained from shareholders, since the company is not obligated to pay dividends unless its fortunes permit their payment. While debt leverage and operating leverage are different phenomena, their effects are parallel. Both high debt leverage and high operating leverage are risky, but both create opportunity for improving profit.

Companies with high operating leverage tend to be those that are quite capital- (as opposed to labor-) intensive; depreciation, maintenance and other expenses associated with capital equipment tend to be fixed. As companies become more automated, increasing their investment in plant, they become more highly leveraged. Electric and telephone utilities have high operating leverage, since most of their expenses derive from fixed plant: the generating and distribution facilities of electric utilities, and the telephone lines, switching facilities, and central offices of telephone utilities. The incremental expenses incurred by the utility—that is, variable costs—associated with a customer making another long-distance telephone call or leaving the porch light on overnight are very small.

Labor- (as opposed to capital-) intensive operations have low operating leverage. Personal-service firms, such as janitorial services or secretarial services, are examples. These companies require very little capital equipment; most of their expenses are people-related. If business picks up, more janitors or secretaries are hired, and they are removed from the payroll again when business slackens. Employee wages and salaries represent the bulk of the expenses and they are variable.

A manager makes the trade-off between risk of loss and opportunity for profit in deciding whether to increase or decrease the company's operating leverage. In the Tamaki example, renegotiating the service contract to a higher fixed monthly fee (from a lower fixed fee plus a percentage of revenue) increases Tamaki's operating leverage. New and smaller firms with limited financial resources are well advised to maintain variability in as many expenses as possible, in order to reduce risk. On the other hand, a stable, secure, well-financed larger company may choose to increase operating leverage in order to provide opportunities for increased profits, accepting the attendant higher risk. Companies with high operating leverage frequently offset this risk by arranging to finance with little debt leverage—that is, by reducing the financing risk. Conversely, a company with low operating leverage is in a better position to assume the risks associated with high debt leverage. Only companies with very stable and predictable revenue streams—such as public utilities—are able to tolerate both high operating leverage and high debt leverage.

SUMMARY

Interpretation of both budget reports and cost accounting reports (the latter to be discussed in subsequent chapters) is influenced greatly by the mix of fixed and variable expenses (costs). Fixed expenses are those that are independent of volume of activity, while variable expenses are those that vary directly with activity volume.

Analysis of budget variances (the comparison of budgeted and actual financial results) requires a clear understanding of how expenses vary with volume. Flexible budgeting provides that variable costs be budgeted as percentages of revenue and fixed costs at absolute dollar levels. Actual results are then appropriately and usefully compared to volume-adjusted budget data.

Audiences of financial reports often make the implicit and erroneous assumption that expenses and costs are variable when in fact the great bulk of them are fixed—or, more accurately, they are fixed in the short term, although by management action they can be made to vary over the long term.

A clear understanding of the interrelationship among volume of sales or revenue, selling price, operating costs (fixed and variable), and profits help managers to analyze many day-to-day operating decisions. Simple or sophisticated models that describe these interrelationships are now widely used to test alternative action plans before final decision—that is, to analyze what-if questions. Such models can also help you focus on the important issues of operating leverage and break-even points.

NEW TERMS

Break-even. Condition of zero profit or loss. Break-even occurs when total contribution equals total fixed costs.

Contribution. The difference between total revenue (sales) and total variable costs.

Contribution margin. Contribution as a percentage of total revenue (sales).

Contribution statement. In contrast to a conventional operating statement (see Chapter 4), a statement that distinguishes fixed expenses and variable expenses in determining operating profit.

Fixed expenses (costs). Those costs that remain unchanged with modest changes in volume of activity.

Flexible budget. A form of budget wherein variable expenses are budgeted in relationship to activity volume (e.g., stated as percentage of revenue) and fixed expenses are stated in absolute dollar terms.

Operating leverage. The extent to which a company's total costs and expenses are fixed. A company with high fixed costs but low variable costs is said to have high operating leverage. A company with high operating leverage has high risk of incurring operating losses but also opportunities for leveraging profits higher.

Variable expenses (cost). Those costs that vary directly and proportionally with modest changes in volume of activity.

Volume-adjusted budget. A budget that has been revised to reflect actual volume of activity during the accounting period. Volume-adjusted budgets are particularly useful when both fixed and variable cost elements are present.

DISCUSSION QUESTIONS

13.1 Indicate which of the following expenses should be viewed as variable:

(a) Engineering salaries, since they vary with the number of design engineers employed.

(b) Utilities expense to light and heat the factory and office, since these expenses vary with the season.

(c) Packaging materials expenses, since these expenses vary with the number of products shipped from the factory.

(d) Discounts allowed expense, since these expenses vary with the volume of sales of the company.

(e) Depreciation expense, since these expenses vary with the size of the factory.

(f) Labor wage rates, since by agreement with the labor union they vary with the rate of inflation.

13.2 What is the break-even point for a service company?

13.3 Under what circumstances is high operating leverage a desirable condition for a manufacturing company? When is it an undesirable condition?

13.4 What additional information is required to convert the fixed-dollar budgets discussed in the previous chapter into flexible budgets, a primary focus of this chapter?

13.5 Many argue that in reality no costs are truly fixed. How would you respond to that argument?

13.6 Wages paid to factory workers have long been assumed to be variable manufacturing expenses. What factors have led to that assumption being less and less valid?

13.7 Distinguish between contribution margin and gross margin. Be specific.

13.8 Give two examples of industries that are characterized by high operating leverage and two that are characterized by low operating leverage.

13.9 If you were the operator of an ice cream and yogurt shop in your town, how would you categorize your expenses and which of those expenses are likely to be variable and which are likely to be fixed? Can you foresee ways in which you could convert some of your fixed costs into variable costs, and some of your variable costs into fixed costs?

13.10 Assume that you operate a small firm manufacturing kitchen cabinets. If you wished to improve your profits in prosperous periods, you might seek to increase your operating leverage. How would you go about doing that? Alternatively, you might seek to reduce your risk by reducing your operating leverage; how would you go about doing that?

PROBLEMS

13.1 What is the break-even point for a company that anticipates monthly fixed costs of $525,000 and variable costs equal to 55 percent of sales?

13.2 Refer to question 13.1 above. If the company could reduce its variable costs to 45 percent of sales by additional automation, an action which would also add $150,000 to its monthly fixed costs:
(a) What would its new break-even point be?
(b) Would its operating profit be improved by this action when monthly sales reach $1.6 million?
(c) Below what monthly sales volume is the company better off foregoing the automation?

13.3 If your department's fixed-dollar budget variance shows a credit balance of $3000 for the month; its flexible budget is comprised of $15,000 of fixed costs and variable costs equal to 30 percent of sales volume; and actual sales for the month fell 20 percent below the budgeted level of $45,000, calculate the variance between actual and volume-adjusted budget expenses for the month.

13.4 The hot dog stand at the local ballpark pays monthly rental of $4000 plus 10 percent of revenue. Labor costs are $3000 per month for the permanent staff plus part-time labor that averages $10 per 100 hot dogs sold. Food and materials expenses average $40 per 100 hot dogs sold. Other fixed expenses are $15,000. During a normal month of baseball season the stand expects to sell 20,000 hot dogs at two dollars each.

(a) In a typical month, how much does the hot dog stand expect to make in operating profit?

(b) What is the break-even point in monthly number of hot dogs sold?

(c) If the stand could increase sales by 10 percent (2000 hot dogs) by decreasing its price to $1.90 per hot dog, should it institute the price reduction?

(d) If the stand could increase sales by 10 percent (2000 hot dogs) at the $2 price by increased advertising at the ball park, should it undertake this additional advertising if it will add $2500 to the stand's monthly fixed costs?

(e) The stand operator is renegotiating the lease arrangement with the park. The ballpark seeks to increase the fixed portion of the rent to $6000 per month, and is willing to consider reducing the percentage of stand revenue that it receives. Should the owner be enthusiastic about this changed rent formula? What is the maximum percentage of revenue she should be willing to pay if the fixed portion of the rent is to increase to $6000 per month?

13.5 The O'Brien Company utilizes flexible budgeting for its manufacturing operations. The budget for the production scheduling department is described by

$$\text{Monthly expense budget} = \$45,000 + (\text{DL1} - \text{DLn}) \times 0.140$$

where DL1 is the actual direct labor for the month and DLn is the normal monthly direct labor.

(a) What is the departmental expense budget during a normal month?

(b) If the normal monthly direct labor cost is $145,000, what would be the budget formula in the more traditional form: Budget = FC + DL1 where FC is the monthly fixed costs and DL1 is actual direct labor cost for the month?

(c) By what percentage is the production scheduling manager expected to decrease expenditures in a slow month when direct labor is 10 percent below the normal level?

(d) If the manager decides to subcontract part of the work that the department performs, fixed costs of $4,400 will be replaced by a variable cost equal to 3 percent of direct labor cost. How would the flexible budgeting formula be affected? Under what circumstances would you recommend this subcontracting?

13.6 The reported selling expense variance at Morphy Corporation for September 1995 was $23,000 credit, measured against the fixed-dollar budget (that is, the budget unadjusted for volume). When the same selling expenses are measured against the flexible budget (adjusted for volume), the variance was $15,000 debit.

(a) Was volume of activity at Morphy above or below normal (expected) levels for September?

(b) If the flexible budget for selling expenses for a month is

$$\text{Expenses} = \$135,000 + (0.07)\ \text{Sales}$$

what was the difference between actual sales and expected sales in September?

(c) How would you evaluate the performance of the sales department at Morphy for the month of September?

13.7 The Wilkinson Maintenance company, a contract janitorial service, reported actual and variance results for April 1996 as follows (debit, or unfavorable, variances shown in parentheses):

	April Actual	Variance from Fixed-dollar Budget
Revenue	$106,000	$4,000
Expenses		
Wages	62,000	(2,200)
Salaries	12,400	200
Supplies	10,200	(600)
Transport	3,600	(200)
Depreciation	6,000	0
Miscellaneous	2,800	200
Total expenses	97,000	(2,600)
Operating profit	$ 9,000	$1,400

Wages are expected to vary directly with volume; management salaries are generally fixed, except that included in salaries is a bonus for the general manager equal to 1 percent of revenue. The general manager believes that janitorial supplies should be budgeted at 7 percent of revenue, while the balance of supplies expense is fixed. The amount of transport expense depends, in part, upon the location of the particular jobs. Depreciation and miscellaneous expenses are fixed.

(a) What was Wilkinson's flexible-budgeted profit for April?

(b) How would you evaluate the general manager's operating performance in April?

13.8 A long-term care facility has a total of 120 beds. Each patient is charged $125 per day for full care, including meals and nursing. The out-of-pocket cost of the food is about $24 per patient per day. The number of nurses employed varies with the number of patients in the facility. When the facility is full, 360 nurse hours are required per day for patient care. The nurses are paid $15 per hour. In April, the facility averaged 83 patients and lost $7,550. Assuming there are 30 days in every month (to simplify calculations),

(a) What is the facility's break-even point in number of patients per day?

(b) If the nurses' wages are increased to $20 per hour, what is the new break-even point?

(c) If the nurses' wages are increased to $20 per hour and the hospital wants to break even with 80 patients in the facility, how much will each patient have to pay per day of care?

(d) If it were possible for the facility to subcontract its food operations, eliminating $47,000 per month in fixed costs and the out-of-pocket cost of the food in exchange for a payment to the subcontractor of $38 per patient per day,

   (1) What is the new break-even point, if salaries to the nurses remain at $15 per hour?

   (2) Would the hospital be more or less profitable when operating at full capacity?

(e) In order to provide more recreation activities, the hospital is considering increasing its fixed costs by $4,000 per month and its variable costs by $3 per patient per day. If the nurses' wages are increased to $20 per hour,

   (1) What would be the break-even point in patients per day if charges are increased to $130 per patient per day?

   (2) If the manager feels that plans should be based upon breaking even at an average occupancy of 80 patients per day, what would the daily charge per patient have to be to reach break-even?

13.9 The Chavez Corporation produces a standard line of fire fighting equipment sold to municipal fire departments. The corporation's operating statement, in conventional format, for the most recent year is

	Year ended September 30 ($000)
Sales	$91,260
Cost of goods sold	49,280
Gross margin	41,980

	Year ended September 30 ($000)
Operating expenses	
Selling	13,680
Development	5,940
Administration	7,740
	27,360
Operating profit	$14,620

Assume that the corporation's budget (in abbreviated form) for the year was

	($000)	%
Sales	$87,000	100%
Cost of goods sold		
Variable	34,800	40
Fixed	13,050	15
	47,850	55
Gross margin	39,150	45
Operating expenses		
Variable	4,350	5
Fixed	21,750	25
	26,100	30
Operating profit	$13,050	15%

How well did Chavez Corporation control its expenses this year? Explain.

13.10 Assume that you are a securities analyst for a large Wall Street firm. You have just received the year-end financial statements for the Dow Standard Corporation, a small manufacturing firm. Reported earnings for the firm were disappointing and you are trying to discern what effects pricing, volume and cost control have had in lowering the firm's profits from expected level. Shown below is your estimate for 1996 prepared late in 1995 (and confirmed as "reasonable" by Dow Standard's management), and the actual results just reported.

	($000)	
	Estimate for 1996	Actual for 1996
Sales	$200,000	$171,000
Cost of goods sold	120,000	112,000
Gross margin	80,000	59,000
Selling expenses	30,000	28,000
General expenses	10,000	9,600
Operating profit	$ 40,000	$ 21,400

In a telephone conversation with the corporation's treasurer, you learn that prevailing prices for the year were about 5 percent below the expected level. The company sells all of its products through independent agents to whom it pays 10 percent commission on sales.

(a) Determine the effect on operating profit of

    (1) the price decrease

    (2) control of selling expenses

(b) Determine what portion of budgeted manufacturing expenses must be fixed if, in fact, the difference between budget and actual for cost of goods sold is attributable solely to changes in physical volume.

(c) Perform the same analysis for general expenses.

(d) As a securities analyst, what is your overall assessment of Dow Standard's performance in 1996?

13.11 A percentage analysis of the budget for O'Malley & Sons for the current year is

Sales (1,000,000 units)		100%
Cost of goods sold		
Variable	40	
Fixed	15	55
Gross margin		45
Selling expenses		
Variable	10	
Fixed	10	20
General and administration expenses		15
Operating profit		10%

By mid-year sales and operating profits were running substantially ahead of the $6 million and $600,000, respectively, that the company planned for the year:

Sales (580,000 units)	$3,400,000
Cost of goods sold	1,800,000
Gross margin	1,600,000
Selling expenses	700,000
General and administration expenses	550,000
Operating profit	$ 350,000

(a) Present a complete but concise analysis of the actual results for the first half of the year. Analyze the effects of volume, selling price changes, and cost control on the operating results.

(b) Because of strong demand for the company's products, O'Malley & Sons is considering raising its selling price by 10 percent. By referring to the original budget for the year, how great a reduction in number of units sold could the company tolerate with this price increase and still earn the same:

(1) Dollar profit for the year?

(2) Percentage of operating profit to sales?

(c) What is the annual break-even volume (in dollars) implicit in the original budget?

(d) If by changing its manufacturing process the company increased its fixed expenses within Cost of Goods Sold by 5 percentage points and decreased its variable expenses by the same 5 percentage points, by how much would its annual break-even volume of sales (in dollars) be increased or decreased?

13.12 Shown below are the operating results for the last six fiscal quarters for a bicycle repair shop. The shop employs a manager and several permanent technicians; it also employs a large number of part-time high school students whose hours of work are increased and reduced as business fluctuates seasonally and for other reasons. (Dollar amounts in thousands.)

	I	II	III	IV	V	VI
Sales	$ 130.0	$ 134.6	$143.2	$148.6	$139.8	$136.0
Expenses						
Repair parts	56.6	58.6	62.0	64.8	60.8	59.2
Labor	47.0	48.0	49.6	50.8	49.0	48.2
Occupancy	13.4	13.4	13.4	13.4	13.4	13.4
Supplies	14.4	14.8	15.2	15.4	15.0	14.8
Total expenses	131.4	134.8	140.2	144.4	138.2	135.6
Operating profit (loss)	($ 1.4)	($ 0.2)	$ 3.0	$ 4.2	$ 1.6	$ 0.4

(a) Develop a flexible budget for the bicycle repair shop based upon these historical results.

(b) Calculate the break-even volume of sales for the shop and verify by reviewing the recent quarterly results.

(c) How much additional business would have to be generated to justify spending $2000 per quarter on additional advertising and promotion?

(d) The landlord who owns the building in which the shop is located is willing to reduce the fixed rent by $3000 per quarter in exchange for a rental supplement equal to 2 percent of shop revenue. Should the shop owner accept these revised rental terms? Why?

___14
INTRODUCTION TO COST ACCOUNTING

Continuing our discussion of managerial accounting, the next several chapters are devoted to what is popularly called **cost accounting.** Cost accounting develops detailed information on the cost of producing a product or service. Although traditionally treated as a subject quite apart from financial accounting, cost accounting is, in fact, simply a subset of it. Just as a subsidiary ledger is part of the general ledger, so cost accounting data are part of financial accounting data. Cost accounting reports amplify and clarify the values of cost of goods sold and inventory, and provide selected supplemental information useful to managers.

Recall from our earlier discussions that many transactions can be recorded in a number of alternative ways—for example, LIFO inventory accounting can be used instead of FIFO, or accelerated depreciation instead of straight line. The resulting financial statements are, of course, affected by these choices but either alternative is both accurate and acceptable. Similarly, in cost accounting we face choices. We arrive at quite different answers to the question, "What does the product cost?" depending upon our choice among alternative costing procedures.

To this point in our study of accounting, we have succeeded in developing financial statements for a variety of companies without referring to cost accounting. Why do we now need to consider a new set of accounting techniques? Where are these techniques to be used? The primary answer: in manufacturing firms.

A manufacturing company typically owns (holds) inventory at various stages of completion. For example, a manufacturer of safety helmets carries raw-material inventory (plastic resins and strapping material), in-process—or partially completed—inventory (for example, helmet shells that have been formed but not finished or assembled), and finished goods inventory (helmets awaiting shipment to customers).*

*Material that is considered raw to this manufacturer—for example, the plastic resin—would be considered finished materials to the company's supplier, the resin producer. It is essential to bear in mind the entity for which we are accounting.

To value properly the manufacturing company's assets, we must account for the increasing value of the inventory as it moves from raw to more finished states. Each of the valuation models presented in Chapter 2—time-adjusted value, market value, and cost models—recognizes that the manufacturing process increases the value of the inventory.

The term *cost accounting* implies the cost model, the basis of cost accounting procedures in general use today. Thus, in accordance with the realization concept, the profit earned by a manufacturing company from the purchase of raw materials, their transformation to finished goods, and the sale of those finished goods to customers is recognized only when the critical transaction occurs: the ultimate sale to the customer. In the transformation process, materials move from the raw state to progressively more complete states. The cost model requires us to reflect in increased inventory values those costs incurred in effecting this transformation. To fail to record these inventory value increases would be to understate profits in periods when manufacturing occurs and overstate profit in the period when the final sale to the customer occurs. If that fact is not now clear to you, it soon will be. Bear in mind, too, that cost accounting is useful in service, as well as manufacturing, firms.

WHAT QUESTIONS? WHY? FOR WHOM?

Early in our financial accounting discussion we asked: What decisions are going to be influenced by the financial information supplied? Who is going to make them? Why does the financial information influence these decisions? To whom are these data supplied?

Consider these same questions for cost accounting information. To answer the question "For whom?" is easy. Unlike the multiple audiences for financial accounting, there is one key audience for cost accounting information: internal management—that is, operating managers within the manufacturing company or service firm.

As you know, financial accounting requires cost data to value inventory and cost of goods sold, but these data could be supplied by the simplest cost accounting system. More elaborate systems are justified only if they supply more extensive useful information, since the cost accounting function exists primarily to serve operating managers by providing data and analyses for day-to-day operating decisions. Typically, no outside authorities—stockholders, banks, security analysts, or governmental regulators—require that these more elaborate data be assembled.

Two of the relevant questions to be answered by cost accounting data are "What is the value of inventory?" and "What manufacturing costs should be matched against sales revenues?" (i.e., "What was cost of goods sold for the period?"). But cost accounting information can shed light on many other operating questions as well.

For example, the marketing department faces these key decisions: what price to charge for the product or service; which products to promote; whether to discontinue a certain product; how much extra to charge to modify (customize) a standard product. While product costs are by no means the sole criterion for determining product selling prices or the composition of the product line, they are certainly relevant to the decision. Note, for example, that marketing is inclined to promote those products lines that offer the greatest margin between selling price and manufacturing cost. The company should consider discontinuing a product when its margin gets very small or turns negative. And if marketplace conditions suggest a price below manufacturing cost, drastic action is typically called for.

Certain companies sell their products or services at **cost plus**—that is, at a price equal to the cost of the product or service, plus a fixed amount of profit, or plus profit as a percentage of the cost. Many defense contractors and certain construction companies price on this basis. In these instances both supplier and customer must agree on the definition of the *cost* of the product or service. In effect, law firms, accounting firms, consulting companies, and other personal service operations bill their clients (customers) on a cost-plus basis.

Manufacturing managers face quite different decisions than do marketing managers. Shall the company perform a certain part of the manufacturing process itself, or shall it subcontract to an outside firm (typically called a **make-or-buy** decision)? Should the company invest in new production equipment? Should it upgrade existing equipment? Should it schedule one long production run of 100 pieces or two shorter production runs of 50 each? To answer these questions, the manager must consider both current production costs and how those costs will be affected by each alternative. Incidentally, the cost data relevant to these manufacturing decisions may not be identical with the data relevant to the marketing decisions outlined above.

Other questions that haunt operating managers are: Is the company operating efficiently? More efficiently this year than last? This month than last month? In plant A than in plant B? On product X than on product Y? Are operations generally proceeding "on plan?" As discussed in Chapter 12, budgeting helps answer these questions by highlighting deviations from plan on an *exception* basis. Cost accounting extends these management-by-exception techniques to particular products or projects.

And beyond strictly financial data, data developed for cost accounting purposes, some of it nonfinancial data, can be useful to, for example, the production-control group in scheduling both the facilities and the work force. These data include detail on labor hours and machine hours required to produce various products.

The cost accounting department also assists development and design engineers. The costs of existing products provide a basis for evaluating the probable cost of a new or redesigned product. Working together, the cost accountant and the industrial engineer (or value engineer) spot opportunities for significant cost reductions through product redesign, changes in manufacturing method, or material substitutions. A comprehensive cost accounting database is invaluable to engineering departments interested in contributing to increased profits.

In providing this cost information, cost accountants are not constrained by rules imposed by outside authorities. External audiences—stockholders, creditors, and government regulators—are largely unconcerned with the company's specific cost accounting procedures. As a result, few generally-accepted accounting principles exist for cost accounting. The cost accountant is free to arrange and rearrange cost data to be most useful to the primary audience, the line manager. Detailed cost information is considered confidential by most manufacturing companies; thus cost information from competitors is seldom available, and company-to-company comparability of cost information is of little concern. Note, however, that accounting methods within a single manufacturing company should be consistent to facilitate comparisons of cost data on different products, from different departments, and from different accounting periods.

A final introductory caveat: Be careful in answering the question "What does product X cost?" Both you and the person asking the question must understand the use to which the cost information will be put. You both also need to understand just what is included and excluded from the cost of product X. That is the next issue on which to focus: Which of all the expenses of a firm are properly included as costs of manufacturing the firm's products?

VALUATION IN COST ACCOUNTING: PRODUCT AND PERIOD EXPENSES

Recall that the fundamental accounting issue is valuation. Early chapters stressed the centrality of the question: How should we value assets and liabilities and, consequently, value revenues and expenses? As we now focus on accounting for the costs of manufacturing, service, and similar operations—that is, cost accounting—the issue remains precisely the same: How shall we value inventory and cost of goods sold?

To repeat, historical costs—the cost value method of valuation—continue to dominate. The question is what cost elements and how much of the historical cost of each element should be included in the valuation of a certain unit of output. And, the question is the same whether output is defined in terms of physical goods or intangible services.

We now must keep in sharp focus the distinction between product and period expenses. This distinction dictates the timing of expense recognition. Recall that product expenses are those that are matched in an accounting period to that period's revenues derived from delivering the corresponding services or physical goods. All expenses not so matched are considered period expenses; they are expensed during the period in which they are incurred, irrespective of what or how much was produced or sold in that period. Once we define product expenses, we define by deduction the period expenses: all nonproduct expenses accrued in the accounting period.

What is so important about this distinction, about the timing of expense recognition? Note that if, in an accounting period, inventory is growing—that is, the number of units manufactured exceeds the number sold—certain manufacturing expenditures of this period are reflected in the Inventory account (an asset); cost of goods sold is less than the total of manufacturing expenditures. Similarly, when inventory declines, more goods are sold than produced; since goods sold include some manufactured in previous periods, costs of goods sold for this period are greater than the period's manufacturing expenditures.

The distinction between product and period expenses is not always clean. We shall review in a moment the considerable gray area between product and period costs, and consider alternatives to resolving the split. While it is important just how the split is made, it is far more important that the resolution be consistent across accounting periods, across products, and across departments, in order to maintain comparability.

Note that the classification—the resolution of the gray area—affects the timing of expenses and therefore of profit. To the extent that more expenditures are categorized as product costs, fewer are period costs and thus:

- In periods when inventory grows, more expenditures are reflected as an asset (inventory), and fewer are expenses of the period—therefore, profit is greater.
- In periods when inventory levels decline, both the inventory reduction and the cost-of-goods-sold value are higher—therefore, profit is lower.

So, we come to the key question at the nub of cost accounting. What are the relevant product costs? Where do we draw this important line between product and period expenses?

DEFINING PRODUCT COSTS IN MANUFACTURING

Why does this problem only now arise? We have dealt with the distinction between product and period costs since Chapter 4. Until now, virtually all of our examples have been drawn from the merchandising industries, retail and wholesale. Here the distinction between product and period expenses is quite straightforward. Merchandise is purchased at a known price; that known price is the historical cost for purposes of both valuing inventory and valuing cost of goods sold when the merchandise is resold to customers. Note that the merchandise is resold in the same condition or state in which it was purchased; it has not been physically altered by the merchandising firm (except perhaps by combining it with other merchandise, or packaging it.)

Manufacturing firms, by contrast, **convert** the materials or merchandise that they purchase into different products or materials. This **conversion** is the fundamental difference between a manufacturing firm and a merchandising firm.

Does this conversion cause the material to become more valuable to the manufacturing company? Of course, and therefore in valuing later stages of inventory—that is, semifinished products (typically called work-in-process or work-in-progress) or completed products (typically called finished goods inventory)—the historical cost of the raw materials alone is inadequate. Including only material costs as product expenses would understate the value of semifinished or finished inventory and thus understate the value of cost of goods sold when that inventory is sold. The other side of that coin is, of course, that period expenses consequently would be over valued.

Surely the managers in the manufacturing firm would like to know what it costs to produce the product. That appears to be a simple question, but it is difficult to answer. Once we move away from confining product expenses to historical material costs, we open the Pandora's box of other possible costs that might be included as product expenses. How about wages paid to manufacturing labor? All labor? Including supervisors and quality inspectors? How about the plant manager or the vice president of manufacturing? And then, beyond salaries and wages, how about maintenance, depreciation on the facilities and equipment, power, and the host of other cost elements inherent in a manufacturing operation?

There is the dilemma. How do we resolve it? Here are some alternatives.

Material Only

Recognize that one possibility surely is to treat manufacturing environments as we have merchandising environments. The historical costs of materials purchased provide a reliable, verifiable, free from bias, and readily available basis for valuing inventories—whether raw, in-process, or finished—and, when the sale occurs, the related cost of goods sold value.

This alternative would deprive manufacturing managers of some potentially useful information, but the work of cost accountants would be greatly simplified.

Before discarding this alternative consider a very highly automated manufacturing plant, one into which raw material is inserted and from which a finished product in due course appears with no human interference. The plant employs no more than, say, a diligent but unskilled overseer whose sole task is to shut off the power to the plant if it begins to run amuck. While such plants are not numerous, they do exist. How different is such a plant from a merchandising operation? In a merchandising operation, materials typically arrive in bulk and leave singly or in small bunches. They are not converted in a manufacturing sense, but they are undoubtedly handled more than in the highly automated manufacturing plant. Both the merchandising and the highly automated manufacturing firms require substantial investments in facilities and equipment, and in both cases the work force consists of material handlers, sales personnel and various administrators. They are really very much alike.

If you are inclined to think that the cost of operating the highly automated manufacturing facility (power, maintenance, depreciation, for example) should be included in the cost of the finished product emanating from the automated facility, why not in a parallel manner include the cost of operating the retail store and wholesale warehouse facilities in the cost of the product delivered from the merchandising facility? In a merchandising operation, the product may be unchanged physically, but it is surely altered in the eyes of the purchaser. Don't make up your mind until we consider some other alternatives.

Moreover, remember that the definition of **direct material**—material directly related to the final product—is not necessarily clear cut. Every manufacturing firm purchases various materials that are used up in manufacturing but don't end up physically as part of the final product—for example, lubricants, solder for the flow soldering machine, cleaning fluids, and compounds. Are these considered direct material? Typically not, but the line between direct and indirect materials is not always sharp.

Material and Labor

A second alternative is to include material, as just discussed, and also wages of those members of the work force directly involved with manufacturing the product, so-called **direct labor.** This sounds like a step in the right direction, but it opens a new dilemma. What is direct labor? What part of the work force is directly involved in manufacturing? Only those that physically transform (convert) the product in the direction of its completed state? Most such transformation is actually done by machines of course. Well, then perhaps machine operators should be included as direct labor. How about material handlers, inspectors (they surely handle the product), and fork-lift drivers? All are important categories of labor, but are they direct labor or **indirect labor?** Moreover, if *directly involved* sounds like the right modifier to define direct labor, are you prepared to convince the department supervisor, production scheduler, maintenance mechanic and stockroom attendant that they are not directly involved? Surely, they think they are essential to the manufacturing process, at least as important as the machine attendant who spends most of his or her time watching an automatic machine tool operate.

Thus, the distinction between direct and indirect labor is fuzzy. Nevertheless, you could decide arbitrarily which personnel to consider direct labor and which indirect labor. We have encountered numerous other accounting situations where we have to make arbitrary calls, and this is no more or less perplexing than the others. Note, for example, that we also have to determine which salaries are in the indirect labor category and which are administrative expenses rather than indirect manufacturing expenses. Is the manufacturing vice president a production person or an administrative person? Once again, of course, being consistent in all these determinations is important.

So, to repeat, a second alternative is to define product expenses as comprised of solely direct material plus direct labor—commonly called **prime costs.**

Recall the discussion in the last chapter of variable and fixed costs, including a clear separation of the two. There is not much doubt that direct materials are variable costs: The more that is produced, the greater the consumption of direct materials, and that relationship is typically quite linear. Traditionally, direct labor is also treated as fully variable. Note the assumption required to justify such treatment: Management can and will add or remove direct labor proportionally with changes in volume of manufacturing. This assumption implies both that direct production workers can be laid off when activities slow and that additional workers can be hired (or brought back from layoff status) when volume of activity increases.

At least two conditions tend to invalidate the assumption that direct labor is variable. First, sound human-relations practices no longer permit adjusting employment levels to match fluctuating production activity with little concern for the welfare of the employees. Increasingly, companies work hard to dampen swings in employment, and many have virtually guaranteed stable employment, sometimes in the face of union pressure or government regulations, but often simply in response to societal pressure or a sense of responsibility. Second, as required production skill levels have increased, training periods for new employees have lengthened and thus the ranks of production workers cannot be augmented on short notice.

Once again we face the short-term–long-term dilemma. Surely production labor can be varied directly with long-term swings in production levels. Attrition will in time reduce employment levels without abusing a company's commitment to employees for stable employment, and new production workers can be trained in months (or years), if not in days or weeks. But, recognize that in the short term, direct labor hours committed to a particular manufacturing unit are quite sticky. The less management really can (or will) cause them to fluctuate as volume of activity changes, the less valid the assumption that direct labor is a variable expense.

Be forewarned: In our study of cost accounting we will typically treat prime costs as fully variable costs, as imperfect as that assumption is. If prime costs were fully variable and if, in addition, they were the only fully variable manufacturing costs, they would equal the incremental cost of producing one unit more of a product, and the amount saved by producing one unit less. However, in most manufacturing environments, some overhead cost elements also vary directly and proportionately with changes in volume of manufacturing activity.

Material, Labor, and Overhead

So, let's take the next step: consider including overhead as part of the definition of product expenses. What is overhead? It consists of all expenses incurred by the manufacturing department that are neither direct material nor direct labor. If this sounds like rather circular reasoning, recall the discussion above about the difficulty of isolating direct material from indirect material and distinguishing among direct labor, indirect manufacturing labor, and still other labor that is not a manufacturing expense.

Surely indirect material and indirect production labor are overhead expenses. So also are the costs of occupying the space in which manufacturing occurs: rent expense, depreciation expense on buildings and improvements, heat and light expenses, maintenance and janitorial expenses, and insurance and taxes on the property. Include also the depreciation, maintenance, repair, and other expenses associated with owning and maintaining the equipment used in the manufacturing department's equipment.

Note that this definition of product expenses includes only expenses of manufacturing. Thus, we must exclude the expenses of the engineering, development, marketing, selling, servicing, administrative, and all other departments that are not strictly manufacturing. But even this definition of product expenses is fuzzy; consider how you would account for the manufacturing engineering department. Is this a manufacturing function or an engineering function? Once again, it doesn't much matter which you choose, so long as you remain consistent in your choice from accounting period to accounting period.

Direct material and direct labor are, by definition, *directly* identified with the product: the material ends up in it and the direct labor workforce works directly on it. Not so with overhead. By definition overhead is indirect. To move forward with this definition of product expenses requires that we find some rational basis for allocating—we will call it **absorbing**—these indirect, overhead expenses into the product. The next chapter considers methods for absorbing overhead.

Recall again the distinction between fixed and variable costs and recognize that overhead includes many expenses which are fixed and relatively few that are fully variable. As a result, product expenses defined according to this alternative do not approximate well the incremental cost associated with producing one more unit of a product, nor the incremental cost saved by producing one less. This fact does not obviate the usefulness of the resulting product costs, but it does mean that volume-adjusted estimates of expenses must be cognizant of the mix of variable and fixed costs.

Material, Labor, Overhead, Engineering, Selling, and Administrative Expenses

We need not confine ourselves to including in product expenses only costs of manufacturing the product. We could also include the expenses associated with designing it, selling it, and administering the entire organization.

Such a definition of product expenses would, however, destroy our efforts to distinguish clearly between product and period expenses. Most of what we have been treating as period expenses would under this definition be absorbed into product expenses. But these other nonmanufacturing expenses are no less real and no less important to the successful mission of the manufacturing firm than those expenses incurred in the manufacturing departments. We could simply eliminate the distinction between product and period costs. After all, aren't managers interested in knowing the full cost of the firm's activities, measured in terms of the products delivered to customers? This fourth alternative definition of product expenses provides exactly that.

As with manufacturing overhead, we would have to find some method of allocating these nonmanufacturing expenses to the products produced; but, if we can find a rational basis—as we will in the next chapter—for allocating indirect manufacturing expenses to the products, we could use the same or a related method to allocate the engineering, selling, and administrative expenses.

Again, as with manufacturing overhead, these expenses are likely to be heavily weighted with fixed, as opposed to variable, expenses. We need therefore to realize that, as with the previous alternative, the resulting product costs do not approximate incremental costs.

IS CONVERSION LIMITED TO MANUFACTURING?

Selecting the third alternative definition of product expenses (material, direct labor and manufacturing overhead) implies that the key activity in the conversion process is manufacturing. To be sure, that is the department that physically transforms materials from one state to another. But by no means is that the only department engaged in activities crucial to delivering satisfaction to the customers, activities for which the customer is willing to pay.

Consider, for example, the engineering department. Hardware design engineers are responsible for a great deal of the value added in a product. And, in a software company, one might argue that software engineers (programmers) carry the primary responsibility for adding value to software products, as the cost of reproducing the computer disk—the manufacturing cost, if you will—is trivial.

And increasingly sales and marketing personnel provide service (both before and after the sale of the product) that is key to customer satisfaction. Why shouldn't the cost of these activities be included in the product expense that is matched against the revenue earned from the customer?

Thus, if we broaden the concept of conversion as it applies to cost accounting, we see that the range of possible product expense definitions just discussed makes sense. Before we return to that range of possibilities, let's review the history of cost accounting in industrial countries.

HISTORICAL PERSPECTIVE OF COST ACCOUNTING

The procedures and rules of cost accounting evolved with the Industrial Revolution, as manufacturing became a key economic activity and manufacturing firms grew in size and scope to the point where managers became distant from shop-floor activities. Only then did managers' questions of the type outlined at the beginning of this chapter become relevant: What does a product cost? how efficient is a section of the manufacturing department? Should a product be redesigned, or phased out, or promoted more aggressively than a related product?

Prior to the Industrial Revolution, virtually all commercial transactions occurred between an owner—a farmer or a craftsman—and a customer. To the extent the owner employed others, he (almost always he, not she) paid them wages on a piece-rate basis, an absolutely variable direct-labor wage. Indirect labor was limited to that portion of the owner's time not devoted directly to production. Overhead was minimal, particularly relative to material and direct labor inputs. Formal cost accounting was clearly unnecessary.

The Industrial Revolution, however, brought opportunities for owners to increase the scale of their operations, to invest substantial amounts of capital, to create hierarchical organizations, and to hire workers on a long-term rather than piece-work basis. In turn, these owner–managers—and increasingly hired managers—needed internal information on costs and efficiencies, in addition to the information always obtained in external marketplace transactions.

The earliest large-scale manufacturing activities were in process-type industries, particularly textiles and steel. In these operations raw materials were converted into a single finished product. Costs were collected for materials and labor devoted to the process, and these aggregated costs were divided by total output to determine cost per unit. Overhead was a relatively small proportion of total costs, as capital investment per employee was minor by today's standards and indirect labor was minimal, as virtually all employees were devoted to the single production process.

With the advent of metal fabrication companies during the late nineteenth century, the process-industry cost accounting techniques were adapted for this somewhat more complex environment. Now the manufacturing activities consisted of many discrete steps rather than a single process, and the labor force consisted of individuals of widely varying skill levels. Supervisors, inspectors, and material handlers now spread their attention and activities across several of the discrete production steps, and thus they became indirect labor rather than direct labor. Purchased parts were combined with fabricated parts, and labor was required to assemble finished products.

Still, overhead remained a relatively small portion of total costs; direct material and direct labor costs were dominantly important. Product expenses were defined to include overhead in addition to direct labor and material, but overhead was a small fraction of the total product cost and indirect labor comprised much of that overhead. Moreover, employee relations were an outgrowth of the pre-Industrial Revolution agricultural and craft worker society. Workers were expected to be hired when work was available and laid off when the work was completed. Thus, labor—all labor, both direct and indirect—was largely a variable cost.

Interestingly, most cost accounting procedures in use today were developed prior to 1925. These procedures are built around the third alternative definition of product expenses discussed above: direct material, direct labor, and overhead. Remember, in the early part of this century, overhead costs were low relative to direct labor and direct material, and these product costs were dominantly variable. Thus, product expenses so defined approached incremental costs, providing information that was extremely useful to managers.

What has happened since 1925? A great deal to manufacturing industries, and unfortunately not much to cost accounting procedures. The direct material-direct labor-and-overhead definition of product expenses continues to be the accepted one for industry today. It has become a progressively less satisfactory definition over the last 75 years.

Modern Manufacturing

How have manufacturing industries changed? Three trends are particularly noteworthy. First, industry has become far more automated, a trend that will surely continue. Automation involves the substitution of investment capital for labor—or, in a cost accounting view, direct labor is replaced by overhead expenses, specifically the depreciation, maintenance, power, and related nonlabor operating expenses of the automatic equipment. Industry in highly industrialized countries has moved to the point where direct labor, instead of comprising 50 or 60 percent of the final selling price to the customer, is now often only three or four percent. Cost accounting systems built to track direct labor costs when those costs predominated now focus a great deal of attention on what has become a minor cost element.

Second, both because of changes in employee relations practices and because of the trend toward automation, manufacturing costs have become very largely fixed rather than variable with volume of activity. Depreciation of capital equipment is obviously a fixed cost (except in those rare instances where the units-of-production method of depreciation is appropriate because the equipment's useful life is a function of the volume produced on it). As mentioned earlier, direct labor is becoming increasingly fixed in nature, simply because managers are committed to a stable employment policy; the potential net benefits of such an enlightened policy are substantial when direct labor is a small part of total manufacturing costs. And, as the indirect labor force has become increasingly populated with highly skilled manufacturing and maintenance engineers and with sophisticated production planners and schedulers responsible for keeping the highly automated plant operating at peak efficiency, the indirect labor force is also essentially a fixed cost, as essential to the company's operations as are the corporate officers, in both boom times and recessions.

Third, manufacturing expenses are less deterministic than they once were; now they, like marketing and engineering departmental costs, are more discretionary. Recall that deterministic costs are those about which one can say the less the better; or put another way, we can estimate in a scientific manner what we should spend on a deterministic cost element. For example, we can determine objectively the direct material costs of a product. We can list the materials that go into the product and then we can price them from outside sources; we can set a standard (or budget) for what the direct material cost of the product should be, and if, by clever purchasing, we can beat that cost (with no sacrifice in quality or delivery), we can be certain that we are better off. Essentially the same can be said for direct labor. Time and motion study procedures permit us to estimate the time required to do manual tasks; we can thus set a standard (or budget) for the product's direct labor cost and, if the labor force requires more time than estimated, we can be certain that something went wrong—problems arose or the force was inefficient.

We cannot be so certain about discretionary costs. Take the costs of manufacturing engineering for a product. We can estimate the engineering hours required to develop the process for a new product or a redesigned product, but engineering is not a repetitive task and we cannot set reliable time standards for the task. Moreover, we are willing to exceed our manufacturing engineering hours estimate if the result is a process with substantially better reliability or lower costs than we originally envisioned. This same situation may apply to employee training or equipment maintenance expenses. We cannot scientifically determine how much we need to spend on training in order to achieve a certain level of competence. The decisions on these expenditures are in the realm of art, not science.

Now suppose in a particular accounting period we spend more than we planned on manufacturing engineering manpower to improve a process. Does this represent poor performance? Not necessarily. It does indicate expenditures in excess of plan, but exceeding the planned expense level may be highly desirable. Suppose the manufacturing engineers discovered mid-project an opportunity, with a 10 percent increase in engineering hours, to leapfrog the primary competitor's quality specifications. To miss that opportunity simply to meet the engineering hours budget would be foolish. Similarly, to continue an unsuccessful project merely because the engineering hours are available is also foolish. But, terminating the project early only results in expenditures below the planned level; it does not spell good performance, since after all the project itself was unsuccessful.

Recall that virtually no expense categories are wholly deterministic or wholly discretionary. Instead they fall somewhere along a spectrum from primarily deterministic to primarily discretionary. More and more manufacturing costs are falling closer to the discretionary end of that spectrum, by comparison with the situation early in this century. As manufacturing activities have become more complex, more automated, subject to more rapid change, and less direct-labor paced, the associated expenses have become less deterministic and more discretionary. The manufacturing engineering and design engineering departments now have much tighter linkages; their tasks are similar. The design engineers design products, while the manufacturing engineers design and operate processes. Decisions on maintenance expenditures for automated equipment require judgment: too much and too little maintenance are both foolish, and the optimum level is difficult to determine scientifically.

Excessive Concern for Manufacturing Costs

Moreover, if a company shortchanges activities in manufacturing, the downstream consequences can be costly, costly in decreased customer satisfaction to be sure, but also in higher warranty service expenditures. Thus, a preoccupation with lowering product expenses, when product expenses are limited solely to manufacturing costs, may have the undesirable result of adding cost to the selling and field service departments. The optimum manufacturing cost is often not the lowest possible manufacturing cost.

So, the cost accounting environment has become much more complex, and yet the traditional cost accounting still assumes that:

(1) The relevant product expenses are solely manufacturing expenses; manufacturing is where conversion occurs—where value is added—and that is where management's cost control attention should be focused.

(2) The key manufacturing cost is direct labor; overhead should be assigned to products based upon the amount of direct labor expended on that product.

(3) Product expenses comprised of direct labor, direct material, and production overhead provide the relevant data for most management decisions (in spite of the fact that overhead is increasingly fixed in nature and is growing as a proportion of total manufacturing expenses.)

(4) Managers should concentrate primarily on lowering product expenses (in spire of the fact that these expenses are increasingly discretionary rather than deterministic in their nature.)

As we proceed in the study of cost accounting, bear in mind these unrealistic assumptions on which so much current practice is built. While subsequent chapters will review and recommend alternatives to the conventional practice, you should have no illusions that traditional practices will be soon altered.

Before leaving this brief history lesson, it is appropriate to note that the term *overhead* grew out of a very different manufacturing environment than today's. When direct labor and direct material dominated, accounting for 80 percent or more of the total product expense, indirect manufacturing expenses were almost incidental. The important work was carried out by the direct labor force; wages to others employed by the manufacturing company, together with the cost of acquiring and maintaining the manufacturing plant facility, were incidental and only a fraction of the cost of direct material plus direct labor. Overhead comprised a necessary set of costs, to be sure, but managers had to almost apologize to the real workers, direct laborers, for the unfortunate existence of overhead. Indeed, a popular synonym for overhead was (and still is) burden, a word that truly describes how people felt about such costs: a burden to the direct labor force.

Today direct labor has in many instances become incidental, and overhead costs dominate product expenses. Overhead may be indirect in the sense that we use that term in cost accounting, but it is surely mainstream. The terms overhead and burden are now wildly inappropriate. The production supervisor, manufacturing engineer, maintenance specialist, production scheduler, as well as the host of other individuals who comprise the indirect work force do not consider themselves in any sense a burden to those relatively few individuals who are directly involved in the conversion process. Indeed, they are precisely the opposite. For these reasons this book favors the phrase indirect costs—when referring solely to manufacturing costs, indirect production costs, or IPC—over the terms overhead and burden.

SOME ILLUSTRATIONS AMONG THE RANGE OF POSSIBILITIES

We have not resolved the dilemma of just what costs to include in the definition of product expenses, and it is probably clear to you by now that a single answer is not going to fit all situations. Consider a couple of quick examples.

We have said repeatedly that a merchandising firm—wholesaler or retailer—does, and probably should, include only direct material costs (i.e., the purchase cost of the merchandise being resold) as product expenses. All other expenses are treated as period expenses. This structure readily provides the merchandising managers with terribly useful information: the margin between selling price and acquisition cost. Surely in comparative terms some merchandise takes up more space, requires more handling, is more difficult to sell, and flows through inventory more slowly. All of these conditions add to the cost of carrying such merchandise; that is, they contribute to higher overhead, or indirect costs. We could distribute this overhead to the various merchandise items (as a percentage of selling price, or based upon the number of days it is in inventory, or on some other basis), but merchandising managers have traditionally not found much use for elaborate cost accounting reports that distribute overhead. They use various rules of thumb—departments having lower annual sales per square foot of occupied space require higher gross margins, or inventory that turns over rapidly requires lower gross margins—but raw gross margins, unaltered by the distribution of indirect costs, remain the key cost accounting data.

Take at the opposite extreme a marketing research firm that charges each customer based upon total costs incurred in each individual marketing research project. Total here means total, everything: not just the salaries of researchers assigned to the particular project and their assistants and aids, but the costs associated with administering the firm, selling future projects, maintaining the library, operating the computer system, renting the space, retaining staff currently between projects (idle time), and so forth. All must be included in the marketing research firm's definition of product expenses. Thus, indirect costs incurred by the firm must be distributed to the various projects in a manner that is equitable for, and explainable to, all clients, since the fully compiled costs are the basis for billing those clients.

These two examples represent the extremes along the range of possibilities for the definition of product expenses. Where do traditional manufacturing and service firms fit? That's the conundrum. They don't ideally all fit the same definition, in spite of the fact that accounting conventions typically so demand. Tradition says that product expenses should include direct material, direct labor, and all indirect costs in manufacturing—but only manufacturing, not engineering or administration or selling.

Chapter 16 addresses the question of how to allocate—or absorb—indirect expenses in this traditional cost accounting environment.

FLOW OF PRODUCT EXPENSES: A MANUFACTURING FIRM

The cost accounting system of a manufacturing firm tracks the costs of converting materials from one state to another. This conversion typically does not take place instantaneously, but rather stretches over a time period as short as minutes or hours or as long as months or, in extreme cases, years. Direct material flows from raw-material inventory into in-process inventory and finally into finished goods inventory. During this period in-process inventory is increasing in value; additional direct material, direct labor, and indirect production costs (IPC) are augmenting the value of in-process inventory as it moves toward its finished state.

Figure 14-1 shows a simplified cost flow chart. The debit and credit of each cash flow is identified by a letter and described in the legend. Take time to understand the flows depicted here. Note particularly the three categories of inventory—raw, in-process, and finished goods—and the fact that all three are assets on the balance sheet.* Product costs become expenses only when the final product is sold. By contrast, the period costs—however defined, but typically including selling, engineering, and administrative expenses—never end up as part of the inventory values;

---

*Sometimes purchased material is used directly upon receipt, with the result that raw material inventory is at or near zero. Similarly, finished goods inventory will be low if most finished products are shipped directly from the factory floor to customers.

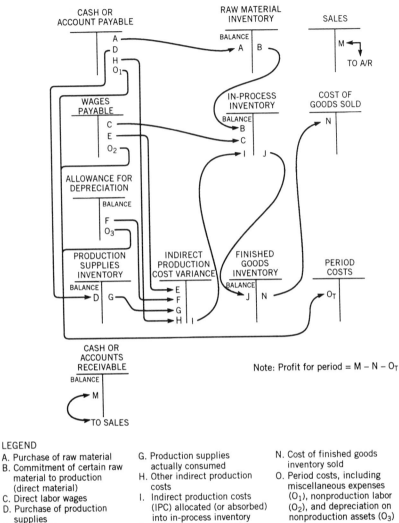

Figure 14-1   Cost accounting flow chart: manufacturing.

LEGEND

A. Purchase of raw material
B. Commitment of certain raw material to production (direct material)
C. Direct labor wages
D. Purchase of production supplies
E. Indirect labor wages
F. Depreciation of production equipment and factory space

G. Production supplies actually consumed
H. Other indirect production costs
I. Indirect production costs (IPC) allocated (or absorbed) into in-process inventory
J. Value of finished goods completed during the period
M. Sale of finished products

N. Cost of finished goods inventory sold
O. Period costs, including miscellaneous expenses (O_1), nonproduction labor (O_2), and depreciation on nonproduction assets (O_3)

they are expenses of the period regardless of how much product is manufactured or sold.

The flow chart shows an opening balance in, and debit and credit entries to, each of the inventory accounts during the period. Their closing balances may be greater or less than the opening balances. That is, more raw material may have been purchased than used (*A* more than *B*), or the reverse may be true. Again, more production may have been completed during the period than started; if so, in-process inventory declined during the period.

Finally, if the amount of physical product sold exceeded the amount produced, N must be greater than J: finished goods inventory declined. This fact means that cost of goods sold for this accounting period includes some production expenditures incurred in previous periods. Or, stated another way, the total of this period's production expenditures was less than the amount shown in cost of goods sold, and the corresponding offset is the decline in the asset value, inventory. Similarly, if production exceeded sales, then J must be greater than N: finished-goods inventory increased. If so, a portion of this period's production expenditures is being put into inventory (an asset). Or, stated another way, of the total production expenditures this period, a portion remains in inventory to be recognized as an expense (cost of goods sold) in future periods when the goods are sold to customers.

In this latter case—where production exceeds sales—you may feel that expenses are understated and profit overstated, since a portion of production expenditures is recorded as an asset. But the assets of the firm have indeed increased and no misstatement of profit occurs unless the items now in finished goods inventory prove ultimately to be unsalable.

FLOW OF PRODUCT EXPENSES: THE MARKETING RESEARCH FIRM

Now consider a service firm, specifically the marketing research firm mentioned earlier. It wants to capture all costs as product expenses to provide the basis for billing customers.

As illustrated in Figure 14-2 this firm uses two *overhead pools,* one for those indirect costs that routinely support the marketing research projects (for example, the cost of space occupied by the line market researchers, the telephone system, the library, the computer facility) and the second pool for general functions of the firm (for example, top management salaries, the remainder of the space costs, promotion expenses, the accounting office.) Why two pools? Typically because the basis for distribution of each pool—that is, the overhead absorption mechanism—is different. For the first pool the overhead absorption mechanism is direct salaries charged to the marketing research project, the assumption being that cost elements in this first pool are driven by (but are undoubtedly not directly variable with) the activity level of the line marketing researchers. The second pool uses for overhead absorption some intermediate level of project cost: for example, direct salaries plus overhead assigned from the first pool plus other direct charges to the project (including services rendered by outside contractors.)

Figure 14-2 illustrates the flows associated with this cost accounting system. Note that all expenses are "absorbed" into jobs in one of three manners: directly (A, C, and $F3$); by means of the service support overhead rate; and by means of the administrative overhead rate. No expenses remain as period expenses to be matched to the accounting period.

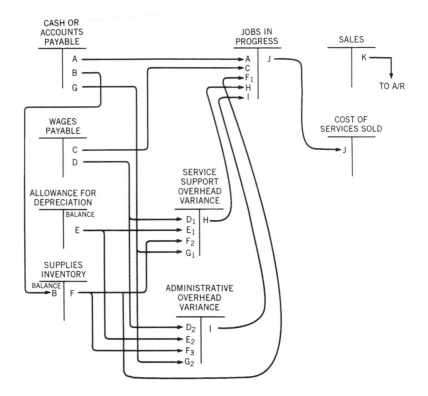

Figure 14-2 Cost accounting flow chart: market research firm.

LEGEND

A. Purchase of miscellaneous materials and outside services chargeable directly to jobs
B. Purchase of supplies
C. Direct labor wages chargeable to jobs
D. Other wages and salaries, including service support functions (D_1) and administrative functions (D_2)
E. Depreciation on equipment used in service support (E_1) and in administration (E_2)
F. Supplies issued from inventory: directly to jobs (F_1); to service support functions (F_2); and to administrative functions (F_3)
G. Other indirect costs (e.g.: telephone, travel, rent, insurance, utilities expenses), including those absorbed as service support overhead (G_1) and those absorbed as administrative overhead (G_2)
H. Service support costs (overhead) allocated to (absorbed by) jobs by means of the service support overhead rate using job direct labor (C) as overhead vehicle
I. Administrative costs (overhead) allocated to (absorbed by) jobs by means of the administrative overhead rate using the sum of all job charges ($A+C+F_1+H$) as overhead vehicle
J. Cost of jobs (projects) completed and delivered to customers during the accounting period
K. Revenue earned on completed jobs (projects) during the accounting period

Raw-material inventory of the type found in manufacturing firms is not present here (although the company maintains a supplies inventory), nor does the concept of finished-goods inventory fit a service firm of this type. But, as with manufacturing firms, some jobs (projects) may remain in process (not yet completed) at the end of the accounting period; these are valued at the sum of the direct charges and the service support overhead and administrative overhead absorbed to that point by these unfinished jobs.

APPLICABILITY OF FINANCIAL-ACCOUNTING GUIDELINES

As mentioned earlier, cost accounting is not as constricted by generally accepted accounting principles as is financial accounting. Since the audience for cost accounting reports is internal management, cost information should be compiled and presented in whatever ways are most useful to managers in making decisions.

Nevertheless, the eight basic concepts of financial accounting presented in Chapter 5 do apply to cost accounting.

Expression in Monetary Terms. Cost accounting tells only that portion of the story that can be expressed in monetary terms. Much that is relevant cannot be so expressed—for example, the condition of the equipment, the skill level of the personnel, and the layout of the facility.

Entity. Cost accounting is concerned with only a portion of the entity—the production (or service) activity. The limits of that activity must be defined carefully, as pointed out several times in this chapter.

Going-concern Assumption. This assumption is particularly relevant to valuing in-process and finished-good inventories, as their valuations would generally be decidedly lower if the going-concern assumption were removed. The value of a partially completed unit is typically dependent upon its ultimately being completed and sold.

Conservatism. When in doubt as to the proper cost-accounting treatment, choose that alternative that minimizes or postpones the recognition of profit. A subsequent chapter will illustrate that this guideline argues for classifying more costs as period costs and fewer as product costs.

Accrual. All cost accounting techniques rest on the accrual, rather than cash, basis of accounting. Cost accounting seeks to improve the match of the cost of producing goods and services to the realization of revenue from their sale.

Realization. Only costs of conversion, not period expenses nor profit, are included in in-process and finished-goods inventory values. All revenue and profit are earned on the particular date when the goods or services are delivered or furnished.

Consistency. To make useful comparisons and to observe trends of costs, data should be compiled and presented in a consistent manner across accounting periods.

Materiality. The cost accountant, more even than the financial accountant, tends to violate this guidelines. There is almost no limit to the detail and apparent precision one can include in cost accounting reports. Thus, one must strike a balance at the point of diminishing returns from increased detail, bearing in mind that:

(1) Information costs money. Operating personnel must keep detailed records and these records must be processed. Final reports must be prepared and reproduced. Users must digest the reports. The more detailed the output, the more detailed must be the input, and the more time must be spent in record keeping, processing, and analysis.

(2) Masses of data tend more to confuse than to enlighten. Too often, the intended user despairs when presented with massive cost accounting reports, either because they are difficult to understand or because time pressures inhibit thorough analysis.

(3) Apparent precision is often spurious precision. You are well aware by now that in all areas of accounting assumptions must be made. We must be content with less than complete information. For example, labor-time reports from factory personnel inevitably contain inaccuracies, and IPC accounting involves arbitrary allocations. The more these data are manipulated, allocated, and processed, the more the final cost accounting reports take on an aura of precision. In fact, of course, imprecise input data cannot be turned into precise output information.

SUMMARY

Cost accounting develops detailed information on the cost of a product or service. That is, its focus is valuation of product costs as distinct from period costs. The primary audience for cost accounting information and reports is internal management rather than external audiences. Cost accounting procedures are less constrained by rules than are financial accounting procedures. While cost accounting is useful for valuing cost of goods sold and inventory, its primary purpose—and the primary test of its usefulness—is to aid managers in making sound manufacturing, marketing, product, pricing, and other operating decisions.

The fundamental difference between merchandising enterprises and manufacturing enterprises is that manufacturing converts materials from one state to another and thereby increases their value. A fundamental cost accounting dilemma is deciding just what categories of costs should be included as part of this cost of conversion. For example, material alone might be included; or material plus direct labor (prime costs); or material plus direct labor plus manufacturing overhead (indirect production costs or IPC); or all of these costs plus engineering, selling, and administrative expenses. Traditionally, the third of these four definitions of product costs is used by most manufacturing companies and is required for the valuation of cost of goods sold and inventory.

Today's typical cost accounting framework has changed little from the framework developed during and following the Industrial Revolution, even as large-scale manufacturing displaced owner-managed craft activities. At that time, direct labor and material dominated the costs of products, with indirect costs (overhead) of substantially less significance. Modern manufacturing—now incorporating much greater automation, changed employee relations practices, and more discretionary but fewer deterministic expenses—has substantially altered the mix of direct and indirect expenses. As a result some of the preoccupation with manufacturing costs to the exclusion of other categories of expenses is increasing inappropriate, as are certain of the traditional cost accounting procedures, particularly those used to absorb overhead into individuals products and services.

The financial accounting guidelines discussed in Chapter 5 are applicable as well to cost accounting. The cost method of valuation is assumed, and the accrual concept requires a clear distinction in an accounting period between the cost of goods sold and the cost of goods manufactured. The principal of materiality is often violated by cost accounting systems that develop excessive detail and apparent but spurious precision.

NEW TERMS

Absorbing (absorption). The process by which indirect production costs (IPC) are allocated to and thereby included in the cost of individual or groups of products or services.

Cost accounting. The set of accounting techniques that develops detailed information about the cost of a product or service.

Cost plus. An arrangement between customer and supplier that provides that the price charged is a function of the cost of performing the contract—that is, cost plus a fixed fee or cost plus a certain percentage of cost.

Convert (conversion). To transform raw material into in-process and finished-goods inventory. The process of conversion distinguishes manufacturing from merchandising and service activities.

Direct labor. Wages paid for time spent on production activities that can be identified directly with products manufactured or services performed. Direct labor is a product cost, generally (but often erroneously) assumed to be variable.

Direct material. The portion of product costs represented by the cost of materials that end up on, in, or otherwise part of the final product. Direct materials are a variable product cost.

Make-or-buy. A management decision whether to purchase a particular part or service from an outside vendor or produce the part (perform the service) within the firm.

Prime costs. A product-cost definition that includes only direct material and direct labor as product costs and excludes all overhead.

DISCUSSION QUESTIONS

14.1 How is cost accounting different from financial accounting?

14.2 Who are the primary audiences for cost accounting information and reports?

14.3   Why is cost accounting less constrained than financial accounting by formal rules imposed from outside the firm?

14.4   What entries on the balance sheet and the income statement are particularly affected by cost accounting procedures?

14.5   How might cost accounting information assist a marketing manager in arriving at answers to the following questions:
  (a)   What price to charge on the new model within an existing product line
  (b)   The minimum price to quote on a large special order from a potential customer with whom the company does not now do business
  (c)   Whether to promote product M in preference to product L

14.6   Assume that you are an engineer in a high-technology company. How might cost accounting information assist you in arriving at answers to the following questions:
  (a)   Whether to recommend to management that a certain part be subcontracted to an outside supplier (rather than continuing to be produced within the company's own factory)
  (b)   What the return on investment will be from a new product that the marketing and developing staffs are considering
  (c)   What the return on investment will be from a new automatic machine being considered by the manufacturing department

14.7   What is the fundamental difference between a manufacturing firm and a merchandising firm and why does the former have greater need for cost accounting?

14.8   Typically across American industry, is direct labor expense increasing or decreasing as a proportion of total costs incurred by manufacturing firms? Why?

14.9   Which of the financial accounting guidelines are the most relevant to the purposes and uses of cost accounting information? Discuss.

14.10   Indicate whether each of the following expenses should be considered a manufacturing overhead expense (a product expense) or an operating expense (a period expense—selling, engineering or general and administrative) or should be divided between the two categories on some basis:
  (a)   Salaries in the accounting department
  (b)   Salaries and wages in the shipping and receiving department
  (c)   Rental on factory space
  (d)   Salaries of the manufacturing engineers
  (e)   Salaries of the vice president of manufacturing and his or her immediate staff

(**f**) Workmen's compensation insurance (insurance coverage for injured employees)

(**g**) Utilities (heat, light, and power) expense

(**h**) Depreciation on delivery trucks operated by the company

(**i**) Operating costs for the company-wide computer network

(**j**) The costs of employment advertising in connection with hiring additional assembly personnel

14.11 What is meant by a *cost plus* contract? In what circumstances are such contracts used in preference to *fixed price* contracts?

14.12 Assume a company anticipates sales of $12 million and operating profits of only $100,000 for the coming year. While it considers $100,000 to be an inadequate profit, it is reluctant to reduce the number of employees, reduce plant capacity, and in other ways cut indirect expenses because it anticipates that in the following year demand for its products will accelerate substantially. Is it possible that the company could increase its reported profits in the coming year by increasing its inventory, even though sales remained at the $12 million level? Explain your answer.

14.13 Indicate whether each of these costs is fixed or variable, as those terms are used in cost accounting:

(**a**) Materials used in the products manufactured; prices of these materials are expected to inflate at the rate of 5 percent per year

(**b**) Rental on manufacturing space; the rental is escalated each year as a function of the Consumer Price Index

(**c**) Depreciation on a particular machine tool the capacity of which has been increasing each year as the company improves its product designs and manufacturing techniques

(**d**) Wages paid to product-assembly personnel; in accordance with the union contract, the wage rate will not change for three years

(**e**) Wages paid to a group of particularly skilled production personnel; in accordance with the union contract, these workers are guaranteed 40 hours of work per week for 50 weeks per year

(**f**) Fuel oil for the factory steam plant; this fuel oil is acquired on a so-called take or pay contract that requires the company to purchase a certain amount of fuel regardless of how much it actually needs

PROBLEMS

14.1 Two companies are identical in size and in products manufactured. They differ only in the design of their cost accounting systems, specifically in how they classify certain expenses between product and period expenses. Company T defines more cost elements as product costs, and Company S defines more cost elements as period costs. For the coming year the companies have prepared the following estimates:

	Company T	Company S
Estimated sales (units)	50,000	50,000
Estimated production (units)	55,000	55,000
Inventory at 1/1/96 (units)	10,000	10,000
Estimated product costs	$250,000	$170,000
Estimated period costs	$130,000	$210,000

If these estimates are realized in the coming year by both companies:

(a) Which company will report higher profits? How much higher will they be?

(b) Which company will have higher inventory values at the end of the year?

(c) Which company will report higher gross margins?

14.2 A new corporation expects in its first year of operations to incur the following costs:

Material for products	$145,000
Direct labor	63,000
Manufacturing overhead	
Variable	78,000
Fixed	190,000
Engineering, selling and	
administrative expenses	230,000
Total	$706,000

If this company produces 150,000 units, ships 130,000 of them (on which it expects to earn total revenue of $5.40 per unit or a total of $702,000), and has 20,000 units in inventory at the end of its first year of operation, what will be its reported first-year profits and value of year-end inventory, if:

(a) It defines product costs as comprising solely direct material

(b) It defines product costs as comprising prime costs

(c) It defines product costs as comprising prime costs plus variable manufacturing overhead

(d) It defines product costs as comprising all costs except engineering, selling and administrative expenses

(e) It defines product costs as absorbing all of its costs, including engineering, selling and administrative expenses

____15
ANALYSIS OF PRODUCT COSTS

Chapter 14 set the stage for this analysis of product costs by distinguishing more clearly between product costs and period costs and by defining, in some detail, alternative definitions of product costs. Recall that product costs may include only material costs, or material and labor, or material, labor and certain elements of overhead, or, at the ultimate, all of the costs of the firm. Recall, too, that cost accounting is relevant not only to manufacturing enterprises, but also to professional service and research environments.

This chapter focuses specifically on manufacturing companies. It uses the definition for product costs that encompasses material, labor, and at least some overhead elements, but excludes nonmanufacturing operating expenses (that is, engineering, development, marketing, and general and administrative expenses). This is the traditional manufacturing cost accounting environment with which you need to be familiar.

Bear in mind that we are interested in product costs for two reasons:

(1) They provide the data required to value accurately inventory and cost of goods sold—the financial accounting reason.
(2) They represent information useful to managers as they evaluate current operations and decide when and to what extent operating plans need to be altered—the managerial accounting reason.

Both reasons are crucial. Traditionally, cost accounting systems have focused almost exclusively on the first reason: increasingly, managers are demanding better information for day-to-day decision making. To fulfill their managerial accounting functions most cost accounting systems require elaboration beyond a simple system that would be required solely for financial accounting.

We have a good deal of latitude for that elaboration. The absence of strict, externally imposed cost accounting rules permits us to tailor cost accounting systems to fit particular needs. A system appropriate for one manufacturer may be distinctly inappropriate, or even unworkable, for another. To fit these varying characteristics and requirements, we need to consider alternative structures for cost accounting systems.

EXAMPLES OF MANUFACTURING COMPANIES

Picture the production activity, and particularly the diversity of tasks, in each of the following companies.

A Manufacturer of a Standard Line of Men's Dress Shirts

Shirts of different sizes, colors, and styles are produced. The raw materials (cloth, accessories, packing material) proceed through the various steps in the process (cutting, sewing, packing) and emerge as finished shirts. Cutting and sewing equipment, together with assembly fixtures, comprise the production fixed assets.

What features of this manufacturing firm influence its cost accounting system? First, the manufacturing activity is broken into jobs; each job specifies one or more steps in producing a specified quantity of a defined style of shirt. Numerous jobs are always in process. A particular completed shirt might have been cut on one job, sewn on another, and finished on a third. The products are standard (i.e., defined by a manufacturer's stock or catalog number), not custom (i.e., designed and produced to individual customer specifications). Thus, the firm can estimate or budget quite accurately its cost by individual stock or catalog number. The production activity is labor intensive; little capital equipment is required. Overhead is therefore likely to be comparatively low, and much of the overhead will vary with volume of activity rather than being fixed in nature.

A Manufacturer of Specialized Machinery

At a manufacturer of specialized large printing presses, a number of different types of presses are manufactured, some standard models and others specially configured for a particular customer. Giant and small machine tools are required, painting and plating facilities, large assembly floors, and extensive material handling capacity, including cranes and a fleet of forklift trucks. Raw-material inventory consists of purchased metal plate and rod, castings, hardware, and major purchased components such as motors, gears, and rollers. In-process inventory consists of machined parts and finished subassemblies in the storeroom, as well as partially assembled presses on the assembly floor, some of which remain in process for a number of months. Presses are shipped to the customers upon completion; no finished press inventory is maintained. However, an extensive spare parts inventory—a form of finished-goods inventory—is maintained to assure rapid parts delivery to existing press users.

What are the characteristics here that define the appropriate cost accounting system? As with the shirt manufacturer, activity is defined in terms of jobs: build X quantity of a component part; assemble Y quantity of a particular subassembly; assemble and test press number 851 for customer Z. Is the product standard or custom? Well, it is some of both: Many standard subassemblies combine with some custom parts in a custom-assembled press. Accurate estimates of the cost of the standard parts and subassemblies are practical, but estimates are more problematic for the custom activity. The manufacturing activity is quite capital intensive (lots of expensive fixed assets are required), but it also requires a good deal of direct labor. Overhead costs are substantial and relatively fixed in nature (i.e., overhead related to the fixed assets doesn't vary with volume of activity).

An Oil Refiner Producing Standard Products

Unlike the last two examples, where manufacturing occurs in a series of discrete steps, defined in terms of jobs, refining is a continuous process. The manufacturing task is to operate the process for a specified period, or until a certain amount of raw material is consumed, obtaining all the finished product possible. The raw material is crude oil, together with various catalysts, chemical agents, and additives. In-process time is relatively short and the direct labor force is small relative to the value of product produced, as only a few operators are required to monitor the process. The process runs around-the-clock, seven days per week.

What are the characteristics that define the appropriate cost accounting system? First, the task is to operate the continuous process; it would be inappropriate to define the task in terms of discrete jobs. Both the inputs and the outputs are standard, and so budgets of product costs here should be highly reliable. Oil refineries represent very large capital investments, contributing to relatively high overhead, most of which is fixed in nature.

A Specialty Chemical Firm, Producing Custom Pharmaceuticals

A speciality chemical firm producing custom pharmaceuticals to be marketed by others formulates a limited number of chemical compounds, which it then packages under contract for large pharmaceutical houses; they in turn market the products under their own trade names. The company has chemical formulation facilities and several packaging lines. The raw materials are largely chemicals and packaging materials. The in-process time is brief, and while the formulated chemicals are inventoried, the finished products—custom-packaged pharmaceuticals for particular customers—are shipped directly from the packaging line to the customers. The chemical formulation requires relatively few skilled operators, while the packaging lines require a large number of semiskilled personnel.

What are the defining characteristics? Here we have both a continuous process—

chemical formulation—and the packaging activity that occurs as a series of jobs. Since there are two distinct departments, distinctly different cost accounting systems can apply to each. Without knowing more about the extent of customization that the manufacturer must provide to the various pharmaceutical-house customers, we can't know just how difficult it would be to budget (estimate) product costs. Overhead is not inconsequential, both because a fair amount of capital equipment is required, and because production scheduling and control is quite elaborate; overhead has both fixed and variable cost elements.

An Assembler of Electronic Instruments

This company manufactures no metal parts or electronic components; all are purchased from suppliers and constitute the firm's raw material. The labor force consists of a large number of skilled and semiskilled assemblers, electronic technicians, and support personnel in the stockroom, scheduling department, and maintenance. The manufacturing equipment consists of assembly fixtures, soldering equipment, simple hand tools, and electronic test equipment.

The defining characteristics here are again unique among these examples. The manufacturing task is composed of a series of jobs: build X quantity of a particular subassembly or finished instrument. The company has a standard line of instruments, and thus is able to estimate (budget) the product cost of each, although these estimates are rather unreliable when a new instrument is first introduced. Overhead is high but driven more by substantial indirect labor expenses than by capital equipment costs, which are modest. Overhead is, as a result, somewhat more variable than for the printing press manufacturer, but less so than for the shirt manufacturer.

NEED FOR ALTERNATIVE STRUCTURES

These simple scenarios should convince you that heterogeneous manufacturing environments have heterogeneous information needs. The same cost accounting system is not going to satisfy the information needs in these very different manufacturing companies. In fact, a rather amazing variety of cost accounting systems is in use today, some highly sophisticated and some quite simple. Parenthetically, be assured that the usefulness of the resulting information does not correlate with the system's complexity; some simple systems are highly effective and have the added virtues of being inexpensive to operate and easy for both accountants and managers to understand.

With this great variety of cost accounting systems, we need a categorization scheme. One defining parameter was discussed in the previous chapter: How inclusive should overhead expenses be? An appendix to Chapter 16 discusses three possibilities: (1) include no overhead, but only prime costs (direct labor and direct material); (2) include variable IPC (overhead) only, while treating fixed IPC as a period cost (**direct** or **variable costing**); or (3) include both variable and fixed manufacturing overhead but no nonmanufacturing overhead (**full-absorption costing**).

The other two fundamental parameters that define cost accounting systems are:

(1) What is the definition of the task for which cost data are being collected? The answer points to either **job order costing** or **process costing.**

(2) For the purposes of valuing cost of goods sold and inventory, should product costs be defined as the actual costs incurred or as some predetermined or budgeted cost? That is, shall inventory and cost of goods sold be valued at what it actually costs to make a product, or at what it should cost? Here the choice is between **actual costs** and **standard costs.**

A subsequent chapter will review the difference between actual and standard cost systems. While it may seem intuitively obvious to you that actual costs should be used, please withhold judgment, for a standard cost system has many benefits.

Before focusing on the first of these two questions—what is the definition of the task—recognize that the cost accountant defines the major structural elements of the cost accounting system with an eye to the needs and peculiarities of his or her company. As a building architect answers certain fundamental structural questions early in the design of a house—Shall it be brick or wood? One or two stories? Face east or north?—so the cost accountant must address structural questions in the design of a cost accounting system.

DEFINITION OF TASK

When a task is best described as producing a given number of units—that is, described in batches of output—the **job order costing system** is appropriate. When the task is defined as operating a manufacturing process for a specified time period, the **process costing system** fits.

What are examples of jobs? When a cabinetmaker receives an order to fabricate a special kitchen cabinet, that order is a job in the cost accounting system and all costs incurred on that job are collected—direct labor, direct material, and indirect production costs (IPC). In a machine shop, a **job order** is often defined as a subtask: perform the required drilling operations on a lot of 100 parts. This lot may have already been milled—another job order collected those costs—and may subsequently be further processed on other job orders. Thus a job may encompass a single activity (drill one hole in a lot of parts) or multiple activities (fabricate, assemble, and finish a kitchen cabinet) and may involve a single unit (kitchen cabinet) or many units (100 machined parts). In all cases, the job is defined in terms of output of a unit or units to a specified stage of completeness.

Contrast these job order environments with the following processes. A coal-burning, power-generating plant produces kilowatts of electricity and typically runs continuously. The plant's task is not defined in kilowatt-hours of power output but rather in terms of the length of time each of the various generators (processes) is on line. Costs of plant operation for a segment of time are collected. Another example is the oil refinery mentioned earlier; the refining task is not defined as producing so many gallons of gasoline, plus so many gallons of kerosene, plus so many gallons of fuel oil. The process is continuous, and thus it is impractical to collect costs for a set number of gallons of output. In process costing, costs to operate the process are collected for a specified period of time, rather than for a specified output.

To recap, a job order costing system fits a batch environment: a manufacturing operation where the task is defined as completing one or more discrete steps on a certain number of units. By contrast, a process costing system fits a continuous production process, where the task is defined as operating the process for a certain period of time or until a certain amount of raw material is consumed.

Determining the cost per unit of production is slightly different under the two systems:

> In job order costing, the cost per unit is determined by dividing the total costs incurred on the job by the number of units realized. The job's costs are collected for as long as the job is unfinished (or open)—as short as hours or as long as months. Thus, the cost of drilling one metal part is determined by dividing the cost of drilling the whole lot of parts by the number of parts produced (100 in the earlier example).

> In process costing, the cost per unit (typically defined in bulk measurement terms such as a gallon, a kilogram, or a square meter) is determined by dividing the costs incurred in operating the process for the prescribed time period by the output derived during that period. Thus, the cost of a kilowatt-hour of electricity is determined by dividing the total cost of operating the generating plant for a period (for example, one month) by the number of kilowatt-hours produced during that month.

EXAMPLES OF ALTERNATIVE COST ACCOUNTING STRUCTURES

Figure 15-1 presents a matrix of cost accounting structures into which each of the five example manufacturers has been placed. The shirt manufacturer defines its work by jobs and standard (budgeted) costs can be developed for each of its standard shirt styles. (By the way, one can imagine a very high-volume, highly automated continuous flow shirt manufacturing plant for which process costing would be the right choice.) It isn't the nature of the product but the organization of the manufacturing activity that drives the choice. Just about the same comments apply to the instrument assembler.

The oil refiner operates a process costing system, using standard product costs, since it operates a continuous process to manufacture standard products. The press manufacturer operates in a job cost environment; some combination of standard and actual costing probably fits here—standard product costs for standard components and assemblies, but actual costs to value custom-produced parts as well as to value the assembling and testing of the finished, built-to-specification presses. Note that standard and actual product costs can be mixed in a single cost accounting system.

The specialty chemical manufacturer is placed right in the middle of Figure 15-1,

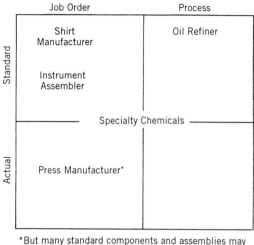

*But many standard components and assemblies may
be valued at standard cost.

Figure 15-1   Illustration of alternative accounting structures.

suggesting that each of the four cost accounting structures, or more likely a combination of them, might be used. The formulation activity may be either a continuous
or a batch process. If continuous, then processing costing fits; if batch, then the
company should use job-order costing. Standard product costs may be applicable
throughout, but if the customized packaging operation must deal with a wide variety
of customer demands, actual costing may best fit this part of the manufacturing
activity.

Job Order Costing

Look a little closer at a typical job order cost system, for instance the shirt manufacturer. The plant consists of three departments: cutting, sewing, and packing. The
shirts move from department to department, increasing in value as they proceed.
The overall task of making a given number (lot size) of a certain model of shirt is
segmented into jobs (or subtasks) defined as performing a certain function (e.g.,
sewing) on the lot of shirts. A single shirt's total cost is arrived at by combining the
costs collected on several jobs (cutting, sewing, and packing) and dividing the total
by the number of shirts produced. Jobs can be of greater or lesser scope; the overall
task can be segmented into larger jobs (e.g., make X shirts of one color and Y of
another) or smaller jobs (sew only the side seams on the body of a particular size and
style of shirt).

Each job constitutes, in effect, a subsidiary ledger account tied to one or more
general-ledger, in-process inventory accounts. As raw material is issued to the job,
the debit balance in the subsidiary ledger account increases, while the raw-material
asset decreases. As direct labor is expended on the job, wages are paid to (or
accrued for) plant employees, and this credit entry is balanced not by a debit to an

expense account but by a debit to the job subsidiary-ledger account. IPC assigned to the job also increases the debit balance—that is, increases the value of in-process inventory.

At the end of an accounting period, some jobs will still be open. When complete, they are closed, and the account balance is moved to finished-goods inventory where it will remain until the shirts are shipped to customers. That is, to close a job, the job subsidiary-ledger account is credited so as to bring it to a zero balance; the offsetting debit is to finished goods inventory, another asset account.

Process Costing

A process costing environment may consist of a single process (e.g., the oil refinery) or a number of processes, in which case each process typically constitutes a separate department. Process costing involves collecting all the costs for the department for the prescribed time period. Generally, a complement of workers is assigned to a process department; virtually all of these workers are considered direct labor. Incidentally, labor time reporting and the allocation of IPC are generally easier and less expensive in process costing than in job order costing.

Material is processed through Department A, as a first step, and is then transferred to Department B and beyond for further processing; between departments it may be stored in a semifinished state, as in-process inventory. The output of Department B may be split between finished-goods inventory and Department C; if so, the output of Department B is a finished product, but a portion is further processed before it too is sent to finished-goods inventory.

Valuing in-process inventory is more difficult in process costing than in job order. In process costing, one may be in doubt at the end of an accounting period as to just how much of the material, labor, and IPC incurred by this department during this period should be assigned to work still in process; this determination is critical, since the balance of the costs represents the cost of the department's output for the period. A simplifying assumption is often made: no change in in-process inventory occurred (i.e., the same amount of work in the same state of completion was in process at the end of the period as at the beginning).

COSTING JOINT PRODUCTS AND BY-PRODUCTS

This is a good place to explore briefly an interesting cost accounting dilemma that arises when two or more different end products emerge from a single process or a single job order. These are called **joint products.** Examples are the various distillates that are derived from a catalytic cracking tower processing oil; the end products made from a steer, including the various cuts of meat and the hide; and the various grades of agricultural products that are realized from a sorting or classifying operation. When one of these end products is not specifically sought and is of substantially less value than the primary product or products—for example, a lesser mineral when gold is mined—it is called a **by-product,** a special kind of joint product. While joint products are more prevalent in continuous processes, where the process costing structure is used, joint products also sometimes derive from a single job order.

The dilemma in costing joint products is to decide what portion of the total labor, material, and IPC incurred is properly assignable to each joint product, or to the by-product. Some logical but inevitably arbitrary allocation method is used, sometimes based upon the relative sales values of the joint products, or their relative weights, or some other criterion. For by-products, any amounts realized from the sale of the by-product may be offset against the process's operating costs, or the by-product cost may be set at zero.

Obviously, no precisely accurate method of assigning costs among joint products exists. This is not the first time we have encountered the need to be arbitrary, even if logical. But the result is that, while joint product costs are adequate for valuing inventory and cost of goods sold, they are typically useless for making other management decisions.

COST ACCOUNTING IN OTHER FUNCTIONS AND IN OTHER INDUSTRIES

Remember that these techniques of product costing in a manufacturing setting also apply to many nonmanufacturing activities. We discussed some in Chapter 14. For example, analogous techniques are widely used in the construction industry. Direct material, direct labor, and indirect construction costs are incurred in excavating, carpentry, concrete work, and landscaping. Some combination of these activities is required to construct a building, road, or dam. The contractor is typically building a single, not multiple, units, and the inventory (the construction project) does not physically move toward its finished-goods state, but in most other respects construction and manufacturing are very similar.

Service industries also must cost account—that is, account for the cost of providing a service. A plumber expends direct materials, direct labor, and indirect costs in completing a repair job, and he or she accounts for these expenditures as a basis for billing the customer. A lawyer incurs direct labor (the lawyer's time and perhaps that of associates and aides) as well as many indirect costs (rent, telephones, and insurance, for example) in completing a client assignment; again cost accounting data are needed for billing purposes, but they are also needed for management analysis and control in any sizable professional services firm.

Many commercial banks view certain departments such as wire transfer, the teller stations, and safe deposit box access as processes, using process costing techniques to generate cost data to assist in pricing customer services and monitoring productivity.

Hospitals and medical clinics cost account. Research universities are required by their external funding sources (primarily the U.S. federal government) to cost account research projects; faculty, graduate students, and research associates are the direct laborers. Local governments cost account various municipal services, including road repair, custodial activities, library operations, and refuse collection.

Even for nonmanufacturing activities within the manufacturing company, cost accounting is useful to cost activities outside the factory. For example, how much does it cost to develop a new product? Or, to make a sale? These costs aren't used in valuing inventory and cost of goods sold, but they are very useful in managing by exception, in making staffing decisions, and in a host of other ways. So, just as manufacturing managers are interested in production costs, sales managers and engineering managers need data on the costs of developing products or effecting sales.

However, a word of caution: It is far more difficult to cost these nonmanufacturing tasks; unlike most production tasks, engineering and selling are relatively unprogrammed. You can estimate quite accurately the materials and labor hours needed to complete a production task; the same is not true of selling or of creative engineering. How knotty is the technical problem; how many different approaches will be tried before a solution is found; how creative is the engineer assigned to the task? How enthusiastic are customers about the product; how tough is the competitive battle on a particular order? A large order may cost no more to close than a small order.

Nevertheless, even for these unprogrammed engineering and selling functions historical-cost information is useful. Knowledge of the labor, material, and indirect expenses utilized on an engineering-design project helps the company track the deployment of its technical resources and provides a basis for forecasting and budgeting the future. Cost accounting is unable to cost the closing of a sale, since one cannot predict whether a particular sales call will lead to a sale, or how many calls will occur before the sale can be closed. However, making a sales call is a definable task for which cost data can be collected and these data help in planning future selling activity.

So, cost accounting is pervasive in our modern society.

SUMMARY

Cost accounting systems are fashioned to provide information that can be most useful to the company's operating managers. A wide variety of cost accounting systems are in use today across a broad spectrum of manufacturing and service enterprises, large and small. This chapter identifies three bases on which cost accounting systems can be categorized; decisions with regard to the following three parameters define the structure of the cost accounting system best suited to a particular situation:

(1) What is the appropriate definition of the task for which data are to be collected? Is the task defined in terms of a job order—produce so many parts or units, or provide a specified service—or as a process—operate the contin-

uous process for a specified period of time? Here the choice is between a job order costing and process costing system.

(2) Shall inventory and cost of goods sold be valued at actual costs or standard costs? The use of standard costs facilitates the comparison between actual and planned production results, and helps pinpoint the causes of deviation from plan.

(3) How comprehensively should the cost accounting system be in incorporating indirect production costs (IPC) in product costs? The possibilities range from including only direct and no indirect costs (so-called prime costs only) to including only variable IPC to including both variable and fixed IPC.

This chapter outlines five quite different production activities and asks the reader to consider which cost accounting structure is most appropriate for each:

(a) A manufacturer of a standard line of men's shirts
(b) A manufacturer of large printing presses
(c) An oil refinery producing standard products
(d) A chemical specialty firm, producing custom pharmaceuticals for sale by others
(e) An assembler of electronic instruments

A special case for costing individual products arises when joint products, including by-products, are derived from a single job or process.

Clearly, a wide variety of cost accounting structures is possible. Indeed, even within a single company the use of different structures for different segments of the business may be appropriate. In designing the cost accounting system, the information needs of the users, line operating managers, should be emphasized. These needs are, in turn, dictated by the nature of the manufacturing or service activity. Moreover, in a few industries such as defense contracting, public utilities and other regulated industries, the cost accounting systems are also influenced by the demands of external audiences, particularly governmental regulatory and contracting agencies.

NEW TERMS

Actual costs (actual costing). Product costs composed of actual rather than standard costs. Actual costing contrasts as a cost accounting structure with standard costing.

By-products. A category of joint products consisting of products of substantially less commercial value than the other joint products derived from the job or process.

Direct costing. A cost accounting structure that defines IPC (overhead) as including only variable indirect production costs, with fixed indirect costs accounted for as period expenses. An alternative name is variable costing.

Full-absorption costing. A cost accounting structure that defines IPC (overhead) as including both fixed and variable indirect production costs (but excludes nonmanufacturing overhead). This structure contrasts with variable (direct) costing,

Job-order (job-order costing). The basis for task definition that specifies both the work to be accomplished and the number of units to be worked on. In job order costing all costs associated with performing the defined task are collected. Job order costing contrasts with process costing.

Joint products. Two or more different end products that are derived from a single process or job order. The cost of each joint product is determined by allocation of the joint costs.

Process costing. A cost accounting structure that defines the task as operating a continuous process for a specified period; all costs associated with the process for the period are collected. Process costing contrasts with job order coasting.

Standard costs (standard costing). Predetermined product costs representing what it should cost, rather than what it actually does cost, to produce a product, perform a service, or operate a process. Standard costing systems value inventory and cost of goods sold using standard costs; standard costing contrasts with actual costing.

Variable costing. A cost accounting structure that defines IPC (overhead) as including only variable indirect production costs, with fixed indirect costs accounted for as period expenses. This structure contrasts with full-absorption costing; an alternative name is direct costing.

DISCUSSION QUESTIONS

15.1 Identify three examples of manufacturing processes that are better accounted for by job order costing systems than by process costing systems. Identify three examples of manufacturing processes where the reverse is true.

15.2 Is a job order or a process costing system typically less expensive to operate?

15.3 What is the essential difference between a joint product and a by-product? In both situations, why is it difficult to determine the costs of individual products?

15.4 In a company where inventory is growing during an accounting period, will direct (variable) costing or full-absorption costing lead to higher reported profits for the period? Why?

15.5 Consider the following set of services performed by the local city government. Is process costing, job order costing, or neither costing system applicable to each service? If process or job order costing is applicable, how would you define the process or jobs for which costs should be collected?

(a) A sewage treatment plant

(b) The public library

(c) The parks and recreation department

(d) The street and sidewalk repair unit within the maintenance department

(e) The municipal water treatment and chlorination plant

(f) The building permit issuing department within the city planner's office

(g) The traffic engineering department (consisting of four traffic engineers and various support staff)

15.6 Why is it difficult to value in-process inventory when utilizing a process costing system?

15.7 Describe in detail how you would determine the amount of labor and material to be charged to a job in:

(a) A factory that manufactures kitchen cabinets

(b) A shop that customizes automobiles

(c) A software development department that designs and writes code for new software programs to be marketed to auto repair shops

(d) A major motion picture production firm

(e) A construction firm specializing in public works projects

15.8 Refer to the five different activities listed in question 15.7. For each, identify the major indirect production costs that you will want to include in a full-absorption product cost, and indicate what difficulties, if any, you think you will have in determining these indirect costs. Which of these indirect costs are fixed in nature, and thus would be excluded from product costs in a direct (variable) costing system?

15.9 In a public statement justifying a price increase on a particular model of automobile, an officer of an auto manufacturing company said, "Our costs have risen significantly in the past year, largely due to inflation, but also because of redesign required by recent federal regulations. Our total costs are now $13,500 on this care that we are pricing at $14,200." What costs do you think this spokesperson is including in "our total costs?" How reliable to you think this "total cost" figure is? What assumptions underlie this "total cost" determination?

15.10 Described below are some manufacturing or service operations. What cost accounting structure would you recommend for each, and why?

(a) An architectural design firm comprised of five architects, two draft-persons, and two office staff members

(b) A large aluminum smelting plant

(c) A construction company specializing in building roads

(d) A manufacturing plant devoted solely to 21-inch television sets

(e) A manufacturing plant devoted to large volume production of a limited line of microprocessor integrated circuits

(f) A large law firm employing 400 individuals, about half of whom are lawyers

(g) An engineering design firm specializing in designing hospitals

15.11 Assume that the Langford Manufacturing Company experiences wide seasonal fluctuations in sales, with sales in the peak season running at twice the monthly rate in the slow season. To gain manufacturing efficiencies, the company's production rate remains essentially constant throughout the year. The company is debating whether to use direct (variable) or full-absorption costing. Will the company's monthly fluctuations in reported profits be less under one of these two cost accounting methods? If so, which one? Why?

15.12 How might cost accounting techniques be used in a marketing organization to provide information helpful to the sales managers? What types of analyses and decisions do the sales managers face for which cost accounting information might be helpful?

15.13 A large law firm states that its associate (young) lawyers charge $150 per hour for their work on a particular case, while senior lawyers may charge $350 per hour and more. Assuming that a lawyer may well charge 1500 or more hours per year to various cases on which he or she works, do these hourly charges represent what the lawyer is paid in salary? What other costs of the law firm do you think are "absorbed" into these hourly rates?

15.14 What cost accounting structure would you recommend for each of the following production or service activities?

(a) A contract janitorial service

(b) A large university that performs both teaching and research

(c) A major metropolitan recycling center

(d) An oil refinery

(e) A highly automated manufacturer of home lighting fixtures

(f) A cannery that processes very large quantities of a single fruit

(g) A cannery that processes small quantities of many different fruits as they become ripe

15.15 Two products manufactured by the Williams Corporation have the following product costs:

	Product I	Product II
Prime cost	$3.75 per unit	$2.75 per unit
Variable (direct) cost	4.25 per unit	3.50 per unit
Full absorption cost	5.50 per unit	5.50 per unit

Note that the full-absorption costs of the two products are the same. What can you deduce about the products and how they are manufactured by comparing all of the product cost data shown above?

PROBLEMS

15.1 The Cowell Specialty Chemical Company produces custom-blended chemicals in large quantities to order for a few customers. One large order consumed all of the production capacity at Cowell for the month of May 1995. Cowell uses a process costing system. Assume that Cowell issued from inventory materials during the month of May valued at $43,000 and labor time cards revealed that a total of 2200 hours was charged to the process during the month; the standard labor wage rate is $12 per hour (including fringe benefits). Output on this one large order totaled 100,000 kg. Factory overhead for the month was $53,000, $15,500 of which was variable and the remainder was fixed. Selling, administrative, and other operating costs for the month totalled $31,000. Calculate the product cost for 1 kg of the custom-blended chemical produced in May, assuming:

(a) Product costs are defined as prime costs only

(b) Product costs are defined as variable (direct) costs

(c) Product costs are defined as full-absorption costs

15.2 The Cowell Chemical Company (see problem 15.1 above) operated one of its processes in order to produce 10,000 kg of chemical X for its customer, Belcher Pharmaceuticals; the aggregate product cost for operating the process to produce 10,000 kg of chemical X was $37,500. The process employed by Cowell results in the production of a low-value by-product, chemical T, for which Belcher has no use. The production of 10,000 kg of chemical X results in 1500 kg of chemical T. Cowell disposed of chemical T, realizing $2 per kilogram. What should Cowell's cost accounting records show as the product cost per kilogram of chemical X sold to Belcher?

15.3 Refer to problem 15.1 above. Do you think the cost per kilogram of this custom-blended chemical would have been much different if Cowell had used standard rather than actual costs in determining product costs? Explain your answer. If Cowell had used standard costs, what additional information would the cost accounting system have revealed, information that would not be available if actual costs are used?

15.4 Whitfield Enterprises modified automobiles to individual customer requirements. In July, 1995 Whitfield commenced and completed Job 453, which called for the installation of an elaborate sunroof in a luxury car. Whitfield's cost accounting department determined that materials valued at $516 had been acquired for this job and/or issued from Whitfield's stock room. Labor time cards revealed that five different workers spent time on this job, charging a total of 116 hours of direct labor to the job; when these hours were multiplied by the appropriate wage rates earned by each of the five workers, the total direct labor cost on this job was $981. Total direct labor cost on all jobs for the month of July 1995 was $16,742. Total shop overhead (indirect costs) for the month was $26,393, of which $6754 was variable and the remainder was fixed. Calculate the cost of this project, assuming:

(a) Project costs are defined as prime costs only

(b) Project costs are defined as variable (direct) costs

(c) Project costs are defined as full-absorption costs

16
ALLOCATION AND ANALYSIS OF INDIRECT COSTS

To include indirect costs—that is, any costs beyond direct material and direct labor—in product expenses requires that the cost accounting system adopt a method of attributing, allocating, assigning, or (in cost accounting parlance), absorbing these indirect costs among all that is manufactured or serviced by the firm. By the very nature of their being indirect, rather than direct, **indirect production costs**—what this book refers to as **IPC**—are difficult to assign to production output.

This chapter discusses two fundamentally different methods of allocating indirect costs. The first, called here the **traditional cost-allocation method,** was developed early in this century and is consistent with manufacturing operations that are heavily weighted toward direct costs, as explained in the brief history of cost accounting outlined in Chapter 14. This quite straightforward method simply aggregates all categories of indirect manufacturing costs and allocates them to the products in some logical but arbitrary manner. This method has its decided shortcomings, as we shall see. Nevertheless, it continues to be the dominant method employed today in U.S. manufacturing operations.

In recent years, in an attempt to respond to the modern trends in manufacturing that were discussed in Chapter 14, managers have become increasingly enthusiastic about a new cost allocation method called **activity-based costing.** This method attempts to identify the particular indirect manufacturing activities that drive, or cause, the indirect costs, and then to allocate IPC to products based upon the amount of each activity demanded by each product.

TRADITIONAL COST ALLOCATION METHODS

Let's restate the challenge. While one can relatively easily determine the value of direct material and direct labor to be assigned to a particular unit of output—time reporting and materials requisition systems will provide the necessary source-document information—determining how much of, for example, the factory rent or the shop superintendent's salary should be assigned to a unit of output is a good bit more challenging. Inevitably, some arbitrariness will be involved in these allocations or distributions. Such, indeed, is the nature of costs that cannot be identified as direct.

To allocate these indirect costs, then, cost accountants must select some rational, consistent, and fair method of dividing IPC among all that is produced. Regardless of the rationality or fairness of the method, the resulting IPC in product expenses is still an arbitrary amount. A different allocation method will result in a different product expense. This fact needs to be emphasized repeatedly, simply because managers overlook it so frequently as they interpret cost accounting reports.

Another complication here is that IPC allocations must be made before we know exactly how much was spent on IPC or exactly how much was produced. We must be able to determine in real time how much things cost, that is, as the things are being produced throughout the accounting period. Typically we can't wait, or don't want to wait, until the accounting period ends. This impatience is particularly true for a company that performs custom work (manufacturing or service) and prices its output as a function of cost; such a company can't wait until the end of the accounting period to total up and allocate actual IPC because rendering invoices to its customers can't wait.

This need for timely data demands, then, that IPC be allocated to the various portions of production *during* the accounting period, not simply at the end. Therefore, we typically predetermine the basis for allocating IPC and then use it throughout the accounting period to assign IPC to in-process inventory. Of course, the amount assigned to (or, in typical accounting parlance, the amount of IPC absorbed by) in-process inventory is likely to be slightly different from the actual sum of expenditures on all IPC cost elements. This small difference is treated as a variance; we do *not* recompute after the end of the accounting period the amount of IPC allocated to each unit of output.

To repeat, in order to provide timely data on final costs of items or services produced, IPC must be allocated throughout the accounting period—before actual IPC expenditures are known—using a predetermined formula and allocation method.

A detailed discussion of procedures for allocating IPC and the meaning of the IPC Variance account follows.

IPC Vehicle

The first step is to determine the **IPC vehicle***—the basis for assigning IPC from the general pool of indirect costs to the particular production segments. The most common vehicles are direct-labor hours, direct-labor dollars, material dollars, machine hours, and units of production. The vehicle chosen must be directly identifiable with the production segments, and must be common to all items produced or

---

*As we shall see, sometimes more than a single IPC vehicle is used.

services delivered. It should represent a fair and equitable basis for the allocation, or absorption, of IPC. In a shop where direct-labor hours is the IPC vehicle, if item A requires twice as many direct-labor hours as item B, item A will cost twice as much in terms of IPC—item A will absorb twice as much IPC as item B. This assumption, while arbitrary, represents a reasonable basis for the allocation. It may be the best assumption one can make, but you must recognize its limitations when you later analyze performance results.

Although direct-labor hours and direct-labor dollars are the most common IPC vehicles, particularly in labor-intensive manufacturing or servicing environments, other vehicles are also possible. For example, in a custom-printing plant, printing press machine hours are probably most appropriate; much of the overhead is connected with the presses themselves, and the IPC that a particular printing job should absorb is assumed to be a function of the number of press hours the job requires. A producer of safety helmets might use units of production as the appropriate IPC vehicle; each helmet would then be assigned the same amount of IPC.

IPC Rate

Next, the **IPC rate** must be predetermined; that is, one must determine before the accounting period begins the amount of IPC that each unit of the IPC vehicle will carry. This calculation requires an estimate of total production activity for the accounting period. This planned activity level is then used to determine both (1) the expected, or budgeted, IPC expenditures to accomplish the planned output, and (2) the quantity of the IPC vehicle—for example, the number of direct-labor hours or machine hours—to be utilized during the accounting period. The IPC rate, then, is simply (1) divided by (2)—the budgeted IPC expenditures divided by the budgeted volume of the IPC vehicle.

For example, assume that a particular manufacturing operation expects to require 1,500 direct-labor hours per month to accomplish its planned production. To support this activity level, the managers expect to spend $38,000 per month on indirect production costs. This operation's resulting IPC rate, assuming that direct-labor hours is the IPC vehicle, will be $25.33 per direct-labor hour ($38,000 divided by 1500 hours). When costing a particular item produced in this manufacturing operation, $25.33 of IPC is allocated to an item for each direct-labor hour consumed in producing it.

Extending the example, the cost of an item that contains $88.60 of direct material and requires 3.5 direct-labor hours to produce (wage rate of $11.00 per hour) is

Direct material	$ 88.60
Direct labor (3.5 × $11)	38.50
IPC (3.5 × $25.33)	88.66
Total product cost	$215.76

Note that this IPC is used throughout the accounting period. In an actual month, the number of direct-labor hours will undoubtedly differ somewhat from the 1500-

hour estimate, and the amount actually spent on IPC cost elements will not total exactly $38,000. Remember, these differences are typically small and we want to avoid reallocations of IPC at month-end. What happens to these small differences between actual operations and planned operations, differences both in direct-labor hours used and in the amount spent on IPC?

IPC Variance

The differences are reconciled (or drawn off) in the **IPC Variance** account. Since actual operations almost always differ somewhat from plan, some debit or credit balance in the IPC Variance account must be expected. Consider the sources of the debit and credit entries in this account. (You may want to turn to the cost flow chart shown in Figure 14-1.) As the superintendent's salary is earned, the rent paid, supplies used, and depreciation on production equipment recognized, the IPC Variance account is debited. (The corresponding credits are to Wages Payable, Cash, Supplies Inventory, and Allowance for Depreciation.) As hours of direct labor are expended to build in-process inventory, IPC is allocated to (absorbed by) this in-process inventory: $25.33 of IPC for each hour of direct labor. Throughout the period, credit entries are made to the IPC Variance account as IPC is absorbed into inventory (with corresponding debit entries to in-process inventory.) At the end of the accounting period, the credit amount in IPC Variance is the total IPC absorbed by production during the period. (In Figure 14-1, the credit entry, I, is the aggregate amount of IPC absorbed, with the offsetting debit entry to In-process Inventory; the value of I is the product of the IPC Rate times the quantity of the IPC Vehicle involved in the manufacturing activity throughout the accounting period.)

Suppose that in a particular month (1) the total amount spent on IPC cost elements was $38,800, (2) 1570 direct labor hours were spent, and (3) thus $39,768 of IPC was absorbed (1570 hours at a rate of $25.33 per hour.) The IPC Variance account at month-end would show:

IPC Variance

38,800	39,768

The IPC Variance account has a net $968 credit balance. (This credit balance in the variance account is frequently referred to as a *favorable variance* in the sense that it represents a negative expense; a debit balance is *unfavorable*.) Production during the period absorbed more IPC than was actually spent.

To repeat: IPC is not redistributed at the end of the accounting period to eliminate the IPC variance. Instead, it is typically charged to Cost of Goods Sold for the period. (In this case, the credit balance is a negative expense serving to reduce cost of goods sold.) In the example above the IPC rate would have had to have been a bit less than the $25.33 rate used in order for the IPC variance to be zero: $38,800 actually spent divided by 1570 hours of actual direct labor equals $24.71. This 2 percent difference (or error, if you will) in the assignment of IPC is simply not material; remember that IPC accounting is, in any event, only an allocation process.

The use of a predetermined IPC rate assures timely cost accounting data; that advantage is well worth the disadvantage of generating small balances in the IPC Variance account.

But return now to consider the $968 credit IPC variance. What are possible explanations of this variance? As you interpret this variance balance, you need to keep in mind the mix of fixed and variable costs in IPC.

First, assume that all IPC cost elements are variable expenses—that is, they vary directly and proportionally with volume of production activity, as does direct material. If this assumption holds, then the IPC variance is entirely a spending variance; it is unaffected by differences between planned and actual volume of production, and the variance simply means the company spent less than planned on IPC. Figure 16-1 illustrates this situation. Note the derivation of the IPC rate: The budgeted IPC expenditures for the anticipated production level are divided by the volume of the IPC vehicle represented by that level. The dotted diagonal line is the IPC budget line and, since all IPC cost elements are variable, the line (1) starts at the origin and (2) defines budgeted, or planned, IPC at all possible levels of production. As production occurs, the IPC rate is applied and IPC is absorbed according to the solid line on Figure 16-1. Here, because all of the IPC cost elements are variable, the dotted and solid lines are coincident. The figure illustrates a condition where actual production level exceeds the planned level. Because all IPC costs are variable, the absorption of IPC—the credit to the IPC variance—defines a volume-adjusted budget for IPC.

Now suppose that IPC cost elements are comprised of some fixed expenses (e.g., depreciation and supervision salaries) and some variable expenses (e.g., utilities and indirect materials). Here the IPC variance is driven by two effects:

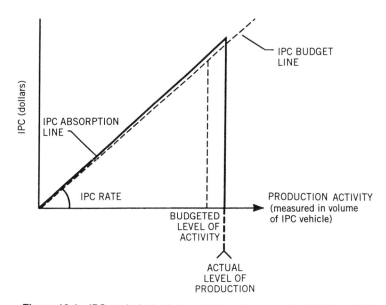

Figure 16-1   IPC analysis: budget and absorption assuming IPC is variable.

(1) Spending on IPC elements above or below the planned level

(2) Production activity above or below the planned level

Figure 16-2 illustrates this more complex IPC situation. The dotted lines show the derivation of the IPC rate. Note that the dotted diagonal line, the line labeled IPC budget line, does not begin at the origin but rather part way up the *Y* axis, a distance equal to the total of fixed IPC cost elements. Remember that these budgeted fixed costs are unaffected by the level of production activity, but also note that they will be completely absorbed only if the production level exactly matches the planned level. If actual production exceeds or falls short of the plan, IPC will be, respectively, overabsorbed or underabsorbed.

Figure 16-1 illustrates what is called a *variable costing* environment, while Figure 16-2 illustrates what is called a *full-absorption costing* environment. The appendix to this chapter will review the advantages and disadvantages of these two methods of costing, methods that differ only in the definition of what cost elements are included in IPC. At that time, we will consider a technique for isolating the spending effect from the volume effect in analyzing the IPC variance under full-absorption costing (that is, when both fixed and variable IPC cost elements are present).

The IPC Dilemma

Before proceeding, let's summarize what we might call the IPC dilemma:

(1) Because IPC is comprised of indirect, not direct, cost elements, we cannot determine with precision how much overhead is consumed in each step of production or by each unit of output.

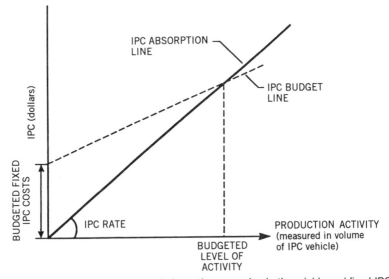

Figure 16-2 IPC analysis: budget and absorption assuming both variable and fixed IPC cost elements.

(2) Thus, IPC must be allocated to production in a necessarily arbitrary manner, utilizing an IPC vehicle.

(3) To assure timely management information, as well as timely evaluation of inventory and cost of goods sold, the allocation must be based upon estimates both of the amount to be expended on IPC elements and of the amount of production across which the IPC is to be allocated; that is, the IPC rate must be predetermined.

(4) It would be a rare coincidence if the amount of IPC absorbed just equalled the amount incurred, resulting in a zero IPC variance. Typically, some IPC variance is generated and is charged off (taken as a debit or credit to the income statement) in the current accounting period.

(5) If all IPC cost elements are variable (a variable costing environment), any IPC variance is a true spending variance, as it compares actual IPC expenditures with planned IPC adjusted for actual level of production. That is, the IPC absorbed defines a volume-adjusted budget for IPC.

(6) If both fixed and variable IPC cost elements are present (full-absorption costing), the IPC variance is driven by two forces:
(a) volume: over-absorption occurs if more than the budgeted (or estimated) quantity of the IPC vehicle was used this period (and under-absorption results from lower than anticipated activity); and
(b) spending: over-absorption is also caused by spending less than the budget on IPC cost elements (and under-absorption results from over-budget spending). Separating these two effects is a complex and confusing business to which the appendix at the end of this chapter is devoted.

MULTIPLE OVERHEAD POOLS

To this point the assumption has been that all indirect production costs would be absorbed by the use of a single IPC vehicle, typically direct-labor hours or direct-labor wages. In certain kinds of manufacturing or processing operations other IPC vehicles, such as machine hours in a contract printing company or direct material costs, are appropriate, but the assumption continues that only a single IPC vehicle is used.

Consider the possibility of using more than one overhead (IPC) pool, with each pool absorbed by the use of a different IPC vehicle. This approach seems particularly sensible when one considers the nature of overhead in a modern manufacturing environment. For example, a recent study of overheads in the electronics industry suggests the following breakdown of cost elements:

Indirect labor	12%
Facilities and equipment	20
Materials overhead	33
Manufacturing engineering	15
Manufacturing administration	20
Total	100%

Perhaps the first and fifth of these cost elements—indirect labor and manufacturing administration should be distributed (absorbed) by the use of an IPC vehicle based upon labor, while the second should be absorbed by machine hours, and the third and fourth by value of direct materials. Three cost pools, three different IPC vehicles, three IPC rates.

While this more elaborate distribution of IPC has a certain logic to it, we must remember that the final result is still simply an allocation of overhead to products. Managers will be misled if they think that the IPC vehicles cause the indirect cost elements or that an increase or decrease in the use of an IPC vehicle (say, direct-labor hours or machine hours) will necessarily cause a proportional change in the IPC cost elements that it is absorbing.

Therein lies the danger. Multiple overhead pools absorbed by multiple IPC rates lend an air of precision and rationality to IPC accounting that is simply not present. Evidence from actual manufacturing facilities indicates that most of the overhead cost elements shown in the tabulation above are, in fact, fixed. Modest swings in volume of activity (measured by direct-labor hours or machine hours consumed) will have little short-term effect on the amounts expended on these IPC cost elements. Yet, these cost elements are being absorbed by IPC vehicles that vary directly with volume of activity.

Moreover, precision is not achievable even with respect to variable IPC cost elements. Assume that utilities expenditures are a variable IPC cost and that the IPC vehicle is direct labor hours. Almost surely the rate of usage of utilities (electricity, gas, and so forth) is not uniform across all categories of direct labor. An hour of direct labor doesn't *cause* the usage of a uniform amount of utilities. Direct-labor hours are simply a convenient basis for allocating IPC—though some direct-labor hours may be spent in assembly (an activity consuming relatively little utilities) and other direct-labor hours may be spent operating machinery that consumes large amounts of utilities, and no labor hours at all may be expended on activities (e.g., the *burn in* of electronic components or assemblies) that consume large amounts of utilities.

Over the last few years a new method of attributing overhead to products has gained in popularity. This method, called activity-based costing, utilizes certain characteristics of products, as well as certain measures of activity, as bases for assigning overhead to individual products. Advocates of activity-based costing argue that the result is better information for managers to use in making key day-to-day pricing, product design, and marketing strategy decisions.

ACTIVITY-BASED COSTING

Chapter 14 suggests a number of ways in which modern manufacturing contrasts sharply with those manufacturing activities that were prevalent during and following the Industrial Revolution when the traditional method of allocating overhead just discussed was developed. A shortcoming of the traditional method is suggested by the fact that IPC rates have been escalating in recent years.

Escalating IPC Rates

Note, for example, the difference in overhead rates for a turn-of-the-century manufacturing enterprise that is highly labor intensive and a contemporary one that is substantially more complex and more automated. The former has relatively low indirect production expenditures while the latter has high IPC because it has a great deal of indirect labor, high depreciation, and heavy expenditures for maintenance and power. Suppose that cost of good sold had the following composition in the two factories:

	1904 Factory	1944 Factory
Direct material	40%	40%
Direct labor	50	10
IPC	10	50
Total	100%	100%

The IPC rate for the 1904 factory is 20 percent (10 divided by 50) while the IPC rate for the modern factory is 500 percent (50 divided by 10). When IPC rates approach several hundred percent or more, as in this example, one faces the question whether labor is the most rational basis upon which to incorporate indirect costs into product costs. Quite clearly direct labor is not in any sense causing or driving the indirect costs today, although it may have done so in 1904, when indirect costs were largely the costs of supervising and otherwise supporting the direct labor force.

What is causing or driving today's very much higher indirect production costs? If it is the quantity or value of the direct material used in the product, then we could shift the IPC vehicle from direct labor to a physical or monetary measure of direct material. In a few cases this is a sensible shift and solves the problem. In other instances (for example, the commercial printing operation mentioned earlier) a shift of the IPC vehicle to machine hours is sensible and solves the problem.

But in many of today's complex manufacturing operations none of these traditional IPC vehicles is appropriate. Why? Because the sheer complexity of the operation is the primary cause of high indirect costs, and none of these traditional vehicles captures this complexity.

Indirect productions costs are associated with activities such as machine set-up, ordering of parts, inspection, material tracking and handling, scheduling, technician support of automated equipment, manufacturing engineering support, and parts expediting. We might argue, therefore, that a product should bear IPC (that is, it should absorb IPC) to the extent that it causes or exacerbates these complexities of the manufacturing process.

For example, if one model of a piece of furniture is made in small lot sizes of, say 20 units, while another model, because it enjoys higher customer demand, is appropriately made in lots of 200, the first model will be more expensive to manufacture than the second even if, once again, the values of direct material and direct labor are the same for the two models. Suppose the costs of scheduling the production of a lot of each unit and the costs of setting up furniture-making machinery and assembly fixtures for each lot is the same—not an unreasonable assumption; the per-unit cost of these activities will be ten times as high for the unit produced in small lot sizes of 20 as for the one produced in lots of 200. An IPC vehicle built around either direct labor or direct material will not be able to capture these important differences between the two units. Traditional cost allocation methods result in identical, or nearly identical, product costs.

Another example: suppose a single plant manufactures both standard motor-generator sets and customized motor-generator sets. The customization is required by a few customers who operate the units in particular demanding environments. Traditional IPC accounting procedures result in the customized sets costing, say, 20 percent more than the standard sets; this would typically be the case if the prime costs (direct materials + direct labor) of the customized sets were 20 percent greater than the prime costs of the standard sets and IPC was absorbed on the basis of direct labor or direct material. Yet, the customized sets are, in effect, the cause of the complexity of the factory; it is the customized units that are difficult to schedule, that require specialized purchasing, that consume hours of final testing and manufacturing engineering time to be certain that the customer's particular specifications are met. Any analysis of this manufacturing plant would quickly convince us that the customized sets should absorb more of the IPC than the amount that is allocated to them by the traditional procedures.

Similarly, an electronic instrument that is comprised of 400 separate parts is typically more expensive to manufacture than another instrument that has only 150 parts, even if the values of the direct material and direct labor for the two instruments are identical. More parts will have to ordered for the first model, and then these parts will have to be received, inspected, inventoried, and moved to the production floor, and all of these activities will have to be tracked. The traditional IPC vehicles are unable to capture these differences in the way in which they allocate IPC to production.

Why are we concerned about this issue? So long as the factory absorbs all of the IPC, the IPC variances are not extraordinarily large, and the cost accounting system yields a product cost that can be used to value inventory and cost of goods sold, isn't the cost accounting system doing its job? After all, recall that we have admitted from the outset of our discussion of IPC that IPC allocations are inevitably quite arbitrary.

The problem is that managers must make day-to-day decisions based upon the information they obtain from cost accounting reports. Note the kind of erroneous decisions that might arise from the examples just cited.

First, and perhaps most important, are pricing decisions. While the extent to which product *costs* influence product *prices* varies widely among industries and companies, in many instances cost plays some role—often an important role (and sometimes a dominant role that is inappropriate in the actual circumstances!)

Assume the instrument that has 400 parts has the same manufacturing cost as the 150-part instrument, according to traditional cost allocation procedures. If that information leads the marketing staff to price the two instruments identically, the price of the 150-part instrument will be uncompetitive in the marketplace and the price of the 400-part instrument will prove so attractive to customers that the company's sales will be skewed in the direction of the instrument which is, in truth, more expensive to produce. The instrument that has 400 parts should be priced higher, and the one with 150 parts should be priced lower; they should not be priced identically.

Similar distorted pricing of the furniture will result, and customized motor-generator sets will sell at such a small premium over standard sets that customers will be induced to prefer customized sets with the result that the manufacturer's profits will suffer.

Second, design engineers of these furniture units, motor-generated sets, and instruments will look to cost accounting information to guide their decisions about product redesigns or designs of the next production generation. Traditional IPC allocation methods, where direct labor is the IPC vehicle, will signal the design engineer to reduce the direct labor demands of the design; note that, if the IPC rate is 500 percent of direct-labor wages incurred by the product, a one dollar savings in direct labor appears to result in a six dollar savings in total product costs. At least, that is what the cost accounting system tells the design engineer although even a cursory look at the plant would convince you that a small reduction in direct labor is unlikely to have more than a trivial effect on actual IPC expenditures.

In fact, the manufacturing engineer in the furniture factory might perhaps best focus on reducing the set-up times required so that the company can better afford to produce certain models of furniture in small lots. The engineer in the motor-generator firm might consider whether the introduction of a new standard motor-generator set might satisfy the demands of a group of customers who have been purchasing customized sets, each slightly different from the next, thus improving the standard-customized mix of manufacturing activity going on in the plant. And, the engineer considering a redesign of the electronic instrument should probably ignore direct labor and focus on reducing the number of discrete parts that comprise the design, as it is material ordering and handling that is the major cause of indirect production costs in the factory.

Cost Drivers

Activity-based costing seeks to identify those activities or product or process characteristics within the manufacturing or service company that cause, or drive, the indirect production costs. The examples just discussed suggest that these **cost drivers** are often not related to the cost value of direct labor or direct material but instead are a function of various characteristics of the product or service or of the manufacturing process that tend to increase the complexity of the manufacturing process and thus drive up indirect production costs.

In recent years industry has produced some dramatic examples of manufacturing costs being lowered sharply by:

- Reducing the amount of in-process time, the amount of time required to complete an activity or build a product

- Reducing the number of parts that must be purchased, and the number of vendors from which they are purchased; the benefits sought are often improved quality and better quantity discounts, but an important related benefit is reduced indirect production activity and thus cost
- Eliminating inventory by means of a just-in-time (JIT) inventory system; the resulting reductions in the amount of capital tied up in inventory are important, but often of more importance is the reduced indirect production activity, and thus cost, that results when parts move directly from vendor to assembly line without having to be inventoried and subsequently issued
- Targeting small market segments with standard products for which set-up times are so low (through the use of so-called flexible manufacturing systems) that small lot-size production is practical and customization of products is reduced or eliminated.

In each of these cases management has focused on an indirect, or overhead, activity and sought to reduce the amount of the activity required. These reductions have been brought about either by changing the design of the product or the design of the manufacturing process.

Once we have defined the characteristics of products and processes that give rise to IPC expenditures—that is, the cost drivers—we can then:

(1) Collect the costs associated with each activity; and

(b) Allocate the costs to the products or services produced on the basis of the demand that each product or service makes on the activity.

The particular characteristics that are selected as the cost drivers—that is, the basis for allocating overhead (IPC)—vary from company to company and depend upon the nature both of the products and services produced and of the manufacturing or servicing processes. Unlike the traditional method of allocating overhead, many of these cost drivers are unrelated to the volume of a production run. In our example of the instrument manufacturer, some possible cost drivers are:

- The number of setups
- The number of discrete moves of material (material handling)
- Parts ordering required (number of orders placed)
- Product updating (number of engineering change orders)
- Product complexity, as measured by number of parts or hours required in final system checkout
- Space consumed (occupancy costs), as measured by the number of elapsed days in process

Indirect manufacturing activities normally are identified by department: purchasing, scheduling, material handling, manufacturing engineering, maintenance, and so forth. Typically the financial accounting system will yield information as to how much the company anticipates spending on each activity, although some reconfiguration of departments and of the company's chart of accounts may be required to align both the organization and the accounting system with this new view of manufacturing overhead. These costs by activity are the *raw* cost data required for the activity-based cost system.

The next step is to select enough cost drivers so that each of the manufacturer's indirect production activities can be assigned to a driver and yet not so many that the process of cost allocation becomes hopelessly complex. (Here, then, is another accounting situation where we must make a reasonable trade-off between the value of the information for decision making and the cost of obtaining the information.) Once we have developed an estimate of the amount of the cost driver to be incurred or consumed for a period across all of the firm's products or processes, we are in a position to determine the rate at which each unit of that activity should be charged as products make demands on the activity.

The zealous designer of the activity-based costing system, in his or her quest for precision and truth in product costs, may be tempted to select a large number of drivers, each to allocate a small segment of the total indirect production activity. This temptation should obviously be resisted in the interest of accounting efficiency. Moreover, because many of these cost drivers are correlated—that is, respond in the same direction and magnitude to changes in process design or production volume— several IPC activities can generally be combined and allocated by use of just one of the drivers.

Recognize that the selection of cost drivers can have behavioral effects, some desirable and some undesirable, much along the lines of those suggested in Chapter 12's discussion of the behavioral effects of budgeting. If the number of parts is selected as a cost driver, design engineers will be motivated to go to great lengths to eliminate or combine parts. To the extent this effort simplifies the tasks of the purchasing, receiving inspection, and material handling departments of the company, the motivation is productive; if this preoccupation with reducing the number of parts leads to a degradation of the performance of the product, the motivation may be dysfunctional. Similarly, using number of setups as a cost driver will encourage longer production runs, but that benefit needs to be weighed against the costs of carrying additional inventory, particularly interest and obsolescence costs.

Note, too, that merely because a cost (e.g., material handling) is driven by a certain characteristic (for example, the number of piece parts in the instrument), does not suggest that the cost is variable and will necessarily increase or decrease as the driver is increased or decreased. Suppose that the number of piece parts is, in fact, reduced. If the expected savings in material handling costs are actually to be realized, separate decisions must be taken to reduce the number of material handlers, the amount of space and equipment devoted to material handling, and so forth.

And, when all is said and done, we are still dealing with the allocation—or, perhaps more accurately, the attribution—of costs to products or services. Allocations of depreciation expenses, no matter how accomplished, are largely irrelevant, as depreciation expenses typically bear no relationship to the cost of adding (or savings from disposing of) capital equipment. And, like all cost accounting methods, activity-based costing involves compromises, approximations, and assumptions about causality. The resulting information is useful but not unassailable as to accuracy and relevance.

When is Activity-Based Costing Important?

You may by now have the impression that an activity-based costing system is substantially more expensive to operate than a conventional IPC cost allocation system utilizing a single cost pool and a single IPC rate. You are correct. The manufacturing process must be studied in detail, cost drivers selected carefully, and the use of each driver by each product must be measured. Measuring these attributes of products can be expensive, although fortunately in many instances the information is already available because it is used for other purposes. For example, the set-up time required for a product is probably well known to the production scheduling staff because the data are required in the scheduling process.

As mentioned earlier, the designer of the cost accounting system must trade off the additional costs of operating an activity-based costing system with the added benefits to be derived from it in terms of improved decision making.

Activity-based costing is advantageous in a manufacturing plant that has the following characteristics:

- Product diversity is high
- The market it serves is fiercely competitive
- The costs of measuring the use of cost drivers is low

A few additional words on the first two of these characteristics is in order.

Activity-based costing has been enthusiastically pursued primarily in those situations where a diversity of products emanates from the same production facility, where direct labor, machines, supervisors, production schedulers, material handlers, and manufacturing engineers spread their attention across an array of product lines and product models. The key dimensions of product diversity appear to be:

- Diverse in the number of parts that each comprises
- Diverse in product size, some large products consuming large dollar values of direct material and direct labor and other products consuming substantially smaller dollar values
- Diverse in lot size, with some products built in very large lots and others built a very few at a time
- Diverse in performance specifications, with some products demanding greater precision, more elaborate final check-out, more attention from manufacturing engineers than other products that readily achieve their less demanding specifications
- Diverse in the extent to which they have are customized for particular customers

Traditional IPC cost allocation methods, including those that use multiple IPC pools and IPC vehicles, in comparison with activity-based costing, will over-cost:

- Products with fewer parts
- Larger products
- Products built in larger lots
- Products with less demanding performance specifications
- Standard (as contrasted with customized) products.

This over-costing results from the fact that a disproportionate share of indirect costs is assigned to these products when in fact spending on these indirect cost elements is being driven by complexity (products with high part count), frequent setups (products built in smaller lots) and difficult-to-meet standards (products that consume extra time on the part of manufacturing engineers and final test personnel).

The resulting cost cross-subsidies (to use an economist's phrase) may be relatively unimportant if the manufacturing company dominates its market. Pricing in such a market is unrelated to cost, and in any case the customer's buying decision does not turn dominantly on price. However, when competition is stiff, errors in pricing or errors in product design that result from a misunderstanding of true manufacturing costs are likely to be exploited by a competitor. The potential for problems is particularly great when some of the manufacturer's competitors are highly focused on only segments of the product line. Thus, if Company A is over-costing and consequently over-pricing simpler, large volume products (i.e., allowing these products to cross-subsidize more complex, low-volume models), Company B will perceive an opportunity to design a manufacturing facility that focuses on just these simpler, large volume products. Company B thereby avoids the high level of expenditure on purchasing, material handling, set-up crews and manufacturing engineering that Company A is enduring and substantially undercuts in price the product offerings of Company A. (These comments are not meant to imply that Company A *should* be setting prices based upon product costs. On the contrary, it should be pricing based upon the realities of the market. In fact, the real danger of the over-costing is that Company A will decide to exit a market in which it is capable of earning reasonable margins over activity-based costs.)

The Future of Activity-Based Costing

Traditional methods die slowly, and surely this truism applies to the accounting profession. Both managers and accountants are reluctant to jettison a system of accounting for product costs that has been in use for many years and that has resulted in a storehouse of comparative cost data. The fact that activity-based costing often results in product cost information that is very much at odds with the information yielded by the traditional cost allocation method contributes to the anxiety.

Note that the rethinking of processes and causal relationships that is inherent in preparing for the possible implementation of an activity-based costing system can have substantial benefits for a company, even if final implementation of the system is a long time in coming. Indeed, if periodically a study is done (outside of the formal cost accounting system) to recost products on the basis of activity costs, the information thereby obtained can go a long way to redirect the pricing, design engineering, process engineering, and capacity planning of the company.

Note, too, that activity-based costing has many applications outside of manufacturing, for example in analyzing selling and engineering costs. (Cost accountants have traditionally devoted little attention to costing these activities.) Selling involves many different activities, from planning the marketing strategy, to developing sales collateral material, to researching potential customers, to calling on customers, to preparing formal proposals and quotations, to confirming the order, and so forth. What cost drivers might be relevant? The elapsed time from first customer contact to final commitment, the number of decision makers in the typical customer organization, the complexity or sophistication of the product, the sales channel utilized and so forth. As in manufacturing, activity-based costing in sales will matter most if a company sells product or services of varying complexity to customers of varying nature and size.

For our purposes here we should recognize the shortcomings of the traditional cost allocation methods and keep an open mind regarding the possible benefits of the somewhat more complex activity-based system of cost allocation. In these days of increased worldwide competition and additional focus on competitiveness we need a cost accounting system that focuses the attention of managers on the key competitive product, pricing, and design decisions. Activity-based costing offers an important step in that direction.

AN EXAMPLE

Figures 16-3 through 16-7 provide a reasonably simple illustration of the differences among the cost allocation methods discussed in this chapter. You should particularly note that these different methods result in quite different final per-unit costs for the three products. The three products were selected to demonstrate that different bases of IPC allocation can result in very different cost accounting data, and thus the diversity of product characteristics in this illustration is somewhat extreme.

Figure 16-3 derives the traditional IPC rate, where direct labor cost is the IPC vehicle. The exhibit shows the per-unit cost for each product utilizing the traditional method of IPC allocation. Note that product M8, although less than half as costly as T6, consumes about the same amount of labor and only about $\frac{1}{7}$ the amount of material; we might say that M8 is labor-intensive, while T6 is material intensive. T4 is somewhere in between.

Figure 16-4 contrasts these per-unit product costs with those derived from the use of, first, direct material value as the IPC vehicle and, then, the use of two IPC pools, one absorbed by direct labor and the other by direct material value. (Incidentally, the necessary and quite arbitrary choices as to which IPC costs should be absorbed by labor and which by material are not explained in this figure; the choices

FIGURE 16-3   Derivation of Per-Unit Product Cost, Traditional IPC Allocation (IPC Vehicle = Direct Labor $)

Derivation of IPC Rate

IPC COST ELEMENT	BUDGET ($000)
Indirect production labor	$1,524
Manufacturing engineering	1,361
Rent and other occupancy	984
Maintenance and repair	1,610
Power	1,067
Depreciation, equipment	1,116
Miscellaneous	582
	$8,244
Budgeted direct-labor wages	$2,461 (179,000 hours)

Overhead rate ($8244 ÷ 2461) = 335% of direct labor

Resulting Product Cost

	Products		
	M8	T4	T6
Direct labor	$133	$ 209	$ 135
Direct material	124	278	843
IPC*	445	700	452
	$702	$1,187	$1,430

*IPC per-unit = 335% of direct labor per unit.

in fact lead to about 55 percent of the IPC costs being allocated by the labor vehicle and 45 percent by the material vehicle.) Note that the material-intensive product, T6, appears very costly when IPC is absorbed by direct material value—T6 costs now about 5.2 times as much as M8 while previously it was only twice M8's cost; T4's cost declines about 15 percent with this shift in IPC vehicle. Of course, the per-unit costs using two IPC pools and vehicles lie somewhere between the per-unit costs that arise from using solely direct labor and solely direct material as IPC vehicles.

Figure 16-5 details the product characteristics and then derives from them the cost drivers to be used in the activity-based cost system; the exhibit spells out how

FIGURE 16-4   Comparison of Product Costs: Alternative IPC Vehicles

	Products		
IPC Vehicle	M8	T4	T6
Direct labor $	$702	$1,187	$1,430
Direct material $	$483	$ 993	$2,512
Both	$604	$1,100	$1,917

FIGURE 16-5 Product Characteristics Relevant to Activity-Based Costing

	M8	T4	T6	Total
		Products		
Annual volume (units)	5,420	6,160	2,220	—
Price per unit	$875	$2,064	$2,467	—
Direct labor hours per unit	9.7	15.2	9.8	—
*Annual direct labor hours	52,574	93,632	21,756	167,962
Average lot size	800	800	250	
*Number of lots per year	6.8	7.7	8.9	23.4
*Number of discrete parts	137	345	423	905
*Number of parts handled†	931.6	2,656.5	3,764.7	7,352.8
Machine hours per unit	6.7	8.8	3.2	
*Machine hours per year	36,314	54,208	7,104	97,626

* = Cost drivers.
†Number of discrete parts times number of lots per year.

much of each driver is affected by each of the three products. Note that T6 is built in smaller lots than the other two products, but actually accounts for more lots per year than M8 and T4, even though its total annual volume is substantially less. It also has a very large number of individual parts (three times as many as M8); many of these are simply parts purchased from subcontractors rather than made in the factory, with the result that T6 utilizes substantially fewer machine hours than the other products but, because of its complexity, more assembly hours than M8.

Figure 16-6 segments the IPC cost elements shown in Figure 16-3 on the basis of activities (data that might not be readily available in the general ledger) and then indicates for each activity the appropriate cost driver. Note that the IPC cost elements listed in Figure 16-3 must be rearranged to correspond with the activities; the total budget for the IPC costs elements remains the same at $8,244,000.

Finally, Figure 16-7 shows the per-unit product costs as derived by an activity-based costing system. A comparison of Figures 16-4 and 16-7 shows that activity-based costing leads to a set of product costs that are bracketed by the extremes shown when the IPC is absorbed solely by labor or solely by material. Consider for a moment the kind of decisions to which this information might lead. If the part count of product T6 were reduced, or if it were built in larger lots, the demands on the materials handling staff, on manufacturing engineering, and on scheduling would be reduced, with the result that IPC expenditures could be reduced. Reducing part count in the next generation of product T6 is a logical goal for design engineering, a goal that is reinforced by activity costing. Since such changes might have no effect on the amount of direct labor or direct material costs of the product, the traditional method of IPC allocation would not highlight this opportunity. Indeed, the use of direct labor as the IPC vehicle would suggest to design engineers that in their quest for lower overall product costs for T6 they lower direct labor cost; in fact, however, direct labor accounts for less than 10 percent of T6's cost (in all four cost compilations illustrated in these exhibits), and Figures 16-6 and 16-7 indicate that direct labor is a cost driver for just over 7 percent of the total IPC.

FIGURE 16-6   Indirect Production Costs Segmented by Activity

Activity and Cost Element	Budget ($000)	Cost Driver
Production supervision		A
Indirect labor	$ 491	
Depreciation and miscellaneous	44	
Occupancy and power	56	
	591	
Material handling		D
Indirect labor	517	
Depreciation and miscellaneous	216	
Occupancy and power	382	
	1,115	
Production scheduling		B
Indirect labor	342	
Depreciation and miscellaneous	106	
Occupancy and power	112	
	560	
Quality assurance		B
Indirect labor	174	
Depreciation and miscellaneous	66	
Occupancy and power	91	
	331	
Manufacturing engineering—production changes		C
Engineering salaries	776	
Occupancy and power	143	
	919	
Manufacturing engineering—process improvement		D
Engineering salaries	585	
Occupancy and power	69	
	654	
Machine operation		E
Occupancy and power	785	
Depreciation and miscellaneous	885	
Maintenance and repair	1,119	
	2,789	
Assembly operations		C
Occupancy and power	413	
Depreciation and miscellaneous	381	
Maintenance and repair	491	
	1,285	
Total	$8,244	

LEGEND: Cost Driver

A =	direct labor	$ 591
B =	number of lots	891
C =	number of part numbers	2,204
D =	number of parts handled	1,769
E =	machine hours	2,789
		$8,244

FIGURE 16-7   Activity-Based Product Costs

Cost Driver	M8	T4	T6	Total
	Product			
A Direct labor	$ 185(31.3%)	$ 329(55.7%)	$ 77(13.0%)	$ 591
B Number of lots	259(29.1)	293(32.9)	339(38.0)	891
C Number of part numbers	335(15.2)	840(38.1)	1,029(46.7)	2,204
D Number of parts handled	224(12.7)	639(36.1)	906(51.2)	1,769
E Machine hour	1,037(37.2)	1,548(55.5)	204 (7.3)	2,789
	$2,040	$3,649	$2,555	$8,244
Units produced	5,420	6,160	2,220	
IPC per unit*	$ 376	$ 592	$1,151	
Direct labor†	133	209	135	
Direct material†	124	278	843	
	$ 633	$1,079	$2,129	

*Annual IPC for product divided by annual units produced.
†From Figure 16-3.

SUMMARY

While determining the value of direct materials and direct labor appropriately as-signed to a particular unit of output is relatively straightforward, distributing the indirect production costs (IPC) is substantially more challenging. Moreover, the resulting allocation is inevitably arbitrary since determining the precise amount of overhead consumed by each product or in each step of manufacturing is impossible; accordingly, IPC allocations are frequently misinterpreted.

Traditionally, indirect production costs have been allocated by selecting an IPC vehicle (often direct labor hours or dollars) that is common to all segments of output and then predetermining an IPC rate that is applied throughout the ensuing account-ing period in order to cost products or services as they are produced. The fact that IPC rates are predetermined necessitates that an IPC variance be developed to draw off in each accounting period the difference between the amount of actual IPC expenditures and the aggregate IPC absorbed.

In an effort to produce more exact per-unit product costs, some companies use multiple IPC pools, each absorbed by a different IPC vehicle, most generally a measure of direct labor or direct material volume consumed by the product. While such allocations are more elaborate and appear more precise, they are still merely alloca-tions; they do not attempt to define why a company spends more or less on IPC.

Increasingly, activity-based costing is being adopted by industry in an attempt to couple more closely the allocation of overhead with the product and manufacturing characteristics that drive, or cause, the IPC. Indirect production activities are the focus of activity-based costing and these activities are traced through to the products to estimate the demand that each product (or service) places on the activity. The system requires that cost drivers be identified to serve as the basis for distributing the expenditures on each IPC activity.

Activity-based costing is important where diverse products—diverse in terms of such characteristics as product complexity, production lot size, and extent of customization—are produced in the same manufacturing facility. In such environments, conventional IPC cost allocation methods—that is, systems using as IPC vehicles measures of volume of direct material or direct labor consumed by the product—tend to over-cost the simpler, standard products manufactured in large lots.

Activity-based costing, although more expensive to implement than conventional IPC cost allocation schemes, produces information that is more relevant to day-to-day decisions that managers must make, such decisions as pricing, product-line configuration, product redesign, and marketing promotion.

This chapter concludes with an illustration of the wide range of per-product costs that can result from the alternative approaches to IPC cost allocation.

APPENDIX: VARIABLE AND FULL-ABSORPTION COSTING

This appendix explains the difference between two alternative definitions of IPC inclusiveness—variable (or direct) costing, which defines IPC to include only the variable cost elements of IPC, the fixed elements being treated as period costs; and full-absorption costing, which defines IPC to include both fixed and variable IPC cost elements. Full-absorption costing is more prevalent than variable costing but results in an IPC variance that is challenging to analyze and potentially misleading to management.

Review of IPC Variance Account

Recall that the IPC variance account is debited as various indirect cost elements are expended, for example, indirect labor wages, power, rent, depreciation, and insurance. Credit entries occur as the IPC rate is applied, by means of the IPC vehicle, to absorb IPC into in-process inventory. Thus, if the IPC vehicle is direct-labor hours, each time an hour of direct labor is charged to a particular job or to a process, IPC is also charged in the amount of the IPC rate per direct-labor hour.

At the end of an accounting period the aggregate debit in the IPC Variance account equals the amount spent (or accrued) during the period on all IPC cost elements, and the aggregate credit is total IPC absorbed into production during the period. Only by shear and infrequent coincidence are aggregate debits equal to aggregate credits; thus some remaining IPC variance balance is typical. What conditions would lead to a zero balance? First, spending on IPC cost elements would have to be smack on budget, no deviation. Second, the amount of production activity—as measured by the quantity of the IPC vehicle to which the IPC rate was applied—would have to be smack on budget, not even off by a few direct-labor hours (or direct-labor dollars or machine hours or whatever the IPC vehicle). Neither of these conditions is likely to be met frequently, to say nothing of both. So, what does the IPC variance mean? That answer depends in part on how IPC is defined.

Interpreting the Total IPC Variance Balance. On page 362 of this chapter appears this IPC variance account:

IPC Variance

38,800	39,768

The account has a net $968 credit balance. Because it has a credit balance, we are tempted to say it is a favorable variance; however, please withhold judgement, as we will see that the forces causing this credit balance may not be favorable. Now to its interpretation.

First, assume that all IPC cost elements are variable expenses—that is, they vary directly and proportionally with volume of production activity, just as we assume direct material does. All indirect fixed expenses, then, are considered under this assumption to be period expenses and are not absorbed into the products. If these assumptions hold, the IPC variance is entirely a spending variance; that is to say it is unaffected by differences between planned and actual volume of production, and the variance simply means the company spent less than planned on IPC. Figures 16A-1 (which resembles Figure 16-1 in the chapter) illustrates this situation. The dotted lines show the derivation of the IPC rate: the budgeted IPC expenditures for the anticipated production level is divided by the volume of the IPC vehicle represented by that level. The dotted diagonal line is the IPC budget line and, since all IPC cost elements are variable, the line (1) starts at the origin and (2) defines budgeted, or planned, IPC at all possible levels of production. As production occurs, the IPC rate

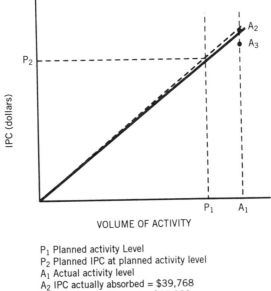

P_1 Planned activity Level
P_2 Planned IPC at planned activity level
A_1 Actual activity level
A_2 IPC actually absorbed = $39,768
A_3 IPC actually incurred = $38,800

Figure 16A-1   IPC accounting: variable costing.

is applied and IPC is absorbed according to the solid line on Figure 16A-1. Here, because all IPC is variable, the dotted and solid lines are coincident.

Figure 16A-1 illustrates a condition where actual production level exceeds the planned level. Because all IPC costs are variable, the absorption of IPC—the credit to the IPC variance—defines a volume-adjusted budget for IPC. Where is actual IPC—the debit to the IPC variance—shown on this figure? It is unrelated to either of the two lines. It is a point at the level of $38,800 (in the example above), below the IPC absorption line. The difference between that point and the absorption line defines the $968 IPC credit variance. Had the point occurred above the absorption line, the IPC variance for the period would, of course, have been negative or debit.

Now suppose that IPC is defined to comprise some cost elements that are fixed—that is, they don't vary with volume of production (e.g., depreciation and supervision salaries)—and some that are variable (e.g., utilities and indirect materials.) Here the IPC variance is driven by two effects:

(1) Spending above or below the plan
(2) Production volume above or below the plan

Figure 16A-2 (which resembles Figure 16-2) illustrates this more complex IPC variance. Once again the dotted lines show the derivation of the IPC rate. Note that the dotted diagonal line, the line labeled IPC budget line, does not begin at the origin but rather part way up the Y axis, a distance equal to the planned expenditures on fixed IPC cost elements. Remember that these budgeted fixed costs are unaffected by the level of production activity, but also note that they will be completely

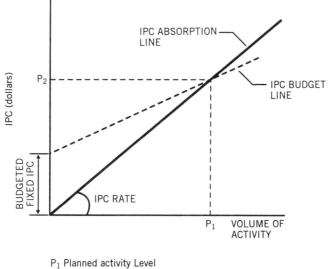

P_1 Planned activity Level
P_2 Planned IPC at planned activity level

Figure 16A-2   IPC accounting: full-absorption costing.

absorbed only if the production level exactly matches the planned level. If actual production exceeds or falls short of the plan, IPC will be, respectively, overabsorbed or underabsorbed.

Figure 16A-1 illustrates a variable costing environment, while Figure 16A-2 illustrates a full-absorption costing environment.

Recall that this is the third dimension for the definition of a cost accounting system first introduced in Chapter 15. In addition to specifying whether the system shall be job order or process, and whether it shall use actual or standard costs in valuing inventory and cost of goods sold (a choice discussed in Chapter 17), one also must specify the definition of IPC. This third dimension is independent of the other two. A company can operate a variable, job order, standard system or a variable, process, actual system or a full-absorption, process, standard system—or any other combination of the three dimensions.

Full-absorption costing is most prevalent in the United States today, but variable costing is gaining in popularity, and for very good reasons. Before discussing the advantages and disadvantages of these two costing schemes, schemes that differ only in the definition of cost elements included in IPC, we need to consider techniques for interpreting the IPC variance in full-absorption costing. Because these techniques are not simple, misinterpretation of IPC variances is widespread and that in turn is a major disadvantage of full-absorption costing systems.

Separating IPC Volume and Spending Variances

IPC variance analysis in full-absorption costing is complex because—and really only because—IPC is comprised of both fixed and variable cost elements. Thus, what follows applies to full-absorption costing but not to variable costing.

In full-absorption costing the IPC rate absorbs both fixed and variable IPC elements. At the planned activity level, the amount of fixed IPC absorbed is just right, just enough and not too much. At any other activity level—above or below plan—fixed IPC will be over- or under-absorbed in relation to budget. The situation is made more complex by the fact that IPC rates are predetermined; that is, the IPC rate used to value inventory and cost of goods sold is not adjusted after-the-fact for actual volume.

Recall the statement above that the IPC variance in full-absorption costing is driven by two effects: spending variations from budget and activity variations from plan. To develop meaningful data for overhead cost control in a full-absorption environment, one must be able to isolate the spending effect from the volume effect. The volume-adjusted budgeting discussion in Chapter 13 addresses exactly this same challenge.

Assume that Department P at the Blume Manufacturing Company expects to require 4500 hours of direct labor per month to accomplish its production plan for the forthcoming year. To support this activity level, the department estimates that total IPC expenditures will be $144,000 per month (including all IPC cost elements, variable, semivariable, and fixed). The resulting IPC rate for Department P for the year is $32 per direct-labor hour ($144,000 ÷ 4500 hours).

This $32 rate is used throughout the accounting period (the year). Since the IPC vehicle is direct-labor hours, if Job 246, for example, consumes four direct-labor hours, it is charged with four times the IPC rate, or $128; in the jargon of cost accounting, Job 246 absorbs $128 of IPC. In general journal format, the accounting entry is;

Dr. Job 246 $128
    Cr. IPC variance $128

Throughout the accounting period, many similar entries are made, as direct labor is expended on Department P's jobs. At the end of the period, the aggregate credit in the IPC variance account equals the total IPC absorbed by all jobs and the aggregate debit is the total amount actually expended on the IPC during the same period.

Assume that for Department P the IPC variance account shows the following at the end of October:

IPC Variance

148,500 | 150,400

At first glance, one might conclude that the Department P supervisor did a good job of controlling IPC expenses: the amount actually spent $148,500, was less than the amount absorbed, $150,400. However, because Blume operates a full-absorption cost system, imbedded in this single variance are two primary effects*:

(1) *Volume:* If Department P was more active this month than planned—that is, utilized more direct-labor hours, the IPC vehicle—more IPC was absorbed than planned.

(2) *Usage or efficiency:* In comparison with estimates (upon which the IPC rate was based), Blume may have used more or less power, more or fewer indirect labor hours, or more or less supplies per unit of productive activity, and so forth.

The task is to separate the single IPC variance into the two components just described: **IPC spending variance** and **IPC volume variance.** That is, the overabsorption/underabsorption effect (volume effect) must be isolated from the spending effect. The $1900 credit balance in the IPC variance account for Department P is the result of some combination of:

---

*Price variation is a third possible effect: Prices per kilowatt-hour for power, or wage rates for indirect labor, may have been more or less than the assumed prices and wage rates in the original IPC estimates. Separating price and usage will be discussed in Chapter 17 but this degree of sophistication is generally not warranted with respect to IPC (although it frequently is warranted for direct material and direct labor). For convenience, this appendix combines the price-and-usage effects.

(1) Production activity above or below expected levels for the month

(2) Total spending on IPC (including both prices paid and amounts used) more or less than planned

Note that the truly useful management information is a comparison of actual IPC spending with a *revised* estimate of appropriate IPC expenditures, that is, a volume-adjusted IPC budget. As illustrated in Figure 16A-1, a volume-adjusted IPC budget is self-defined under variable costing. But not so in full-absorption costing; the volume-adjusted IPC budget must be derived.

IPC Budget Equation (Line). IPC expenditures can be rebudgeted or reestimated based upon the actual activity level in Department P in October. The relevant comparison is not with the original $144,000 estimate, since actual activity turned out to be above the original plan. The data compiled at the beginning of the year to establish the IPC rate indicates how total IPC expenditures are expected to vary with changes in volume. (Refer now to Figure 16A-3.)

At the beginning of the year, Blume's cost analyst estimated total IPC expenditures at several different activity levels; these data were needed for the companywide budgeting exercise that led finally to the production activity plan calling for 4500 direct-labor hours per month. The analyst estimated that total IPC expenditures at this planned production level would be $144,000. She further estimated that at 4000 direct labor hours total IPC expenditures would be $138,000 or $6000 less, and at 5000 hours total IPC expenditures would be $150,000 or $6000 more. These points are labeled A, B, and C, respectively, on Figure 16A-3. By fitting a line to these three points, the analyst developed an algebraic expression for the IPC budget line. The intersection with the y axis (at $90,000) signals the fixed-cost portion of IPC. The slope of the line, equivalent to $12.00 per direct-labor hour, represents the

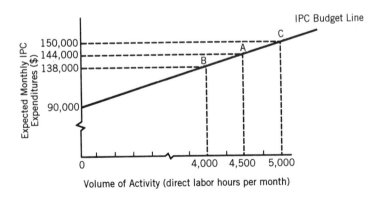

IPC budget equation: Total monthly IPC expenditures = $90,000 × $12 (directed labor hours)

Figure 16A-3 IPC budget estimates.

variable cost portion of IPC. (Note that $12.00 would be the IPC rate in a variable cost system, since all fixed IPC costs would be charged as period expenses.)

The form of this IPC budget line is

$$IPC = F + vX$$

In this example, the equation becomes

$$IPC = \$90,000 + \$12.00 \times (\text{direct-labor hours})$$

The slope and shape of this budget line is valid for only modest variations in production activity (for example, 20 percent above or below the planned level). If actual production greatly exceeds or falls way short of the planned level (e.g., by 50 percent), the straight-line relationship between IPC and volume probably will not hold. Nevertheless, the straight-line approximation in Figure 16A-3 is adequate for most purposes.*

Blume Manufacturing now has the information to separate the single IPC variance into its spending and volume variance components, because now a volume-adjusted IPC budget can be calculated based upon the actual production volume in Department P in October. A comparison of this volume-adjusted IPC budget to actual IPC expenditures reveals how well Department P controlled spending on IPC.

Assume that during October Department P utilized 4700 direct-labor hours. Indeed, the aggregate credits in the IPC variance account verify that direct-labor hours must have numbered 4700: Each direct-labor hour absorbed $32 of IPC and total IPC absorbed during the month was $150,400, or 4700 hours times $32 per hour.

Activity at the rate of 4700 direct-labor hours is, obviously, somewhat above the original plan of 4500. Accordingly, total IPC expenditures for October should logically be above the planned $144,000 per month, since certain IPC cost elements vary with volume. However, total IPC expenditures should not be as high as $150,400, the amount of IPC absorbed (i.e., 4700 hours times $32 per hour), since still other IPC cost elements are fixed and are unaffected by this increased production activity.

From the IPC budget line (and equation), one can determine what should have been spent on IPC in October, given that activity was equivalent to 4700 direct-labor hours instead of 4500. Substituting 4700 hours in the equation yields a volume-adjusted IPC budget of

$$\text{Volume-adjusted IPC} = \$90,000 + 12(4700) = \$146,400$$

Interpreting the Separated Variances. Now the single IPC variance shown above can be separated into these two variances, shown in T-account format:

---

*With more data points a more complex curve (and resulting budget equation) could be developed to describe the variation in IPC with variations in volume. Typically, such added sophistication and complexity are not warranted.

IPC Spending Variance		IPC Volume Variance	
Actual IPC expenditures	Volume-adjusted IPC budget	Volume-adjusted IPC Budget	Absorbed IPC (IPC rate × quantity of IPC vehicle)
148,500	146,400	146,400	150,400

Note several things about these two variances:

(1) The accounting system is still in balance, debits equal credits; the credit balance in the IPC spending variance equals the debit balance in the IPC volume variance.

(2) The algebraic sum of the two separate variances equals the total IPC variance:

$$\begin{aligned} \text{IPC spending variance} &= (\$2,100)\ \text{debit} \\ \text{IPC volume variance} &= \underline{\ \ 4,000}\ \text{credit} \\ \text{Total IPC variance} &= \$1,900\ \text{credit} \end{aligned}$$

(3) IPC volume variance is always favorable when actual production activity exceeds plan and always unfavorable when it falls short of plan. Here activity was above plan. This is probably not news to Blume's managers and is

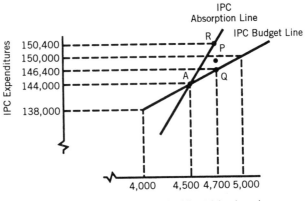

Explanation
Point P = Level of actual IPC expenditures, October 1993 = $148,500
Point Q = Volume-adjusted IPC budget = $146,400
Point R = Absorbed IPC (4,700 hours × $32/hour) = $150,400
IPC spending variance = point Q - point P = $2,100 unfavorable
IPC volume variance = point R - Point Q = $4,000 favorable
Total IPC variance = point R - point P = $1,900 favorable

Figure 16A-4 Graphical depiction of IPC variance analysis.

FIGURE 16A-5   Algebraic Definition of IPC Variances

Assumptions

X = Activity level, measured in units of IPC vehicle
X_e = Planned activity level
X_a = Actual activity level
F = Budgeted fixed IPC costs
v = Budgeted slope of variable IPC costs
   (rate of variation of budgeted IPC with changes in X)
P = Actual IPC expenditures

Therefore,

$$\text{IPC rate} = \frac{F + vX_e}{X}$$

IPC Variances

$$\text{Total IPC Variance} = P - \left[\frac{F + vX_e}{X_e}\right]X_a$$

$$\text{IPC Volume Variance} = [F + vX_a] - \left[\frac{F + vX_e}{X_e}\right]X_a$$

$$\text{IPC Spending Variance} = P - [F + vX_a]$$

Example: Department P, October, Blume Manufacturing Company

X_e = 4,500 direct-labor hours
X_a = 4,700 direct-labor hours
F = \$90,000
v = \$12 perdirect-labor hour
P = \$148,500

$$\text{IPC Volume Variance} = [90,000 + 12(4,700)] - \left[\frac{90,000 + 12(4,500)}{4,500}\right]4,700$$

$$= 146,400 - 150,400 = 4,000 \text{ Cr.}$$

$$\text{IPC Spending Variance} = 148,500 - [90,000 + 12(4,700)] = 2,100 \text{ Dr.}$$

itself not worth the analysis. However, only by isolating the IPC volume variance can you deduce the IPC spending variance.

(4) The IPC spending variance is indeed useful. Blume's managers now know that IPC expenditures during October were \$2100 more than the adjusted spending plan—that is, the plan adjusted to actual activity volume.

This more detailed variance analysis is depicted graphically in Figure 16A-4 and algebraically in Figure 16A-5. The graph, similar to the IPC budget graph in Figure

16A-3, contains a line not shown on the earlier graph: **the IPC absorption line.** This line begins at the origin and passes through point *A*—the same point A shown in Figure 16A-3 (4500 hours and $144,000 of IPC); its slope is the IPC rate, $32 per hour.

In Figure 16A-4, point *P* is the level of actual IPC expenditures for October, assumed earlier at $148,500. Point *Q* is the volume-adjusted IPC for October, based upon 4700 direct-labor hours. Point *R* shows the amount of IPC absorbed into Department P jobs during October; note that the predetermined $32 IPC rate was, in effect, too high. The distances between these points represent the following IPC variances; a negative number indicates a debt balance.

$$Q - P = \text{IPC Spending Variance}$$
$$R - Q = \text{IPC Volume Variance}$$
$$R - P = \text{Total IPC Variance}$$

Why is All This Important?

Why does the interpretation of IPC variances in a full-absorption cost environment warrant such extensive analysis? The reason is simple: Surprisingly few managers know what over-or under-absorbed overhead means. As a result, misinterpretations of overhead variances is widespread. You need to be alert to the need to separate spending and volume effects whenever you are interpreting variances in an environment that contains both fixed and variable cost elements—and, as Chapter 12 pointed out, that includes almost all environments. Full-absorption costing predominates in manufacturing today, and analogous systems are used in many other kinds of operations, including most research, consulting, and professional service firms.

Example: Variance Analysis at Garcia Auto Repair Shop

Figure 16A-6 is a cost report for Garcia Auto Repair Shop for the months of March and April. Business was slow in March, but picked up briskly in April. Gross margin was below plan in March and well above plan in April, as might be expected with this swing in activity. As a manager, you need to interpret the overhead (or IPC) variance accounts for the two months. Overhead variance was $6000 unfavorable in March and favorable by $4000 in April. Volume alone may have accounted for these variances: low volume in March lead to underabsorption of overhead, while April's high volume created an overabsorbed condition. On the other hand, good or poor expense control at the auto repair shop might be the cause. Garcia needs to isolate the volume effects in order to judge performance in overhead expense control.

Figure 16A-6 derives the overhead budget equation, as well as the volume-adjusted budget for each month. The overhead variance analysis shows that in spite of the overall negative, or unfavorable, overhead variance in March, Garcia Auto actually spent $4000 less than plan—the overhead spending variance was $4000 credit. Furthermore, although April's sales level and gross margin were very favor-

FIGURE 16A-6   Garcia Auto Repair

Mechanics' wage rate = $20 per hour
Overhead rate* = 150% of wage rate or $30 per mechanic hour
Customer billing rate = 120% of cost (labor and overhead)
= $60.00 per mechanic hour

| | March | | April | |
	Budget	Actual	Budget	Actual
Sales	$240,000	$210,000	$240,000	$270,000
Labor expense	80,000	70,000	80,000	90,000
Overhead absorbed	120,000	105,000	120,000	135,000
Overhead variance	—	(6,000)UNF	—	4,000F
Gross margin	$ 40,000	$ 29,000	$ 40,000	$ 49,000
Mechanic hours	4,000	3,500	4,000	4,500

Overhead Variances

March
Overhead Variance

111,000	105,000
Balance:	
6,000 Dr.	

April
Overhead Variance

131,000	135,000
Balance:	
4,000 Cr.	

Overhead Spending Variance

111,000	115,000†
Balance:	
4,000 Cr.	

Overhead Volume Variance

115,000	105,000
Balance:	
10,000 Dr.	

Overhead Spending Variance

131,000	125,000‡
Balance:	
6,000 Dr.	

Overhead Volume Variance

125,000	135,000
Balance:	
10,000 Cr.	

*Overhead rate determined as follows:
Expected overhead expenditures when wages paid to all mechanics total $80,000 per month

Variable cost elements	$ 40,000
Fixed cost elements	80,000
Total	$120,000

Therefore, overhead budget equation $= 80,000 + \dfrac{40,000}{80,000}$ (mechanic wages)

Overhead rate $= \dfrac{80,000 + (40,000/80,000)}{80,000} = \$1.50$ per dollar of mechanic wages

†Volume-adjusted overhead budget $= 80,000 + \dfrac{40,000}{80,000} (70,000) = \$115,000$

‡Volume-adjusted overhead budget $= 80,000 + \dfrac{40,000}{80,000} (90,000) = \$125,000$

able compared to budget, control of overhead spending was unfavorable—the overhead spending variance is $6000 unfavorable. Had overhead spending in April been on plan, gross margin for the month would have been $55,000, or $6000 more than actually earned.

Advantages of Variable Costing

While full-absorption costing has long been the traditional structure for industrial cost accounting systems, recently variable costing has gained popularity as its advantages become more widely recognized. What are those advantages?

First, the clear and consistent separation of variable and fixed manufacturing costs readily yields data for those many analyses that require a focus on incremental or variable costs: make-or-buy decisions, capital-investment decisions, and certain marketing decisions. These decisions are discussed at greater length in Chapter 18.

Second, as we have just seen, IPC variance analysis is a great deal simpler under variable costing than under full-absorption costing.

Third, under full-absorption costing, if planned production volumes decrease over several years, the predetermined IPC rate spreads fixed production costs over fewer units of output, with a resulting increase in the IPC rate. As volume decreases, each unit appears to cost more. As planned volume increases over several years, the IPC rate now spreads the same fixed production costs over more units of output; each unit bears a smaller share of IPC, and therefore appears to cost less.

This sounds sensible enough: the concept of economy of scale. But here the "scale" is unchanged. No change in the capacity or configuration of the factory or service operation occurs. The change is simply of output from an operation of certain scale. The change in product costs here, then, arises solely from the accounting treatment of fixed IPC. (Remember that direct material, direct labor and variable IPC all are assumed to vary directly and proportionally with changes in volume.)

These changes in overhead (or IPC) per unit, illustrated in Figure 16A-7, are easily misinterpreted and may lead to unfortunate decisions. For example, suppose prices are set at a certain mark-up over cost—an illogical but frequent pricing rule. A company utilizing full-absorption costing will increase prices when planned production volumes decline, with the result that orders may decline further, and decrease prices when production volumes increase, just when strong demand suggests no need to lower prices. Under variable costing, all fixed production costs are treated as period costs, and unit costs are unaffected by modest changes in production volume.

Of course, the fact that certain production costs are fixed makes them no less real. There is no suggestion that a given product "costs" less under the variable costing method (or structure) than it does under the full-absorption method. On the other hand, if the level of fixed costs cannot be altered in the short run—that is, if in fact they are fixed regardless of short-term swings in production output—it makes more sense to treat them as period costs, just as selling expenses and administrative expenses are treated.

FIGURE 16A-7   IPC Rates at Alternative Planned Volumes: Full-Absorption and Variable Costing

	Planned Volume of Activity		
	Normal	Slow	High Output
Estimated production, in units per month	2,000	1,500	2,500
Estimated IPC			
Variable ($1.50/unit)	$3,000	$2,250	$3,750
Fixed	4,000	4,000	4,000
Total	$7,000	$6,250	$7,750
IPC rate, full-absorption	$3.50 per unit	$4.17 per unit	$3.10 per unit
IPC rate, variable costing	$1.50 per unit	$1.50 per unit	$1.50 per unit

Dangers of Variable Costing

While these are valid arguments for variable costing, there are also dangers. First, because product costs are lower under variable costing than under full-absorption costing, cost of goods sold are stated correspondingly lower and total period costs correspondingly higher. Thus, margins (sales less product costs) appear more favorable under variable costing than under full-absorption costing, but, of course, higher period expenses just offset that difference. Note that these gross margin differences between variable and full-absorption product costs can be extreme in a situation where fixed IPC costs represent a major portion of total product costs (e.g., in a highly automated, capital-intensive plant utilizing low-cost material and very little direct labor).

Finally, a disadvantage of variable costing is that the accounting profession does not now sanction it as a generally accepted accounting principle to value inventory and cost of goods sold. Before you cast aside variable costing for that fact alone, recognize that it still can be used for internal management reporting; then, as financial statements are prepared for external audiences, the values for inventory and cost of goods sold can simply be restated to their equivalent full-absorption costs. Fortunately, these adjustments are easily made.

Effects on Net Profit

Recall the earlier statement that under variable costing lower product costs are just offset by higher period costs (since they now include fixed IPC). This, in turn, suggests that net profit should be just the same under the two methods, but that is not quite the case. Variable costing and full-absorption costing result in identical operating profits if (but only if) in-process and finished-goods inventories remain the same during the period. When finished-goods inventory increases during a month, full-absorption costing includes in the valuation of that inventory a portion of the month's fixed production costs; variable costing, by contract, treats all fixed production costs as period expenses of the month. Thus, in time of expanding inventories, profit is higher if calculated under full-absorption costing; the reverse is true when inventories decline. Figure 16A-8 illustrates the effect on operating profit of the two methods. Part A of the figure assumes that production and sales are equal at 1000 units—that is, no change in inventory. Part B of the figure assumes that production exceeds sales, that is, finished-goods inventory increases. Part C makes

FIGURE 16A-8   The Effect on Profit of Changes in Inventory: Full-Absorption and Variable Costing

Assumptions	Full-Absorption Costing	Variable Costing
Normal (planned) production level	1000 units	1000 units
Product cost/unit		
Direct labor	$ 4	$ 4
Direct material	3	3
Variable IPC	2	2
Fixed IPC	2	0
Total	$ 11	$ 9
Fixed IPC (period cost)	—	$ 2,000
Selling price/unit	$ 20	$ 20
Other (nonmanufacturing) period costs	$ 6,000	$ 6,000
Opening inventory (1000 units)	$11,000	$ 9,000

A. Inventory unchanged, as production and sales are both 1000 units

Sales	$20,000	$20,000
Product costs	11,000	9,000
Margin	9,000	11,000
Period costs	6,000	8,000
Operating profit	$ 3,000	$ 3,000

B. Inventory increases by 200 units as production (1000 units) is greater than sales (800 units)

Sales	$16,000	$16,000
Product costs	8,800	7,200
Margin	7,200	8,800
Period costs	6,000	8,000
Operating profit	$ 1,200	$ 800

C. Inventory decreases by 100 units, as production (1000 units) is less than sales (1100 units)

Sales	$22,000	$22,000
Product costs	12,100	9,900
Margin	9,900	12,100
Period costs	6,000	8,000
Operating profit	$ 3,900	$ 4,100

the opposite assumption. When production exceeds sales, profits are $400 higher under full-absorption costing than under variable costing. The corresponding offset is to the value of finished-goods inventory.

NEW TERMS

Activity-based costing. A cost accounting procedure that traces costs to products according to the activities for which they are responsible; while volume-related costs are traced using conventional volume measures such as direct labor or direct material, the many IPC costs unrelated to volume are assigned to products by identifying the product-by-product consumption of so-called cost drivers.

Cost drivers. The basis by which IPC expenditures are allocated to products in an activity-based costing system; examples of cost drivers not correlated with volume of production are number of setups, number of discrete parts, number of times handled.

Indirect production costs (IPC). Those elements of total product cost which, unlike direct material and direct labor, cannot be identified directly with products manufactured or services performed. IPC is allocated to—absorbed by—products or services in a rational, although necessarily arbitrary, method that is predetermined before the beginning of the accounting period.

IPC rate. The amount of IPC to be allocated to a product or process as each unit of the IPC vehicle is consumed by that product or process. IPC rates are generally predetermined as follows:

$$\text{IPC rate} = \frac{\text{Estimated IPC expenditures at planned production volume}}{\text{The estimated quantity of the IPC vehicle at that planned volume}}$$

IPC spending variance. A comparison of actual IPC expenditures to volume-adjusted (rebudgeted) IPC.

IPC variance. The difference between actual IPC expenditures for the accounting period and the aggregate of all IPC absorbed during the same period. When actual IPC expenditures exceed the amount absorbed, the variance has a debit balance and IPC is described as underabsorbed.

IPC vehicle. An activity or cost (such as direct-labor hours or direct-labor dollars) common to all production activity in the enterprise that is used to allocate IPC to those productive activities.

IPC volume variance. A comparison of volume-adjusted (rebudgeted) IPC to the IPC absorbed by actual production during the period.

Traditional cost-allocation method. The IPC cost-allocation method that selects an arbitrary IPC vehicle with which an IPC rate is calculated for assignment of IPC costs to production activities.

DISCUSSION QUESTIONS

16.1 In the traditional method of allocating indirect production costs (IPC), how is the IPC rate determined?

16.2 Why does an IPC rate need to be predetermined—that is, set before the beginning of the accounting period, rather than after the fact?

16.3 What are the most common IPC vehicles in use in industry today?

16.4 In a single IPC Variance account in a full-absorption costing system, two conditions may drive, or cause, the variance. Explain why each of the following may contribute to an IPC variance:

(a) Actual production volume above or below planned (budgeted) volume

(b) Expenditures on indirect production cost elements above or below planned (budgeted) level

16.5 What factors are causing the continuing trend toward more costs being classified as indirect costs and thus fewer being classified as direct costs?

16.6 Explain why an activity-based costing system is likely to lead to more useful product cost data than a traditional system when:

(a) Similar products are produced in quite different quantities within the same factory

(b) Similar products are produced, some of which are standard and others are customized for individual customers

(c) Similar products are produced, some of which have many more component parts than others

16.7 Give three examples each of activities and cost drivers as these terms are used in activity-based costing.

16.8 Do you think an activity-based costing system would be more or less expensive to operate than a cost accounting system utilizing the traditional method for allocating indirect production costs? Why?

16.9 Suppose a product has proven to be uncompetitively priced in the marketplace. Management has urged engineering to redesign the product so as to reduce its manufacturing cost, and thereby permit more competitive pricing. The product cost detail is

Direct material	$ 42	
Direct labor	22	
IPC	88	(IPC rate = 400% of direct labor)
Total	$152	

If the redesign is targeted to reduce the product cost to $100, how much direct labor will the engineer have to *design out* of this product in order to achieve the target? Is reduction in direct labor the most productive avenue to lower total product cost? How is activity-based costing likely to motivate the engineer toward other redesign targets?

16.10 Refer to question 16.9. If this product:

(a) Were produced in large volumes in a factory where the manufacturing lot sizes were typically small, would you expect its product cost under activity-based costing to be higher or lower than $152?

(b) Used very few subcontracted parts while the typical product made in the factory used many subcontracted parts, would you expect its product cost under activity-based costing to be higher or lower than $152?

(c) Remained in process in the plant for twice as long as the typical product made by the company, would you expect its product cost under activity-based costing to be higher or lower than $152?

PROBLEMS

16.1 The Simic Motor Company's cost accounting system uses machine hours as the IPC vehicle. The company's plans for next year foresee the use of 180,000 machine hours and total IPC expenditures of $2,146,000.

(a) What should be Simic's IPC rate for next year?

(b) If the company had chosen direct-labor wages as its IPC vehicle and expected total wages paid next year to be $523,000, what would Simic's IPC rate be?

16.2 Mehban and Sons produces industrial blending equipment, primarily Model 431 and Model 631 which have the following characteristics:

	Model 431	Model 631
Direct material per unit	$261	$388
Direct labor hours per unit	14.5	16.1

Mehban's standard labor wage rate is $11.50 per hour. Mehban's production plan for 1995 calls for

Total direct material cost	$12,820,000
Total direct labor hours	836,000
Total IPC expenditures	16,377,000

(a) Assume that the IPC vehicle is direct material cost. What are the total product costs for each of the models? By what percentage does the cost of Model 631 exceed the cost of Model 431?

(b) Assume that the IPC vehicle is direct labor hours. What are the total product costs for each of the models? By what percentage does the cost of Model 631 exceed the cost of Model 431?

16.3 Refer to problem 16.2 Assume Mehban and Sons used activity-based costing and the two models had the following additional characteristics:

	Model 431	Model 631
Number of lots per year	10	20
Average lot size	2,000	300
Number of parts per units	85	105

Assume that the cost drivers, and the cost in 1995 of the activities to which they are relevant are as follows:

	1995 Plan	Activity $
Direct labor hours	836,000	$ 4,161,000
Number of lots (set-ups)	65	5,385,000
Number of parts handled	5,810	6,831,000
(Total)		($16,377,000)

Calculate the per-unit product cost for each of the models using activity-based costing. By what percentage does the cost of Model 631 exceed the cost of Model 431?

16.4 One of the factories owned by the Magasi Group experienced an IPC variance of $37,000 (debit) for the month of October. The total IPC absorbed during the month was $872,000.

(a) What were actual IPC expenditures in October at this factory?

(b) If the IPC vehicle is direct-labor wages and the IPC rate is $3.75 per direct-labor wage dollar, what were total direct-labor wages for the month?

(c) If the IPC rate is predetermined on the basis of a planned activity level for October of $250,000 in direct-labor wages, was activity in October above or below planned level? What was the planned level of IPC expenditures upon which the IPC rate was based? Were actual IPC expenditures in October above or below this planned level?

16.5 After a careful study of the variability of its IPC cost elements, the Taylor Corporation determined that IPC could be budgeted according to the following flexible budget:

$$IPC = \$110,000 + 7.6 \text{ (direct-labor hours)}$$
where direct-labor hours is the IPC vehicle.

(a) What would Taylor's full-absorption IPC rate be for January when 13,600 direct-labor hours were expected?

(b) What would Taylor's variable IPC rate be for January when 13,600 direct-labor hours were expected?

(c) If in March the plant's activity (as measured in direct-labor hours) was expected to decline by 10 percent from January's level, what would the full-absorption IPC rate be for March? Does this IPC rate increase by 10 percent? Why or why not?

(d) What is the variable IPC rate for March and how does it compare to January's rate?

16.6 In May Kimball Corporation's total production can be summarized as follows:

Total direct material consumed	$5,981,000
Total direct labor wages earned	$1,692,000
Total expenditures on IPC elements	$5,312,000
Total number of units produced	558,000

(a) If Kimball's IPC rate is $3.10 per direct-labor dollar, what was Kimball's IPC variance for May? (Note whether the variance has a debit or credit balance.)

(b) If, alternatively, Kimball's IPC rate is $10 per unit produced, what was Kimball's IPC variance for May? (Note whether the variance has a debit or credit balance.)

(c) Is it possible for one IPC vehicle to lead to a debit variance, when the use of an alternative vehicle would have resulted in a credit variance? Explain how this could occur.

16.7 A comparison of planned and actual production results for Armstrong for the month of October was

	Planned	Actual
Hours of direct labor	45,000	44,000
Average direct-labor wage rate	$11.30	$11.10
Machine hours used	13,000	13,200
Direct materials consumed	$489,000	$502,000
IPC expenditures	$363,000	$355,000

(a) Based upon this information can you determine whether Armstrong's operating efficiency was above or below plan?

(b) If Armstrong's IPC vehicle is direct-labor hours, what was the IPC rate for the month, and what was the resulting IPC variance for the month?

(c) If Armstrong's IPC vehicle is machine hours used, what was the IPC rate for the month, and what was the resulting IPC variance for the month?

16.8 The Grubbe Corporation's production plans for the coming year are

Expected direct-labor hours	450,000
Expected IPC expenditures	
Variable cost elements	$3,169,000
Fixed cost elements	$5,338,000

(a) What is Grubbe's variable IPC rate? What is its full-absorption IPC rate?

(b) During the month of February, Grubbe's actual production results were

Actual direct-labor hours	38,000
Actual IPC expenditures	
Variable cost elements	$260,800
Fixed cost elements	421,700

What was the balance for February of Grubbe's total IPC variance account, assuming full-absorption costing? Assuming variable (direct) costing?

DISCUSSION QUESTIONS FOR THE APPENDIX

16A.1 What additional information does management derive from the two variances, IPC spending and IPC volume, that is not available from the single total IPC variance account?

16A.2 Explain (in words rather than symbols) what constitutes the credit balance in the IPC spending variance account for a particular accounting period; this same value also appears as the debit balance in the IPC volume variance.

16A.3 Do you agree or disagree with each of the following statements, and why?
   (a) Variable costing provides more useful information for management decision making than does full-absorption costing.
   (b) Variable costing tends to undervalue inventories as compared with their values as determined by full-absorption costing.
   (c) In periods when business is slow, a company may be willing to accept a contract for goods or services at a price below the full-absorption cost of those goods or services, but should not be willing to accept a contract where the price is below the variable cost.
   (d) As manufacturing becomes more automated, the differences in product costs arrived at by full-absorption costing and those arrived at by variable costing continue to increase.
   (e) A company's reported profits will be the same under both full-absorption and variable costing if and only if its physical inventories remain the same from the beginning to the end of the accounting period.

(f) The IPC volume variance is not determined under variable costing because it is irrelevant.

16A.4 The higher the fixed element of IPC as a percentage of total IPC, the greater the potential for significant overabsorption or underabsorption of IPC, assuming a full-absorption accounting system. Explain.

16A.5 What are the advantages and disadvantages of variable costing as compared with full-absorption accounting?

16A.6 Do you think variable costing or full-absorption costing provides better information for pricing decisions? (Remember the appropriate but limited role that product costs should play in all product pricing decisions.)

16A.7 The IPC variances for Fox Limited in November are

$$\text{IPC spending variance} = \$0$$
$$\text{IPC volume variance} = \$3000 \text{ credit}$$

Was production in November higher or lower than normal? Can you determine whether actual IPC expenditures in November were higher or lower than the amount that would be budgeted for IPC at normal volume?

PROBLEMS FOR THE APPENDIX

16A.1 The Effinger Manufacturing Company has developed the following IPC budget for a month:

$$\text{IPC} = \$45,300 + 0.8 \text{ (direct-labor wages)}$$

For the month of August, the planned level of output (upon which the derivation of the IPC rate is based) was $23,000 of direct-labor wages and the actual level of output was equivalent to $25,600 of direct-labor wages while actual IPC expenditures totaled $63,700.

(a) Without further calculation, determine whether the IPC volume variance will have a debit or credit balance.

(b) Calculate the IPC rate assuming:
(1) Variable costing
(2) Full-absorption costing

(c) Calculate for August the:
(1) Total IPC variance (debit or credit?)
(2) IPC spending variance (debit or credit?)
(3) IPC volume variance (debit or credit?)

16A.2 Refer to problem 16.8 in the end-of-chapter problems for Chapter 16. What were the values at the end of February of Grubbe's IPC spending and IPC volume variances?

16A.3   The total IPC variance account for the Whittlesey Company for January was as follows:

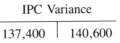

IPC Variance

137,400	140,600

If the IPC vehicle is direct labor hours and the IPC rate was determined using the following estimates:

Expected fixed IPC = $104,800
Expected variable IPC = $33,000
Expected direct-labor hours = 5,000

separate the total IPC variance into its spending and volume components.

16A.4   Refer to problem 16A.3. Assume the company used a variable rather than a full-absorption costing system.

(a)   What would be the company's IPC rate?

(b)   What additional information would you need to calculate the IPC variance under variable costing?

16A.5   The Noda Company has a total IPC variance for May of $2,100 credit. The IPC vehicle is units of production; production in May was 105 percent of the normal number of units. The IPC rate is $21 per unit and the company's IPC budget equation is $90,000 + 6.00 (number of units).

(a)   What was the "normal" (expected) monthly volume of production?

(b)   What was the IPC volume variance in May?

(c)   What was the IPC spending variance in May?

___17

STANDARD COST ACCOUNTING SYSTEMS

We now turn to the interesting opportunity to bring the budgeting techniques (described in Chapter 12) to bear on cost accounting. We shall see that so-called standard costing facilitates *management by exception* by utilizing the techniques of setting budgets (standards) and then tracking the difference between actual and budget (that is, developing variances) for product costs.

Standard costing sounds complex—and, in a sense, it is—but the benefits of standard cost accounting systems over actual cost systems have led most manufacturers of standard (or even semistandard) products to use them. While standard cost systems may be difficult to conceptualize, they are typically less expensive to operate day to day than are actual cost systems. Furthermore, while it may seem intuitively obvious that actual costs are in some sense better, more proper, or more accurate than standard costs, please withhold judgment until you know more about standard costing.

Recall that *standard* or *actual* costing is the third parameter that must be fixed when designing a cost accounting system. (The other two are *job order* or *process* costing and the comprehensiveness of the IPC or overhead definition—from prime costing to full-absorption costing.) The question now is: Shall the cost of a product be defined as what it actually costs to produce, or as the estimate of what it should cost to produce?

Remember that this decision is independent both of the choice between job order costing and process costing and of the choice among the alternatives for including IPC in product costs. Standard costs can be used with either a job order or a process costing system, so, of course, can actual costs. Similarly, one can use the standard or actual IPC, regardless of how broadly or narrowly IPC is defined, the IPC cost elements can be included at their actual or standard values.

WHAT ARE STANDARD COSTS?

Thus far we have been tracking actual material costs as materials flow into and out of raw-material inventory, then to in-process inventory, then to finished-goods inventory, and finally to cost of goods sold. Similarly, as actual direct-labor hours are spent, each is valued at the actual direct-labor rate paid, and this direct-labor cost increases the value of in-process inventory.

Alternatively, one could track standard costs of materials, labor, and IPCs as they flow through in-process inventory to finished-goods inventory and finally to cost of goods sold. To employ a standard cost system requires that:

(1) Standards are set—that is, someone (for example, a cost accountant or an industrial engineer) must determine in advance—in effect, budget—prior to actual production:

 (a) The number of direct-labor hours required per unit of output and the hourly wage rate

 (b) The number of pounds, kilos, meters, feet, or pieces of direct material required per unit of output and the budgeted price per pound, kilo, meter, foot, or piece

 (c) The appropriate amount of IPC to be assigned to each unit of output

Setting standards is simply detailed budgeting applied to product costs.

(2) The differences between actual costs and standard costs be identified in some appropriate, and hopefully useful, manner. This step, of course, is simply variance analysis (see Chapter 12) applied to product costs.

The cost model requires that a unit in inventory be valued at its *historical* cost—the cost of direct labor, direct material, and IPC incurred in making the unit. A standard cost system simply defines historical cost as what it *should* cost to produce the unit: the unit's predetermined or standard cost.

ADVANTAGES AND DISADVANTAGES OF STANDARD COST SYSTEMS

The primary disadvantage of standard cost systems is the expense associated with setting standards: predetermining, or budgeting, the standard costs for all the various products the company manufactures. In order to value inventories and cost of goods sold at what they *should* cost to produce, rather than what they actually *did* cost, someone must determine what they *should* cost. Depending on the variety of the products produced, and the complexity of the manufacturing processes, setting these standards can be quite complex and costly.

Mitigating this disadvantage is the usefulness of the cost standards themselves. They can assist managers in making a host of everyday operating decisions, such as:

(1) Pricing standard products, as well as products to be customized for a particular customer

(2) Make-or-buy decisions (i.e., whether to subcontract certain manufacturing or servicing activities)

(3) Decisions to redesign products to reduce cost or to enhance performance

(4) Production scheduling, for which the standard labor times and standard machine hours are necessary data inputs.

And there are important advantages of standard cost systems. First, standard cost systems provide variance information to line operating managers. Differences between incurred (actual) production costs and budgeted (standard) production costs are highlighted to facilitate management-by-exception. If the direct-labor standards accurately assess how much labor *should* be expended to produce a unit (or group of units), the difference between actual and standard direct-labor costs is relevant to managers who are responsible for efficiency and cost control. A job-by-job analysis of this difference, or variance, helps managers pinpoint troublesome production jobs. Analysis of the sum of the variances on all jobs within a particular department helps managers evaluate departmental efficiency. Similarly, variances can be developed and analyzed for direct material and IPC.

In addition, standard costing eliminates two shortcomings of actual cost systems. First, under an actual cost structure, physically identical units of finished-goods inventory typically have different values if they were produced on different job orders (job order cost structure) or during different periods (process cost structure). These differences are useful for certain decisions—and they are highlighted by standard cost variances—but they are a nuisance when valuing inventories and cost of goods sold. Recall the discussion in Chapter 9 of the techniques of valuing merchandise purchased at different prices: the first-in, first-out (FIFO) and last-in, first-out (LIFO) methods. The same problem arises in valuing inventories of manufactured products. The use of standard costs eliminates the problem by assuring that physically identical units have identical product costs.

A second shortcoming of actual cost systems is that record keeping is extensive, cumbersome, and costly. Standard cost systems are typically easier and less expensive to operate. Differences between actual and standard costs are drawn off, or isolated, at each manufacturing step. Once this difference, or variance, is removed, there is no longer a need to keep track of the actual costs of prior manufacturing steps as the product proceeds step-by-step from raw material to finished-goods inventory.

In summary, standard cost systems are gaining in popularity over actual cost systems for three primary reasons:

(1) Variance information points up exception areas—products, departments or cost categories where costs are not in line with plan.

(2) Standard cost systems are less expensive to operate, both because cost flows are simpler and because like inventory items are valued identically (at stan-

dard) even though manufactured at different times and therefore at different actual costs.

(3) Standard costs are handy reference data for many managers—for marketing managers in making pricing and product-line decisions, for purchasing agents in making buying decisions, for production schedulers in loading the shop, and for top management in making investment decisions.

INTERPRETING ACTUAL-STANDARD PRODUCT COST VARIANCES

Standard-cost variances are general-ledger accounts that compare actual performance (actual costs) with budgeted or planned performance (standard costs) for selected segments of the operation. A wide variety of variances is possible. Variances can be developed, for example, for individual departments in a manufacturing or servicing company. Then, within the individual department, they can be developed for specific products, departmental functions, and individual cost elements (for example, labor or material). These variance data help managers at many levels—project leaders, department managers, plant managers, division general managers—focus on exception areas.

Figure 17-1 shows a variance report for the month of July for one department, Department M, of the Exeter Manufacturing Company. To simplify the example, assume that Department M produces only one product, Malex, and that Malex is produced entirely within this department.

You see immediately on Figure 17-1 that Department M's total annual expenses exceeded the standard by about 6 percent. What do you conclude? That Department M controlled expenses poorly during July, since the total expense variance is negative (debit, or unfavorable) $3900? But, don't be too hasty. More analysis is re-

FIGURE 17-1   Exeter Manufacturing Co. Variance Report Manufacturing Department M ($000) for July

	Standard July	Actual July	Variance*
Direct labor wages	$18.0	$19.2	($1.2)
Direct materials used	27.1	29.6	(2.5)
Indirect production costs			
Supervisory labor	2.2	2.2	—
Fringe employment	4.1	4.4	(0.3)
Supplies	1.2	1.4	(0.2)
Maintenance	4.0	3.6	0.4
Heat, light, and power	1.7	1.9	(0.2)
Rent and other occupancy	6.1	6.0	0.1
	$64.4	$68.3	($3.9)
Units of Malex produced	4,000	4,320	320 units

*Indicates effect on earnings. Amounts in parentheses reduce earnings.

quired before reaching conclusions regarding performance. The causes of variation between actual and standard need to be pinpointed before corrective action can be formulated, if indeed any action is warranted.

Note the important nonfinancial information at the bottom of Figure 17-1: the number of Malex units produced, standard and actual. The department produced 320 more units (8 percent more) than expected; that is, the aggregate standard for each cost element assumes production of 4000 units, not 4320. Now recall our discussion of variable and fixed costs in Chapter 13. Because in July actual production quantity exceeded budget (standard), actual expenditures on variable costs will exceed standard even if the plant was efficient. So, one obvious and major cause of expense variation is a shift in volume of activity—in this case, more Malex units produced. This shift in output volume may alone explain the variances in direct labor wages and direct materials. It may also influence some of the indirect production cost (IPC) elements, particularly those such as supplies expense, heat, light, and power, and fringe employment costs that are more variable than fixed. On the other hand, changes in output volume should not affect rent and other occupancy costs; these expenses are fixed.

In addition to volume of productive activity, the other key causes of variation between actual and plan (between actual and standard) are price changes and efficiency. Exeter may be paying more than standard prices for material; or perhaps changes in the work force mix have caused the average wage rate to vary from standard. Of course, the third cause—but the one we tend to think of first—is efficiency.

To summarize, in addition to the effect of volume changes, two other factors influence how much is spent on direct labor wages: the efficiency of the labor force and the wage rates paid. Obviously, the same can be said about direct materials expenditures: Exeter may be more efficient or less efficient in the use of materials, and in addition it may be paying more or less than standard prices for the materials acquired in July. We turn now to isolating these effects: volume; price or wage rate; and efficiency or usage.

SEPARATING PRICE AND USAGE VARIANCES

To repeat, even when production volume is exactly on plan, actual expenditures may deviate from plan for one or a combination of the following reasons:

(1) Efficiency deviated from plan. How? Perhaps more material was wasted or had to be scrapped; or improved labor efficiency resulted in fewer direct-labor hours; or efficient use of equipment consumed fewer kilowatt-hours of power; or carelessness or inefficiency caused more production supplies to be consumed.

(2) The price paid per unit of input deviated from plan. For example, changed specifications or quantity-discount terms resulted in lower prices for a certain material component; a recent labor-union agreement caused wage rates to be

higher than planned; a power company rate increase resulted in higher charges per kilowatt-hour.

If standards (or indeed any budgets) are established with respect both to usage and to price, then separate variances can be generated. While such refinement is not warranted for all variances, it is particularly appropriate for direct labor and direct materials, both because they are large costs and because the necessary data to set the standards are generally at hand. In arriving at product cost standards, the cost engineer estimates the number of hours of direct labor required, as well as the labor-wage rate, and the quantity of materials (measured in terms of units, weight, length, or area), as well as the price per unit of measure.

With these standards the cost accountant can develop separate **wage rate variances** and **labor efficiency (or usage) variances** and also separate **purchase price variances** and **material usage variances.** Conceptually, price and usage variances can be calculated for all other Department M expenses shown in Figure 17-1 (expenses that comprise the department's IPC). However, establishing separate usage and price standards for the IPC elements is difficult, and the resulting information is typically only marginally useful.

Figure 17-2 provides the information needed to develop material and labor vari-

FIGURE 17-2   Exeter Manufacturing Co., Background Data for Analysis of Material and Labor Variances for July

A. Standard Material and Labor Costs (Per Unit of Malex)

MATERIAL: STANDARD QUANTITY	×	STANDARD PRICE	= STANDARD MATERIAL COST
Item A	24 grams	$0.20/gram	$4.80
Item B	2 units	$1.08 each	2.16
Subtotal, material			$6.96

LABOR: STANDARD HOURS	×	STANDARD WAGE RATE	= STANDARD LABOR COST
Skill P	0.21 hours	$14.00	$ 2.94
Skill Q	0.12 hours	12.00	1.44
Subtotal, labor			$ 4.38
Total standard material and labor costs			$11.34

B. Actual Results, July

Quantity produced (from Figure 17-1)	4,320 units
Direct material used	
Item A	103,000 grams
Item B	8,700 units
Total material cost (from Figure 17-1)	$29,600
Direct labor hours used	
Skill P	895 hours
Skill Q	510 hours
Total labor cost (from Figure 17-1)	$19,200

FIGURE 17-3   Exeter Manufacturing Co., Variances (Combined) for Material and Labor for July

Material Variance		Labor Variance	
Actual total material cost	Standard material cost of output	Actual total labor cost	Standard labor cost of output
$29,600	4320 units × $6.96 = $30,068	$19,200	4320 units × $4.38 = 18,922
	Balance = $468 Credit	Balance = $278 Debit	

ances, including separate usage and price variances, in Exeter's Department M for July. Part A of the exhibit shows standard costs of material and labor for one unit of Malex. Note that separate standards have been established for the quantities and the prices of the inputs (material and direct labor). Part B of the exhibit details the actual results for the month of July. Obviously you need both sets of data—standard and actual—in order to develop variances.

Figure 17-3 derives a single variance for each of direct material and direct labor. These variances combine the effects of variations in price (wage rate) and usage (efficiency). The $29,600 actual material cost for the month compares with the standard cost of $30,068 (4320 units produced times standard material cost per unit of $6.96) resulting in a credit, or favorable, balance of $468. (Note that the standard cost has been adjusted for actual volume produced—4320 units of Malex. That is, the $30,068 standard is the volume-adjusted budget for material). This single variance doesn't tell you whether the favorable balance arose from lower material prices or reduced material usage, or some combination of the two—or perhaps some inefficiency in the material use was more than offset by actual prices well below standard, or vice versa. Similarly, the total labor variance is a $278 debit, but the separate effects of wage rate variations and labor efficiency or inefficiency are not discernable.

Figure 17-4 separates the total material variance ($468 credit) into its price and usage variance components. (The total labor variance can be decomposed in an exactly analogous manner.) The price variance compares actual and standard prices for the actual volume of material used; thus, neither the total production volume nor the efficiency of material usage (i.e., extent of wastage or scrap) affects this variance.

The credit entry to this purchase price variance (actual material quantity used times standard prices) is balanced by the debit entry to the usage variance. Thus, the usage variance compares actual and standard usage, both valued at standard prices. Variations in material prices do not affect this variance, as standard prices determine both the debit and credit entries.

Now, how should we interpret these variance data? Note that the $468 credit in the total material variance (Figure 17-3) shows the combined effect of actual prices

FIGURE 17-4 Exeter Manufacturing Company Separate Price and Usage Variances for Material for July

Material Purchase Price Variances		*Material Usage Variances**	
Actual total material cost*	Actual material quantity used × standard prices	Actual material quantity used × standard prices	Standard material cost of output†
$29,600	A: 103,000 grams × $0.20 = $20,600	$29,996	4320 units × $6.96 = $30,067.20
	B: 8700 units × $1.08 = $9,396		
	Total A + B = $29,996		
	Balance: $396 Credit		Balance: $71.20 Credit

*Actual material quantity used times actual prices.
†This variance can be verified as follows:

Material	Standard Quantity	Actual Quantity	Physical Quantity Variance	Standard Price	Variance (in $)
A	4320 units × 24 grams/unit of Malex = 103,680	103,000	680 grams	$0.20 per gram	$136.00
B	4320 units × 2 units/unit of Malex = 8640	8700	(60) units	$1.08 per unit	(64.80)
				Total	$ 71.20

below standard ($396 credit) and efficient material usage ($71 credit). Note also that the arithmetic sum of Figure 17-4's separate price and usage variances equals the corresponding total variance in Figure 17-3 (with allowances for rounding):

Material purchase price variance	$396 credit
Material usage variance	71 credit
Total material variance	$467 credit

Thus, indeed the single variance has been decomposed into its two component parts.

Still more detailed analysis is possible. Price and usage variances for each of materials A and B and for each of labor skills P and Q could be developed if actual expenditures for the month were available at this level of detail. (Certain of this detail is shown in the second footnote in Figure 17-4.) This additional detail can be incorporated into the cost accounting system, at some additional cost, of course, if the benefits seem to outweigh the accounting time required. If not—that is, if the total material price variance is sufficient—the cost accounting system and resulting management reports should not be burdened with additional detail.

Indeed, managers in certain instances find even the amount of detail in Figure 17-4 to be excessive. For example, if wage rates are dictated by the long-term labor union agreement, Department M's wage rate variance from month to month will approximate zero. When a new labor union agreement is negotiated, standard wage rates are revised accordingly and once again wage rate variances will be nil. In this case, the cost accounting system should be designed to yield only a single labor variance, as indicated in Figure 17-3. When interpreting this single labor variance, one can be confident that any debit or credit balance is attributable solely to efficiency.

A strong argument for separating price and usage variances is that the two effects—price and efficiency—are the responsibility of different managers within the organization. Material prices are negotiated by the purchasing department; the efficiency with which materials are used—that is, the extent of spoilage, waste, or rework—depends to a large degree upon the care and competence of the direct labor force. If the variances suggest corrective action, that action should be taken in the purchasing department, if the problem relates to price, and on the production floor, if the problem is usage. Another argument for separation is that a favorable price variance might lead to an unfavorable usage variance if, for example, the company purchases lower-cost but inferior materials, resulting in high wastage or spoilage. And, at other times the reverse can be true.

In summary, any expense variance, including a variance for any of the IPC cost elements, can be broken down into its price and usage components if (1) separate quantity and price standards can be established and (2) the benefit of this additional detail outweighs its cost.

THE EFFECTS OF TIGHT AND LOOSE STANDARDS

The discussion thus far of standard costing may imply that standards—that is, budgeted product costs—can be set with precision. In fact, they are no more than estimates, even if rigorously arrived at. Moreover, managers frequently adopt the philosophy, or policy, of setting standards on the tight side. The magnitude of variances are, of course, greatly influenced by the philosophy that managers adopt. Some managers set standards tight (low and therefore a challenge to achieve) for the reason mentioned in Chapter 12: they believe standards provide an incentive, a goal, toward which the organization should strive. If standards are set tight, negative (debit) variances typically occur. Managers who believe in **tight standards** anticipate substantial debit variances and plan accordingly.

Because tight standards lead to low product costs and debit variances, they result in low values for inventory and cost of goods sold. In the long run, these two effects—low product costs and high debit variances—exactly offset each other. But not necessarily so in the short run. In fact, a company's profits are unaffected by the tightness or looseness of standards only if production volume equals sales volume and thus inventories are unchanged over the period. If inventories grow when standards are tight, the value added to inventory is low (by comparison with the value added under looser standards) and the debit variances generated in the production of these inventoried products reduce profit in the current period.

To illustrate, assume that a company incurred actual production costs for a particular month of $470,000; it sold 90 percent of its output and placed the other 10 percent in inventory. The income statement and balance sheet implications of tight and loose standards are as follows:

	Tight standards	Loose standards
Aggregate standard costs of everything produced (assumed)	$450,000	$480,000
Variances	20,000 Dr.	10,000 Cr.
Balance Sheet Effect:		
Increase in inventory*	45,000	48,000
Income Statement Effect:		
Cost of goods sold†	405,000	432,000
Variances	(20,000)	10,000
Total Expenses	$425,000	$422,000

The $3000 lower profit with tight standards is matched by the $3000 lower value of inventory. Opposite effects result when inventories are reduced.

OTHER VARIANCES IN STANDARD COSTING

This discussion has not been exhaustive in touching all the possible variances used in practice. As mentioned in Chapter 12, managers often find it useful to develop variances on, for example, revenues or sales, as well as on costs and expenses. Recall that any comparison between actual results and budgeted or expected results is termed a variance. Deviations from standard or budgeted sales revenue can result from variations in numbers of units sold (volume effect) or from variations in sales price realized (price effect), or from some combination of the two. Using procedures just explained, these two effects can be isolated and reported.

Another example involves so-called **mix variances.** If a process combines several different materials to create a final product, one can predetermine a standard mix of these materials. A debit total material variance can be caused by greater use of a higher-priced material in substitution for a lower-priced material, even though the total pounds of raw material used equalled the standard quantity. Thus, in addition to volume, purchase price, and usage variances, a material mix variance could be calculated. Mix variances can also be calculated with respect to labor, when a variety of skill levels staff a certain process or job, and for sales revenue, when a company markets a range of product lines.

*10 percent of production volume, valued at standard costs.
†90 percent of production volume, valued at standard costs.

SOME FINAL CAVEATS

This discussion of standard cost systems needs to conclude by repeating several caveats. First, remember that it costs time and money to develop, compile, and analyze accounting detail. These efforts must be balanced against the benefits derived from the additional information. Striking the balance between two little and too much detail is a challenge that is too often struck on the side of excessive detail.

Second, don't be misled by the business jargon that refers to debit variances as unfavorable, or negative, and credit variances as favorable, or positive. Any deviation from standard—favorable or unfavorable—is worth investigating. The standard represents the plan and managers need to understand the reasons why actual operations deviate from that plan, whether these deviations add to or reduce profits.

Third, one must consider the accuracy of the standards before hastily judging the meaning of variances. Variances can arise strictly because standards were poorly set. Sometimes standards and budgets are little better than top-of-the-head guesses, particularly in companies operating with understaffed accounting departments or in volatile industries with rapidly changing product lines. In other companies with extensive cost histories and a staff of industrial engineers to establish and revise standards, cost standards may be very accurate indeed. In practice, the need for accuracy depends on the uses to which the standards are put. For example, where labor-hour standards are the basis for employee compensation—either as piece work (so much per unit produced) or as a group bonus—the standards must be set with precision, using detailed time studies or other sophisticated engineering techniques.

Regardless of how they are set, standards or budgets should be reviewed periodically for reasonableness. This review must take into account changes in the products, manufacturing methods, and staffing. Generally, standard product costs are reviewed when a major error is suspected and otherwise not more frequently than once per quarter nor less frequently than once per year.

Finally, recall from Chapter 12 that employees are motivated both positively and negatively by standard costs and by budgets. Some managers argue that standards and budgets should be set low (tight) to spur employees to be more efficient; they feel that high (loose) standards promote, or at least condone, a lax attitude toward cost control. Other managers argue that standards and budgets set too tight are likely to be ignored by employees as being unreasonable and therefore irrelevant.

SUMMARY

The third parameter to be specified in the design of a cost accounting system is the use of actual or standard product costs. Standard costing systems bring the benefits of budgeting and variance analysis to product costs. To implement these systems, product costs must be estimated (that is, predetermined or budgeted) in detail—an expensive activity and one prone to error under certain circumstances—including the amount of material to be used, prices of the material components, labor hours, wage rates, and machine hours. These data typically have important uses outside the cost accounting department, for example by the scheduling, marketing, and design engineering departments.

Despite appearance to the contrary, standard cost systems are typically less expensive to operate than actual cost systems because inventory valuation procedures are simplified. Moreover, of course, the differences between standard and actual are useful to management in monitoring performance by department or by product line and deciding what, if any, corrective action needs to be taken. On the other hand, some standard cost accounting systems generate more detail than is really useful.

The decomposition of material and labor variances into their price (wage rate) and usage (efficiency) components is often warranted, since these decomposed variances have relevance to different parts of the organization. These same techniques are useful in analyzing revenue by decomposing sales variances into price and volume components.

Some managers pursue the philosophy of setting tight standards to challenge operating units to improve cost performance. If so, debit variances must be anticipated, and managers should be aware that such a policy will result in lower reported profits when inventories are growing.

NEW TERMS

Labor efficiency variance. A comparison of actual and standard direct-labor hours, both valued at standard wage rates.

Loose standards. Contrasted with tight standards, loose standards are higher estimates of standard product costs.

Material usage variance. A comparison of actual and standard material quantities used, both valued at standard prices.

Mix variance. A comparison of the standard mix of an input or output (for example, materials or labor skills used, or product lines sold) to the actual mix achieved with respect to that input or output.

Purchase price variance. A comparison of actual and standard prices for the actual quantity of material acquired.

Tight standards. Contrasted with loose standards, tight standards are lower estimates of standard product costs.

Wage rate variance. A comparison of actual and standard wage rates for the actual number of hours of labor used.

DISCUSSION QUESTIONS

17.1 Explain how standard costing facilities management-by-exception.

17.2 In addition to the choice between standard and actual costing, what other choices must the designer of a cost accounting system make in order to define fully that system?

17.3   Is an actual cost accounting system more or less expensive to operate than a standard cost accounting system? Why?

17.4   What are the two parameters that must be specified in order to define the standard direct-labor cost of a product? What are the analogous two parameters for direct material?

17.5   Are both IPC spending and IPC variance accounts relevant to standard costing or only to actual costing? Explain.

17.6   Is an IPC rate predetermined only for an actual cost system or for both an actual and a standard cost system? Explain.

17.7   Explain a material mix variance. Give an example of a manufacturing environment where a material mix variance might be particularly applicable?

17.8   Under what circumstance might you reasonably assume that the labor wage rate variance will be zero and thus you need determine only a single direct-labor variance?

17.9   What are the primary advantages of standard cost systems over actual cost systems? Disadvantages?

17.10 For what purposes might a manufacturing company use information regarding direct labor standards in addition to determining standard costs of goods sold and standard inventory values?

17.11 What are some characteristics of manufacturing environments where it is easy (inexpensive) to determine standard costs?

17.12 Why are LIFO and FIFO techniques of inventory valuation more applicable to actual cost systems than to standard cost systems?

17.13 Give an example of a circumstance where a debit (negative) material usage variance should not lead to the conclusion that the manufacturing force was inefficient in the use of materials.

17.14 Do you agree that different segments of the organization are typically responsible for (and thus should be particularly interested in) price and efficiency variances for both material and labor? Explain.

17.15 What is the effect of so-called tight standards on the valuation of inventories?

17.16 Would you recommend that standards be set a little tight, a little loose, or at the best estimate of future actual costs? Explain your reasons.

17.17 How would you determine for a particular manufacturing company how often its product cost standards should be revised?

17.18 Why is the material purchase price variance often determined at the time the material is received into inventory while the material usage variance is determined later, when the material is withdrawn from inventory for use in the manufacturing process?

PROBLEMS

17.1 In producing 1000 kg of Sankret, the manufacturer purchased and used the following materials:

	Kilograms	Purchase Cost
Material P	310	$263
Material T	595	280
Material W	140	455
	1,045	$998

The standard material cost per kilogram for this product is $1.05.

(a) Calculate the total material variance on the 1000 kg produced.

(b) Assuming the following additional detail on standard material costs, calculate the purchase price variance and the material usage variance for the production of the 1000 kg of Sankret.

Material	Standard Quantity	Standard Price
P	$0.30	$0.90 per kilogram
T	0.60	0.52 per kilogram
W	0.15	3.00 per kilogram
	$1.05	

17.2 In Department M during October the actual wage expense was $14,860 for 1060 hours actually worked. The standard labor wage rate was $14.10 per hour and the aggregate standard labor cost for that which was produced in Department M for the month was $15,200. Calculate for the department for October:

(a) Total labor variance

(b) Wage rate variance

(c) Labor efficiency variance

17.3 In-Flite Services, Inc. produces airline meals for several airlines operating out of the nearby international airport. For the month of July its labor variances were as follows:

Wage rate variance:	$1,400 debit
Labor efficiency variance:	$2,300 debit

If the company's standard wage rate was $9.75 per hour and its actual wages paid in July were $38,600,

(a) By how many hours did its actual labor hours exceed the standard?

(b) What was the total standard labor cost for the month?

17.4 The Williams Corp's Plant 63 manufactures only Product D, which has the following standard cost:

Direct material	$2.65
Direct labor	1.15
IPC	4.60
	$8.40

The IPC vehicle is standard direct labor dollars and the standard wage rate is $9.00 per hour. For the month of January, the plant's actual production was

Units of Product D	15,000
Total wages paid	$17,400
Actual direct labor hours worked	2,000
Total material used	$39,000 (valued at standard purchase prices)
Actual IPC expenditures	$72,000

Calculate all variances permitted by these data.

17.5 Refer to Problem 17.4 above. Suppose that Plant 63 decided at the beginning of January to loosen its cost standards on Product D to

Direct material	$2.75
Direct labor	1.30
IPC	5.20
	$9.25

If in January Plant 63 sold only 10,000 units of Product D (recall that it produced 15,000 units), by how much would its profits be affected (higher or lower?) for the month by the use of the "looser" standards?

17.6 The following production variances were recorded for February for Factory S:

Material purchase price variance:	$1,100 Credit
Material usage variance:	$3,650 Debit
Labor wage rate variance:	$1,600 Debit
Labor efficiency variance:	$0
IPC spending variance:	$600 Debit
IPC volume variance:	$1,200 Credit

The IPC rate was $25 per standard direct-labor hour, the standard wage rate was $10 per hour, and the production for the month was equivalent to $40,000 of standard direct labor.

(a) How many hours of direct labor were worked during the month?

(b) What were the actual total wages paid for the month?

(c) Was actual production above or below the plan (normal) for the month?

17.7 To develop a sales price variance, the Whittesey Company accounted for each sale as follows:

> Dr. Sales price variance: units sold times standard price
> Cr. Sales: units sold times standard price
> Dr. Accounts receivable: actual value of sale
> Cr. Sales price variance: Actual value of sale

(a) In a particular accounting period, what was the average discount from list price provided to customers if actual sales were $348,900 and the sales price variance account balance was $14,550 debit?

(b) Describe in T-account format the debit and credit entries that would have to be made to develop both a sales price variance and a sales volume variance for an accounting period.

17.8 The High-Glos Paint Company's most popular paint is manufactured from three primary ingredients. The standard cost of a liter of paint is

Ingredient	Amount Used (liters)	Standard Cost
B	0.4	$0.60
M	0.3	1.30
S	0.3	0.30
Total	1.0	

On a particular job to produce 2000 liters of paint, the following actual quantities of materials were used:

Ingredient	Amount Used (liters)
B	822
M	573
S	605
Total	2000

Calculate a material mix variance for this job.

17.9 The Lyman Smith Corporation manufactures a single product that it processes in a single department. The standard cost of the product is

Raw materials:	5 pounds at $2.00 per pound =	$ 10.00
Direct labor:	3 hours at $12.00 per hour =	36.00
Indirect costs:	$24.00 per direct-labor hour =	72.00
		$118.00

All inventories are recorded at standard costs; the inventories at October 1 are

Raw materials:	5,000 pounds at $2.00	$10,000
Work in process:	100 units*	6,400
Finished goods:	200 units at $118	23,600

The following are transactions for the month of October:

(a) Purchased 50,000 pounds of raw materials for $101,200.

(b) Started 10,000 units into process; however, because of spoilage it was necessary to issue 51,000 pounds of raw material.

(c) As of October 1, the work force was granted a wage increase of $0.30 per hour. This increase had not been anticipated when the standard cost of $12.00 per labor hour was established. Total direct labor hours worked were 29,500 (and thus the accrued wages payable for the month were 29,500 × $12.30) $362,850.

(d) During the month 9900 units were completed and transferred to finished goods. (Assume the other 100 units are in-process inventory and are half completed.)

(e) The predetermined IPC rate was $24.00 per standard direct-labor hour.

(f) Actual indirect costs for the month were $692,000.

(g) In October 9700 units were sold for $180 per unit.

Assignment:

(i) Trace the transactions through T-accounts (create and name T-accounts as you think appropriate).

(ii) Calculate all relevant variances.

(iii) Calculate cost of goods sold for the month. Include all variances, as the company follows the practice of charging all variances to cost of goods sold each month.

17.10 The Saugatuck Corporation operates a process, standard, variable costing system. Process A (also referred to as Department A) produces product X using raw materials P and R. The following data apply to the month of July.

Beginning and ending in-process inventory: 0		
Material purchases:		
Material P:	Quantity	450 pints
	Dollars	$2,200
Material R:	Quantity	100 pounds
	Dollars	$1,040
Material usage:	Material P	460 pints
	Material R	89 pounds
Labor usage:	Hours	860
	Dollars	$8,900

Note: The in-process inventory includes all the materials for 100 units but only one-half of the labor—and therefore one-half of the indirect costs—have as yet been expended on these units.

Variable IPC expenditures $7,300

Standard prime cost per pound of product X output

Direct labor: $20.00 (at $10.00 standard wage rate per hour)

Direct material:

Material P $5.00 (at standard price of $5.00 per pint)

Material R $2.00 (at standard price of $10.00 per pound)

IPC vehicle: pound of product X produced

Variable IPC rate: $16.00 per pound of product X

Amount of product X produced in July: 450 pounds

Assignment: Calculate all relevant variances.

17.11   The Fast-Fill Gasoline Co. set monthly sales volume and price standards for each of its retail gas stations. Actual prices were changed frequently during the month in response to competitive conditions but the standard prices were set for each grade for the month. Standards for August for station 836 were

Grade	Volume (gallons)	Price per gallon	Revenue
A	21,500 (15.4%)	$1.35	$ 29,025
B	73,000 (52.3%)	1.30	94,900
C	45,000 (32.3%)	1.27	57,150
	139,500 (100.0%)		$181,075

Actual results for August were

Grade	Volume (gallons)	Revenue
A	20,100 (14.7%)	$ 27,035
B	71,500 (52.3%)	93,665
C	45,200 (33.0%)	57,420
	136,800	$178,120

Calculate, in the following order, for the month of August:

(a) The total sales price variance

(b) The sale mix variance

(c) The sales volume variance

(*Note:* the three variances should add to the total difference of $2,955 between budgeted revenue and actual revenue.)

____18

COST ANALYSIS FOR OPERATING DECISIONS

This book has focused on management decisions and thus it concludes appropriately with a review of some common and recurring operating decisions for which managers seek relevant cost data.

Chapter 10 discussed how analysis of the two primary accounting system outputs, the balance sheet and the income statement, influence many decisions. Recall that analysis of liquidity may lead to more borrowing or to repaying a portion of present indebtedness. A review of working capital may reveal that inventory is too high or too low, that customers should be pressed for speedier payments, or that more or less trade credit should be used. Capital-structure analysis suggests when to raise more permanent capital, whether to use more or less borrowed funds, and what should be the dividend policy. And finally a review of profitability—expenses relative to sales, and profit relative to investment—can influence a host of operating decisions.

The cost accounting chapters stressed managers' use of product cost reports to evaluate operating efficiency, to decide when and where to take corrective action in manufacturing (and similar) operations, and to influence the marketing and pricing of individual products.

In addition to these important decisions, some having long-range implications for the company, managers—and particularly middle managers—face numerous operating decisions, some every day, that collectively determine the operation's success and financial health. Accounting systems should be designed to yield data to inform these day-to-day decisions. Moreover, not only must the data exist in the accounting system but they must also be disseminated in useful format to decision makers, who in turn must understand the relevance (and shortcomings) of the data.

EXAMPLES OF OPERATING DECISIONS

The following are examples of prevalent operating decisions discussed in this chapter.

(1) The production engineer is considering whether to fabricate a particular part or subassembly within the company or subcontract it to a vendor—the classic make-or-buy decision. If the company has the internal capability and capacity, or could acquire it, the primary decision criterion is typically cost. The engineer can request from the cost accounting department the standard costs for internal manufacture and can obtain the vendors' price quotations, but is this the appropriate comparison?

(2) The sales manager is considering whether to accept a particular large order from a nonregular customer. The price offered is low, but what is the minimum acceptable price? Is it ever wise to accept an order at a price below cost?

(3) The financial analyst in the treasurer's department is analyzing the return on a proposed investment to automate a production step. What are the true costs of the new and old methods?

(4) The design engineer and the material manager are trying to determine when and if a particular redesigned product should be introduced to the market. The decision is complicated by the existence of a good deal of raw and semifinished inventory that would be rendered obsolete by the new design.

(5) The product-line manager in marketing is evaluating the effect on sales and profit of varying the marketing inputs—price, promotional effort, product repackaging, change in incentive to the sales force, and so forth.

Outside of the manufacturing industries, managers face many similar, as well as some different, operating decisions. Service firms encounter pricing and product-line decisions, as well as make-or-buy decisions, and so do many nonprofit operations. Capital expenditure decisions are prevalent in virtually all organizations. Interrelationships of volumes, prices, and costs permeate public activities and private; highly competitive companies and regulated ones; service and manufacturing firms; large companies and small.

IMPORTANCE OF FRAMING ALTERNATIVES

All of these operating decisions involve choices among alternatives: make-or-buy, accept or decline the special order, introduce the product or don't, accept or reject the capital equipment investment proposal, select among a spectrum of possible prices and promotional plans. Sometimes the decision is of the go–no go type, deciding either to take an action or not; at other times the decision is among a broad set of alternatives, but even here one of the alternatives is typically to do nothing.

The optimum decision is possible only if all relevant alternatives are evaluated. If only suboptimal courses of action are considered, the decision will necessarily be suboptimal. One cannot overemphasize the importance of properly framing the alternatives, taking particular care to analyze all relevant alternatives. A common failing is to consider only the obvious courses of action, without considering explicitly other less-obvious but more beneficial options. Once a problem is framed as a choice between two mutually-exclusive action alternatives, the analysis focuses solely on that choice. If the problem is reframed in a broader context, other options may become apparent.

This admonition—consider all relevant alternatives—seems so simple and obvious as to insult your intelligence. Poor problem definition is so prevalent, however, that a couple of examples help to demonstrate the point.

(1) The make-or-buy decision is typically viewed in its narrowest context: Given the part's design, in-house capabilities, and vendor price quotations and specifications, should the work be subcontracted? Another alternative might be to improve, expand, or upgrade the company's in-house capabilities, particularly if similar parts are used in other products, or if other parts might be redesigned to use the new in-house capability. Still another alternative might be to redesign the part to take particular advantage of a known vendor capability. Or perhaps the part can be combined with one or more other parts and subcontracted as a unit; or perhaps the search for vendors has been too restricted geographically, since the part's light weight makes air freight feasible.

(2) The evaluation of automatic equipment frequently narrows immediately to a choice between the present method, at zero incremental investment, and the proposed method with high initial investment. Perhaps this decision should first be framed as a make-or-buy decision; that is, perhaps among the acceptable alternatives is subcontracting the operation so that no in-house method is used, present or proposed. Or perhaps a larger capital investment, involving equipment with broader capabilities, more versatility, or higher operating speeds, would be justified if the evaluation were more comprehensive.

(3) The marketing manager, when considering the relative effects of price, promotion, and sales-force incentive, might consider entirely different methods of marketing: independent agents instead of a company sales force; direct-mail promotion instead of magazine-space advertising; cents-off coupons instead of price discounts to wholesalers.

DIFFERENTIAL CASH FLOWS

Once all relevant alternatives have been framed, the analyst must then focus on the financial differences among them. Only the differences between alternatives are relevant to the decision. One need not define all of the economic consequences of each possible course of action but rather only that subset of consequences affected by the choice. Any conditions and financial flows unaffected by the particular decision may be ignored.

For example, if the selling price and unit volume are unaffected by the make-or-buy decision or the decision to redesign, one need not project total revenues, costs, and profits to be realized from the product, but rather only those few cost elements that are affected by the decisions.

If the present method of manufacture and the proposed automated method (necessitating a capital expenditure) both utilize the same factory floor space and supervisory attention, these costs can be ignored. Attention is appropriately focused instead on the differences in economic consequences that arise because the two methods utilize different amounts of power, direct labor, supplies, and so forth.

Moreover, it is the *cash-flow* differences among the alternatives that are particularly relevant. Cash flow is the ultimate financial objective, for it is cash flow that is used to repay borrowings, to pay dividends to shareholders, to support community and societal programs, and to pay salaries, wages, and bonuses to the staff.

Finally, the *timing* as well as the amount of those cash flows is critical; every rational person always prefers the inflow of a sum of cash today rather the same inflow a year from now, since the cash can be used profitably during the intervening year to make investments, to repay borrowing, or to pay extra salaries or bonuses. Money always has a time value whether in the hands of individuals, profit-seeking companies, nonprofit organizations, or government units.

Important among the cash flows of a profit-making company are income taxes. To the extent that an operating decision affects the company's taxable profits, its cash flow is also affected. Thus, the decision to invest in new capital equipment affects future depreciation expenses for the company; while depreciation expense itself is not a cash flow, and thus should not be included in the analysis of alternatives, the fact that depreciation expenses reduce income taxes must be included. Scrapping (throwing away) inventory does not directly involve a cash flow, but because the book value of that scrapped inventory is deducted from taxable income, the resulting cash savings in income taxes should be included in the analysis. Tax increases may also result; if a fixed asset is sold for an amount in excess of its book value, the difference is taxable and the cash outflow for this added tax must be considered in the decision.

To summarize, the key to operating decisions is the *differences* among alternatives in the *timing* and *amount* of *cash flows*.

This emphasis on cash flow may suggest that differences in reported profits are irrelevant to the kinds of operating decisions discussed here. While theoretically accurate, the statement is a bit too global. Certain situations provide strong incentive for managers to concentrate attention on parameters other than cash flow. For example, some management bonus plans are tied to current reported earnings (accrual, not cash basis). The price paid by an acquiring company for the shares of an acquired company may be a multiple of current period profits, not cash flows. Companies that operate in a regulated environment (e.g., utilities and certain government defense contractors) often respond more to regulatory constraints or pressures than to the timing and amount of cash flow.

PROBLEMS IN DETERMINING DIFFERENTIAL CASH FLOWS

Most accounting systems do not report costs and expenses in a way that facilitates determining differential cash consequences of decisions. The problems arise for one or more of the following reasons:

(1) Accounting systems are based upon the accrual concept of accounting, and yet many operating decisions would be better served by a cash-basis system. While accrual-basis reports are more valuable for many purposes and particularly for audiences external to the company, maintaining records and issuing reports that facilitate the separation of cash and noncash expenses and revenues is also important.

(2) Some expenses—both product and period—vary with volume of activity, while others are fixed. If the operating decision being analyzed affects volume to a modest extent, variable costs will be affected and fixed costs will not. (Recall the discussion in Chapter 13.)

(3) Many expenses are allocated among products or segments of the business. For example, the IPC rate is used to prorate or allocate costs among products, and sometimes corporate marketing or development expenses are allocated—necessarily somewhat arbitrarily—across all product lines or divisions. These arbitrary allocations are seldom equivalent to incremental cash flows and as a result can lead to faulty financial analyses.

Thus, frequently one cannot simply accept data from existing accounting reports and plug them into the analysis. Return now to the five examples outlined at the beginning of this chapter and consider the adjustments to accounting data needed to focus on differential cash flows.

The Make-or-Buy Decision

The Arata Corporation is considering whether to produce part number 4783 in its own shop or to subcontract the fabrication to Schreiber and Associates. Assume other alternatives have been considered and eliminated and the two alternatives are equivalent in quality, delivery, and other nonprice considerations. Schreiber has quoted $473 per 100 parts and the analyst determines (from cost accounting records) that the standard full-absorption cost of in-house manufacture is $557 per 100. The decision seems obvious: subcontract.

Recall, however, that full-absorption costs include certain allocated indirect production costs (IPC). Will these costs be avoided if the part is subcontracted? Most will not be. If the decision is to subcontract, part number 4783 will no longer carry these allocations, but the costs will not evaporate. A reallocation of the IPC will occur or negative IPC variances will result. What the decision maker needs to know is the amount by which Arata's total IPC will increase or decrease as a result of this decision.

Assume the detailed standard product costs for 100 of these parts are

Direct labor	$120	
Direct material	173	
Variable IPC	120	(100% of direct labor)
Fixed IPC	144	(120% of direct labor)
Total	$557	

The IPC vehicle here is obviously direct labor, and the total IPC rate is 220 percent of direct labor. What cash flows will be saved if Arata subcontracts? Surely material. How about direct labor? If Arata will shift the displaced direct-labor employees to other productive activities or dismiss them, then the direct-labor cost will also be avoided by subcontracting. But note that restrictive labor contracts may preclude reassignment of direct labor and enlightened employee relations or government regulations may preclude dismissal. Thus, one cannot be certain that in all subcontracting cases direct labor is an avoidable cost.

The analysis of IPC savings is even more difficult. Variable IPC includes those elements of overhead that vary with production volume. If direct labor is eliminated by subcontracting, one is inclined to assume that the associated variable IPC will also be saved. However, note that variability is defined with respect to changes in total activity, not to changes in the mix of that activity. A decision to subcontract may increase the work of the purchasing and inventory control departments, but decrease the work of the factory supervisors and production control. Thus, even variable IPC may not be entirely differential with respect to this make-or-buy decision.

The analysis of the fixed IPC product costs is still more complex. Prominent among the fixed IPC cost elements are rent on the manufacturing space and depreciation of production equipment. If the factory and its equipment are unaffected by this decision—a reasonable assumption—then the portion of these costs allocated to part number 4783 is irrelevant. It does not follow, however, that all fixed IPC costs are necessarily irrelevant. For example, if the shipping and receiving function is part of fixed IPC, the decision to subcontract increases fixed costs to the extent that shipping and receiving takes on added tasks. Any such difference in fixed costs must be considered.

Make-or-buy decisions are aided by a variable-cost system (or a full-absorption system that clearly separates fixed and variable IPC). The assumption that variable manufacturing costs are differential to the make-or-buy decision, while fixed manufacturing costs are not, is typically a useful approximation, though, as just pointed out, not completely accurate. This approximation is almost surely preferable either to ignoring all overhead in the analysis or to assuming that all IPC costs are differential. Applying the approximation to this example, the make alternative at $413 (total standard cost of $557 less the fixed IPC of $144) compares favorably with the buy alternative at $473. Part number 4783 should be made in-house.

Accept a Low-Priced Order?

The sales manager at Sedwick Company must decide whether to accept a particular order from a distant, foreign customer. The order is large, but the price is low. The customer is offering only $71,000 for merchandise having a normal list price of $97,000. Sedwick's cost accounting group estimates standard manufacturing cost for this merchandise at $75,000.

The marketing ramifications here are numerous. Will Sedwick have trouble serving this foreign customer? If the order is not taken at this low price, might the customer return later and offer a higher price? Would Sedwick be setting a dangerous precedent if other customers learn about this price? In addition to all these important but noncash considerations (or, at least, nonimmediate-cash), the sales manager must consider the present cash consequences before making a decision.

The decision framework seems simple: accept the order or decline it. This statement, however, is not a complete description of the possible alternatives. How busy is the company? If by accepting this order Sedwick commits its factory so that other higher-priced orders would have to be declined, the consequences are different than if, by accepting this order, Sedwick merely puts to use capacity that would otherwise remain idle. The company's ability to serve other customers is critically important in decisions of this type. Again, framing the alternatives is the important first step.

Assume the following with respect to prices and costs:

Normal price	$97,000
Price offered	71,000
Standard manufacturing cost	
Direct labor	20,000
Direct material	25,000
Variable IPC	15,000
Fixed IPC	15,000
Total standard cost	$75,000

If Sedwick is operating below capacity, with no reasonable expectations of selling this added capacity, then the relevant alternatives are to take the order or do nothing. Which alternative is better? Direct labor, direct material, and variable IPC are probably incremental or differential to this decision. Since the sum of these three cost elements is $60,000 and the customer is offering $71,000, Sedwick is better off taking this order than not—better off by $11,000. If the labor for this job would, in the absence of the job, be standing idle, then even direct labor is not differential, and acceptance of the order becomes very compelling.

Assume on the other hand that, if this order is declined, Sedwick has a high probability of selling all the merchandise it can produce at normal prices. Now the decision is between two order opportunities. The decision is simple: decline the order since the normal-price order will cause Sedwick to be $37,000 better off ($97,000 price less $60,000 variable cost), while the foreign order will improve Sedwick's condition by only $11,000.

Note that the full-absorption product cost data were not used. Would these data be relevant in deciding whether to expand the factory's capacity so that, for example, both the normal-price business and the foreign order could be accepted? No, the full-absorption costs are not differential to that decision either, because (1) they contain noncash expenses (primarily depreciation), (2) they involve arbitrary allocations, and (3) they do not capture for the analysis the immediate cash outflows to acquire the expanded facilities. In fact, for almost no operating decisions are full-absorption product costs differential.

Return to the initial assumptions and recall definitions introduced in Chapter 13. We say that the acceptance of this foreign, low-priced order contributes to Sedwick $11,000, the difference between the cash inflows and cash outflows brought about by the decision. The term contribution implies contribution to fixed overhead and profit. That is, the acceptance of this order will contribute to Sedwick $11,000 of cash that it otherwise would not have had. Recognize that this order will not provide $11,000 of reported profit to the company: in fact, the order itself will incur an accounting loss of $4,000 ($71,000 price less $75,000 standard manufacturing

FIGURE 18-1   Bidding by Marking-Up Full Costs: Skilling Construction Co.

Basic Assumptions:	
Total estimated overhead for a period (assumed	$180,000
to be 100% fixed)	
Overhead applied as percentage of labor	
Bid price = 120% of estimated total cost	
Job M: Estimated materials cost	$ 14,000
Estimated labor and direct supervision cost	$ 7,000
A. Bid Price for Job M in Slow Period	
Estimated total labor (all jobs) for period	$ 60,000
Overhead rate = ($180,000 ÷ 60,000)	$3 per direct labor $
Total cost of Job M:	
Material	14,000
Labor	7,000
Overhead ($3 × 7000)	21,000
Total	$ 42,000
Bid Price of Job M = (120% of $42,000)	$ 50,400
B. Bid Price for Job M in Busy Period	
Estimated total labor (all jobs) for period	$ 90,000
Overhead rate = $180,000 ÷ $90,000	$2 per direct labor $
Total cost of Job M:	
Material	14,000
Labor	7,000
Overhead ($2 × 7000)	14,000
Total	$ 35,000
Bid Price of Job M = (120% of $35,000)	$ 42,000

cost). The added activity (and absorption of overhead) will lead to a favorable IPC variance, but the cost accounting of the order itself will reveal a $4000 loss.

This type of contribution analysis is very useful in establishing bid prices during periods of slack activity. Under such conditions, accepting business at less than full cost may be essential to survival. Figure 18-1 illustrates the dilemma created by blindly bidding as a mark-up of full costs. When times are lean and the company's business is slow, this bidding rule causes Skilling Construction to increase prices in a vain attempt to cover overhead, thus driving away more business. When the company is very busy and fixed overhead is spread over a larger volume of activity, total costs of construction are lower; the company then reduces its prices and more bids are won at exactly the time when the company will have difficulty handling the work. In fact, Skilling should be pricing just opposite to this decision rule: price lower when business is slack and raise prices when the company's capacity is being strained.

Capital-Investment Decisions

Capital-investment decisions occur throughout both the private and public sectors of the economy. Elegant procedures, generally referred to as capital budgeting or engineering-economy techniques, have been devised to aid such decisions. These procedures require that the analyst develop a complete outline of the cash inflows and outflows occasioned by each investment alternative under study. Again, the emphasis is on the magnitude and timing of differential cash flows.

Figure 18-2 presents the accounting data developed by Lipinsky Manufacturing Corporation relating to a proposal to automate one manufacturing step. Once again,

FIGURE 18-2 Lipinsky Manufacturing Corp.:
Proposal to Automate Operation R

Present cost of completing Operation R:	
Material	$2.00 per part
Labor	3.40
IPC (200% of labor)*	6.80
	$12.20 per part
Estimated cost of completing Operation R (after automation):	
Material	$2.00 per part
Labor	1.40
IPC (200% of labor)*	2.80
	$6.20 per part
Investment to automate:	
Equipment and installation	$600,000
Estimated life	6 years
Annual maintenance expense	$10,000
Estimated salvage value	0
Estimated annual volume	40,000 parts per year

*Assume one-half of total IPC is variable.

to isolate cash-flow consequences these data must be reconstructed, since they were developed on the accrual basis and include both noncash and allocated expenses. Note that the full cost of manufacture is $12.20 per part under the present method and $6.20 under the proposed method; the apparent savings is $6.00 per part. The investment to automate is $600,000 with an estimated life of six years and estimated additional annual maintenance charges of $10,000.

Figure 18-3, part A illustrates the type of analysis that results from the uncritical use of the accounting data. This analysis assumes that IPC will be saved at a rate of 200 percent of direct-labor savings. Indeed, some of the variable IPC will probably be saved, if much of the variable IPC is labor-related, including fringe benefits. But correspondingly much of the fixed IPC that has been allocated to this operation R— rent, building maintenance, heat, and manufacturing management—will continue to be incurred by Lipinsky even if the labor time required for Operation R is reduced. Only cash savings that can truly be identified with this automation investment should be included.

So, the first problem in Part A is that the operating savings of $240,000 are overstated. But there are other problems. Deducting depreciation on the new equipment—$100,000 per year, assuming straight-line depreciation and zero sal-

FIGURE 18-3   Lipinsky Manufacturing Corp.: Analysis of Proposal to Automate Operation R

A. Analysis of Accounting Return—Misleading

Operating Costs

Present (40,000 parts × $12.20) =	$488,000
Proposed (40,000 parts × $6.20) =	248,000
Operating Savings	$240,000
Less: Depreciation	(100,000)
Maintenance	(10,000)
	$130,000

Savings ÷ initial investment = $\dfrac{130,000}{600,000}$ = 21.7%

Savings ÷ average book value of investment = $\dfrac{130,000}{300,000}$ = 43.3%

B. Analysis of Cash Flows—Required for Return on Investment Calculation

	Present	Proposed	Difference
Material	$ 80,000	$ 80,000	0
Labor	136,000	56,000	80,000
Variable IPC	136,000	56,000	80,000
Annual maintenance	0	10,000	(10,000)
Net annual cash flow			$150,000
Initial (time-zero) cash flow		($600,000)	
Return on investment*		13.0%	

*Discounted cash flow or internal rate of return method.

vage value—is incorrect, since depreciation is a part of IPC; there is some double counting here.

This misleading analysis indicates a ratio of annual savings to initial investment of 21.7 percent—a quite handsome accounting return. Indeed, the investment is still more attractive (43.3 percent) if the estimated annual savings is compared to the investment's average book value—that is, the book value of the equipment at the end of three years when it is one-half depreciated.

The shortcomings of this analysis are (1) the operating savings associated with fixed IPC are illusory, since the decision to invest will not materially alter the company's fixed IPC cash expenditures; (2) the savings are reduced by the depreciation expense, although depreciation is not a cash outflow to Lipinsky; and (3) no recognition is given to the timing of the cash flows—the fact that the investment occurs at time zero while the returns are spread out over six years.

The second analysis in Figure 18-3 overcomes these deficiencies. Depreciation is ignored. The discounted cash flow or internal-rate-of-return technique* takes explicit account of the timing of the cash flows. The assumption is made that variable IPC will be saved in proportion to labor savings. (By no means is this assumption valid for all capital investments; each element of the IPC should be analyzed separately.) Apparent savings in allocated costs (fixed IPC) are omitted. The resulting return on investment is a much less attractive 13.0 percent, a rate that will be acceptable in some circumstances, but not in others.

Both of these analyses have still another shortcoming: income taxes are ignored. Income taxes are very real cash costs and are affected both by the operating savings and by the depreciation expense that is deductible for tax purposes. Figure 18-4 extends the analysis of Figure 18-3 to derive an after-tax return on investment. Note that this exhibit assumes sum-of-the-years-digits depreciation so as to accelerate the tax savings derived from depreciation.

The first part of Figure 18-4 simply derives the difference in income taxes. The $150,000 annual operating savings adds to taxable income, while the depreciation represents a shield against taxes; the difference between them is the net increase or decrease in taxable income. In the first year the depreciation is greater than the savings and thus Lipinsky receives both the benefit of the operating savings and a small income-tax benefit. In subsequent years the depreciation shield reduces. The second part of Figure 18-4 details, year-by-year, the amount and timing of the after-tax cash flows. These flows equate to an after-tax return on investment of 7.5 percent, a rate that would not be attractive to most companies. Thus, a careful study of net cash flows reveals that an investment proposal which at first seemed quite attractive is in fact a marginal investment opportunity, or worse.

When to Introduce a Product Redesign

The design engineer and material manager at Carlos Manufacturing are considering when to introduce a product redesign. The marketing manager is pressuring for

---

*While the techniques used here are mentioned in Chapter 2, a full description of them is beyond the scope of this book. See any beginning finance or engineering economy textbook.

FIGURE 18-4 Lipinsky Manufacturing Corp—Proposal to Automate Operation R: After-Tax Analysis

Calculation of Difference in Income Tax:		Year					
	0	1	2	3	4	5	6
Operating savings (see Figure 18-3, Part B)	—	150	150	150	150	150	150
Depreciation (SOYD)	—	171	143	114	86	57	29
Increase/(decrease) in taxable income	—	(21)	7	36	64	93	121
Increase/(decrease) in taxes (50% rate)		(10.5)	3.5	18	32	46.5	60.5
After-tax cash flow:							
Investment	(600)	—	—	—	—	—	—
Operating savings	—	150	150	150	150	150	150
Income taxes	—	10.5	(3.5)	(18)	(32)	(46.5)	(60.5)
Total cash flow	(600)	160.5	146.5	132.0	118.0	103.5	89.5
After-tax return on investment* = 7.5%							

*Discounted cash flow or internal-rate-of-return method.

early introduction, but the production manager and controller are anxious to avoid having to scrap raw and semifinished goods inventory. Some facts relevant to this decision are outlined in Figure 18-5. The new model, designated Mark II, is less expensive to manufacture but should enjoy the same reception and command the same selling price as Mark I. Note that Figure 18-5 compares only the variable product costs, not the full-absorption costs.

Because the Mark II design is radically new, any Mark I raw or in-process material in inventory at the time of introduction will be scrapped. All of Carlos's managers agree that the new design should be introduced not later than six months from now, when all existing Mark I inventory has been exhausted, but the marketing manager is arguing for immediate introduction. The controller is asked to study the economic consequences of the decision.

The economic comparison shown in Figure 18-5 is inappropriate, even though it correctly identifies the consequences to the company's income statements. If introduction is delayed six months, all inventory will be used up, and therefore no inventory write-off will occur, but cost of goods sold will reflect the higher unit cost of Mark I. On the other hand, if introduction is immediate, the lower unit cost of Mark II will be reflected in the cost of goods sold for the full six months, but the inventory of Mark I materials, now carried on the balance sheet at $140,000, must be written off.

The key point here is that existing inventory (carried at historical costs) cannot be affected by the decision to use or to scrap the material. These are, in economists' terms, **sunk costs.** The incremental cost of turning the inventory now on hand into finished units of Mark I is something less than total variable cost, as the inventory is

FIGURE 18-5   Carlos Manufacturing Corp.:
Introduction of Model Mark II

Facts	Mark I	Mark II
Variable cost of manufacture		
Direct material	$ 1.00	$ 1.40
Direct labor	2.00	1.30
Variable IPC	2.00	1.30
Total variable cost	$ 5.00	$ 4.00
Expected sales per month (units)	10,000	10,000
Inventory		
Raw (dollars)	$ 20,000	—
(units)	20,000	—
In-process (dollars)	$120,000	—
(units)	40,000	—

	Costs Throughout Next Six Months	
Erroneous Economic	Introduction	Immediate
Comparison	in 6 months	introduction
Cost of goods sold: Mark I	$300,000	—
Mark II	—	$240,000
Write-off inventory: raw	—	20
in-process	—	120,000
Total expenses	$300,000	$380,000

a sunk cost. Therefore, the write-off does not represent a cash flow, although it affects the company's profit-and-loss statement. (But consider another step of complexity: These sunk costs are deductible for income taxes if the inventory is scrapped, resulting in a positive cash impact through a reduction in taxes.)

A more careful analysis of this decision recognizes that a third alternative may be attractive: introduce in four months, using up the in-process inventory and scrapping the raw material; that is, it may be economic to convert the in-process material into finished goods. Accepting the problem as first stated—introduce now or six months from now—without questioning whether other alternatives are viable may obscure the optimum decision.

A correct economic comparison requires more data than are available in Figure 18-5. What we need is an analysis of the cash costs to the company of each of the three alternatives. Once again, variable product costs are more appropriate to the analysis than full-absorption costs. The cost to complete the in-process inventory will be less than the cost to complete the raw material inventory and both costs will be less than the $5.00 total variable cost of a Mark I unit.

Cash inflows can be ignored, as they are assumed to be the same under all three alternatives. The analysis can be further limited to just those out-of-pocket (that is, future) cash costs for Carlos over the next six months; the comparison of costs beyond that period is unnecessary, as it is obvious that the lower-cost Mark II unit should by then be in production.

Varying Marketing Inputs

The fifth example cited at the outset of this chapter involves the product-line manager's analysis of the effect that price, promotional effort, product redesign, and other factors have on the sales volume and profit of the company. The product manager needs a clear understanding of the interrelationships of volume, price, costs, and profits. This understanding is fundamental to many operating decisions. Every operating manager can well use a simple model describing these relationships to analyze a broad range of what-if questions. These analyses were described in Chapter 13, and you are urged to review that material.

SUMMARY

The primary users of accounting data, operating managers, have been the focus throughout this book and particularly in this chapter. As important as the traditional accounting statements are—operating statement, balance sheet, cash flow, and cost accounting reports—detailed financial data should also be available to managers to help analyze economic consequences of operating decisions.

The key to such operating decisions is the difference in cash flows (both amounts and timing) among the relevant alternatives. The first challenge is to frame properly the alternatives, searching for less obvious options that may prove optimal. Deriving the differential cash flows from traditional accounting data is complicated because (1) accounting records are maintained on an accrual, not a cash basis, (2) variable and fixed expenses are likely to be affected quite differently by the decisions, and (3) many accounting reports, particularly cost accounting reports, include expenses that have been allocated in an arbitrary way that can confuse decision makers.

NEW TERM

Sunk costs. Cash-flow expenditures incurred in the past that cannot be altered or affected by decisions now or in the future.

DISCUSSION QUESTIONS

18.1 Describe how you would go about analyzing a make-or-buy decision when:

  (a) You have the in-house production capability and it is not being used to full capacity

(b) You do not have the in-house production capability (but could acquire it)

(c) You have the in-house production capability and demand for its use exceeds capacity

18.2 Describe both the quantitative and qualitative considerations that should inform a decision about accepting a large order (for products your company manufactures) from a customer with whom your company does not currently do business.

18.3 As a senior manufacturing manager, you are faced with the following problem: the design engineers at your manufacturing company have developed a new generation of products that includes a major part that requires a fabrication technique not currently available at your company. Identify as many alternatives as you can for solving the problem.

18.4 In most cost analyses in connection with marketing decisions, is it reasonable to assume that variable (direct) manufacturing costs approximate differential future cash flows? Explain.

18.5 Why are differential cash flows more important than differential profits in making most operating decisions?

18.6 Are depreciation expenses, because they do not involve the flow of cash, irrelevant to operating decisions? Explain.

18.7 What are sunk costs? Give three examples of sunk costs.

18.8 In comparing alternative capital investment opportunities, how are differences in timing of cash flows incorporated into the analysis?

18.9 Give three examples of incomes or expenses that do not involve the direct flow of cash except as they affect income taxes.

18.10 Explain the method of analysis you would use to decide whether to lease a car (for, say, a four-year term) or to purchase the car (financing 80 percent of the purchase price by means of a 36-month bank loan). Are there any nonfinancial considerations that would enter into your decision?

18.11 A production manager reporting to you (you are the manufacturing vice president) has recommended the investment of $35,000 in a new automated machine tool for her department. Her analysis compares production costs on the proposed tool and on the tools currently owned by your company. What other alternatives might you suggest she explore?

18.12 A hospital administrator is evaluating bids from two contract building-maintenance firms for complete janitorial service and external maintenance of the hospital for the next year. What other alternatives might the administrator consider besides selecting between the two bidders?

PROBLEMS

18.1 Perform the analysis that would help you decide whether to accept an order for 3000 units of product T46 from the Sturgis Corporation in Australia. The list price of product T46 is $93.00 and its manufacturing costs are

full-absorption cost	$61.80
variable (direct) cost	48.15
prime cost	37.30

Sturgis has offered you a contract price of $160,000. State any assumptions that you think are important to your analysis.

18.2 Perform the analysis that would help you decide whether to subcontract the manufacture of part D2, which your production department has been fabricating for the past three years and that now has the following cost:

full-absorption cost	$23.16
variable (direct) cost	15.38
prime cost	14.81

The Jordan Machine Shop has offered you the following prices:

Annual quantity	Price per unit
more than 10,000	$16.75
5001 to 10,000	18.40
2001 to 5000	21.16
2000 or less	25.30

You anticipate that you will require 6500 units of D2 in the coming year. State any assumptions that you think are important to your analysis.

18.3 Refer to problem 18.2. Suppose your company does not currently own the necessary equipment to produce part D2. (The manufacturing cost data shown in the problem represent estimates.) You could purchase the necessary, specialized capital equipment to produce D2 for an investment of $58,000; the equipment is expected to have a five-year useful life. The expected demand for product D2 is as follows:

	units
Year 1	6,500
Year 2	8,500
Year 3	4,500
Year 4	2,500
Year 5	0

Formulate the cash flow analysis that would be useful in deciding whether to make this capital investment. State any assumptions that you think are important to your analysis. Would you make the investment?

18.4 The Weinstein Company manufactures and markets standard wooden kitchen cabinets. The standard cost of the most popular of these units is

Direct material	$ 52.50
Direct labor	30.90
IPC	26.25
Full-absorption cost	$109.65

The cost accountant at Weinstein estimates that the variable (direct) cost of the unit is $99.15. The IPC vehicle at Weinstein is direct-material dollars.

(a) A large residential building contractor approached Weinstein during the early fall, Weinstein's slow season, and offered to buy 500 units at $105 per unit. Would you accept the order? Why or why not? What factors did you consider in making this decision?

(b) During Weinstein's busy season, the company is considering whether, in order to meet demand, it should work overtime or subcontract the manufacture of these units. The subcontractor has bid $119.10 per unit for 1000 units. If these units are built in-house on overtime, labor costs would be about 150 percent of the standard shown above. Weinstein expects to be able to sell these units at $144 each. What would you do, and why? What factors did you consider in making this decision?

(c) A design engineer has proposed substituting less expensive material that would require the expenditure of some more labor. The effect of such a substitution would be to reduce direct-material cost by $3.00 and increase direct labor by $3.30. What would be the new standard full-absorption cost of the unit? Would you make the substitution, and why? What factors did you consider in making this decision? Would your answer be different if the IPC vehicle were direct-labor dollars?

18.5 Tripoli Toy Company was a medium-sized toy manufacturing company. Its engineering department aggressively sought product cost reductions through redesign (value engineering). One attractive opportunity was to substitute a molded-plastic chassis (frame) for the present fabricated sheet-metal chassis on a particular toy.

The engineering department had proven the technical and economic feasibility of the substitution. The tooling required for the molded-plastic chassis, purchased for $10,000, had already been used to manufacture prototype quantities.

The comparative full-absorption manufacturing cost data on a per-unit basis were as follows:

	Plastic	Metal
Material	$0.88	$0.41
Labor	0.13 (0.02 hours)	0.75 (0.12 hours)
IPC	0.18	1.07
	$1.19	$2.23
Tooling	$10,000	fully depreciated

Estimated annual usage was 12,500 units. The IPC rates were $8.92 per direct-labor hour (full absorption) and $2.75 per direct-labor hour (variable or direct). The plastic unit would be molded by a subcontractor and minor additional processing would be required at Tripoli. The raw material for the metal frame was sheared to size by a metal distributing company and then punched, formed and finished at Tripoli. The 0.12 hours of processing labor were represented by

> 0.06 hours for punching
> 0.04 hours for forming
> <u>0.02</u> hours for finishing
> Total 0.12 hours

(a) Should the substitution be made?
(b) Assuming the following existing inventories (relating to the metal unit), the question remains as to when the substitution should be effected:

	Number of Units	Inventory Value
Raw material	3,000	$1,230
Work-in-process	4,200	<u>5,544</u>
		$6,774

The work-in-process units had been punched but not formed or finished; the scrap value of the metal parts was about $0.05 per unit.

18.6 Tripoli Toy (see problem 18.5) was approached by Breakfast Bounty, Inc. (BBI) with an offer to purchase up to 10,000 units of a small game that was introduced by Tripoli two years ago. Units sold to BBI would be modified slightly from Tripoli's standard design and would carry the BBI label rather than the Tripoli label. BBI would offer these to its customers through a coupon or premium on or in cereal boxes at what would appear to customers as a bargain price.

The primary terms of the offer were as follows:

Delivery   During April, May and June: not less than 1500 nor more than 3500 in any single month; BBI to give 30-days notice of the exact quantity required

Terms: Net 30 days
Price: $5.35 per unit

Tripoli's standard full absorption cost for the unit was estimated at

> Direct material $1.27
> Direct labor (0.35 hours)   2.19
> IPC   <u>3.12</u>
> $6.58

(See problems 18.5 for IPC rates.) Sales of the comparable standard game were 5000 units in the first year, 12,000 units last year, and (estimated) 15,000 units this year and next year, after which volume was expected to fall off. The list price to the consumer was $28.50 and Tripoli received a price of $11.00 from its distributors.

Tripoli's sales manager was anxious that the company not jeopardize the near-term profit potential from this game by diverting either Tripoli's own production capabilities or retail customer demand to BBI. The manufacturing manager was attracted by the timing of the deliveries requested by BBI: right in the heart of Tripoli's slow season. (By early or mid-June Tripoli was typically operating at or near full capacity.)

Should Tripoli accept this offer from BBI? Explain your answer in detail.

CASES

PIRELLI CORPORATION

Tanya Rosenblatt reviewed the trial balance at June 30, 1994 and was encouraged with what she saw. She had been anxious to study the interim financial statements for the second quarter. As president of Pirelli, she was under considerable pressure from the company's board of directors to improve profitability. For the past several days she had been pressing the accounting manager, Ted Yamata, to prepare the second-quarter financial statements. Ted told her that he would require another day or two to complete the end-of-period adjusting entries and prepare the statements, but offered to give her the preliminary trial balance that appears in Figure P.1.

Company Background

Tanya Rosenblatt, together with a group of investors, purchased Pirelli Corporation in 1990 from the entrepreneur-founder who wished at that time to retire. As a company active in the hazardous materials clean-up business, Pirelli had grown rapidly in the decade of the 1980s as government regulations on materials usage and disposal increased in response to national concerns both for the environment and for employee health. However, under the leadership of the former owners, the company had been only marginally profitable. Rosenblatt and her outside investors felt that they could both broaden the client base of the company and increase its profitability.

Traditionally, the company had focused on toxic clean-up work for the large electronics companies. Since acquiring the company in 1990, Rosenblatt had extended the company to serve the oil companies, primarily their retail gasoline outlets, and an increasing number of municipalities. Sales growth for the past three years had been in excess of 25 percent per year, placing considerable strain on the financial resources of

FIGURE P.1   Pirelli Corporation: Trial Balance Worksheet, June 30, 1994

Account Number	Account Name	Preliminary Trial Balance	
		Debit	Credit
110	Cash	$ 120,611	
120	Accounts receivable	915,691	
121	Allowance for doubtful accounts		$ 16,410
125	Advances to employees	48,800	
130	Supplies inventory	117,167	
131	Fuel inventory	12,350	
140	Prepaid expenses	81,950	
151	Equipment—office	135,510	
153	Equipment—field	481,967	
159	Accumulated depreciation		83,973
161	Intangible asset—customer list	136,000	
162	Accumulated amortization—customer list		112,000
165	Intangible asset—goodwill	265,000	
166	Accumulated amortization—goodwill		26,500
210	Accounts payable—trade		102,216
220	Bank loans—short-term		200,000
231	Interest payable		5,933
241	Accrued wages and salaries payable		160,473
243	Accrued bonuses payable		
251	Customer advance payments		20,000
253	Deferred income		35,100
271	Miscellaneous accruals		83,371
291	Dividends payable		
311	Notes payable—long-term		570,000
411	Capital stock		600,000
421	Retained earnings		116,463
501	Contract revenue		2,216,193
503	Other revenue		56,702
601	Project labor—professional	154,740	
603	Project labor—staff	436,960	
609	Fringe benefit expense—project	149,826	
611	Supplies—project	98,471	
621	Subcontract expense—project	138,420	
701	Professional salaries	412,050	
703	Other salaries and wages	226,763	
709	Fringe benefit expense	153,122	
801	Office supplies expense	33,606	
811	Depreciation expense—field equipment	17,500	
812	Depreciation expense—office equipment	5,800	
821	Fuel expense	6,420	
825	Other vehicle expense	7,995	
831	Advertising and promotion expense	21,672	

FIGURE P.1   (*Continued*)

Account Number	Account Name	Preliminary Trial Balance	
		Debit	Credit
833	Dues expense	2,448	
841	Rent expense	68,840	
843	Insurance expense	11,550	
845	Occupancy expense	29,366	
847	Telephone expense	18,861	
851	Travel expense	41,693	
855	Staff training expense	12,963	
891	Interest expense	14,700	
893	Bad debt expense	5,580	
895	Amortization expense	8,450	
897	Other expenses	16,802	
901	Miscellaneous income		4,310
	Totals	$4,409,644	$4,409,644

the company and requiring the company to borrow substantial additional funds. Tanya knew—and her board of directors reminded her frequently—that improved profitability had to accompany this growth if the demands of creditors and the expectations of stockholders were to be met.

In 1990 the Pirelli Company enjoyed an excellent reputation among its customers. As a result the acquisition price paid by Rosenblatt and her investors was considerably above the value of the net assets (or net worth) of the company. Accordingly, a portion of the purchase price was ascribed to the customer list asset, an asset to be amortized over five years, and another portion to goodwill, an asset to be amortized over 40 years. The amortization of the value of the customer list could be deducted for income tax purposes, while the amortization of goodwill could not.

The acquiring group paid $2 million for the Pirelli Company, $800,000 in cash to the former owner and $1.2 million in the form of a 10-year term loan bearing interest at 8 percent per year.

First-Quarter Operations

Tanya and the rest of Pirelli's management team paid particular attention to quarterly (rather than monthly) financial results. Accordingly, Ted Yamata and the accounting staff were careful to develop a comprehensive set of end-of-period entries at the conclusion of each quarter so as to state as accurately as possible the asset and liability position of the company, and thus its profit for the quarter.

When Ted gave Tanya the preliminary trial balance (Figure P.1), he cautioned her that the apparent profit (the difference between revenues and expenses on this trial balance) would change as a result of the end-of-period entries, and would probably decrease somewhat because depreciation and amortization of assets had not yet been recorded.

Tanya had some concern that Ted was excessively conservative in accounting for revenues and expenses. Over the past three years she and Ted had often engaged in friendly and productive arguments about just what end-of-period accounting adjustments were appropriate. Ted found these discussions useful since accounting for certain of the end-of-period adjustments required knowledge that only the top management of the firm possessed, including plans, problems and commitments. As he explained to Tanya, "While financial statements are historical documents, the values assigned to certain assets and liabilities are substantially influenced by the company's future plans."

Each quarter Tanya and Ted spent about an hour together reviewing the proposed end-of-period adjustments. Ted separated these adjusting entries into what he called *recurring* and *nonrecurring* adjustments. The recurring adjustments were the routine entries that occurred at the end of each fiscal quarter and about which there was relatively little uncertainty. The nonrecurring adjustments, on the other hand, changed from quarter to quarter, depending upon the particular activities and decisions undertaken by the company during the quarter.

Recurring Adjustments

Ted reviewed with Tanya each of seven recurring adjustments:

(1) A portion of the acquisition cost of the firm's fixed assets, principally equipment and vehicles, was assigned as depreciation expense to each fiscal quarter. The offsetting credit was accumulated in a single contra account, Accumulated Depreciation. Depreciation of the office equipment was $6000 for the second quarter of 1994, while depreciation of the field equipment and vehicles was $18,000.

(2) Pirelli maintained an Allowance for Doubtful Accounts, although its experience with customer bad debts had been quite good. Ted's policy with regard to this account was that the contra account should not exceed 2 percent of the outstanding customer accounts receivable (shown on the trial balance) nor should the increase in the allowance in any single quarter exceed one-half of 1 percent of total sales for the quarter. Tanya had long felt that, given the company's strong record of collecting accounts receivable, the allowance was excessively high; she knew of no customer accounts currently outstanding that were very likely to prove uncollectible. Nevertheless, over the years she had become convinced by Ted that the allowance was prudent and therefore she approved the policy.

(3) Included among the prepaid expenses was the $12,000 remaining balance on the $36,000 annual premium for a general insurance policy. The cost of this insurance policy was amortized (allocated) across its 12-month term.

(4) Interest on the note to the former owners was accrued for the quarter. Interest is paid annually, at the end of the year.

(5) As fuel oil was purchased for the company's vehicles, its cost was expensed to account number 821. At the end of each quarter, the motor pool manager made an estimate of the fuel oil inventory and supplied this information to the accounting department. Accounting then made the necessary adjustment to increase or decrease the Fuel Expense account and the Fuel Inventory account. The motor pool manager estimated that the value of fuel inventory at June 30, 1994 was $3000 less than at March 31, 1994.

(6) The value assigned to the customer list at the time the company was acquired was being amortized over a five-year period at the rate of $6800 per quarter, and the goodwill was being amortized over a 40-year period at the rate of $1650 per quarter.

(7) The company's Board of Directors met each quarter and frequently declared a dividend. Tanya confirmed that the board had met in June and had declared cash dividends on the company's common stock totalling $10,000. The dividend was scheduled to be paid on July 15.

Nonrecurring Adjustments

Ted then reviewed with Tanya other end-of-period entries that might be made to state more accurately the value of assets and liabilities at June 30 and thus the profit for the second quarter of 1994.

(8) Ted recalled from Monday's staff meeting Tanya's report on a $1 million law suit that a subcontractor had filed against Pirelli in June, alleging breach of contract in connection with a job that had been completed in March. Tanya reported that the firm's lawyers believed that the lawsuit was without merit; they felt that the worst-case outcome of this suit would be an out-of-court settlement for about $10,000. Ted proposed that the company reserve this amount as a liability at June 30; Tanya felt that no accounting action should be taken until preliminary settlement discussions had occurred between the two sets of lawyers.

(9) Tanya recalled that in the fourth quarter of 1993 the completion of a contract with the City of Concord had been clouded by a lingering disagreement as to whether the site clean-up had been adequate. Pirelli's management and city officials agreed to have the work checked by an independent third party. As a precaution against possible additional expenditures that might be required on this job, Ted reduced contract revenues by $20,000 and established this amount as a deferred income. In response to Ted's inquiry, Tanya reported that the third party had confirmed the adequacy of Pirelli's work and that the City of Concord was now fully satisfied.

(10) Pirelli's management had for some time been discussing the advisability of improving the appearance of the company's entrance and main lobby. The estimated cost of this remodelling and redecorating was $60,000. Ted wondered whether it might be desirable to being to accrue—at the rate, say, of $15,000 per quarter—for this anticipated expenditure.

(11) The discussion of lobby redecorating caused Tanya to wonder if there were perhaps expenses charged to the current quarter that properly belonged in future accounting periods. She mentioned that Pirelli had contracted and paid for exhibit space at a fall convention. She asked Ted how the $3000 for this exhibit space had been accounted for. Ted reviewed the check register and determined that it had been charged to account number 831, Advertising and Promotion Expense. Tanya argued that this amount should be shown as a prepaid expense as of June 30, not as an expense of the current quarter. Ted responded by noting four arguments for making no adjustment at this time: first, the commitment for the exhibit space was not cancelable; second, advertising and promotion expenditures by their nature tended to benefit more than a single accounting period and yet they were typically recorded as an expense when paid; third, the amount was small, and thus not really material in the accounting period; and fourth, showing the $3000 as an expense in the current period was conservative.

(12) In reviewing the gross profit earned on each of the jobs completed during the quarter, Tanya and Ted were surprised to see that the margin on the Sunfield Oil Company project was particularly handsome, well above management's expectations. Ted suggested that his chief cost accountant review with Tanya the detail of charges to this job. In so doing they discovered that the billing had not yet been received from a subcontractor for a major portion of the work on this job. Both Ted and Tanya agreed that a proper matching of expenses and revenues for the quarter required that this consulting fee, estimated to be about $16,000 should be included in expenses of the current quarter.

(13) Tanya and Ted next reviewed the aging of the accounts receivable, a report that showed by individual customer name the amounts past due. They noted that $15,000 of the amount due from the City of Millport was now 150 days past due, and that $5000 was 90-days past due from TPL Developers, a commercial real estate development firm that had declared bankruptcy in May. Tanya felt certain that the City of Millport would ultimately make payment and that this slowness in payment was not unusual for municipalities. However, she agreed that Pirelli was unlikely to recover more than a small fraction of the amount due from TPL Developers.

(14) Ted proposed to Tanya that a portion of the year-end management bonus be included as an expense of the current quarter. He argued that the company's record of improved profitability was almost certain to cause the Board of Directors to declare a handsome year-end bonus for the top executives, in accordance with a long-standing but informal board policy. They agreed that, judging by the profit earned during the first half of the fiscal year, year-end bonuses were likely to aggregate $75,000 or more. No bonus expense had been included in the first quarter, but Ted urged that one-third of the annual bonus be included as an expense of each of the final three quarters of the fiscal year, including the quarter for which he was now developing adjusting entries. Tanya felt that bonuses should be included in

the fiscal period in which they were awarded, although she was uncomfortable with the possibility of a large bonus expense falling in the fourth quarter and thus depressing reported profits for that quarter.

After some additional review of the preliminary trial balance, Tanya and Ted could find no other adjustments that needed to be made—or even potential adjustments about which they might argue! Ted assured Tanya that he could complete the June 30 financial statements for her in about an hour.

Assignment

(a) Prepare in general journal format the adjusting entries that you think should be made at June 30, 1994.

(b) Record these entries in adjustment columns on a trial balance worksheet, and complete the worksheet to determine the adjusted trial balance.

(c) From the adjusted trial balance, prepare an income statement for the six-month period ended June 30 and a balance sheet as of June 30, 1994. (Note: The second-quarter income statement would be determined by deducting the first-quarter income statement from the six-month income statement that you have just prepared.)

(d) If Pirelli had failed to make these end-of-period adjusting entries, would its six-month income have been overstated or understated, and by how much?

(e) Review your financial statements. If you were Tanya or a member of Pirelli's board of directors, would you be pleased with the company's results for the first six months of 1994? Do you have any particular concerns about the company's current financial position?

ANALYTICS CORPORATION

Analytics Corporation produces a limited line of analytical instruments for use in research laboratories in industry and in universities. The entrepreneur-founder of the company, Alex Wong, had earlier in his career worked for a division of a Fortune 500 company that served the same market, although with a substantially broader product line. By the late 1980s he was convinced that a market opportunity existed for two instruments that incorporated some emerging expert-systems technology. When he was unable to convince his employer of the attractiveness of the opportunity, Wong began to develop a business plan for a new company.

Early in 1987 Wong resigned his division manager position to devote full time to the development of his product ideas and the search for venture capital. He immediately incorporated the company as Analytics Corporation. By the middle of that year he had assembled a small team of four individuals, including a chief engineer, Sally Garvin, a software engineer, and a technician in addition to himself. Periodically during this formative year Wong and Garvin invested personal funds (which they obtained through second mortgages on their homes) to cover the various start-up expenses of the company. By late in the year, Wong had obtained commitments from three venture capital firms to provide $1.5 million of equity capital and a stand-by credit line of $1 million that would be available to the company as long-term, noninterest-bearing debt if certain product development milestones were met on schedule. The company commenced formal operations in January, 1988.

Negotiations with the venture capitalists had been protracted, although ultimately successful. The venture capitalists spent several months checking personal references and in other ways satisfying themselves that Wong and Garvin—but particularly Wong, as president—had the experience, the breadth of technical and market knowledge, and the personal drive that would maximize the company's chances for success. They were impressed with the founders' technical educations, including Wong's masters degree in computer science and Garvin's Ph.D. in electrical engineering following an undergraduate degree in physics. Wong's general management experience was viewed by the investors as highly desirable. Garvin was well known in the industry as both an innovator and an effective manager. Garvin, who had split her time over the previous 10 years between industry and university research, had demonstrated solid capability in project management as well as an entrepreneurial flair. Neither Wong nor Garvin had much experience in accounting and finance, but the venture capitalists were confident that they could provide guidance to the company in the financial area.

In return for their $1.5 million equity investment the venture capitalists received 45 percent of the common stock of the company. Wong and Garvin were left with 30 percent and 15 percent of the common stock, respectively, in return for their year's work, their investments, and their product designs. The remaining 10 percent of the common stock was reserved for key employees that would have to be attracted to the company over the next two years or so.

By late in 1988, the company had commenced shipments of its first product, the Model 4100. Early in the second year, 1989, a second instrument, the Model 7400, was introduced. Over the next few years other instruments—as well as equally important improvements and accessories for the existing instruments—were introduced. By early 1995 the company's offerings included three instrument families, with a number of individual models offered in each family. While the life of an individual model was seldom longer than three or four years, by pursuing a product-family concept Analytics had succeeded in lengthening the time period between major product redesigns, thus leveraging its engineering efforts. Nevertheless, the company continued to struggle, as it had in its very early years, to control its development expenses, as the pressure was relentless to redesign products both to incorporate new technology and to reduce their manufacturing costs.

Analytics faced formidable competition in its marketplace. Customers were generally sophisticated and demanded accuracy, reliability, on-time delivery, and competitive pricing from their instrument suppliers. Analytics found itself competing simultaneously with the state-of-the-art instruments offered by its large domestic competitors and by one Japanese company, and lower-priced instruments offered by an English company selling through a U.S. distributor. Discounts from list price were commonly offered by competitors, sometimes in the form of accessories or additional features that were included with the instrument at no charge to the customer.

The competitive environment caused Wong to emphasize the importance of manufacturing in Analytics' overall strategy. As a result, Analytics invested heavily in fixed assets, including cleanroom facilities, certain machining and joining equipment, and test fixtures and chambers. As the company's sales grew, Analytics moved twice to new facilities, once in 1990 and again in 1994, as it struggled to increase manufacturing capacity and reduce the use of overtime.

Over the company's seven-year-life the concentration of sales had moved from the education market to the industrial market. To accommodate this shift Analytics increased its field sales force, opened regional offices, and increased the number of models offered in each instrument family in its efforts to target particular customer needs. In 1993 Analytics began an aggressive exporting program, opening sales offices in both the European and Japanese markets. All of these marketing efforts had the effect of increasing the company's selling expenses.

The financial performance of the company was at the same time both satisfying and troubling to Wong and to the venture capitalists, two of whom served on the company's board of directors. The company had obviously met an important market need and had been welcomed by its customers, as evidenced by the rapid growth in sales. The company earned an operating profit in its second year and had been profitable four of the five previous years, the exception being the recession year of 1991. Nevertheless, overall profitability had not met the projections that Wong had incorporated in the business plan that he used to convince the venture capitalists to invest in the company; the representatives of the venture capital firms reminded Wong frequently of that short-fall. Wong was disappointed that Analytics seemed always to be short of funds to make the investments in working capital and fixed assets that he viewed as essential for the company's long-term success.

In mid-1990 when Analytics suffered a severe cash shortage, the venture capitalists agreed to invest an additional $500,000 in equity and to fulfill its $1 million note obligation. Then in 1993, bowing to pressure from the bank and recognizing that their long-term note would not be repaid in the foreseeable future, the venture investors agreed to convert their $1 million debt into common stock. As a result, by early 1995 the common stock of the company was owned 55 percent by the venture capitalists, 22 percent by Wong, and 23 percent by other members of management, a few of whom were no longer employed by the company. In addition, grants under a broadly based employee stock option plan had resulted in outstanding and unexercised stock options equivalent to about 7 percent of the common shares issued.

The 1990 cash crisis had caused the board of directors to demand that a new chief financial officer be recruited. After a lengthy search, Wong hired Roland Hirata, a young and promising manager at the international accounting firm that did Analytics' annual audit. Although Hirata was an accomplished accountant he had little formal training or experience in general business management. Wong was confident that his own experience would complement well the technical accounting skills that Hirata would bring to Analytics.

The venture capitalists helped Wong develop a strong banking relationship with

Analytics Corporation, Balance Sheet ($000), December 31

	1988	1989	1990	1991	1992	1993	1994
Current Assets							
Cash	$ 235.5	$ 69.7	$ 72.0	$ 86.8	$ 105.5	$ 123.6	$ 140.6
Accounts receivable	184.2	472.1	967.7	1,061.4	1,570.6	1,810.1	2,453.7
Inventory	253.6	551.2	708.3	715.5	1,436.1	1,857.7	2,783.2
Other	31.7	41.6	91.3	79.6	106.3	95.6	146.1
Total Current Assets	705.0	1,134.6	1,839.3	1,943.3	3,218.5	3,887.0	5,523.6
Plant and equipment	1,036.4	1,853.3	3,375.9	5,146.6	5,971.6	7,463.2	9,305.5
Less depreciation	(61.6)	(212.0)	(371.6)	(630.7)	(1,035.2)	(1,426.9)	(1,881.4)
Intangible assets, net	64.1	62.8	67.1	65.5	62.2	59.3	55.6
	1,038.9	1,704.1	3,071.4	4,581.4	4,998.6	6,095.6	7,479.7
Total Assets	$1,743.9	$2,838.7	$4,910.7	$6,524.7	$8,217.1	$9,982.6	$13,003.3
Current Liabilities							
Accounts payable	$ 139.1	$ 210.9	$ 443.3	$ 436.1	$ 748.8	$1,157.6	$ 1,850.6
Notes payable	0.0	405.0	530.0	470.0	1,010.0	1,150.0	2,130.0
Accrued liabilities	44.6	71.7	143.6	149.9	216.3	298.3	385.7
Total current liabilities	183.7	687.6	1,116.9	1,056.0	1,975.1	2,605.9	4,366.3
Long-term Liabilities							
Term loan due to bank	0.0	600.0	600.0	2,300.0	2,800.0	3,500.0	4,100.0
Note due to shareholders	0.0	0.0	1,000.0	1,000.0	1,000.0	0.0	0.0
Total long-term liabilities	0.0	600.0	1,600.0	3,300.0	3,800.0	3,500.0	4,100.0
Owner's equity							
Capital stock	1,650.4	1,661.6	2,183.1	2,189.3	2,191.6	3,206.4	3,216.6
Retained earnings	(90.2)	(110.5)	10.7	(20.6)	250.4	670.3	1,320.4
	1,560.2	1,551.1	2,193.8	2,168.7	2,442.0	3,876.7	4,537.0
Total Liabilities and Owner's Equity	$1,743.9	$2,838.7	$4,910.7	$6,524.7	$8,217.1	$9,982.6	$13,003.3

Analytics Corporation, Income Statement ($000), Years Ending December 31

	1988		1989		1990		1991		1992		1993		1994	
Sales	$1,073.2	100.0%	$3,230.7	100.0%	$5,761.6	100.0%	$6,355.7	100.0%	$9,781.6	100.0%	$11,890.8	100.0%	$15,677.1	100.0%
Cost of goods sold	561.1	52.3	1,841.0	57.0	3,382.4	58.7	3,819.8	60.1	5,809.2	59.4	6,626.9	55.7	8,783.5	56.0
Gross margin	512.1	47.7	1,389.7	43.0	2,379.2	41.3	2,535.9	39.9	3,972.4	40.6	5,263.9	44.3	6,893.6	44.0
Selling expenses	281.6	26.2	604.1	18.7	852.7	14.8	972.4	15.3	1,525.9	15.6	1,914.4	16.1	2,571.0	16.4
Development expenses	221.1	20.6	455.5	14.1	662.6	11.5	699.1	11.0	704.3	7.2	986.9	8.3	1,081.7	6.9
Administrative expenses	99.6	9.3	289.5	9.0	611.5	10.6	654.1	10.3	995.5	10.2	1,193.7	10.0	1,591.1	10.1
	602.3	56.1	1,349.1	41.8	2,126.8	36.9	2,325.6	36.6	3,225.7	33.0	4,095.0	34.4	5,243.8	33.4
Operating profit	(90.2)	(8.4)	40.6	1.2	252.4	4.4	210.3	3.3	746.7	7.6	1,168.9	9.8	1,649.8	10.5
Interest expense	0.0		60.9	(1.9)	121.6	2.1	241.6	3.8	369.1	3.8	577.1	4.8	571.1	3.6
Profit before taxes	(90.2)	(8.4)	(20.3)	(0.6)	130.8	2.3	(31.3)	(0.5)	377.6	3.9	591.8	5.0	1,078.7	6.9
Income taxes	0.0		0.0		9.6	0.2	0.0		106.6	1.1	171.9	1.4	428.6	2.7
Net income	($ 90.2)	(8.4%)	($ 20.3)	(0.6%)	$ 121.2	2.1%	($ 31.3)	(0.5%)	$ 271.0	2.8%	$ 419.9	3.5%	$ 650.1	4.1%

First Security Bank in Atlanta. The bank had considerable experience in lending to high-technology companies but the credit markets in the 1990s had caused many banks, including First Security, to become somewhat more risk averse. Wong and Hirata spent a considerable amount of time informing the Bank about the company's plans and encouraging the loan officer, Ruth Sanchez, to support these plans with additional credit. By 1994, Analytics had a $2.5 million line of credit (subject to certain restrictions that at the end of 1994 limited Analytics' borrowing under the line to about $2.1 million) and a $4.1 million term loan that the Bank had increased from time to time to assist the company in acquiring fixed assets, including lease-hold improvements.

In early 1995 Wong and Hirata were preparing for another visit to the Bank to request additional credit to finance the growth that the company anticipated in 1995 and 1996. However, by this time Sanchez was evidencing real discomfort with the amount that Analytics was then borrowing and was pressuring Wong and Hirata to consider a public offering of the company's common stock. Analytics' board of directors, on the other hand, felt that now was not the time to seek an initial public offering (IPO) of the company's stock both because the over-the-counter stock market had declined 18 percent over the past four months and because Analytics' recent earnings record was not as attractive as the directors and management felt it could and should be. Investment bankers suggested that Analytics might command a price-per-share of $14 in an IPO at this time; the company felt that with continued growth, improved earnings, and a stronger stock market it should be able to command a per-share price of $25 or more.

Wong had just received the final financial reports for the year 1994. These together with financial statements (balance sheet and income statement) for each year of the company's short history appear in the attached exhibits. Wong realized that he must reconcile some conflicting pressures: the company's sales growth opportunities over the next two years; the company's need to continue aggressive investments in marketing and product development; the directors' expectations for improved profitability; the need ultimately to go public to provide both liquidity for the investors and additional capital for the company; and the Bank's reluctance to increase Analytics' credit lines. Wong promised the directors that he would present his recommendations at the board meeting scheduled for the following week.

SOFTWARE ASSOCIATES, INC.

Software Associates, Inc., located in a suburb of San Diego, was a rapidly growing firm specializing in developing, producing and marketing standard computer software for commercial customers. Founded in 1987 the company had grown both by the acquisition of other software companies and by internal expansion of its original product line and markets. By the mid-1990s the company was considered a leader in its market and had grown to a middle-sized company.

Software Associates' (SA) initial market was in the medical field, providing accounting and administrative software systems to doctors' offices and small clinics. The company next expanded into the hospital market and thence into supplying software for other professional firms such as architects and consulting engineers. By acquisition it gained access to the market for software for retail stores and just recently it had acquired a company that offered an opportunity for entry into supplying software systems for manufacturers.

SA used a variety of marketing channels. To reach some of its smaller customers, including its traditional small doctors' offices, it relied on direct mail. Later it found that, as the computer software market matured, sales through dealers (including, for example, Businessland) became essential. Still later, as it expanded its attention to the large retail chains and to manufacturers, SA began to license its software to VARs (value-added resellers), companies specializing in developing, installing and debugging specialized, turn-key software/hardware systems for individual customers or groups of customers. Thus, by 1994 SA was selling through many marketing channels, including a small direct-sales force focused on so-called national accounts.

Software Associates went public in 1991 when the IPO (initial public offering) market was reasonably hot, after which its acquisition program accelerated, with most acquisitions done on a stock-for-stock basis.

Ralph Witkins recently joined SA as chief financial officer following 10 years of increasingly responsible positions with a manufacturer of high-technology instruments. Witkins found the career transition somewhat more challenging than he had anticipated. "Financial statements for software firms are not very comparable with those for hardware firms," he noted to SA's president. "Cost of goods sold is almost an irrelevant concept, margins are vastly different—either very low or very high—

FIGURE S.1 Software Associates, Inc., Income Statements

	Years ended December 31			
	1993		1992	
Net revenues	$307,239	100.0%	$197,241	100.0%
Cost of revenues	60,432	19.7	42,111	21.4
Gross profit	246,807	80.3	155,130	78.6
Operating Expenses				
Research and development	39,231	12.8	30,103	15.3
Sales and marketing	88,937	28.9	52,932	26.8
General and administrative	10,332	3.4	6,555	3.3
Total operating expenses	138,500	45.1	89,590	45.4
Operating income	108,307	35.2	65,540	33.2
Other income and expenses	3,467	1.1	2,888	1.5
Income before income taxes	111,774	36.4	68,428	34.7
Provisions for income taxes	34,650	11.3	21,896	11.1
Net income	$ 77,124	25.1%	$ 46,532	23.6%
Net income per share	$ 2.47		$ 1.56	
Note: The aggregate depreciation expenses are	$ 7,929		$ 5,067	

$ in thousands, except per share amounts

and traditional balance sheet ratios, like inventory turnover, don't mean much." These differences between software and hardware companies caused Witkins particular difficulties as he attempted to assess the prices that SA should pay for various companies that SA was considering acquiring.

SA's financial statements for the most recent two years appear in Figures S.1 and S.2. Witkins noticed particularly the very large gross margin that the company appeared to earn; the company's high operating expenses, particularly product development and marketing; the company's abundant liquidity as measured by the current ratio; the company's long accounts receivable collection period; and the large amount of capitalized software development costs. He decided that he had better study the footnotes to SA's audited financial statements to gain further insight into the company's accounting policies. After reading the excerpts from the "Notes to the Financial Statements" that appear in Figure S.3, he pondered whether the company's accounting policies were appropriate. Most particularly, he asked him-

FIGURE S.2   Software Assocatiates, Inc., Balance Sheets

	December 31	
Assets	1993	1992
Current Assets		
Cash and cash investments	$ 14,386	$ 9,671
Accounts receivable, net	68,275	45,901
Inventories	7,851	5,621
Other	8,630	5,682
Total current assets	99,142	66,875
Software development costs, net	29,714	21,386
Property, plant and equipment, net	27,824	18,250
Other assets	8,311	4,409
Total assets	$164,991	$110,920
Liabilities and Stockholders' Equity		
Current Liabilities		
Accounts payable	$ 14,321	$ 8,502
Accrued compensation	6,940	4,795
Notes payable	3,243	3,877
Income taxes payable	7,408	4,963
Other	3,809	2,610
Total current liabilities	35,721	24,747
Notes payable	27,618	23,850
Owners' equity		
Common stock	21,818	18,358
Retained earnings	79,834	43,965
Total stockholders' equity	101,652	62,323
Total liabilities and stockholders' equity	$164,991	$110,920

$ in thousands

**FIGURE S.3   Excerpts from "Notes to Financial Statements"
Software Associates, Inc.**

(1) **Inventories.** Inventories are stated at the lower of cost (first-in, first-out method) or market. Cost includes labor, material, and manufacturing overhead. Inventories consist of raw materials and supplies, work-in-progress, and finished goods.

(2) **Revenue Recognition.** Revenue is generally recognized when the software has been shipped and the invoice has been sent to the customer. Revenue from products relicensed through VARs is recognized at the time such fees are reported to the company. In December 1991 the American Institute of Certified Public Accountants (the "AICPA") issued SOP 91-1 that requires that revenue for technical support and software update rights must be recognized ratably over the contract period. Service revenue, which accounts for approximately 30 percent of total net revenue in each year, is recognized as services are performed and invoices are rendered to customers.

(3) **Software Development Costs.** The company capitalizes internally generated software development costs in compliance with Statement of Financial Accounting Standards No. 86 "Accounting for the Costs of Computer Software to be Sold, Leased or Otherwise Marketed." Capitalization of software development costs begins upon the establishment of technological feasibility of the product. The establishment of technological feasibility and the ongoing assessment of the recoverability of these costs require considerable judgment by management with respect to certain external factors, including, but not limited to, anticipated future gross product revenue, estimated economic life and changes in software and hardware technology. Amortization of capitalized software development costs begins when the products are available for general release to customers and is computed separately for each product as the greater of (1) the ratio of current gross revenue for a product to the total of current and anticipated gross revenue for the product, or (2) the straight-line method over the remaining estimated economic life of the product. Currently, estimated economic lives of three of five years are used in the calculation of amortization of these capitalized costs. Amortization is included in the cost of revenue in the accompanying statements of income.

Software development costs capitalized were $24,861,000 and $16,714,000 for the years ended December 31, 1993 and 1992, respectively. Amortization of capitalized software development costs were $16,180,000 and $10,855,000 for the years ended December 31, 1993 and 1992, respectively.

---

self if the accounting policies were conservative in a financial sense, and did they provide information useful to management.

As he thought about SA's business, he realized that in many ways it was more like the book publishing business or the motion picture producing business than it was the manufacturing business where he had spent most of his working life. The only real manufacturing that SA performed was reproducing the disks on which the software programs were encoded and assembling the accompanying users' manuals.

SA's vice president for development had long argued that her operation at SA was analogous to both the development and production operations at a company producing hardware. That is, while some of the activities in her area truly constituted new product development, writing computer code for a software package after it was conceptualized and diagrammed was the key value-adding function at SA and thus analogous to the manufacturing operations of a hardware company. She argued that imposing on SA's operations cost accounting techniques appropriate to traditional hardware manufacturers resulted in financial statements that were useful to no one, neither managers within the company nor analysts outside.

DISCUSSION QUESTIONS

1. Compute and analyze the relevant financial ratios for Software Associates. Compare and contrast them with the ratios developed for Analytics Corporation (see the Analytics Corporation case on page 445).

2. Is Witkins correct in assuming that this business is more analogous to the book publishing or motion picture producing business than it is to a traditional manufacturing business? What are the similarities? Differences?

3. What are some alternative methods of accounting for software development costs? What would be the impact of these alternatives on the reported financial statements (both income statement and balance sheet)? What difficulties do you anticipate you would encounter in implementing the procedures in Note 3 on Figure S.3?

4. Are software development costs an element of manufacturing overhead at SA? If so, are they included in the valuation of inventory? If not considered manufacturing overhead, how are they included in the income statements?

5. How useful are cost accounting data to marketing managers at SA in making pricing decisions? How useful are they to development managers at the company?

6. Assume that SA's common stock is publicly-traded and that you are a securities analyst. How confident should you be in the financial statements issued by this company? What are the risks? Are they greater or less than the risks inherent in the financial statements of Analytics Corporation?

7. Assume that you are SA's banker. Assess the value as collateral for borrowing of each of the following assets: accounts receivable, inventory, software development costs, and property, plant, and equipment.

8. Construct a Cash Flow Statement for 1993.

9. If the price-earnings ratio of SA's common stock is 18, what is the ratio of the market value of the stock to its book value?

10. If SA continues to grow rapidly (say, 40 percent per year), how soon do you think it will need to seek additional long-term financing (either debt or equity)? What are the key assumptions you make in answering this question?

TRITEX CORPORATION

In early 1995, Ms. Jennifer Williamson was promoted from Vice President of Marketing to President and Chief Operating Officer of Tritex Corporation. Tritex had, in the preceding several years, experienced a flattening in its growth together with declining profit margins. The company's founder, Mr. Samuel Yoblinski, was by 1995 spending only about one-third of his time at Tritex. At the urging of several of the company's board members, he finally turned the day-to-day operations over to Ms. Williamson, although Yoblinski retained the title of chief executive.

Williamson believed that the company had fallen behind the industry in new product development. She had confidence that the sales organization which she had built, now under the leadership of the vice president of marketing, Samuel Prince, could effectively sell more advanced systems at healthy profit margins if reasonable differentiation in specifications between Tritex and its competitors could be established. The market for the types of systems built by Tritex was highly competitive; while in the industry's early years competition turned largely on advanced performance specifications, in more recent years price and quality had also become critical competitive factors. Williamson intended to spend time with the company's development people helping to orient projects to those improvements that she felt would be particularly meaningful to customers.

Over the past five years, manufacturing at Tritex had become increasingly automated in an attempt to meet the product cost goals that were required in light of declining industry price levels on systems that were the workhorses of Tritex's product line. All Tritex systems were manufactured in its Watertown factory, each proceeding along essentially the same production path. The Zeus system had substantially greater capability than the original Apollo line; unlike the Apollo line it was computer based and thus involved a good deal of software and commanded a price nearly three times that of the Apollo. In recent years, Tritex had been pressed by its customers to customize both the Apollo and Zeus systems but now dominantly the Zeus system. This customization involved incorporating peripherals manufactured by others and providing the customer with additional software that was drawn from a library of programs developed by Tritex and assembled and integrated to meet each customer's particular needs. Customized systems required extra labor hours primarily in final assembly, test, and calibration.

Williamson knew that she must place heavy emphasis on improving Tritex's profitability. For the years 1993 and 1994 Tritex's return on equity was well below the average of companies in its industry. Moreover, the board of directors repeatedly pointed out that the pretax margins of about 2 percent earned by Tritex in each of the last several years were woefully inadequate for a high-technology system manufacturer, which Tritex claimed to be.

Figure T.1 contains Tritex's 1994 income statement. Williamson was concerned about the substantial overhead variance shown (underabsorbed overhead). When she reviewed the statement with the production manager, he pointed out that overhead expenditures had accelerated a great deal in recent years as customized systems

FIGURE T.1 Tritex Corporation, Income Statement, 1994

	$000	%
Sales	$22,932	100%
Cost of goods sold	12,493	54.5
Material and labor variances	116	0.5
Underabsorbed overhead	520	2.3
	13,129	57.3
Gross margin	9,803	42.7
Operating Expenses		
Sales commissions	988	4.3
Marketing	4,807	21.0
Research and engineering	1,520	6.6
General and administrative	2,004	8.7
	9,319	40.6
Operating Profit	$ 484	2.1%

became a larger fraction of Tritex's business, the manufacturing engineering department nearly doubled, and personnel were added in the materials area to cope with material flowing to and from subcontractors. Tritex's overhead rate had more than doubled over the past decade until now it was well over 300 percent of direct labor. Williamson wondered whether she should insist on a reduction in the overhead to get the rate down closer to 200 percent; she felt sure that at a rate between 200 and 250 percent no underabsorbed overhead would have occurred in 1994.

Bruce Voss, the company's controller, pointed out that the underabsorbed overhead in 1994 was simply a result of sales volumes, and therefore production volumes, falling well below the levels anticipated when the 1994 overhead rate was set late in 1993. Had the overhead rate been set higher, the underabsorbed condition would have been avoided. Figure T.2 shows the information required to derive the overhead rate, as well as the standard product costs for the three product categories that comprised Tritex's current line: Apollo, Zeus, and custom systems.

After reviewing the information in Figure T.2 Williamson asked Voss whether perhaps the real problem was that the Apollo systems were simply unprofitable. The Apollo system had been built by Tritex for many years, but had come under severe price pressure during the last three years. She understood that Apollo had an anticipated (standard) gross margin of 19.8 percent—a percentage that she thought was dangerously low in the high-technology systems business—but she wondered if perhaps its net margin after all expenses might be negative. She urged Voss to produce a product-by-product profit and loss statement, one that would absorb not just manufacturing costs but all costs and expenses into the individual products. The results of Voss's analysis are shown in Figure T.3.

Williamson was frequently reminded of the confusion that overhead allocations seemed to cause the line operating managers at Tritex—as well as herself. While Tritex had always distributed manufacturing overhead to products on the basis of

FIGURE T.2   Tritex Corporation: Overhead Rate, Production in Units and Standard Product Costs (1994)

Derivation of 1994 Overhead Rate

Cost Element	Budget ($000)
Indirect production labor	$1,524
Manufacturing engineering	1,361
Rent & other occupancy costs	984
Maintenance and repair	1,610
Power	1,067
Depreciation, equipment	1,116
Miscellaneous	582
	$8,244
Estimated direct labor wages	$2,461 (179,000 hours)
Overhead rate ($8244 ÷ 2461)	335 percent

Estimated Production in Units, 1994

Apollo	5,400
Zeus	3,850
Custom	2,300

Standard Product Costs, 1994

Product	Direct Labor Hours	Direct Labor $*	Material	Overhead†	Total
Apollo	9.7	$133	$124	$ 445	$ 702
Zeus	15.2	$209	$278	$ 700	$1,187
Custom	29.6	$407	$392	$1,363	$2,162

*Standard labor wage = $13.75 per hour.
†At 335% of direct labor standard cost.

direct labor cost she wondered if perhaps direct material or some combination of direct labor and direct material costs would be more appropriate.

She was aware that engineers in the manufacturing engineering department seemed confused as to how to treat overhead as they considered various make-or-buy alternatives, particularly for subassemblies of systems, some of which were manufactured internally and some of which were subcontracted. She recalled an analysis of such a decision, shown in Figure T.4. Prince also reminded Williamson of a pricing decision that the company faced. Prince's marketing analyst had recently developed the price-volume estimates for the Zeus system that are shown in Figure T.5. Prince wondered how he should use these in deciding on a possible increase or decrease in Zeus's price.

As Williamson pondered these questions, and reviewed again the relatively poor profit performance of recent years, she wondered if the company was using the right cost accounting system. She was somewhat aware of recent and widespread criti-

FIGURE T.3 Tritex Instruments: Product-by-Product Income Statement,* 1994

| | Product | | | |
	Apollo	Zeus	Custom	Total
Sales	$ 4,742	$8,510	$9,680	$22,932
Cost of goods sold	3804	4,164	4,525	12,493
Material and labor variance[a]	35	39	42	116
Underabsorbed overhead[a]	158	174	188	520
	3,997	4,377	4,755	13,129
Gross margin	745	4,133	4,925	9,803
Operating Expenses				
Sales commissions	0	691	297	988
Marketing[b]	1,183	1,344	2,280	4,807
Research and engineering[c]	204	503	813	1,520
General and administrative[d]	414	744	846	2,004
	1,801	3,282	4,236	9,319
Operating profit	($1,056)	$ 851	$ 689	$ 484
For reference:				
Number of units sold	5,420	3,508	2,093	
Price per unit	$ `875	$2,426	$4,625	

*Bases of allocation:

[a]Variances and underabsorbed overhead allocated among products on the basis of cost of goods sold.
[b]Marketing expenses allocated among products on the basis of estimates of sales effort expended on each product category.
[c]Research and engineering expenses charged to products based on estimates of time spent.
[d]General and administrative expenses allocated among products on the basis of sales dollars.

FIGURE T.4 Tritex Corporation, Make-or-Buy Decision: Subassembly #2861 for Product Zeus

Purchase Price

Quantity per year	Price per unit
4,000	$360
5,000	$330
6,000	$310
7,000	$305
8,000	$302

Estimate of In-House Manufacturing Cost*

Direct labor hours per unit	3.9
Direct labor $ per unit	$ 53.63
Direct material $ per unit	118.81
Overhead $ per unit	179.64
	$352.08

*Assume 6000 units per year at lot sizes of 500.

FIGURE T.5   Tritex Corporation, Analysis of Pricing Decision, Zeus

	Current	Lower Prices		Higher Prices		
Price per unit	$2,426	$2,300	$2,400	$2,500	$2,600	$2,700
Volume (units per year)	3,850	4,300	3,925	3,750	3,425	3,150

FIGURE T.6   Tritex Corporation: Information Relevant to Activity-Based Costing

Activities	Budget 1994 ($000)
Assembly supervision	$1,285
Assembly set-up	582
Purchasing	847
Receiving and stores	1,511
Production control & scheduling	738
Software troubleshooting	691
Manufacturing engineering	1,263
Quality assurance—assembly	416
Quality assurance—checkout and calibration	911
	$8,244

Product Characteristics	System Products		
	Apollo	Zeus	Custom
Annual volume (units)	5,400	3,850	2,300
Price per unit	$875	$2,426	$4,625
Standard D.L. hours per unit	9.7 hours	15.2 hours	29.6 hours
Average lot size	1,000	600	20
Number of part numbers	137	416	475
Computer memory capacity	0	X	$6X$
Average time in check out	4 hours	11 hours	23 hour
Standard direct material $ per unit	$124	$ 700	$1,363

cism of traditional cost accounting techniques—some writers seemed to feel that these techniques were a primary factor in the country's loss of competitive position in world markets. She had seen some discussion of a new technique called activity-based costing which was viewed by some companies as providing more useful data for pricing, product-line, make-buy and other operating decisions. Figure T.6 provides some product-line and overhead information germane to activity-based costing.

INDEX